NETNOGRAPHY

Robert Kozinets knows his stuff: over the past 25 years, he has almost single-handedly established netnography as a methodological framework for qualitative Internet research. This third edition of his essential guide to netnographic research practices provides a very welcome update to the framework, taking in even more of the complex and ever-changing landscape of current social media platforms and their uses, and offering a wealth of ideas for working with qualitative social media data. Whether they're already calling themselves netnographers or have yet to discover the field, this book will inspire and enable many more researchers to investigate social media practices from a qualitative perspective.

Axel Bruns, Professor in the Digital Media Research Centre, Queensland University of Technology

If anyone had any doubt that this is the golden age for research, Rob Kozinets has made the case and provided the field guide that shows why this is so. *Netnography* is a fun locution for a big set of ideas about how to exploit new research methods to explore the biggest social, political and economic issues of our time.

Lee Rainie, Director of Internet and Technology Research, Pew Research Center

Netnography is a must-read for anyone engaged in or contemplating qualitative research on social media. Online behavior is at once a psychological, social, and technological phenomena, and qualitative approaches require both rigor and context, which Robert V. Kozinets offers in abundance. Both history and methodology are meticulously detailed in what ought to be a guidebook for social media researchers.

Howard Rheingold

Robert V Kozinets

NETNOGRAPHY

The Essential Guide to Qualitative Social Media Research

⑤SAGE

Los Angeles | London | New Delhi
Singapore | Washington DC | Melbourne

Los Angeles | London | New Delhi
Singapore | Washington DC | Melbourne

SAGE Publications Ltd
1 Oliver's Yard
55 City Road
London EC1Y 1SP

SAGE Publications Inc.
2455 Teller Road
Thousand Oaks, California 91320

SAGE Publications India Pvt Ltd
B 1/I 1 Mohan Cooperative Industrial Area
Mathura Road
New Delhi 110 044

SAGE Publications Asia-Pacific Pte Ltd
3 Church Street
#10-04 Samsung Hub
Singapore 049483

Editor: Michael Ainsley
Editorial assistant: Amber Turner-Flanders
Production editor: Imogen Roome
Marketing manager: Susheel Gokarakonda
Cover design: Shaun Mercier
Typeset by: C&M Digitals (P) Ltd, Chennai, India
Printed in the UK

Library of Congress Control Number: 2019937404

British Library Cataloguing in Publication data

A catalogue record for this book is available from
the British Library

ISBN 978-1-5264-4469-1
ISBN 978-1-5264-4470-7 (pbk)

At SAGE we take sustainability seriously. Most of our products are printed in the UK using responsibly sourced
papers and boards. When we print overseas we ensure sustainable papers are used as measured by the PREPS
grading system. We undertake an annual audit to monitor our sustainability.

This book is dedicated to my parents, Mickey and Anne, who lovingly cared for me, encouraging and supporting me in all my interests and peculiarities – even if they didn't always quite understand what I was doing.

Also, to Sidney Levy. You are missed and never forgotten.

And to Mila Steele. This book would not have taken shape without your ambitious vision.

One of the radical spirits in current thought has
defined the task of this somber age as learning anew
to be human.
George Steiner

When you are philosophizing, you have to descend
into primeval chaos and feel at home there.
Ludwig Wittgenstein

CONTENTS

ACKNOWLEDGEMENTS

For the third iteration of this book there are several Sage people to thank. Katie Metzler and Patrick Brindle made the last two editions happen. Mila Steele and John Nightingale were enormously helpful in getting this book off the ground and written. My gratitude to Amber Turner-Flanders and Imogen Roome, who helped everything run smoothly. Michael Ainsley, the book's managing editor, brought the project to completion with grace and effectiveness, especially considering that he was also a new father during the time he was working on it. Many thanks to all of you, and to everyone at Sage who helped make this book happen.

ABOUT THE AUTHOR

Robert V. Kozinets has developed research methods and theories that are widely used around the world today. In 1995, in a dissertation study, he invented the term netnography – and began developing the techniques behind it. Along the way, his techniques were sharpened by presentations at many of the world's top universities and work with major corporations, non-profits, and government agencies. Asking questions about methodology, sociality, technology, community & commodification, activism, scientific representation, ideology, utopia, and desire, his research pushed disciplinary boundaries to open up a more integrative, moral, and expressive form of studying and theorizing the world around us. He is the Jayne and Hans Hufschmid Chair and a Professor of Public Relations and Advertising at the University of Southern California's Annenberg School for Communication and Journalism.

INTRODUCING: NETNOGRAPHY, QUALITATIVE SOCIAL MEDIA RESEARCH METHODS, AND THIS BOOK

CHAPTER OVERVIEW

This chapter will be full of introductions: an introduction to social media, netnography, qualitative social media research, and this book. Over five billion people around the world use different types of social media, and this new edition of the book responds to the need for updated and improved ways to investigate and understand those uses. The chapter's opening section will broadly explore some of the contours of social media today, looking at global usage patterns, exploring the most popular types of social media platforms, and encouraging some personal reflection on your own use. The next section of the chapter will introduce netnography, defining it as a form of cultural research that uses a set of specific qualitative practices to investigate social media. Netnography is affiliated with and distinct from other forms of digital anthropology and media anthropology. Like other forms of anthropology, it uses techniques that value immersion in a culture. However, these terms are redefined in particular ways in netnography. Netnography is different from other methods because it uses specific techniques and a pragmatic approach to investigate online traces. The chapter's final section will introduce the contents of the book, demonstrating how the approach has been updated for a rapidly evolving world of social media. The five main sections of the book are devoted to methodology and history, empirical initiation, data collection, data analysis and interpretation, and communicating netnographic research.

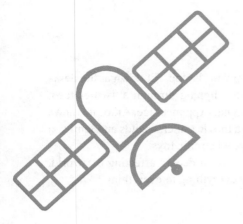

'We will become the Network Nation, exchanging vast amounts of both information and social-emotional communications with colleagues, friends, and "strangers" who share similar interests, who are spread out all over the nation. Ultimately, as communication satellites and international packet switched networks reach out to other cities and villages around the world, these social networks facilitated by computer-mediated communications will become international; we will become a "global village" whose boundaries are demarcated only by the political decisions of those governments that choose not to become part of an international computer network. An individual will, literally, be able to work, shop, or be educated by or with persons anywhere in the nation or in the world.'

(Starr Roxanne Hiltz and Murray Turoff (1978) *The Network Nation: Human Communication via Computer*, p. xxv)

SOCIAL MEDIA RESEARCH
Exploring the Universe of Social Media

Take out your phone. Turn on your tablet. Boot up your laptop. Sit down at the desktop. Lo and behold: the wonders of social media. Flipping through a Twitter feed, checking Facebook updates. A Snapchat beep. A WhatsApp message. All of it – news to read, sports, research material, interconnected, a movie trailer, friends and family, a fitness influencer, merging and built into seductive electronic toys.

This is social media. This is a world within a world deeply affecting the world. Fast, current, zooming by, expanding, connecting everything to everything.

Redefining Social Media

Accurate and succinct definitions of social media are surprisingly hard to find. In a useful exception, Ulrike Gretzel (2017b: 1) defines and then explains social media as:

> Web-based communication platforms or applications that take advantage of Web 2.0 technologies, which make it possible for users without technical expertise to easily produce and publish content on the Internet. Social media encompass a variety of different types, such as social networks, review sites, instant messaging applications, and video and photo sharing sites.

For our purposes, we can define social media as applications, websites, and other online technologies that enable their users to engage in a variety of different content creation, circulation, annotation, and association activities. Netnography is a way to study social media that maintains the complexities of its experiential and cultural qualities.

From Virtual Communities to Instagram Nano-influencers

When I started writing about virtual communities, Internet studies was still a relatively small field. No one would hear about social media for another fifteen years. Blogs were at least seven years away from wide recognition and the beginning of their growth. When the first edition of *Netnography* was published in 2010, social media was still a bit of a novelty. In 2009, when I wrote the first chapter of the first edition of the book, there were about 150 million active users on Facebook, and around a million Twitter users.

Just nine years later, social media have become a major part of the fabric of contemporary human society. About 5 billion people, roughly two-thirds of the world's population, are connected through their mobile phones, and about 4 billion of them use these devices to connect to broadband. Ninety-five percent of Americans own a cell phone, with 77 percent of them smartphones. All of these connections potentially link people to one another through a variety of social media sites and other interaction platforms, as well as to the affordances of apps and the agency of algorithms. From its humble beginnings in work machine networks, today's social media is an unprecedented, global, amplified, electrifying technocapitalist experience.

Social media today thus comprise a complex social system that reflects and reveals human society and is also, itself, a unique social phenomenon. *Netnography* is designed to help you make sense of that system and the way people interact with and within it.

Netnography and Social Media's Evolution

Social media has evolved dramatically over the past decade, emerging as a commonplace, influential, and yet still deeply misunderstood phenomenon. *Netnography: The Essential Guide to Qualitative Social Media Research* responds to the need for a more expansive, inclusive, applied, and up-to-date way to understand social media. The book continues to evolve the two prior volumes and extends them into a new, internally structured system for mixed qualitative methods inquiries using social media data. The emphasis in netnography today is on a qualitative research approach to social media data, rather than on ethnography, anthropology, marketing research, or any one field or methodological approach.

This volume is a near total reboot. It refocuses netnography on social media's vital, and ever-challenging new realities. It offers researchers a detailed and specific approach to conducting qualitative research using social media as the basis of its datasets. Netnography encompasses interviews, data scraping, archival work, online observation, and active engagement with new forms of data collection, visualization, thematic analysis, and field-level rhetorical representation. This edition intensifies the focus on technique but maintains a strong grounding in social scientific theory that seeks, more than ever, to bridge fields such as communication, computer science, cultural studies, anthropology, and psychology. This chapter provides three types of general overview. To begin with, it examines the current terrain of social media. It then introduces and overviews netnography. And finally, it outlines the contents of this book.

Do We Really Need Another Name for Online Ethnography?

Netnography? Do we really need a new name for ethnography, even if it is done online?

Coining a new name for something that already has a perfectly good word to represent it is needless complexification. Unfortunately, we see a lot of this needless complexification in the worlds of business and academia, where audiences reward superficial innovation by scholars or consultants but often do not have the patience or ability to judge its validity in relation to historical precedent.

As you will see in the historical overview contained in Chapter 2, when I first coined the term in 1995, the act of doing social media research of any kind was still emergent, sketchy, and mostly unnamed (and, generally speaking, just not done at all). It was clear to me that the procedures that worked well in the physical terrain of qualitative research, such as asking for consent, did not translate to the online environment. So, encouraged by the feedback of my peers, I began developing netnography as a new discipline that adapted ethnographic and qualitative research methods to the novel and still emerging contingencies of social media environments. Since that time, however, the term 'online ethnography' has come to be accepted as denoting the general category of applying ethnographic research concepts and procedures to online environments such as social media.

As well, a range of different researchers working in different fields have coined a host of new terms for online ethnographic work. These new terms include 'cyber-ethnography' (Ward, 1999), 'virtual ethnography' (Hine, 2000), 'network ethnography' (Howard, 2002), 'webnography' (Puri, 2007), and 'digital ethnography' (Murthy, 2008), as well as a long list of ancillary techniques developed in marketing research agencies such as 'mobile ethnography' and 'show & tell ethnography'. So the question then becomes whether these names actually mean something above and beyond the mere idea of online ethnography. Do terms such as these tell us anything beyond the mere fact that an ostensibly 'ethnographic' type of research can be performed using networked computing devices? Otherwise, this is mere mindless neologizing – renaming for naming's sake, rather than designating in order to add specific meaning and value to the state of our knowledge.

If we are giving a new name to a particular way of doing something, like ethnography, then that new name should signify the approach is significantly different from other ways of doing that same thing. Thus the name netnography – a portmanteau combining network, Internet, and ethnography – has always stood for a cultural focus on understanding the data derived from social media data, characteristics that the approach shares with all other types of online ethnography. However, it differs from other types of online ethnography in its praxis, the specific way that the idea of online ethnographic work is put into practice at the level of action, or boots on the ground.

Netnography 3e is a Recipe Book for Qualitative Social Media Research

Christine Hine, whose term 'virtual ethnography' is still widely used, has written that 'ethnography is strengthened by the lack of recipes for doing it' (Hine, 2000: 13). Netnography differs from virtual ethnography and from most approaches to ethnography in its fundamental disagreement with Hine's statement. When I tried to learn ethnography from within a business field, I found the lack of clear direction for doing it frustrating and disheartening. Why couldn't ethnographers just state what they were doing, and perhaps offer some options to guide me in the different choices I needed to make?, I wondered. I appreciate the flexibility of the ethnographic method that Hine is celebrating. But that high regard for flexibility assumes a type of hands-on mentorship and a basic level of knowledge and ability that is not always the case. I believe it also relates to a more general type of mystification in qualitative research, particularly regarding interpretation, that is both unnecessary and counter-productive.

Pedagogically dismissive attitudes, which seemingly glorify obfuscation, have led to major misunderstandings of ethnography such as Lubet's (2018) critique of ethnography as a form of inaccurate reporting. Lack of a clear guiding recipe to follow may have also led researchers to play fast and loose with research ethics – for example in the inhumane treatment of Brazilian Yanomami populations by ethnographers (Tierney, 2001), or with ethnographers' complicity in a range of colonialist, misogynist, and exploitative ventures (Bosk and De Vries, 2004).

This edition of *Netnography* embraces the provision of clear direction. It provides its readers with a number of basic recipes for getting social media research done. At this point in its development, after over two decades of adjustment, elaboration, and refinement, three editions of this book, and hundreds if not thousands of peer-reviewed articles, research projects, and dissertations based on its principles, netnography is a detailed, sophisticated, and differentiated set of techniques. Clear recipes, names, flowcharts, and directions give this edition of *Netnography* an unprecedented depth. They give you, the netnographer, clearly elaborated choices. By providing adequate and in-depth explanation of the methodological reasoning behind the guidance, there is no loss in flexibility. In fact, you can think of the many exercises in this book as fulfilling the same task as recipes. As you learn to become a better chef, you become freed to experiment with adapting and creating your own recipes. But first, you must be given the recipe for the soufflé!

Netnography as an Organized Set of Research Tools

Netnography today is not merely another name for online ethnography, but a set of general instructions relating to *a specific way to conduct qualitative social media research using a combination of 25 different research practices grouped into three distinct categories of data collection, data analysis, and data interpretation 'movements'*. There is an immense amount of detail and flexibility in the way that netnographic researchers can apply, adapt, and combine the data collection operations of *investigation (simplification, search, scouting, selecting, and saving), interaction (interview, involvement, innovation, and informed consent), immersion (reconnoitering, recording, researching, and reflecting), and the data integration methods of analysis (collating, coding, combining, counting, and charting) and interpretation (theming, talenting, totalizing, translation, turtling, and troublemaking).*

Netnography provides new terminology for a new field that needs additional systematizing, and still will. Many of these ideas, if not most of them, came from my examination of published research by authors such as you. These authors have been changing and altering the early practices of netnography to help them better fit to the contingencies of particular field sites, topics, and academic fields of knowledge. They also have changed and systematized some of the ways to communicate to readers and fellow academics about them.

Netnography has become a syncretic amalgam of research practices and viewpoints from computer science, cultural studies, media anthropology, education, nursing, and my own native fields of marketing and consumer culture research. For example, as you will learn in this book, there is a particular netnographic praxis for collecting investigative data that specifies simplifying, searching, scouting, selection, and saving operations that is entirely unique to netnography and not found in this form in any other account of online ethnography. Similarly, netnographic practices espouse and describe a particular variant of ethnographic participant observation called 'engaged data operations'. They commit to a cultural understanding of social media through an integration of data analysis and hermeneutic interpretation operations. They detail the use of an immersion journal. In terms of ethics, netnography provides a simple, flowchart-based approach to help you navigate the complexities of the research ethics of these methods and ensure compliance with the most rigorous current standards of research ethics practice. From those guidelines, it is able to offer detailed, up-to-date, and appropriate data collection and presentation procedures to accommodate the latest research ethics requirements such as the European Union's GDPR regulations.

These procedures and practices offer the online social scientist a new conceptual terminology alongside these fully adapted research practices. These terms, principles, and operations, and many others you will learn in this book, are what the netnography name signifies.

Netnography = your choice from among 25 explained, illustrated with exercises, research practices or recipes performed with various types of social media data, incorporating up-to-date research ethics standards, and dedicated to helping you produce reflectively curated and insightfully communicated work about social media itself and its cultural inclusions, reflections, and effects.

If you decide to call your work an online ethnography, it will be unclear exactly what principles and procedures you followed. You will be cooking data without a recipe, producing a dish without a name. The onus would then be on you to explain and justify what you have done, because online ethnography is a generic category, like calling your soup 'soup'. The same is true for the many under-specified, dated, one-hit wonder versions of online ethnography like cyber-ethnography and webnography. The point of this book is not to critique other forms of online ethnography, which might all prove useful to certain researchers in particular contexts for specific goals. It is to ensure that the name 'netnography' stands for something specific, relevant, actionable, and useful. When you call your work a netnography, and you cite this book and other contributions to the now-considerable netnographic methodological canon in the social sciences in reference to your research stance and research practices, you are indicating that you more or less followed the procedural roadmap laid out in this book. Name the procedures and your fellow researchers will easily know which recipes you followed. Calling your work a netnography does not just mean that netnography as a technique has become a rigorous, legitimate, detailed, contemporary, and ethical technique. It means that *your* netnography is rigorous, detailed, current, and ethical.

More About Social Media

What we know about social media has changed radically since the first edition of this book was written. Not only are social media platforms gaining mass memberships worldwide, but some large sites are dominant, and particular sites dominate in particular regions or countries. Facebook currently has about 2.2 billion monthly active users, Instagram 800 million, Twitter 330 million, and Reddit 250 million. Among the Chinese social media sites, WeChat has about a billion monthly active users and Sina Weibo 376 million. In Russian online social media, VKontakte has about 480 million accounts and Odnoklassniki 200 million registered users. These are the mass audience social media sites, and they contain significant proportions of the population in their countries or regions. Seventy three percent of the American population say that they use YouTube, and 68% say that they use Facebook (Smith and Anderson, 2018). They are also using social media frequently. Seventy-four percent of Facebook users say they visit the site daily, and 51% say they visit it several times a day. Similarly, 63% of Snapchat users and 60% of Instagram users say they visit the platform daily.

The use of some social media sites is more stratified, and sometimes specialized, than in the past. For example, more than twice as many American women use Pinterest compared to men (41% versus 16%). Among young people aged 18–24, 78% use Snapchat (Smith and Anderson, 2018), versus only 7% among those aged 50 and over. And LinkedIn, which is a network for professionals, is somewhat unsurprisingly over five times more popular with high-income college graduates than those with a high school diploma or less (50% versus 9%). The median American social media user uses three social media platforms, and many Americans use several, with young adults showing the greatest variety of use. In fact, people are so immersed in social media that an American group has declared a 'National Day of Unplugging', held on March 9–10, to encourage people to disconnect from their devices and provide a 24-hour respite period.

Table 1.1 Global social media statistics, 2018

World Region	Population (2017 Est.)	Population % of the world	Internet Users 30 June 2017	Penetration Rate (%Pop)	Growth 2000–2017	Internet Users %
Africa	1,246,504,865	16.6 %	388,376,491	31.2 %	8,503.1%	10.0 %
Asia	4,148,177,672	55.2 %	1,938,075,631	46.7 %	1,595.5%	49.7 %
Europe	822,710,362	10.9 %	659,634,487	80.2 %	527.6%	17.0 %
Latin America/Carribean	647,604,645	8.6 %	404,269,163	62.4 %	2,137.4%	10.4 %
Middle East	250,327,574	3.3 %	146,972,123	58.7 %	4,374.3%	3.8 %
North America	363,224,006	4.8 %	320,059,368	88.1 %	196.1%	8.2 %
Oceana/Australia	40,479,846	0.5 %	28,180,356	69.6 %	269.8%	0.7 %
WORLD TOTAL	7,519,028,970	100.0 %	3,885,567,619	51.7 %	976.4%	100.0 %

Source: www.internetworldstats.com. Copyright © 2017, Miniwatts Marketing Group. All rights reserved worldwide.

THINKING ABOUT YOUR OWN SOCIAL MEDIA USE

1.1

Where is your mobile phone right now? Is it next to you? Take a look at your phone (or the bookmarks on your browser).

- What social media sites are there?
- Do you use any of the sites mentioned in the opening to this subsection of this chapter?
- Which ones?
- How often do you visit these sites? Do you visit them more than once a day? How many do you visit more than ten times a day?

If you aren't aware of your own social media use, why don't you try using a tracker to help you understand how many visits and how much time you are spending on social media. Here are some popular current social media usage trackers you can consider:

- Social Fever
- SPACE – Break phone addiction
- AppDetox – App Blocker for Digital Detox
- OFFTIME – Distraction Free
- MyAddictometer – Mobile addiction tracker
- Quality Time
- Moment – Screen Time Tracker
- Forest – Stay Focused

Table 1.2 Percentage of U.S. adults who use each social media platform

	Facebook	Instagram	Pinterest	LinkedIn	Twitter
Total	68%	28%	26%	25%	21%
Men	67%	23%	15%	28%	21%
Women	69%	32%	38%	23%	21%
Ages 18–29	88%	59%	36%	34%	36%
30–49	79%	31%	32%	31%	22%
50–64	61%	13%	24%	21%	18%
65+	36%	5%	9%	11%	6%

Note: Race/ethnicity breaks not shown due to sample size.

Source: Survey conducted March 7–April 4, 2016. Pew Research Center, 2017.

Table 1.3 Among the users of each social media site, the percentage who use that site with the following frequencies

Platform	Less often	Weekly	Daily
Facebook	7%	15%	76%
Instagram	22%	26%	51%
Twitter	33%	24%	42%
Pinterest	43%	31%	25%
LinkedIn	51%	31%	18%

Note: Numbers may not add to 100 due to rounding.

Source: Survey conducted March 7–April 4, 2016. Pew Research Center, 2017.

Social Media Studies

An SMS is a message. Social media studies, abbreviated as SMS, is an arm of media studies that investigates and develops theory about the online messages that people leave for and send each other. It is a communications subfield, but intersects with Internet research and many other social sciences. Netnography is a tool for social media studies: studies specifically built to understand this global, grassroots, corporate collective communication phenomenon. One that is redistributing power based on new mediagenic metrics.

I hesitate to call social media globally ubiquitous, however. We must recognize that 2.5 billion citizens of the world currently live their lives without an Internet or mobile phone connection. These people, who constitute a full third of the world's population, may have either no access, or only sporadic access to the vast networked infrastructure of information and communication that the other 5 billion have at their fingertips. But for most of the world today, social media is a natural part of their everyday experience. Social media inform them, entertain them, annoy and delight them alongside, as much as, and often more than, any other form of communication and information.

In 1978, when Starr Roxanne Hiltz and Murray Turoff, a husband and wife research team of Rutgers University professors, published their classic book, *The Network Nation*, they predicted many elements of the social media dominated society we currently live in. Along with other early information technology prognosticators like Alvin Toffler, Hiltz and Turoff predicted an interconnected world where home computers would be as commonplace as telephones, and where the barriers of time and space that once limited our access to other people would shrink to near zero.

To their immense credit, they were extrapolating from a very small base. As they note, 'the first computerized conferencing system was created in 1970' and, at the time of the book's writing, its uses were limited to 'tens of organizations and a few thousand people' (Hiltz and Turoff, 1978: xxv). And yet despite these samples being small and early, they clearly resembled us in many ways. Recreational uses, for play and gaming, were huge then, as they are now. The psychological and sociological impacts on social and family life were there. So were the Internet's destruction of the press and its impact upon television viewership. As well as the way these new technologies would alter concentrations of wealth and power, making software, hardware, and online retailing entrepreneurs the richest Americans in the world.

Hiltz and Turoff also foresaw the abuse of surveillance power. They thought these technologies would 'allow for the invasion of privacy in rather unique ways' (p. xxvi). However, extrapolating from their time, they clearly underestimated the vast impact of large corporations and their increasing power, and the related rise of a neoliberal mantra of a free, open, and deregulated online environment. Their pragmatic focus on shopping, learning, and working were also typical of the early Internet researchers, but made it difficult for them to perceive the social and recreational uses that have driven social media development over the last two decades, resulting in much of its ecosystem-like complexity.

But there was one thing that Hiltz and Turoff gave voice to with great precision, and that was their prediction that the networked world of the future would 'dramatically alter the nature of social science research concerned with the study of human systems and human communication processes' (p. xxvi). Indeed, it has done so, and those dramatically transformed social science research practices are the focus of this entire book. As this chapter now proceeds to introduce and describe netnography, we will begin to take a much closer look at how our contemporary networked world of networked communications transforms sociality and the way we approach our understanding of it.

WHAT IS NETNOGRAPHY?

DEFINING NETNOGRAPHY YOUR OWN WAY

1.2

Before we turn to the next section of this chapter, which defines netnography and explains why it is different from other ethnographic methods, you may want to have a look at Figure 1.1. This word cloud was constructed in 2018 from the then-current netnography entry in Wikipedia (we will be learning more about using word clouds as an analytic technique in a later chapter).

Exercise: Look at this netnography word cloud from Wikipedia. From your examination of it, what would you guess is the current definition of netnography? What would you suppose are the main differences of netnography's approach? When you have given those two questions some thought, move on to the next section.

(Continued)

Figure 1.1 Netnography word cloud

Netnography is a form of qualitative research that seeks to understand the cultural experiences that encompass and are reflected within the traces, practices, networks and systems of social media. These cultural experiences can be engaged with, communicated through, and then reflected upon, forming the three fundamental elements of netnography: investigation, interaction, and immersion. Ethnography is about more than rote practice, however. It is a way of viewing data and thinking about how to understand the world. It is in this viewpoint about understanding the world as a cultural matter that netnography is most like traditional ethnography. Grand philosophical details, such as what constitutes 'participation' in netnography, are not as important to the approach as the empassioned quest for social truths and cultural understandings.

Netnography is Not Merely Ethnography Done Online

You can think of netnography as a particular set of actions for doing research within and about social media: initiating the netnography, investigating social media sites and experiencing and/or downloading and saving their data, interacting with people through interviews and other methods, immersing in the data and reflecting on it, analyzing, interpreting, integrating analysis and interpretation together, and instantiating your netnography by communicating it to your research audiences. Those actions, operations, or procedures are things that we can also call research practices. Research practices are tied into positions, which are ways that people make sense of their own actions and behavioral options, and research positions tie practices to disciplinary structures and social positions.

Netnography has always been the ethnography of online network actors and interactions. But now it is becoming much more: a set of sub-routines, suggested, inflected, and then reflected back through multiple literature bases as a type of crowdsourced scientific method, legitimate, established in multiple fields, yet still growing.

As a type of ethnography, netnography is tied into the current qualitative research practices and positions of anthropology and sociology. It has always been a shifting assemblage of existing legitimate and novel research practices and principles. Netnography was invariably a metamorph, adapting to and being adapted by its computer and data science surroundings, a shifting yet specific set of related data collection, analysis, ethical and representational research procedures.

Like ethnography, netnography subscribes to the methodological connections and principles that animate how its practices relate to:

- views of the world (or ontologies),
- how to study and understand that world (epistemologies), and
- priorities for studying what is important within it (or axiologies).

Also in common with ethnography, the positions and practices of netnography are fundamentally:

- focused on human experience and cultural understanding,
- grounded in deep appreciations of the context of people's everyday life,
- bound to explore social systems of shared meaning, and
- informed by a sense of self-awareness of the researcher and/or of cultural participants.

WIKIPEDIA ON NETNOGRAPHY

1.3

Exercise: Go to Wikipedia. Search for the entry on netnography. Examine the definition of netnography there. Do you agree with it? What would you change about it, if anything? If you feel strongly, go ahead and make the change you wish to see in the world (of Wikipedia)!

Differentiating Netnography

However, despite sharing similar foundations and perspectives, the differences of netnographic practice from other types of research are well worth noting from the outset. Doing so will help prevent confusion. We can start this disambiguation by explaining the relation of netnography to *online traces*. When people post images, video, or text online, or when they comment, share, or do anything else that is accessible online to anonymous or networked others, what they leave behind are *online traces*. Online traces can be textual, graphic, photographic, audiovisual, musical, commercially sponsored, genuinely grassroots, political, fannish, and many other things. Today, these online traces are plentiful, variegated, complex, and widespread. They are also a free form of public social information from which we all draw benefit. One of those benefits is the ability to research them. For over twenty years, collecting and interpreting these traces has formed the core of a netnographic investigation. And from the beginning of netnography, traditional ethnography has had little to say about online traces, what they are, what they mean to social scientific research, how to search for them, how to collect them, what ethical responsibilities accompany their use, the ways that they interact with research searches and search engines, how to analyze them, how to describe them in publications, and so on.

Netnography is centered on the study of online traces. Some netnographies exclusively collect and analyze online traces. Others extend beyond online traces to other forms of data collection and creation. However, the focus on online traces which, when collected, become online data, is a key distinguishing element of netnography. Netnographies start either with social media sites, or with particular topics that are subsequently explored through social media. After collecting, reflecting, and interacting with online traces, netnographers will often, but certainly not always, extend these online explorations with other forms of data collection. This extended data collection can include in-person interviewing, personal observation, online interviewing, mobile interviewing, and mobile recording.

Netnography fits into the general category of digital anthropology, defined as the cultural study of human relations with and through digital technology. So, for example, inspired by Boellstorff's (2008) ethnography of Second Life, Gehl (2016) conducted a digital ethnography situated entirely on the Dark Web Social Network, a social networking site which is accessible to web browsers equipped with a special privacy-ensuring router. However, not all digital ethnography, online ethnography, or digital anthropology is netnography. A digital ethnographer might, for example, study how mobile phone use affects behavior around the family dinner table, or the experiences of Indian immigrants working for technology companies, without ever looking at or considering online messaging and content. These two examples would not be netnographies because all netnographies involve collecting, participating, and interpreting online traces.

There is, of course, considerable variance even in what anthropologists mean when they talk about digital ethnography or digital anthropology. Pink et al. (2015) argue that digital ethnography does not necessarily have to engage with digital technology in its method or its research focus. In fact, Pink et al. (2015) valorize a non-digital data focus as one of the key principles of their variety of digital ethnography: it examines digital life from a purely human angle. Frömming et al. (2017: 13) sidestep the issue of whether digital ethnography needs to embrace digital data and techniques by focusing their view of the future of ethnography on 'digital environments' which is the term they use for the 'mutual permeation of the virtual with the physical world' in sites such as Minecraft or Second Life (immersive virtual worlds), expansive digital social environments like Facebook or Instagram, smartphones, tablets and wearable technologies, and blogs, forums, e-commerce sites, and virtual communities.

Pink (2017: 9–10) views digital anthropology and digital ethnography as fields that are currently 'flourishing' and creating 'a new generation of anthropologists'. She writes that the current time is an intellectual moment wherein anthropologists 'are beginning to make sense of the digital elements of the environment'. Further, she finds 'that digital technologies and media bring with them a body of theoretical, methodological and practical implications. Many of the themes and issues they raise are in fact already part of the subdisciplines of visual and media anthropology.' Although I agree that some areas of anthropology are struggling productively with the changes wrought by digital technologies and media, these areas still unfortunately represent relatively small islands of activity within the greater field. In this book, I draw not only on anthropology and its subfields, but also on a range of other disciplinary fields, such as computer science, communication, cultural and media studies, and many more, in order to develop netnography as an expansive set of qualitative social media research practices that center on the collection and understanding of online traces.

Specificity, Dynamism, and Pragmatism

The second difference between netnography and ethnography is one of specificity. Data collection, analysis, ethics, and representational practices are dramatically altered in netnography because collecting and using online traces are different from the types of data collected and used by traditional ethnographers. As a result, the rules of engagement for someone conducting a netnography turn out to be very different from the ones used by physically embedded, face-to-face ethnographers. This difference between physical and online traces, interactions, algorithms, and socialities is a key element requiring the specific adaptation of netnographic practices and positions from those of the more general fields of ethnographic and digital ethnographic inquiry.

Traditional ethnographic techniques and understandings can of course be applied to new developments, but without specificity in relating the procedures used, the results can be unstructured and willy-nilly. This was the state of the art when I was conducting my dissertation in 1995. People were using online data from bulletin boards, but there were no explicit guidelines about what to do, how to do it, and why to do it. I hungered for an instruction set, a body of knowledge to help me in this new domain, and one to which I could contribute as the method grew and changed. I developed netnography so that I could answer those questions about what type of research procedures to follow in social media. Other scholars found those answers and procedures useful, adopted them, and added to them. In this way, we all built netnography.

Research methods are made of practices pursued with scientific intent. Every recognized, legitimate particular form of research has clear affiliations, roots, and sets of practices. If we do not know the affiliations, roots, and sets of practices that govern a significantly different research approach such as netnography, then we leave it up to individual authors to create their own particular procedures every time they use it. We depend upon individual authors to claim (or have claimed for them) a uniqueness to their findings that may make it difficult to generalize. Uniform adherence to a standard set of practices simplifies communications, or at least helps to aggregate common knowledge so that the wheel of method turns smoothly even as it is – inevitably – being reinvented.

Netnographic techniques require frequent updating because they are both specific and located in dynamic social and technological contexts. New technological developments bring new social science research approaches to the fore, such as using mobile phones and their cameras for interviews or in-the-moment explorations of daily life. Evolution of the social media space means that sites become larger, more complex, more global, and more various. Because its procedures deliberately embrace adaptation and flux, netnography eagerly incorporates these new developments into its research repertoires in order to help triangulate and contextualize online traces. Public postings offer the potential for the participant ethnographer to become a public research figure, a type of public intellectual, online activist, or action researcher. Netnographic research practices follow the rules of online and internet research ethics, which are in a state of near-constant change. And the many visual, mobile, multiple, and storytelling representational options for netnographies require development separately from those of the more familiar modalities of ethnographic research. This edition of *Netnography* includes a range of novel culturally- and technologically-based techniques to help you gather, create, co-create, and analyze online traces.

The third and perhaps most important differentiator is netnography's pragmatic approach. Netnography's focus and forte has always been to present researchers with a nuts-and-bolts, workbench-level approach to cultural social media research. We can also call it a recipe. This pragmatic level is layered onto the richly abstract theoretical bases of traditional ethnographers and the many innovations of contemporary digital ethnographers across multiple disciplines and institutions. This includes those many researchers doing fascinating work while employed in a myriad of business and industry applications, such as marketing research and consumer insight inquiry. Although we will likely never see their work published, I have had very regular contact with them, and they have greatly influenced the practical development of netnography.

The goal of this book is to offer a rich background for researchers from a variety of fields, enabling them to understand the bases of netnography in the study of the cultural contexts and contents of a plethora of online communicative acts and interactions. As well, netnography is focused on providing a clear set of how-to oriented instructions for academic, industry, and other researchers. These guidelines for the practice of netnography are there to help all researchers begin actually discovering, collecting, deciphering, and developing answers and theory from online traces using a range of comprehensible techniques.

SUMMARIZING NETNOGRAPHY

1.4

Netnography is a specific type of qualitative social media research. It adapts the methods of ethnography and other qualitative research practices to the cultural experiences that encompass and are reflected within the traces, networks, and systems of social media. Netnography differs from the more general field of digital inquiry by its emphasis on online traces, interactions, and socialities. It is different from other forms of online or digital ethnography because it specifies particular procedural guidelines. Finally, netnography is a pragmatic, how-to, workbench-level approach to studying social media using a cultural lens.

THE RELATION OF NETNOGRAPHY TO OTHER ACADEMIC FIELDS

Applications and publications that use netnography are burgeoning across fields as diverse as Information and Library Science, Computer Science, Psychology, Media Studies, Travel, Hospitality, and Tourism Studies, Sexuality and Gender, Nursing, Drug Policy Research, Game Studies, Education, Media Anthropology, Geography, and Sociology. In the field of Accounting, for example, Guo (2018) studied an online forum set up by a professional accounting group to explore how people develop the professional identity of being an accountant, and how that related to participants' professional insecurities. D'Ambra and colleagues (2017) used netnography to understand how the use of e-books changed readers' experience of reading. They identified a *New York Times* article about the topic, and another in the publication *Scientific American*. They then downloaded and analyzed the comments left on these articles on the publications' websites. Palo and Manderstedt (2017) used a diverse range of data, including Instagram posts, Twitter messages, reviews, blog posts, podcasts, and YouTube movies, to understand how textual features are understood by engaged child readers. In the field of food sociology, Cronin and colleagues (2014) used netnography to examine discussions of over-consumption of food and alcohol, and then illustrate and develop a theory of their 'carnivalesque' qualities. Contributing to the language studies field, Sultana, Dovchin, and Pennycock (2014) used a netnography of Facebook groups to study the use of the 'linguistic, social and cultural practices' of young Bangladeshi and Mongolian adults. In economic geography, Grabher and Ibert (2014) used their netnographic study of online hybrid professional-hobbyist communities to conclude that the physical 'distance' in these communities should not be considered a deficiency, but rather an asset that helped them to collaboratively learn in ways different from face-to-face learning.

There are many other examples. In the field of Library and Information Studies, for example, Moreillon (2015) used netnography to study how school librarians use Twitter and hashtags as a cultural tool and affinity space to gain and build a sense of professional identity, as well as to promote professional development in a grassroots, social media-created community of practice. Roland et al. (2017) used social network analysis along with netnography to identify and study another kind of Twitter hashtag-based online community of practice, this one dealing with health care. They found that these communities exhibited new characteristics such as social control, common purpose, flat hierarchy, and network-based achievement along with some of the traditional markers of such collectives. Exploring online sites with netnography has also helped us understand how online communications are used to share knowledge about dangerous practices and drugs. In one such study, McVeigh et al. (2016: 1) explored the 'plethora of communal folk pharmacological advice and recommendations for DNP manufacture and use, together with associated harms and outcomes'. DNP is a cellular metabolic poison that causes thermogenesis and results in fat burning and weight loss. Their study provided a rich and grounded examination of the knowledge, attitudes, and motivations of DNP users, and also illustrated the important role that public online sites play in their information sharing. Their study concluded by calling for more study of, and engagement with, these online groups, and the use of this understanding to formulate appropriate and effective policy responses. These examples from the fields of Computer Science, Child Education, Food Sociology, Accounting, Language Studies, Economic Geography, Library and Information Science, Health Communication, and Drug Policy Research are just a small sampling of the hundreds of netnographies that have been conducted and published within numerous academic fields and subfields, as well as in the Marketing Research, Advertising, Public Relations, and Tourism and Travel academic fields and industries.

The reason for its success across academic fields is probably because netnography is a coherent method that has proven very useful for revealing communities of practice, interactional styles, group exchanges, alterations in communication and information systems, learning in the wild, online norms, digital practices, discursive styles, innovative forms of collaboration and organization, and manifestations of creativity. This book captures the waves of exciting new social media research appearing across almost every social science academic field since the publication of the first edition of *Netnography*. Every month that goes by, more and more examples of the diverse forms and fields of netnography are taking hold, and overview articles are beginning to appear with increasingly useful and systematic discussion of researchers' varied methodological and operational choices (Bartl et al., 2016; Costello et al., 2016; Heinonen and Medberg, 2018; Tavakoli and Wijesinghe, 2019; Whalen, 2018; Wu and Pearce, 2014).

INVESTIGATING DIGITAL ANTHROPOLOGY

1.5

The lines between different forms of social science investigation are in flux and they are often unclear. As an exercise, investigate the current meaning and boundaries of the field of 'digital anthropology'. What do you think this term means? Does it include netnography? How is it related to netnography?

To finish this initial investigation of digital anthropology, use an online resource to look up a few digital anthropology articles in peer-reviewed journals. Have a quick read through these articles to understand where the current research interests lie in this important and growing field.

Digital Anthropology and Netnography

It would not be an exaggeration to say that anthropologists have greeted the rise of digital culture with skepticism. In the early 2000s, when the Internet's rise was well under way, a survey of the top 50 anthropology departments in the United States found that almost 30% of anthropologists explicitly rejected the idea that online anthropology could be an important research area (Forte, 2002). Although netnography is definitely a form of digital anthropology, it has always been a hybrid creation of many academic fields. For its formulation, I was indebted to early digital anthropologists such as Arturo Escobar (1994) and his early and controversial advocacy of 'anthropologies of cyberculture'. Although it emerged out of my work in the field of consumer culture research, netnography was originally developed based on scholarship I had seen in cultural studies by scholars such as Henry Jenkins (1995) and Nancy Baym (1995). In fact, it was adapted for my own project of bringing cultural studies into the mainstream of consumer research using a brand studies-related lens to investigate media fan communities.

Netnography draws on the work of many communication and information studies scholars, such as Sherry Turkle (1995), Joseph Walther (1992), Ronald Rice (1984), Margaret McLaughlin (1995), Annette Markham (1998) and Stephen Jones (1995).

I also drew on the work of psychologists like Sara Kiesler and her colleagues (Kiesler et al., 1984) and computer science-based human-computer interface scholars like Brenda Laurel and Joy Mountford (1990). I am indebted to the scholars who work in these fields, and am glad that netnography is a creation whose DNA traces to such exciting fields of scholarly inquiry. I hope that future scholars studying and using netnography will build on this common basis in multiple fields to extend, expand, and integrate not only the approach but also the combined impact of these academic domains.

As the social media field sites in which netnography is situated have grown and spread, the approach's focus has become broader and has touched upon diverse areas of inquiry. In anthropology, for instance, there is a growing corpus of 'ethnographic approaches to digital media' scholarship that Coleman (2010) divides into broad and overlapping categories of 'cultural politics', 'vernacular culture', and 'prosaics'. These studies cover a wide swath of contemporary human engagement with technology.

All netnographies are, by virtue of their engagement with social media, a form of digital anthropology. And although some digital anthropology is recognizably netnographic, such as Daniels' (2009) study of racism online, much of it expands the scope of investigation to consider human experiences with technology as broadly as possible, such as with the ethnographies of software developers and hackers. Another important and closely related field that broadens netnography's focus is media anthropology.

Media Anthropology and Netnography

Media anthropology (also called 'the anthropology of media') is an 'ethnographically informed, historically grounded, and context-sensitive analysis of the ways in which people use and make sense of media technologies' (Askew, 2002: 3). It also explores 'the dynamics of all these social processes of media consumption, production, [and] circulation' (Ginsburg et al., 2003: 23). It would be hard to deny that an understanding of social media communication should form a part of more general ethnographic look at how people use and make sense of media technologies, and thus that netnography should play a key role in media anthropology investigations.

Every day, people are intimately involved not only in the social processes of media consumption, but also in its production and circulation. Ordinary citizens become elevated, some rapidly gain celebrity status. The dynamics of media's social processes have dramatically shifted, and continue to alter. For example, consider the netnography of the relation between hijab-wearing, fashion, and social media identity construction by Kavakci and Kraeplin (2017). This article showed how the broad links between morality, religion, economy, and technology are exhibited through celebrity and in both the global attention economy and the Islamic culture industry. These interdependencies become visible through the investigation of social media identity. Kavakci and Kraeplin's (2017) study concludes that 'the identities of their hijabi women's social media personalities are heavily influenced by Western secular norms and their motivations may often be market-driven, even when bound closely with the mediated Islamic cultural and religious imagery and semiotics' (p. 865). The resulting identity of a stylishly attired but modestly covered Muslim woman is known as a 'hijabista' – a hijab-wearing fashionista.

It is worth noting that, from its inception, netnography was influenced by and used for fan studies in the Cultural Studies vein – an arm of Media Studies and Media Anthropology. The market-based enthusiasm of fan studies, with its passionate connection to its topics, was already a part of online ethnographic work. As we will see in Chapter 2, the Age of Virtual Community in social media studies contained several important studies of the online message board and the conversational groupings that were gathering around general and specific media properties such as soap operas (Baym, 1993), *The X-Files* (Clerc and Lavery, 1996) or *Twin Peaks* (Jenkins, 1995). These early fan studies (and, arguably, 'fannish' studies, such as Howard Rheingold's and Annette Markham's) were marked by a close personal, intellectual, and emotional engagement with the online phenomena they investigated, as well as in the novel processes of investigation itself. Netnography shared and still shares this fan-oriented and fan group-derived emphasis on media, community, and passionate engagement.

OUTLINE OF THIS BOOK

This book is arranged as a series of logical steps that lead you from a conceptual and historically-grounded understanding of netnography, online ethnography, qualitative social media research, and theories about online social interaction to the initiation, development, data collection, analysis, interpretation, and communication of your own netnography project. As part of the book's hands-on approach, you will learn about each step in netnography. You will put this new approach and its specific procedures to use. You will practice these new procedures in a series of practical exercises, including working with a downloadable dataset in spreadsheet format.

You will also create your own research project. You will learn how to prepare data, how to search for relevant traces, how to collect these traces, and how to organize your data, as well as different methods for analyzing and interpreting it, and integrating those analyses and interpretations. As you do so, you will be confronted with realistic methodological and contextual choices. For instance, you will need to consider how to deal with data protection regulations, or how to theorize the complex, changing, and corporate/surveillance capitalist control structure of much of contemporary social media. You will also, as a final step, consider how to communicate the output of your research. The particular manner in which you will move through this learning process is detailed in the remainder of this chapter. The pace at which you do it is under your control (or, if you are using this book for a course, completely out of your hands).

Methodological and Historical Introduction: Chapters 1 to 4

Netnography's initial chapter offers three introductions: an introduction to the field of social media, an introduction to the method of netnography, and an introduction to this book. It provides a clear definition of social media, and then proceeds to define netnography in a similarly transparent fashion. It positions netnography in relation to similar types of research, such as digital anthropology and online ethnography. This first chapter should clear up a lot of questions that people have about netnography and how it relates to other ethnographic forms of online research. Netnography is a specific type of qualitative social media research method that differs from the more general field of ethnographic and digital ethnographic inquiry by its emphasis on online traces, interactions, and socialities. It differs from other forms of qualitative social media research because of its particular procedural guidelines. Finally, this chapter explains how netnography is a pragmatic, how-to, workbench-level approach to studying social media using a cultural lens.

Chapters 2 and 3 will provide a historical basis for understanding social media both as a concept and an institution, and ethnographic social media research as a distinct and interdisciplinary field of inquiry with a history stretching back several decades. In these chapters, the history of social media will be divided into three temporal periods: the Age of Electronic Communications (late 1960s to early 1990s), the Age of Virtual Community (early 1990s to early 2000s), and the Age of Social Media (early 2000s to date). Chapter 2 examines the first two ages. The first age began with the Arpanet and the early years of (mostly corporate) networked communications. For the public around the globe, the Age of Electronic Communication was built on the back of private American online services such as CompuServe and GEnie, and successful public experiments with online services in Europe such as Minitel in France. On the research side, Usenet and the Bulletin Board System proved amenable to an ethnographic approach, and research intensified and developed through the 1990s as the Age of Virtual Community advanced. The second age saw a flowering of experimentation and developments, as corporate, journalistic, and academic communications all emphasized this new form of 'community'. During the second age, a developing field of ethnographies of online environments explored and wrote about life online as an evolving cultural context.

Chapter 3 will demonstrate how the Age of Social Media advanced through three overlapping waves. First, dynamic webpages were forms of social media that were more individual-centered and audience-driven. Then, social networking sites mainstreamed the online interactional format and commercialized online social experience. Finally, visual platforms offered more vivid and creative impressions of contact. Throughout the historical overview, we will observe how the sociotechnical infrastructures of different platforms alter the experience of sociality by offering new social affordances. With an overview of important sites in China (WeChat and QQ), and Russia (VKontakte), we will learn about some of the global developments in social media. We will also discover the netnographic research conducted using sites of social media such as Twitter, Friendster, Reddit, LinkedIn, Facebook, Flickr, You-Tube, Instagram, and Snapchat. Numerous netnographies have already shown how social media offer alternate news channels to the public, are used in life transitions, play a role in processes of credibility and trust formation, become involved in various forms of resistance and activism, and how they are creating new ecosystems of online entrepreneurs and influence networks.

Chapter 4 will delve into a theoretical overview of online sociality. The chapter will investigate utopian and dystopian views of social media and technology by interrogating the ideological and empirical bases of claims of community and also by examining the structure-agency effects of social media technologies on human sociality. On one side is a consocial perspective that leads us to see social media less as a solid institutional arrangement and more as a momentary construction that enables the possibilities provided by individual life projects and trajectories. On the other side are theories positing considerably more determinist effects. The chapter will further examine social media's structure-agency dimension by deploying four distinct but overlapping theoretical lenses: technogenesis, affordance theory, intersectionality, and networked individualism. The chapter's concluding section will consider the central role that marketing, finance, and media industrialization in general play in social media. These capitalist forces have led to a variety of production processes dedicated to monetizing the communitarian dimensions of social life online, with important attendant effects upon both society and our researching of it.

Empirical Initiation: Chapters 5 and 6

Chapter 5 marks the official beginning of the 'how-to' portion of the book. The chapter's methodological overview will present the four elements that distinguish netnography from every other research method. The chapter also offers a broad view of the four general categories of research operations. Then, the chapter explains the six steps of netnography: initiation, investigation, immersion, interaction, integration, and incarnation. Next, the chapter offers some advice and ideas regarding the conduct of netnography in research teams. Much netnography is conducted by groups of researchers, rather than individuals working alone.

With this overview in place, Chapter 5 moves into a discussion and exercise-driven exploration of the first stage of the netnographic research process, initiation. The initiation stage focuses the netnographic project on a particular research question. Chapter 5 will teach you about the two major parts of a research question, and will also unpack the two key initiators of netnographic research questions. Through a series of exercises, you will learn how to develop your own effective netnographic research questions. The chapter examines a number of research questions that have been used in prior netnographic research, analyzing their components and direction in order to provide you with clear guidelines and a strong foundation upon which to base your own netnographic project. Throughout the remainder of this book, you will build on the research questions that you initiate in this chapter.

However, before your netnography project begins in earnest, you should be aware of the ethical procedures that must guide your work. This is the function of Chapter 6. In this chapter, you will learn the fundamental principles behind research ethics, and in particular how netnography follows standards that are adapted to the current contexts that govern ethnographic and online research. The chapter will tell you the percentage of recent online ethnographies published that failed to include any mention at all of ethical guidelines or standards. Applying the two main moral philosophy stances – deontological and consequentialist – to the task of qualitative social media research is the next step in the chapter, which will proceed to identity and quantify a 'consent gap' representing the percentage of the public that has clearly stated their preference for their social media data not to be used in any research investigation. Furthermore, the chapter will explain how ethical practices can be tainted by taking prior detrimental advice. The core of the chapter is an integrated flowchart to ensure that data collection and presentation procedures are research ethics compliant. The flowchart presented in Figure 6.3 is a central tool to help you through the remainder of the book, because data ethics are involved across all of the active operations of data collection, analysis, and communication.

Data Collection Operations: Chapters 7 to 10

Chapter 7 will explore the methodology and implications of netnographic data collection in general, with a specific focus on investigative operations and sampling issues. The chapter will begin by explaining what the terms 'data' and 'data collection' mean in the context of practicing netnography. It will then explore the implications of observer choice on the creation of data from social media traces, interactions, interviews, and researcher experiences. Investigative, interactive, and immersive data collection operations will be introduced and overviewed. The three operations can be used together, in combination, or separately in qualitative social media research. Which operation(s) to use must be determined in deference to the research question and other elements of the research context. The next subsection of the chapter will explore ethics in investigative data operations, including the right to use public versus private sites and data in research, and the need for and forms of researcher disclosure. There will be important practical concerns discussed about how to deal with data in which message posters are anonymous or pseudonymous. The final subsection will foreshadow the way in which the procedures of the next three chapters will build on the base of methodology developed in this chapter.

The focus on data collection continues in Chapter 8 with a full description and development of investigative operations. In netnography, investigation is an unobtrusive process focusing on the selection and collection of social media data. Building upon Chapter 7's reorientation of the notion of data, this chapter will outline netnography's specific investigative practices. There are five of these: simplifying, searching, scouting, selecting, and saving. Simplifying translates the research questions and focus into a consistent set of search terms or keywords. Searching involves the entry of keywords, search terms, hashtags, trends, and their variations into search functions and engines. Scouting operations provide the initial filter to narrow down the choice set from which you will select your data sites. Selection practices apply specific relevant criteria in order to decide which data sites to choose for your dataset. Selection also involves data ethics concerns such as sensitive topics, vulnerable populations, and weighing benefits against risks. Saving operations include capture, cut and paste, and scraping from any manner of devices, including mobile phones. Saving is also implicated in ethical procedures of data security. This chapter will describe, illustrate, and provide numerous examples to help you learn about these five practices that, together, constitute the process of investigative data collection operations in netnography.

Chapter 9 will focus on interactive data collection operations. Interactive data is co-produced and elicited, rather than simply observed and recorded. Before detailing the elements of interactive data collection, the chapter will consider the nature of online engagement as the appropriate frame for netnography, replacing the more perplexing former term drawn from traditional ethnography, 'participation'. The chapter will then present procedural operations under the general categories of interviews, involvements, innovations, and informed consent. The appropriate way to conduct interviews will be covered, focusing especially on online interviews. After that, the chapter will discuss, describe, and provide examples of involvements, or naturalistic immersive interactions. Then, under the general name of innovative research approaches to interaction, the chapter will discuss the use of research webpages, digital diaries, and mobile ethnography. The chapter's final section will provide the reader with a more exhaustive treatment of informed consent procedures in netnography, including a sample form that can be adapted to your own research project.

Finally, Chapter 10 is dedicated to exploring the nature and practice of immersive data operations in netnography. It will open with a critical inquiry into the ethnographic notion of field and field site. This critique will reveal that the concept of a field site is so destabilized by the nature of netnography as to be inaccurate. Instead of field sites, netnographers have data sites. Instead of fieldnotes, netnographers keep immersion journals. The chapter will then specify and explain the four core immersive operations in netnography: reconnoitering, recording, researching, and reflecting. Reconnoitering is a type of orienting towards data sites, guided by the metaphor of the researcher's focus alternately employing a telescope and microscope. In reconnoitering operations, researchers seek deep data that is resonant, reveals lead users, provides exceptions to the rule, or reveals the macro inherent in the micro. Recording is the detailed, specific chronicling of the netnographer doing the research. Researching requires researchers to deliberately reveal, systematize, and evaluate the theoretical viewpoints they consciously and unconsciously impress upon the data during its inscription and analysis. Reflecting operations encourages researchers to develop self-awareness, emotionality, and empathy, completing the set of ethnographic immersion operations. The final subsection of Chapter 10 will provide an overview of the research ethics implications of immersive data operations in netnography before proceeding to the next chapter, which will describe netnography's integration movement.

Data Analysis and Interpretation Operations: Chapters 11 to 13

Integration is a combination of analytic and interpretive data operations in a pragmatic quest to answer research questions in netnography. Chapter 11 opens with a short science fiction story that analogizes a key problem regarding how social scientific analysis obscures contextual understanding. After the metaphorical story, the chapter will define and explain integration, analysis, and interpretation. Integration, analysis, and interpretation will connect to netnographic research, research questions, deductive, inductive, and abductive approaches to research. Those connections will subsequently be explored and discussed. An adaptation of Benjamin's immanent criticism method will be developed and its application explained. The analysis and interpretation exercises of upcoming chapters will be foreshadowed. There are several data-processing tools available to netnographers, including printed hardcopies, word processors, spreadsheets, and qualitative data analysis software. These options will be compared and discussed to close the chapter and prepare the reader for the next two chapters, in which data analysis and interpretation explanations and exercises will be provided.

Data analysis is a research process in which a particular phenomenon is broken down into component parts in order to study and understand it. The various subsections of Chapter 12 break down analysis into five component operations. First, the decisions involved in analysis will be discussed. Levels of analysis will be related to researchers' decisions about what is to be treated as a whole or a part. Analysis and its outcomes will also be related to sociologies of knowledge in which extant theoretical frames are adopted or new ones are made. The basic principles of qualitative data analysis will be overviewed. Following that, this book's more specific focus on data analysis operations for netnography will be introduced, detailed, and illustrated using examples and practice exercises. First, collating operations will be discussed as the preparation of data for coding. Second, coding operations, which lie at the heart of data analysis, are detailed as initiations into the processes of abstraction and reflection that lead to theory development. Third, combining operations unite conceptually-related codes to form new, higher-order elements called pattern codes – and thus reveal more abstract structures and patterns. Fourth, counting operations are a quantifying procedure that allows researchers to more precisely compare various elements in qualitative data. Fifth and finally, charting operations create and use visualizations, maps, graphs, tables, and other displays of data. Researchers today have many tools for grasping a holistic sense of the data, as well as a sense of its component parts and how they fit together. This subsection will consider maps, network graphs, and word clouds. Together, collating, coding, combining, counting, and charting form the constituent elements of the analytic process advanced in this chapter.

Chapter 13's emphasis on interpretation rounds out this section on data integration, analysis, and interpretation. Interpretation is the process of making sense of, and discovering meaning in, collected and analyzed data. In this chapter, the use of hermeneutic interpretation in netnography will be introduced and clarified. Then, the application of assemblage theory to netnographic data interpretation will be introduced and developed. Thereafter, the six interpretive practices will be introduced, developed, and explained with examples and exercises. Theming is the operation that reassembles the component pieces of an abstractly analyzed phenomenon, creating a new conceptual whole from these parts. Talenting is a way to produce theming interpretations using artistic expression. Totalizing operations explore the reassembled conceptual whole and its meaning. Translating operations transport the researcher as they move back and forth between worlds of data and theory. Turtling operations are based on a famous metaphor of turtles standing on each other's backs and refer to the operation that will (re)connect data as well as the holistic phenomenon itself to the context(s) from which it was taken. Finally, troublemaking operations critique underlying and taken-for-granted notions in the service of developing a more robust and ethical interpretation. Throughout the chapter, numerous explanations and exercises will be provided to practically guide the reader through the process of data interpretation in netnography.

The Future Communication of Netnographic Research: Chapters 14 and 15

The book's penultimate chapter, Chapter 14, will forecast the future by reading the communication of netnographic research in the past, as it has occurred through particular research outlets. After presenting general guidelines for writing research, the chapter will present a new concept: the method-embedded research communication triangle, which will identify four key research elements to communicate: (1) the method of netnography, (2) the netnographic data operations, (3) the netnographic dataset, and (4) the data. Chapter 14 describes each of the four elements in turn, providing examples and exercises, and illustrating certain important concepts, such as legitimation from institutional theory and rhetorical writing in the sciences.

The communication of method is a rhetorical act. Strategies may differ and depend upon the various characteristics of an audience. Netnography currently has

25 different research operations (26 if you include research question-asking conceptions as operations). These 25 (or 26) operations are grouped into three distinct categories of data collection and two categories of data integration operations (i.e., analysis and interpretation). You must describe, explain, and justify the particular procedures employed in your research project. Datasets and data also need to be presented in the communication of your netnography. Chapter 14 will provide numerous examples of different types of netnographic method and procedural descriptions, datasets, and data drawn from a variety of published netnographies. The final section of this chapter will discuss some of the hallmarks of excellence in published netnographic research. Following this, the final chapter offers a vision of The Future of Netnography. Don't peek: save this chapter for last.

With this introduction to the book now complete, we will turn in the next chapter to a new examination of the history of social media.

CHAPTER SUMMARY

The book's opening chapter was a series of introductions. First, we were introduced to netnography by way of its relation to social media – the applications, websites, and other online technologies that enable users to engage in a variety of content creation, circulation, annotation, and association activities. Over five billion people around the world have access to different types of social media, and this edition of the book responds to the need for updated and improved ways to investigate and understand how they use them. The chapter's opening section broadly explored some of the contours of social media today, looking at global usage patterns, exploring the most popular types of social media platforms, and encouraging some personal reflection on your own use. The next section of the chapter introduced netnography, defining it as a form of cultural research that uses a set of specific practices to investigate social media. Netnography is affiliated with other forms of digital anthropology and media anthropology through its focus on cultural understanding. Netnography is different from other approaches because it uses specific techniques and a pragmatic, step-by-step approach to investigate online traces. The chapter's final section introduced the contents of the book, demonstrating how the approach has been updated for a rapidly evolving world of social media. The five main sections of the book are devoted to methodology and history, empirical initiation, data collection and creation, analysis and interpretation, and communicating impactful research customized to any academic field.

KEY READINGS

Frömming, Urte Undine, Steffen Köhn, Samantha Fox, and Mike Terry (2017) *Digital Environments: Ethnographic Perspectives Across Global Online and Offline Spaces.* Bielefeld, Germany: Transcript Verlag.

Gretzel, Ulrike (2017) 'Social media activism in tourism', *Journal of Hospitality and Tourism*, 15(2): 1–14.

Pink, Sarah (2017) 'Foreword', in Urte Undine Frömming, Steffen Köhn, Samantha Fox, and Mike Terry (eds), *Digital Environments: Ethnographic Perspectivces Across Global Online and Offline Spaces* (pp. 9–11). Bielefeld, Germany: Transcript Verlag.

Pink, Sarah, Heather Horst, John Postill, Larissa Hjorth, Tania Lewis, and Jo Tacchi, Jo (eds) (2015) *Digital Ethnography: Principles and Practice.* London: Sage.

A HISTORY OF
SOCIAL MEDIA

CHAPTER OVERVIEW

This chapter and the next will explore the history of social media and cultural approaches to its study. For our purposes, the history of social media can be split into three rough-hewn temporal divisions or ages: the Age of Electronic Communications (late 1960s to early 1990s), the Age of Virtual Community (early 1990s to early 2000s), and the Age of Social Media (early 2000s to date). This chapter examines the first two ages. Beginning with the Arpanet and the early years of (mostly corporate) networked communications, our history takes us into the world of private American online services such as CompuServe, Prodigy, and GEnie that rose to prominence in the 1980s. We also explore the internationalization of online services that happened with the publicly-owned European organizations such as Minitel in France. From there, we can see how the growth and richness of participation on the Usenet system helped inspire the work of early ethnographers of the Internet. As well, the Bulletin Board System was another popular and similar form of connection that proved amenable to an ethnographic approach. The research intensified and developed through the 1990s as the next age, the Age of Virtual Community, advanced. Corporate and news sites like Amazon, Netflix, TripAdvisor, and Salon.com all became recognizable hosts for peer-to-peer contact and conversation. In business and academia, a growing emphasis on 'community' began to hold sway, with the conception of 'virtual community' crystallizing the tendency. A developing field of ethnographies of online environments began to see life online as an evolving cultural context. It was against this conceptual and empirical background that netnography was developed and initially defined as a method for exploring cyberculture and online community. However, the electronic winds of change were already swirling. The translation of Livejournal and webpages into weblogs transitioned online socialities from more collective and communal forms such as newsgroups into more individualized and commodifiable formats, helping to usher in the current age, the Age of Social Media.

THE AGE OF ELECTRONIC COMMUNICATIONS: 1960s–1990s

THE QUEST FOR SOCIAL MEDIA HISTORY

2.1

Instructions: Spend 10 minutes investigating the origins of social media. What can you find? When did your sources say that social media began? Discuss with a peer who engaged in a similar exercise. What can you learn from this? Now have a look at Figure 2.1, and then read on.

Social media histories usually start with an obligatory recounting of the early days of the Internet's founding in the 1960s, including the first message sent over the Arpanet in 1969, immortalized in Werner Herzog's documentary *Lo and Behold, Reveries of the Connected World* (Herzog, 2016). From there, many histories skip a few decades, jumping to Tim Berner Lee's development in 1989 of protocols to link hypertext documents together into what became known as the World Wide Web. Five years later, we usually learn about the launch of Mosaic Netscape, the world's first browser. Then, in 2004, Facebook was created and the age of what we have come to know as social media began. However, those unavoidable histories actually miss a lot of the action. Although those particular milestones are certainly important to our understanding of social media – and thus of netnography – many important developments actually helped establish the world of social media between Charley Kline first sending his 'lo' message in 1969 from UCLA to Stanford and Mosaic's browser launch in 1994. Figure 2.2 depicts a map of the original four Arpanet sites. As you can surmise from the figure, the precursor to today's Internet was something like a connection of four computers into a network, producing a device similar to an email server.

As you might imagine, bandwidth was exceedingly precious in the early years of the online world. Because it was originally funded by the government, merely social forms of communication were prohibited or severely constrained in those days. Hinting at the entrepreneurial and ideological motivations that comprise many contemporary social media communications, a 1982 handbook on computing at MIT's Artificial Intelligence Lab warned users that 'sending electronic mail over the Arpanet for commercial profit or political purposes is both anti-social and illegal' (Stacy, 1982: 9). However, the same handbook also stated that 'personal messages to other Arpanet subscribers (for example, to arrange a get-together or check and say a friendly hello) are generally not considered harmful'. These are netiquette types of rules, the stated social norms that many of us are familiar with from FAQs and other guides to specific online behavior. Archival work could be done on documents such as these

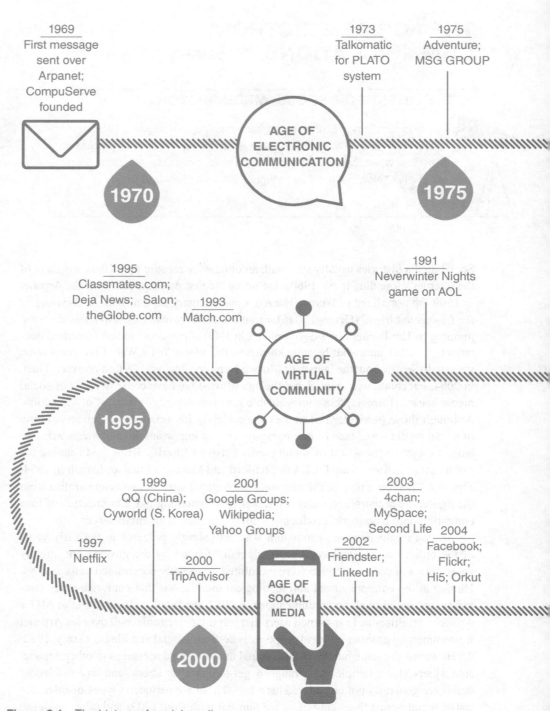

Figure 2.1 The history of social media

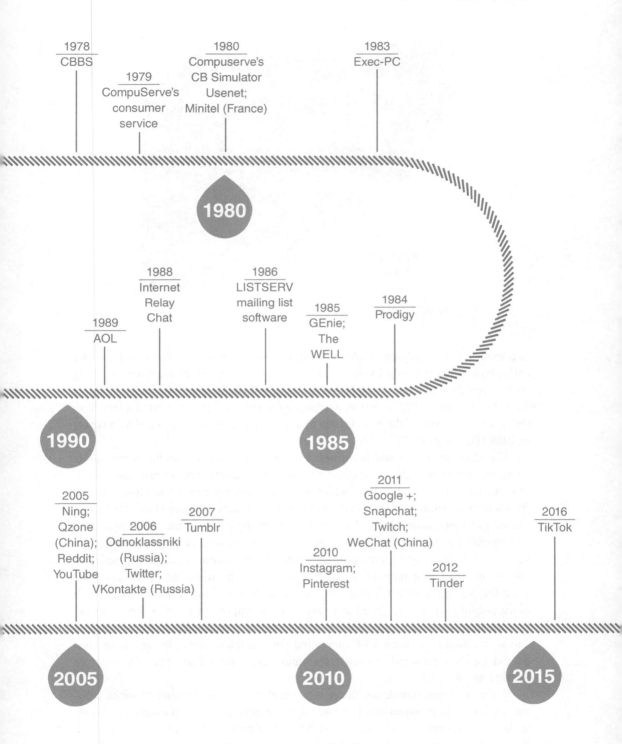

1978
CBBS

1979
CompuServe's
consumer
service

1980
Compuserve's
CB Simulator
Usenet;
Minitel (France)

1983
Exec-PC

1980

1989
AOL

1988
Internet
Relay
Chat

1986
LISTSERV
mailing list
software

1985
GEnie;
The
WELL

1984
Prodigy

1990

1985

2005
Ning;
Qzone
(China);
Reddit;
YouTube

2006
Odnoklassniki
(Russia);
Twitter;
VKontakte (Russia)

2007
Tumblr

2010
Instagram;
Pinterest

2011
Google +;
Snapchat;
Twitch;
WeChat (China)

2012
Tinder

2016
TikTok

2005

2010

2015

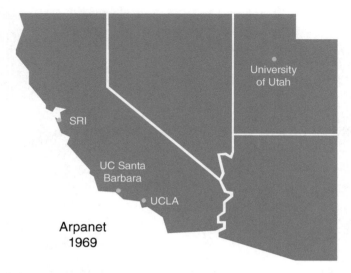

Figure 2.2 Original Arpanet sites

to provide a historically-grounded and netnographic-type portrayal of social media's early days. What it would likely reveal about the early years of the Arpanet, along with its middle and latter years, is that it was full of conflicts and misunderstandings from the clashings of the different worldviews of people – as captured in a report on the first two decades of the Net, written in a scientific journal published NASA report in 1989 (Denning, 1989).

The ideological war and harmful behaviors in the Arpanet archives remind us about the importance of privacy, and one-to-one or selective communication. This, of course, is email. And email – which we must consider one of the most success-ful social applications of information technology to date – began in the 1960s and started to spread around 1973. Very early. Before the Arpanet, the phone networks had already been using their own digital-to-analog modems. Because email is not intended for the public production and distribution of content, it would typically not be included as a form of social media. Yet the introduction of listserv soft-ware for managing email lists made individual-to-individual private email much more public and social. Email lists are thus an important form of communica-tion existing in a hazy gray zone between public and private, individual media and social media. A number of interesting netnographies have, in fact, been con-ducted on data gathered from listservs and other email lists. See, for example Pentina and Amos (2001).

In the academic world, our understanding of the evolving nature of social com-munications was exponentially increased by the perceptive work of a number of early social media researchers who were attuned to the cultural elements of the phenomenon. Among the first was a husband-and-wife team: computer scientist Murray Turoff and sociologist Starr Roxanne Hiltz. Together, they wrote one of the earliest books about how people were beginning to use computer networks (or 'computer conferencing') to socialize, congregate, and organize, reflecting brilliant sociological insights that established Hiltz as a luminary. Published twelve years before the World Wide Web, *The Network Nation* (Hiltz and Turoff, 1978) foresaw a world of commonplace social media – and its researching. Hiltz and Turoff, along with other perceptive scholars of the early social networks like Jan van Dijk, Barry Wellman, and Manuel Castells, wrote that online technologies were creating new social universes, media and relational phenomena with vast effects upon culture, politics, and economies. Each of them appreciated the role of situated, contextualized research of online phenomenon. Each of them also paid attention to the institutional interweaving of science, systems, networks, and media with the public and private interests of people and organizations as they intermingled online. These early researchers informed us that the interconnected networking technologies and ever-more-sophisticated communications systems would have massive social and cultural implications that would keep ramifying and accelerating change.

COMPARING SOCIAL MEDIA YESTERDAY AND TODAY

2.2

What sorts of activities do you think are unique to today's social media? When do you think they started? Write down your assumptions about social media's history. Then, read on.

....
....
....
....
....
....
....
....

Again and again in our historic exploration, we will see that the easy-to-use software structures, affordances, and patterns of behavior and communication, which are familiar and institutionalized in contemporary social media, were established many years ago in systems such as Minitel, Bildschirmtext, CompuServe, GEnie and BBS. Politics, ideology, conflict, and vicious disagreement have always been a part of the online social experience. The easy crossover between types of social communications and accompanying acts, expressed, for example, in the desire to meet someone in person who one has met online – this too has long been a part of online experience. Sexuality, dating, intimate relationships, rip-off schemes, and religion – all of these can be found in the half-century long history of social media. The origins and contours of all of these institutionalized elements of social media are matters with which all contemporary netnographers should be familiar so that they are not caught up in the ostensible 'newness' of social phenomena that, in all likelihood, have been going on since before they were born.

Private American Online Services in the Seventies and Eighties: CompuServe, Prodigy, and GEnie

Figure 2.3 CompuServe screenshot showing file interface

And so, let us enter the time portal and traverse it back to 1969, the year of the Beatles' last public performance, the year that Boeing debuted the 747, Woodstock was held, and the Arpanet was founded. Although rarely heralded for it, 1969 is also noteworthy for another milestone event in the history of social media: the founding of CompuServe. The brainchild of a subsidiary of an Ohio insurance company, CompuServe was the first major commercial online service provider in the United States. It ended up dominating the North American domestic private in-home online communication and information access industry in the 1980s. A screenshot of a late 1980s CompuServe interface is depicted in Figure 2.3. Compu-Serve remained a major influence through the mid-1990s. For early users, it offered up a veritable cornucopia of video-text services with a recognizably strong social media component.

In 1980, CompuServe offered the first public, commercial multi-user chat program, arguably one of the earliest and most successful of the original social media applications. The 'CB Simulator', as CompuServe's online text chat system was called, led to all sorts of interesting gatherings, foreshadowing the social fecundity of later connective media. Using the CB Simulator on CompuServe in the early 1980s, people were dating online, talking through text. Users organized real world events to meet one another. An online wedding occurred on the medium. And an online ethnography of events transpiring on CompuServe's CB Simulator was written by Lindsy van Gelder (1991), which might possibly stand as the world's first netnography.

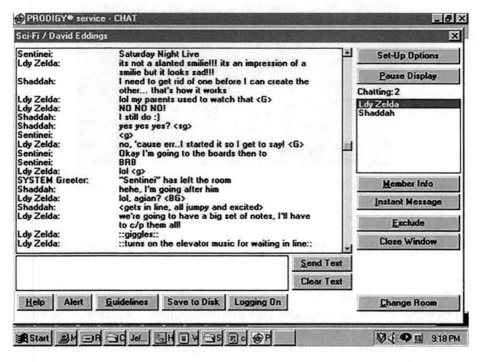

Figure 2.4 Prodigy chat function screenshot, showing the textual inventiveness of conversants

CompuServe hosted a series of popular online games, such as the Island of Kesmai, a historically important multi-user dungeon game and precursor of the MMORPG genre noted for its innovative use of pseudo-graphics. CompuServe revolutionized social media by introducing the GIF file format that greatly simplified the exchange of visual images, and which remains one of the standard visual file formats to this day. Finally, it offered its users a vast variety of message forums that covered a diverse number of topics, providing a bulletin board-like experience that used a combination of communal 'sysop' and compensated management. In 1984, the American companies CBS, IBM, and Sears together launched Trintex, a competitor to Compu-Serve. Changing its name to Prodigy, the new videotex competitor used advertising and its own fully staffed newsroom to grow the market. And in the same year, General Electric entered the market with its GEnie offering.

Figure 2.5 GEnie screenshot of an 'Apple Mafia' technology aficionado group

Throughout the late 1980s and early 1990s, CompuServe, Prodigy, and GEnie offered American consumers an established and increasingly sophisticated variety of online media and social media experiences. Figure 2.4 provides a glimpse into the early world of chat rooms that was already fully developed well before this screenshot of a Prodigy interface was taken in the early 1990s. GEnie, for example, was known for its sophisticated online games, which included massively multiplayer games and those with 3D graphics. GEnie also had a well-developed system of 'RoundTables', that included message boards, chatrooms, and libraries for permanent files, all organized around particular topics such as Astrology, Aviation, Comics and Animation, Health, Music, Pets, Jerry Pournelle, ShowBiz, Sports, Religion and Philosophy, New Age beliefs, and many others. One such GEnie roundtable, used by Apple computer aficionados, an organic early manifestation of a self-organizing online brand fan community, is depicted in the screenshot shown in Figure 2.5.

By the early 1990s, CompuServe, Prodigy, and GEnie were offering their users thousands of moderated forums. The post, reply, thread, and subthread structures of these forums and roundtables closely resembled the moderated bulletin board systems that persist to this day on the contemporary web, such as those on Facebook, Reddit, BBS, Usenet, and in Twitter feeds. In the early 1990s, both CompuServe and Prodigy transitioned from developing and offering their own private online services to offering users access to the World Wide Web. Eventually, they succumbed to the marketing might of America Online, or AOL, a company that began in 1983 as a gaming platform for early consoles and home computers.

Internationalization, Expansion, and Ethnography

One of the most interesting and successful early social media application-running devices appeared in 1978 in France as a creation of French R&D, financed by public money, and designed for public benefit: a socialist Internet. Minitel was a publicly-owned service of France Télécom that eventually offered thousands of different online services to over 25 million French citizens. Among its offerings were message boards that allowed ordinary users to create, distribute, and receive content on a plenitude of different topics. In 1986, French university students used Minitel to coordinate a national strike, providing one of the earliest examples of social media activism. Systems similar to Minitel were introduced (albeit less successfully) in a range of different countries in the 1980s, including Germany's Bildschirmtext, Finland's TeleSamp, Italy's Videotel, and Viditel in the Netherlands. Just as social media does today, all of these services provided different ways for regular users to produce and publish content, as well as to connect, circulate, and comment on others' content in a variety of ways.

And while France and many of the European nations were experimenting successfully with the publicly-funded progenitors of social media, two American universities, one private and one public, were collaborating to create and launch a for-the-public-benefit online socialistic experiment of their own: a massively successful social media innovation called Usenet. Conceived in 1979 and established in 1980, Usenet is one of the oldest public access computer network communications systems still in use. Like CompuServe, Usenet's protocols and interface institutionalized a number of core elements of social media that persist to this day, such as topical forums, subject lines, posts, replies, and the resulting forms of message threads and subthreads, including branches to new threads, sub-forums, and different forums.

On Usenet, people posted messages or 'articles' onto the Arpanet (the early Internet). These 'articles' were deliberately entered into particular newsgroups that were organized by topical categories. The major 'big nine' categories of the Usenet were one of the early attempts to organize collective interests (such as an interest in science) and motives (such as a desire to discuss a subject with others) into neat categories. The interface placed message threads into the following categories utilizing consensual guidelines about subject and topic: alt, rec, comp, humanities, misc, news, sci, soc, and talk. The majority of posts on Usenet are response posts, which are called message threads. In all, Usenet provided a satisfying and flexible social experience, and from its inception met all relevant criteria for social media. This accessibility and variety is likely the reason why Usenet newsgroups were the sites of two of the earliest online ethnographies: Henry Jenkins' (1995) study of online fans of *Twin Peaks*, and Nancy Baym's (1993) research on a soap opera-based online group.

Usenet and Early Online Ethnographies

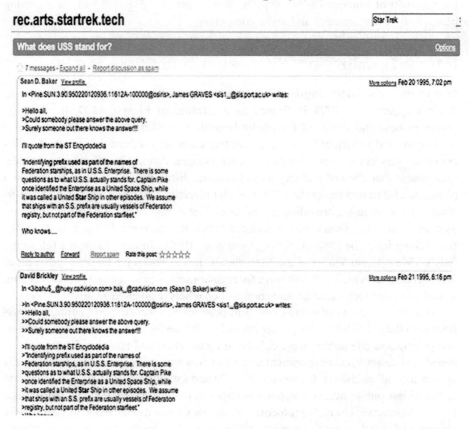

Figure 2.6 Archived version of 1995 Usenet Newsgroup, viewed through Google Groups interface

Early netnographies had to begin with an explanation of what being online meant, and a general mapping of the relevant online social space. In an essay originally presented to the *Society for Cinema Studies* in Los Angeles in 1990, and later published in book chapters in 1992 and 1995, Henry Jenkins began by explaining the nature of Usenet and detailing some of its technological characteristics and capabilities (Jenkins, 1992, 1995). At the time Jenkins presented it, the Usenet reached over 50,000 participants. Jenkins then detailed the content and type of information that people shared on Usenet, which ranged from discussions about government, technology, and science to those about news, hobbies, and popular culture, and included digital sound files and graphic images, as well as both short and very long textual discussions. Even at that early stage of the Internet's development, Jenkins still felt the need to note the tendency for the researcher to be overwhelmed by online data: 'The problem

[when] working with the net becomes not how to attract sufficient responses to allow for adequate analysis but how to select and process materials from the endless flow of information and commentary' (Jenkins, 1995: 52). Then, in the most detailed and rigorous terms yet devised, Jenkins introduces the idea, opportunity, and challenge of conducting ethnographic research online:

Ethnographic research has often been criticized for its construction of the very audience it seeks to examine, via the organization and structuring of focus groups, rather than engaging with the activist or pre-existing cultural community as they conduct their daily lives (the focus of more traditional forms of ethnography). Here, the computer net groups allow us to observe a self-defined and ongoing interpretive community as it conducts its normal practices of forming, evaluation, and debating interpretations. These discussions occur without direct control or intervention by the researcher, yet in a form that is legitimately open to public scrutiny and analysis. (1995: 52–3)

Although he describes his work as ethnography, Jenkins decides to adopt a more distanced stance from the data. In direct contrast to his traditional ethnographic work among *Star Trek* and media fans, he does not discuss his own participation in the group. In fact, he valorizes the lack of engagement in the quote above as a benefit of the method. Further, there is no mention of self-reflection or use of fieldnotes in the essay. This early online ethnography is distanced and written in a more objective style than some of Jenkins' other work: the discursive data allows the analyst, who seems to be observing from a privileged position above or beyond the social site, to 'trace the processes by which television meanings are socially produced, circulated, and revised' (ibid.). Attuned to sampling issues, Jenkins then discusses the 'social specificity' of the audience he studies – an early adopter group 'who tend to be college-educated, professionally-oriented, technologically-inclined men, most of who are involved either with the academy or the computer industry' (ibid.). They are not, as Jenkins explains, representative of general populations. However, as time reveals, and as I would later theorize by connecting the work of Eric von Hippel with netnography, this group provided a window on activities and tastes that were later to become mainstream. Although Jenkins introduces, justifies, and briefly explains his use of online ethnography, he never enters into an explanation of its underlying procedural elements. Indeed, this is not its purpose. To get a sense of the application that Jenkins employed, we can see one of the mid-1980s forms of the original Usenet interface in Figure 2.7. Some of the Usenet was archived and became searchable using Google Groups, appearing similar to the graphic shown in Figure 2.6.

The other noteworthy early online ethnography is Nancy Baym's much more participant-embedded and experience-close interpretation of a soap opera-based online group (Baym, 1993), for which the Usenet rec.arts.tv.soaps newsgroup was the source of data. Her article expands the methodological elements of her online

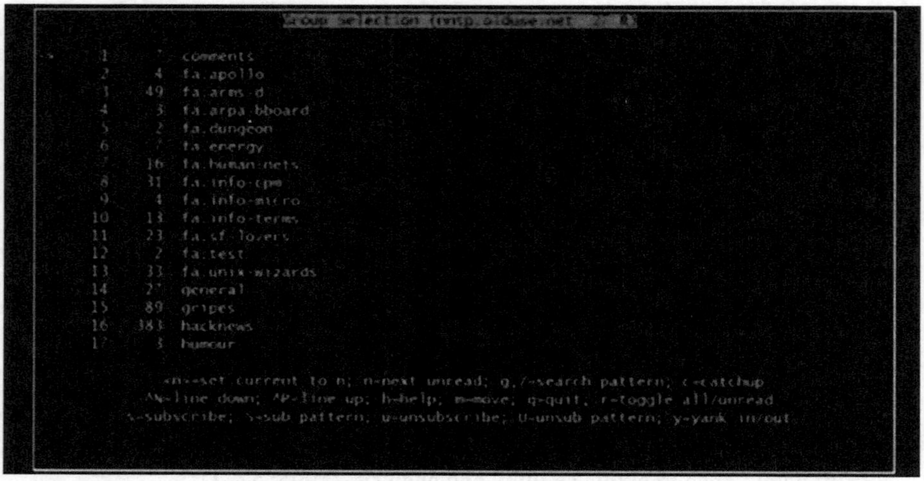

Figure 2.7 Usenet interface screenshot as it appeared approx. 1987

ethnography. She explains that her work is 'part of an ongoing ethnographic study of communication in the r.a.t.s [rec.arts.tv.soaps] newsgroup community' and that her 'position in the group is that of a participant at least as much as a researcher' (p. 144). Then, she explains the nature of her participation. As 'a long-time fan of soap operas' she had an emotional and intellectual engagement with both the topic matter and the forum for its discussion (Baym, 1993: 144). She was 'thrilled' when she discovered the group, and 'had been reading daily and participating regularly for a year' before beginning her research within it. In a nod to the 'member check' practices of Lincoln and Guba (1985), Baym reveals that she shared her research work with the group members and 'found them exceedingly supportive and helpful. They have acted as research participants as well as subjects and have treated me more as an ambassador than a researcher' (Baym, 1993: 144).

An accounting of her analytic procedure follows. Unlike Jenkins, she uses the term 'data' to refer to the discussions and conversations she collected. She discusses saving the messages, collecting and analyzing them, their content, and 'the demographic information [they contain] about the senders'. She also uses a type of online interview, where she posts a set of open-ended questions to participants, which were answered by 18 participants. As well, she includes personal email correspondence with ten other participants in the newsgroup.

She then discusses her ethical stance. Beginning with self-disclosure, she posts two notices 'explaining the project and offering to exclude posts by those who preferred not to be involved' (an early form of opting-out, it seems, and no one declined to participate). Baym changes all names and email addresses, but keeps the gender of the authors, where known, intact. Trying to maintain a sense of their original context, she explains that they are presented 'in a mono-space font', with the spelling and grammar 'remaining as they were written' (p. 145).

BBS and Correll's Lesbian Cafe

Figure 2.8 Screenshot of the Bulletin Board System, or BBS, early 1990s

Figure 2.8 depicts the early, white text on black background format of the bulletin board system, or BBS, which was similar in many ways to Usenet. Online in 1978, BBS was a social media platform that became interrelated with these early American and international online services. Similar to the early message boards, BBS was largely a text-based system, but that system, like the others, was flexible enough to allow a wide range of new social activities, such as the Australian Buddhist 'buddhanet' conversation group captured in Figure 2.8. Message boards and multi-user chat were present, as were some basic social networking features, such as the ability to leave messages on a user's profile. In terms of topics, BBS offered a wide variety of special interest boards that included sports, entertainment, politics, religion, music, dating, and alternative lifestyles. Imaginative areas popped up, where users could commune and role play in themed fantasy areas, such as those based on being on a pirate ship or in a medieval castle.

Shelley Correll, who was then a doctoral student at Stanford, conducted one of the earliest online ethnographies on a computer BBS called the Lesbian Cafe. Her article, published in the *Journal of Contemporary Ethnography* (Correll, 1995), is interesting not only as an early ethnographic work, but also because of its emphasis on a powerful tripartite inter-combination. Correll links the experience of being online in a BBS, an early but intense form of bulletin board, with sociality (the need to be social), the sense of reality (related closely to what to believe, what to care about, and what is true – as found in both media and religion), and the perception of community (who am I? what groups do I identify with and belong to?).

The shared sense that users of the BBS have of a 'common reality serves to maintain a community that carries out many of the same functions as do geographically anchored communities', argues Correll (1995: 298). She tells us a lot about her involvement with the online group, and also about her research methods. These techniques had not been institutionalized and the early works are highly instructive for their procedural attention to detail, because social media was still feeling very new in the 1990s and yet the networks had established vibrant microcultures of their own.

Women who regularly participate in the Lesbian Cafe's online discourses 'do so to be around their own kind of people', Correll states. She was already a member of the online Lesbian Cafe BBS when she begins her participant-observational study. She doesn't mention keeping fieldnotes. But she does state that she asked the founder of the cafe for permission to conduct the study. She posted a note to the group describing her study, and asking for interview volunteers. Every week Correll posted a new note to the group, telling them that they were still being observed by her. Most likely, she captured those observations in data files and fieldnotes. She conducted open, exploratory, and then semi-structured email interviews with 13 female members. She conducted a semi-structured telephone interview with the founder of the cafe. She then conducted eight in-person interviews with members in Atlanta, Georgia, and then the eight of them 'went to a real lesbian bar in Atlanta' (p. 278). Her methods are clear to us, and these are participatory, ethically attuned, and enhanced with in-person, telephone, and email interviews.

It wasn't all utopian and rosy, though. There were lots of unwelcome haters, those who came to the BBS to send messages that bashed, trolled or criticized lesbians. None of these trolls agreed to be interviewed by Correll. However, when asked, all of those 'bashers' self-identified as males. Correll sees them as consequential, and a manifestation of the half-full glass. The haters actually 'provide a source of conflict that serves to increase community solidarity' through a clarification of in-group and outgroup membership (p. 298). The Lesbian Cafe, and other online bulletin and message boards like it, serve 'many of the same functions' and have 'many of the same features' as traditional communities based upon geographic considerations. In fact, this interest-based segmentation is quite historically significant, as Schouten and McAlexander (1995) astutely point out in an article about consumption subcultures published the same year as the Lesbian Cafe article. Correll misses many important differences, but hey, we can cut her some slack; she was a ground-breaking first-year PhD student at the time, just beginning a successful academic career.

Correll concludes her forward-thinking article with a statement that wisely side-steps future debates about technology ushering in the demise of sociality. She sees two notions, 'community' and 'locale', as ideas which are not diminishing, as Putnam (2000) and others such as Turkle (2011) feared, but are 'only being reformulated' (p. 298). Sociality reformulated in the forge of social media becomes almost a single minded-focus through the online scholarship of the 1990s. As we are about to learn, Correll's (1995) focus on linking online experience with notions of community, and of linking online sociality with imaginary notions of spatiality, will become core themes of the scientific literature for almost a decade.

THE AGE OF VIRTUAL COMMUNITIES: 1990s–EARLY 2000s

Throughout the 1990s and early 2000s, the social web continued to expand as more companies and individuals offered more specialized and different sorts of online experiences. Companies of various sorts incorporated social media features into their purchasing and especially their review features. These social media features helped transform and begin to disrupt the retailing, entertainment, travel, and journalism industries of the 1990s – and also lay the groundwork for the rise of social networking sites.

Fairly early on in its history, online retailer Amazon allowed customers to rate and review books and other products, creating a social media phenomenon that grew to encompass an entire genre of funny reviews – a genre embraced by the company itself (see www.amazon.com/gp/feature.html?docId=1001250201, the Amazon site's listing of its own 'funniest reviews'). Amazon's embrace of social media and incorporation of online sociality into its pioneering of online retailing experience was one of the reasons it grew to become the largest and most important retailer in the world. Elsewhere (Kozinets, 2016), I examine several of these funny reviews to make the point that, even when engaging in supposedly rational economic behavior, such as rating products on a retail site, consumers use those directed connective opportunities to 'fulfill a wide range of social, communicative, emotional, and identity-focused needs', including 'cultural connection, witty repartee, social commentary, entertainment, personal revelation, self-promotion' and revenge-seeking (p. 836).

In the entertainment industry, Netflix began operating in 1997 as an online DVD rental concept with a major social component. The original Netflix site and model leveraged users' online interactions. Users created profiles that could be viewed by other users, and contributed long and often highly detailed reviews. They could also recommend films to one another personally, and one user could see both the ratings and the detailed comments that other users gave to particular films. At that time,

Netflix was far more than a place for people to go and rent movies. It was also a hub of online social activity, recommendation, review, and discussion – all of it revolving around the world of entertainment. Its redesign strongly emphasized its automated recommender systems, fully eliminating the earlier communal components. Working with this more recent, and 'de-communified' incarnation, Shen (2014) used netnography to understand customers' experiences, and discourses of satisfaction or dissatisfaction, with Netflix and other firms' recommendation systems.

Different stories can be told for the online travel site TripAdvisor. In 2000, TripAdvisor launched a site that featured official travel reviews from newspapers, guidebooks, and magazines. However, the site offered its users a button where they could add their own reviews. Adding this interactive feature generated massive interest, helping to create the world's largest travel website, and a pioneer of specialized social media. Also noteworthy among these early social media innovations was the world's first recognizable social networking site, classmates.com, an American platform, launched in 1995, dedicated to helping users find former class members and colleagues from school, work, and the military. Numerous travel netnographies have used TripAdvisor as a source of data. For instance, Mkono (2011: 253) used '41 online tourist reviews of two Victoria Falls, ethnic-style restaurants' to study how foreign food is 'othered' and reflects touristic representations of 'the Other'. Researchers in other fields have also found TripAdvisor's cultural form and rich conversations theoretically informative. In the accounting field, Jeacle and Carter (2011: 293) found that TripAdvisor builds its role as a 'trusted intermediary for the "independent traveler"' by enacting an online version of an objectively abstract system with calculative practices.

Change in the world of citizen journalism began to take shape when salon.com began operating in 1995, providing one of the earliest combinations of news and online reader commentary. Following Salon.com's (and others') early example, the comment sections to online news and journalism sites have grown to become important sites of social media and netnographic investigation. Netnographic research using the comments sections of online publications has turned out to be highly productive because many of these publications are specialized and cater to particular interests or particular groups. For example, Sandlin (2007) used an online lifestyle magazine and its discussion boards as the site of her online ethnography. More recently, Elvey et al. (2018: e443) looked at the comments to articles posted on *PulseToday*, a widely read online version of *Pulse* magazine, the United Kingdom's most read new magazines for medical general practitioners. Using what they called a 'tracer term' of 'access to care' for their search of the archives of the online magazine, they narrowed their dataset to 'about 300 comments containing around 21,000 words associated with the 331 articles'. Their analysis was 'an iterative process' that involved reading the entire dataset 'repeatedly', discussing the classification categories with the research team, refining the classifications, and then grouping them together into themes. Their findings revealed not only a general sense of being overworked, but also the ambivalence and 'complex mix of resistance and resignation' that general practitioners feel about their changing roles.

The Time of Community

As the Internet grew throughout the 1990s, it was becoming increasingly obvious to academics, programmers, entrepreneurs, and others that more and more people were using online experiences for activities that were much more than 'information superhighway', library-like exchanges and market-like transactions. As the last section explored, there was already a range of platforms and software applications that offered numerous different sorts of social experiences such as live (single and multi-user) chat, (some massively) multiplayer gaming, email lists, and message or bulletin boards. The WELL, or Whole Earth 'Lectronic Link, was a dial-up bulletin board system that began in 1985, and was similar to the online message boards one would find on BBS systems, CompuServe, and Usenet.

Although he never uses the word 'ethnography' to describe his work, or 'ethnographic' to describe his writing, the prolific author and Internet pioneer Howard Rheingold used the WELL as a type of ethnographic field site when he researched and wrote his book in 1992. Rheingold used a combination of participation in online communities, observation of posts, and email, in-person, and other forms of interviews to gain insights into the phenomenon. His use of extended self-description is obviously based on careful note-keeping of his own participation in the online discourse. The text of *The Virtual Community: Homesteading on the Electronic Frontier* is filled with long verbatim quotes from online group members, described and offset in particular fonts and textual ways to preserve as many of their contextual elements as possible. And among the many different scholarly sources that Rheingold draws upon for his many explanations and elaborations, anthropologists make a strong showing. For example, to explain whether online communities have a culture, he turns to Clifford Geertz for a definition that is also a somewhat one-sided explanation about why we find culture anywhere:

> Culture, according to Geertz, is 'a set of control mechanisms – plans, recipes, rules, instructions (what computer engineers call "programs") – for the governing of behaviour'. (Rheingold, 1993: 187)

Based on his observations of online interest-based forums, support groups and role-playing games, Rheingold noted that people in online communities 'exchange pleasantries and argue, engage in intellectual discourse, conduct commerce, exchange knowledge, share emotional support, make plans, brainstorm, gossip, feud, fall in love, find friends and lose them, play games, flirt, create a little high art and a lot of idle talk' (1993: 3). His engaging and ethnographic style of combining recounting of his own participation and observation with large inclusions of data collected from conversations on the WELL and direct quotes from interviews also proved to be an engaging way to introduce readers to what was already at that time becoming recognized as a new and meaningful social phenomenon.

Among participants and researchers at the time, who were rapidly discovering these new niche areas within a wider web of static webpages and slowly increasing online professionalization, a prevalent shorthand was the notion of 'community', preceded by the moderator 'virtual'. Virtual and online were often held in contraposition, and as somewhat inferior to, something termed 'RL', i.e., real life – embodied, physical presence. In a definition that, like his book, emphasizes emotional commitment, longer-term connections, and personal exchanges, he defined 'virtual communities' as 'social aggregations that emerge from the net when enough people carry on ... public discussions long enough, with sufficient human feeling, to form webs of personal relationships in cyberspace'.

The Virtual Community

2.3

THINKING ABOUT COMMUNITY ONLINE

What does the word community mean to you? What sorts of communities do you identify with? What communities do you participate in? In what ways do your experiences online feel like they bring you into contact with a 'community'? Do different online experiences offer you different sorts of community experiences? How would you describe those different types of community experience? When Howard Rheingold was writing his book about online experience in the early 1990s, he was struggling with exactly those sorts of questions. But he had a much more limited world of social media than you do to develop these ideas with actual experience.

Rheingold's (1993) timely use of the term 'virtual communities' for his book's title is highly significant. A powerful term, 'community' suggested the sense that being online was a human social experience. Sociologists, psychologists, anthropologists, cultural studies scholars, communications scholars, literary scholars, and a range of other social scientists and humanities scholars not only began adopting the virtual community terminology but also naturalized the community-based perspective that those online media were place-like locations where that ephemeral feeling called community could grow. The anthropologist Arturo Escobar (1994: 218) wrote that an anthropological understanding would be important 'not only for understanding what these new "villages" and "communities" are but, equally important, for imagining the kinds of communities that human groups can create with the help of emerging technologies'. In other words, Escobar envisioned anthropologies of virtual communities to be useful for guiding the development of the very notion of community and connectedness as it would become altered by these then-nascent, but looming, technological transformations.

However, the modifier 'virtual' suggested that these new forms of social connection were somehow not quite real, and perhaps best viewed with some suspicion. Indeed, early Internet scholars like Steven Jones (1998) were already unpacking and dissecting these notions. A range of scholars, including Jones and Doheny-Farina (1998), questioned the level of commitment that people had to 'electronic communities'. As Jones put it:

> In the physical world, community members must live together. When community membership is in no small way a matter of subscribing or unsubscribing to a bulletin board or electronic newsgroup, is the nature of interaction different simply because one may disengage with little or no consequence? (1998: 4)

The thought that spatial proximity leads to a magic sense of community is naïve, however. Past and contemporary unfortunate events too numerous to mention bear witness to the fact that merely living together does not guarantee some sense of easy breezy togetherness.

One way social media relate to community, emphasized by many of the early pioneers of what is now recognizable as online ethnography – Markham, Correll, Turkle, and Rheingold, especially – is the emotional reality of online communications, the fact that these interactions stir us, move us, and inspire us. This fact is taken as a phenomenological foundation and draws our attention to James Carey's (1989: 18) distinction between viewing communications as a 'transmission' or language broadcast across distances for the purpose of controlling the masses, and a 'ritual' view that saw communication as 'the sacred ceremony that draws persons together in fellowship and commonality'. At the time, there was much excitement about the public, democratizing, utopian potential of these novel communication forms, 'the sense that we are embarking on an adventure in creating new communities and new forms of community' (Jones, 1998: 9; Schuler, 1996). Could we actually learn from the mistakes of the past? Could we direct future media into more socially positive directions than the media of the past?

Or could it be that these new technologies were just another broken promise? Carey (1989) talked about a technophilic 'rhetoric of the electrical sublime', a 'mythos of the electronic revolution' (Carey and Quirk, 1970). Perhaps, as Beniger (1987: 353) warned, electronic communication and its aptitude for 'personalization' were hastening the sharp drop in interpersonal relations, moving from 'traditional communal relationships' to 'impersonal, highly restricted associations' that would later be captured in terms such as 'filter bubbles'. Beniger (1987: 353) disparagingly terms this state 'pseudo-community' and finds it to be one in which impersonal associations masquerade as personalized communication, leading to insincere, inauthentic, and ultimately unsatisfying social relationships.

Maybe these new communities are destinations for the contemporary 'imaginative diasporas', the 'cosmopolitans and the new professionals who lived in the imaginative worlds of politics, art, fashion, medicine, law and so forth' (Carey, 1993: 178) – and reflect their interests, tastes, and values – including their desire, and lack of it, for social commitments. Perhaps it was that community is simply far too complex, too loaded and rich a concept to simply distinguish, or deny, its presence or absence from any communication medium – especially one so multifaceted as these new forms of communication. Fernback (1997: 39) points out how 'infinitely complex and amorphous' the concept is in academic discourse: it 'has descriptive normative, and ideological connections' and also 'encompasses both material and symbolic dimensions'. The idea of community includes notions of territory, social interaction based on a geographic area, self-sufficiency, common life, consciousness of a kind, institutions of solidarity, primary interactions, culturally distinct groups, and the possession of common ends, norms, and means (Bell and Newby, 1974; Effrat, 1974; Jones, 1998). Answers about such contingent, complex, and crucial matters are not easy to find. Decades later, we still struggle with these same questions. Box 2.3 provides you with an exercise that gives a taste of one such conceptual struggle.

Life Online as an Evolving Cultural Context

For Internet researchers in the mid-1990s, tackling ontological dilemmas about the difference between the virtual and the real was the order of the day. The subtitle of Internet research pioneer Annette Markham's book (Markham, 1998) is instructive: *Researching Real Experience in Virtual Space*. Her book, *Life Online*, is likely the first book-length ethnography of online social experience. It explores and captures her wonderment regarding the way that online communications allow her to extend the body's traditional limitations:

> By logging onto my computer, I (or a part of me) can seem to (or perhaps actually) exist separately from my body in 'places' formed by the exchange of messages ... I can exchange in activities with people of like interests around the globe, using nothing but my computer, my imagination, written text, and the capacity of digital code to process and mediate aspects of my life online. (1998: 17)

Markham's fascination and confusion between the body and the computer, the virtual and the real, the embodied and the communicative, the truth and the lie, is perhaps most powerfully illustrated in an exchange she has with a long-term Prodigy member who educates her on the joys of virtual dating, virtual bodies, virtual sex, and even 'virtual massage' (p. 171). That sort of conceptual confusion between embodiment and digital virtuality was common in writing at the time. In 1991, another Internet research pioneer, Allucquére Rosanne Stone, had written a chapter about virtual existence

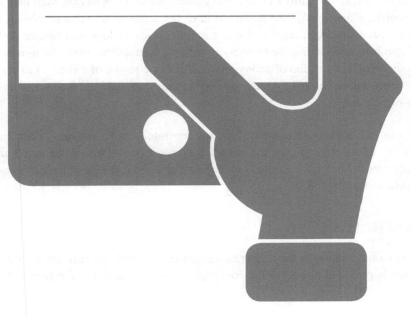

CONSIDERING THE PHYSICALITY OF ONLINE 'CYBERSPACES'

2.4

What do you think about the relationship between your body and social media? Have you ever thought about it? When you are using your mobile phone, your tablet, or your laptop, are you aware of your body? Does your neck start to hurt after a while, or your back start to ache? Do your eyes get strained? How about the stress to your thumbs from typing on your phone? Or your wrists from writing on a keyboard? Where in your body are you when 'you' are online? One of the early pioneers of internet ethnography, Annette Markham, was concerned with these sorts of questions.

called 'Will the Real Body Please Stand Up?'. As Hine (2000) cautioned, the virtual community experience and its ethnographic investigation had to deal with both 'a sense of being disembodied' and 'a connotation of being "not quite" ... not exactly the real thing'.

Yet Markham's (1998: 25) fascinating engagement with her online existence was profoundly shaped by the nature of her methodological engagement with it. She began with a straightforward, if highly philosophical, question: 'How do people make sense of the concept of reality in or through online interaction?' Her initial plan was to act as an 'anonymous, distant observer', a lurker who merely listened to and archived eight months of her chosen online community's conversations 'without participating'. However, as she tried, over and over again, to make sense of the data she collected in her context, the many 'fascinating' discussions she had saved about 'the body and sexuality in cyberspace', she was vexed by a lack of meaningful progress.

> After several painstaking weeks of trying to write the first analysis of metaphors, I realized something was missing from the scene. Now, three months later, I realize *I* was missing. I was surprisingly absent from my own study, which I now realize is an ethnography. I was beginning to understand that cyberspace is not simply a collection of texts to analyze; rather it is an evolving cultural context of immense magnitude and complex scope. I wanted to say something meaningful about the way people experience these new cultural contexts, but I had never really experienced them myself.

And so, aware that what she wanted to do, what she must do in order to be able to reveal the perceived reality of this novel context for social behavior, Markham alters her project. Consciously, she begins to craft her study as an ethnography of these virtual social spaces, reading and citing scholars such as John van Maanen (1988). She also inserts herself, quite profoundly, into the data and the text. She moves from a methodological position of anonymity and distance to one of closeness to her own experience and writes a highly reflexive ethnography, something I would later call 'an auto-netnography':

> Even as I do this ethnography, I am not separate from it. The more I become a part of the ethnography, the more it becomes a part of me. In the end, I am not sure if I will have learned more about cyberspace, the participants, or me. (Markham, 1998: 83)

Early Netnography

In fan culture, canon is the authoritative source material, the real story. This short section is provided to give some background on the founding of netnography, the particular spin on online ethnography that is the subject of this book, as well as to continue the analysis of community, culture, and its online investigation that so consumed researchers working in the era when netnography began. Although I had been active on CompuServe for a time in the late 1980s, the more recent story of netnography begins, strangely and appropriately enough, in a Wendy's in Toronto in 1995. Surrounded by fellow members of a *Star Trek* fan club I had joined as part of my ethnographic investigation into fan culture, one of my key ethnographic participants turned to me and said, 'You know what you need to do? You need to go online. Online for *Star Trek* fans is like a 24/7 Convention!'

My experience was not like Nancy Baym's, where she had been an active member of her online field site for a year, contributing expertly and passionately about soap operas with other soap opera fans. Online fandom was something I had explored, but not particularly deeply or seriously, and had not considered much until that moment. But in that instant, in the Wendy's, in a very organic way, I was drawn into the world of online communications by in-person communication during my ethnography. I upped my Internet game, and started moving online. Exploring those online sites, I knew no one. I didn't even know my fellow crew members' online handles. I started down the path of netnography as a stranger in a strange online world. Like Nancy Baym, however, I did have a solid grounding in the central topics that the participants on those message boards would be discussing.

I learned. I learned that there were tens of thousands of sites dedicated to *Star Trek* and *Star Wars* online, and all sorts of technology, and weird religions, and conspiracy theory science besides. Webpages. Usenet groups. They made up the majority of most of my data collection. My earliest published fan netnographies used the rec.arts.star-trek (Kozinets, 1997a) and alt.tv.x-files (Kozinets, 1997b) Usenet newsgroups, but I was also looking at a variety of fan sites dedicated to shows currently popular at the time such as *Babylon 5* and *Space: Above and Beyond*.

Because watching and listening could get me only a certain type of knowledge, and because I had learned that posting research questions onto general bulletin boards could be problematic, I decided to code and post my own 'Star Trek Research Webpage' with lots of information and accompanying research questions. I began getting responses to it via email, and continuing those conversations, eventually communicating with 65 different people from 12 different countries (Kozinets, 2001: 70). As well, throughout 1996, I began participating in groups and collecting data on consumer activism with Jay Handelman. In that research, we used 11 relevant Usenet groups, including alt.activism, misc.activism.progressive, alt.society.labor-unions, and talk.politics.theory (Kozinets and Handelman, 1998). Between 1996 and 1998, as I finished at Queen's and started at Northwestern, I was conducting a number of online ethnographies, and combined online and ethnographic projects, including one situated in the massively multiplayer video game Quake and another long-term one, begun in 1998, that focused on online interactions centering around food and beverage consumption, including wine and coffee.

Netnography in the Age of Virtual Community

As a doctoral student, I was also reading everything I could about the topic of online community. Was the online world 'virtual' or was it real? Was the phenomenon of online 'community' good or was it bad for us? How could I do this kind of ethnography in an ethical and effective way? How should I handle all of this data? I closely read all of the online ethnographies I could find. Jenkins, Baym, Correll, and Markham were core figures on my academic altar, and I turned to them daily – and those they cited – for wisdom about how to approach the mysteries of online ethnography. It should be no secret, then, that my work would end up closely reflecting the notions of community and culture in wide circulation at the time. So when I presented my netnography paper in Tucson in October of 1996, as a final-year PhD student at my very first conference, the *Association for Consumer Research*, I had no idea that the definition I presented would still be in play two decades later – because that definition is where I started with netnography, but it is almost nothing like what netnography is now.

I was very focused on the product at first, more than the process itself. 'The textual output of Internet-related field work' was my initial attempt to define exactly what it was I was doing (Kozinets, 1997b: 471). Then, 'a written account of online cyberculture, informed by the methods of cultural anthropology' (ibid.). It was a convenient shorthand, text-centric, focused only on the Internet, and dependent on the definition of 'cyberculture' – which I broadly defined the next year in another published conference paper as 'the complex field of social forces in which human bodies, machines, and scientific discourses intersect' (Escobar, 1994; Kozinets, 1998: 366).

Ethics emerged as an important concern almost immediately. Along with the broad definition, I discuss the ethical gray zone that netnography operates within. I include the fact that, when asked, one of the newsgroup members who I had contacted did not want their public posting about a UFO sighting quoted in the research. The first published netnography was, in a way, not only about television shows but also about the public discussion of UFOs, government secrecy, and conspiracies.

Similarly, it was concerned from the beginning about the sampling frame for a netnographic study and the amount and type of data required. I state that I analyze all of the online data using 'a holographic sampling frame' (Denzin and Lincoln, 1994: 202) – a way to screen and pre-select masses of data that are representative of the whole and pertinent to the particular research question. I report the amount of data collected at exactly 83,150 words, and also provide a reader-orienting estimate that it would amount to about 600 pages of single-spaced, single-sided, regular-sized pages if printed. I tell the reader about how many times I read those 600 pages of data through in the course of analyzing them (nine times).

Whether intentional or not, I do not fully recall, but those first definitions avoid the word 'community'. However, in the 1998 paper I refine and redefine netnography as 'a written account resulting from fieldwork studying the cultures and communities that emerge from on-line, computer mediated, or Internet-based communications, where both the field work and the textual account are methodologically informed by the traditions and techniques of cultural anthropology' (Kozinets: 1998: 366). The use of community and culture in this 1998 definition weighed quite heavily on the formulation of a later marketing research journal article, which I wrote two years later and which served, for many, as their introduction to the approach: '"netnography", or ethnography on the Internet, is a new qualitative research methodology that adapts ethnographic research techniques to study the cultures and communities that are emerging through computer-mediated communications' (Kozinets, 2002a: 62).

What was meant by 'cultures and communities'? Merely that online communications bear culture, and that linguistic symbols always come preloaded with reams of almost infinitely-extensible meaning. As well, this early definition reflected my sense that the connections people make online form relationship networks. Did it also mean that netnography was focused mainly on studying the symbolic dance of Carey's 'ritual' communication, the sacred ceremony that draws persons together in fellowship and commonality? Did it mean studying and focusing on the more emotional, more committed, closer relationship types of communities that Correll found in the Lesbian Cafe, and Rheingold found on the WELL? Well, to some extent, it did. Although it was possible to lurk on them, of course, those early Usenets were structured differently from the more deliberately anonymous and distant platforms like Instagram, Tumblr, or Twitter today. The Usenets were more egalitarian and group-directed, and many of the members were familiar to one another. As many of the early virtual and online community scholars had pointed out, this was part of their appeal: online discussions mix communicative acts with social connection. As I wrote in 1998, 'what began primarily as a search for information [online, often] transforms into a source of community and understanding'. Those were the days of virtual community. As a product of those days, netnography reflected my interest in examining those closer and more committed types of online relationships. But netnography could not remain an offshoot of those types of relationships forever, with them built into its very definition. Indeed, social media was transforming quickly and netnography had to be twisted and reshaped to suit its dynamic research environment. Like its early definitions' highlighting of newness, netnography's early emphasis on community would have to change as both the technique and the environment it studied morphed into something very different.

BLOGS ENTER THE SCENE

As Figure 2.9 clearly shows, the blog form was already established in the early years of the millennium. Around 1994, as far as anyone could tell, people started dynamically updating their formerly static webpages and the format that eventually came to be known as a blog was born. As Reed (2005: 240–1) recounts, 'in 1999 the first automated weblog-publishing systems emerged; these allowed unskilled individuals to run blogs easily and free of charge. As a consequence, interest in weblogging (or "blogging")

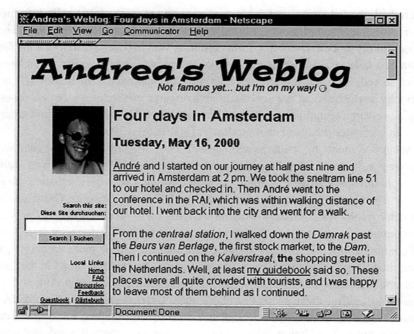

Figure 2.9 Early weblog or blog screenshot, circa 2000, exhibited on Netscape browser

has soared.' Blogs, when open to public comments, were a lot like message boards, with some important differences. Similar to message boards, they (optionally) allowed members of the public to make comments anonymously, initiating and continuing conversations that often took wild turns and ended up in unexpected places. But different from those message boards, they took place in an online environment directed by the blog creator, tended to focus on the content creator's interests and posts, and were usually moderated by them. Blogs offered people a form of individualized, personalized, and cultivated communication that was also scalable, searchable, and – as companies and bloggers eventually discovered – salable. In many ways, blogs heralded a new age of social media. They spread rapidly throughout the world and remain important backbones of social media activity on the Internet. In many countries, Japan for example, blogs are currently much more popular than they are in other nations.

Online ethnographies of blogs followed soon after the user-friendly social media formats became established. In one of the earliest, Reed says that his

fieldwork began in August 2001 when I started reading weblogs and began contacting directory members [i.e., bloggers] to organize individual interviews offline. Gradually I was invited to join the mailing list and to attend pub gatherings; members also encouraged me to start my own weblog (running a weblog remains crucial to my participation in the UK blogging scene). Lately, I have begun to visit individuals at home and work (from where many of them blog) in order to get a better appreciation of posting culture. As well as continuing to meet up with bloggers offline, I sustain conversations through email and instant messaging and through weblog exchanges. (2005: 225)

Reed's ethnographic work reflects its positioning at a point in time when online communications were still very collegial and communal. His analysis, however, reveals notes of narcissism, exhibitionism, immediacy, publicity, and celebrity culture – core constituting elements of the coming Age of Social Media.

In 2006, I published some initial guidelines for adapting netnography to the world of blogs: 'Unlike the more communal and democratic forums like newsgroups', the blog is a 'near-autocracy where the owner remains the undisputed star' (Kozinets, 2006a: 137). Its individualized personalization and perspective is its defining feature, and this move to individualization indelibly changed social media from a flatter and more communal experience to one increasingly based upon audiences and micro- and macro-celebrity star power. Another important element mentioned in the methodological overview is the ability of blogs to gain attention from mass media news outlets. This was something new – comment pages on Usenet groups generally had not broken major news stories, destroyed stock values, or led to respected journalists, such as Dan Rather, retiring. Blogs had star power and mass media appeal – by the mid-2000s, the homestead of virtual community was transforming into a recognizably mass form of media.

Kretz and de Valck (2010) studied 60 fashion and luxury blogs for the narratives they provided to associate the blogger and various fashion brands. They discovered a vocabulary of personal brand association, ranging from implicit photographs to explicit endorsements. McQuarrie and colleagues (2013: 153) looked deeply into 10 popular fashion blogs written by women. Their detailed, contextual, and cultural look at the professionalization of social media in the early 2010s concluded that 'a focus on consumers' newfound capacity, courtesy of the web, to acquire a mass audience requires a new theorization'. There 'is no offline equivalent of a verbal-visual blog, a Yelp restaurant review, or user-generated video content', and (perhaps ignoring decades of fan and zine culture) previously 'only professionals holding an institutional position could publish their writing', make and share high quality video, or receive major funds in exchange for personal endorsements, advertising and promotional consideration. McQuarrie et al.'s (2013: 136) cultural analysis coined a term for this new ability to 'reach a mass audience' by virtue of the empowerment of 'the web': 'the Megaphone Effect'. Writing in the journal *Celebrity Studies*, Ashleigh Logan (2015) explored the self-presentation of female fashion bloggers on Twitter who identify with Kate Middleton, and also play a part in establishing and maintaining a community-like foundation of Twitter followers. Among this group, assuming a leadership role also means building their own group of followers. It also means playing with linguistic alterations and the creation of entirely new vocabularies of identity symbols, such as identifying as a 'replikate' or a 'copykate'.

From a research perspective, blogs were held to contain some interesting analytic characteristics that were later attributed to general social media data. The first was aggregation. If one scanned a selection of blogs about a particular topic, patterns could reveal facts about the general population of blogs considered, or an even wider population. The second was trending elements. If one wished to monitor and aggregate the content from a number of blogs over time, patterns in their content might inform us about upcoming trends. These qualities in blog data led to numerous types of quantitative or automated content analysis, data-monitoring software products being developed, often under the rubric of 'social monitoring' or 'social listening' tools. From an online ethnography perspective, all analytic movements into aggregation and the discerning of trends are potentially informative. However, the scale of the inquiries needs to be kept small enough to maintain a close look into their cultural elements. For a successful netnography, social media from platforms such as blogs need to be analyzed as a particular form of communication, and treated with their narrative forms, story-revealing, and self-promotional megaphone effects kept in mind. That transformation, and its ramification for online interaction and ethnography, became increasingly evident as Twitter rose to prominence. We will see as our investigation of social media's history continues in the next chapter that these changes happened alongside the commercialization and mass adoption of social networking sites, creating dramatic changes to the conceptualization and practice of netnography.

2.5   NETNOGRAPHY ON BLOGS

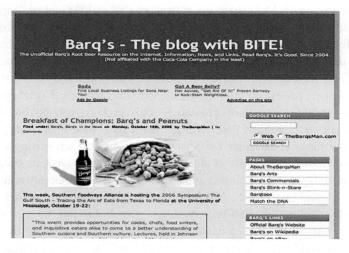

Figure 2.10   Barq's – The blog with bite! landing page screenshot, 12 November 2006

To demonstrate netnography with a brief analysis for a methodological chapter (Kozinets, 2006a) in a book about research methods (Belk, 2006), I focused on a blog by the anonymous and self-proclaimed 'Barq's Man' who had created 'Barq's – The Blog With Bite', as a tribute to Barq's Root Beer, a soda pop brand he enjoyed and which contained a lot of nostalgic meaning for him. The results revealed that blogs were capable of revealing intensely personal first-person stories about particular topics and also revealing upcoming trends with immediacy. The Barq's blog was also covered in prominently-featured advertising. As Figure 2.10's screenshot of the landing page reveals, the front page of the blog contains an advertisement for 'business listings for soda near you!', as well as another asking 'got a beer belly?' and offering 'a proven remedy'.

CHAPTER SUMMARY

This chapter examined the first two ages of the history of the phenomenon we currently know as social media, as well as overviewing some of the cultural research that ethnographically pursued its investigation. The first age was the Age of Electronic Communications, which ran from the late 1960s to the early 1990s. Beginning with the Arpanet and the early years of (mostly corporate) networked communications, the Age of Electronic Communications included the growth and spread of private American online services such as CompuServe, Prodigy, and GEnie, as well as the publicly-owned European services such as Minitel in France. Several important early ethnographers of the Internet developed their research in the context of the rapidly expanding Usenet and BBS networks. Business and academia increasingly employed and emphasized notions of 'community', a tendency cemented with the publication and spread of Howard Rheingold's influential book. Research intensified and developed throughout the 1990s as the Age of Virtual Community congealed and advanced. The chapter proceeded to describe how a developing field of ethnographies of online environments conceptualized life online as an evolving cultural context, and also that it was against this conceptual and empirical background that netnography was initially developed and defined. In the chapter's final section, which provided a very short history of blogs, we learned how the post-Dotcom crash rise of the weblog format helped bring about the current age of social media by transitioning online socialities from more communal to more individualized and mass media-connected formats.

KEY READINGS

Baym, Nancy K. (1993) 'Interpreting soap operas and creating community: Inside a computer-mediated fan culture', *Journal of Folklore Research*: 143–76.

Correll, Shelley (1995) 'The ethnography of an electronic bar: The Lesbian Cafe', *Journal of Contemporary Ethnography*, 24(3): 270–98.

Hiltz, Starr Roxanne, and Murray Turoff (1978) *The Network Nation: Human Communication Via Computer.* Cambridge, MA: MIT Press.

Jones, Steve (ed.) (1998) *Cybersociety 2.0: Revisiting Computer-mediated Community and Technology,* Vol. 2. Thousand Oaks, CA: Sage.

Markham, Annette N. (1998) *Life Online: Researching Real Experience in Virtual Space*, Vol. 6. Lanham, MD: AltaMira.

Rheingold, Howard (1993) *The Virtual Community: Homesteading on the Electronic Frontier*. New York: Addison-Wesley.

MEDIA: COMMUNICATING AND CONNECTING IN THE 21ST CENTURY

CHAPTER OVERVIEW

In the previous chapter, we learned the early history of today's social media. We saw how computerized digital transmission networks were set up to allow people to easily exchange information, providing them with radically new communication capabilities. These accelerating capacities, designed as affordances that people seek uses for, and then adjust to, become new consumption rituals layered onto pre-existing rituals. We reviewed how the Age of Electronic Communications commenced with the Arpanet, then grew through private American online services and publicly-owned European networks. As Usenet systems along with other message board and bulletin board services and protocols expanded, peer-to-peer online gatherings experienced a burst of growth, and ethnographers began to notice and explore these assemblies. Corporations were early to the space, and the collectives were increasingly accepted and encouraged as a new form of community, expressed virtually and online. Static webpages became more dynamic. The profile became more important. The social network and the web log formats grew in popularity, setting the stage for much bigger changes to come.

This is the second half of the history lesson. This edition and this chapter offer a fuller engagement with the most essential as well as some of the most recent ethnographic research on social networking sites, microblogs, news forums, visual and video channels, virtual worlds, and games. This is the story of how the realm of early hobbyists and technology functionaries became the advance guard for a vast army of social media content managers and creators that involves about two out of every three people on the planet. Creative, smart people of all shapes, stripes, and sizes, from everywhere on Earth, are partaking almost every day in a vast variety of different online social experiences, increasingly doing their work and their shopping, getting their ideas, wasting their leisure time, developing their relationships, and seeing their world from the technocultural affordance vantage points of these media.

Figure 3.1 Before the Internet, ham radio was social media

Source: Wikimedia Commons

THE AGE OF SOCIAL MEDIA: EARLY 2000s–DATE

Media are a key concept in netnography. As a term, 'media' is narrower than the concept of 'communication'. However, media is also considerably wider than the systems of television, newspapers, radio, and motion pictures that have made up traditional conceptions of the notion. I follow Nick Couldry's (2012: xiii) definition of media as 'institutionalized structures, forms, formats and interfaces for disseminating symbolic content'. As Couldry emphasizes, the fact that 'virtually all symbolic content' in our contemporary world is now digital, and that 'many platforms carry both mass produced content and interpersonal communication' means that 'the old research divide between "mass media" and general "communication"' have already become hopelessly blurred, a point that I make continuously in these two chapters when I say that media have been social for a very long time. Media are also 'inescapably entangled with power relations' (ibid.; see also Castells, 2007). We can think of the role of media in social systems as being one that facilitates the flow of communications and relationships not merely across regions, nations, and societies, but across different nodal connections and sub-systems of capital, flowing in the form of both social and informational exchange that, together, form ecosystems of great complexity that have major impacts upon the systems in which they are embedded, including the Earth's own living environs.

Well before computers came onto the scene, media were already social. The idea that media's social aspects, applications, and implications are linked with their computer mediation is simply false. Over the years, many media have been social. Party-line telephony provided a collective telephone experience that began in the late 1800s. Fanzines or zines are small-circulation works created by single individuals or small groups of people, usually produced by enthusiasts of particular cultural phenomenon for fellow enthusiasts (Jary et al., 1991; Wertham, 1973). Later, fanzines provided voices for political and feminist protest (Triggs, 2010). They began in the 1930s or earlier. These fan publications most likely formed out of the activities of the early science fiction and futurism fans, shared and discussed at the early science fiction conventions that began popping up around the time of the 1939 New York World's Fair.

Another example is a technological affair, as short-range radio use exploded into the consumer domain when government opened up the space for public use, communication, and innovation. Ham and Citizens Band (or CB) radio is a system of short-range radio transmission and reception that uses technology and bandwidth to enable ordinary citizens to communicate with one another free of restriction and centralization (Bartlett, 2013). CB radio dates to the 1940s, and ham radio to the early 1900s. The media lesson for contemporary social media thinkers is this: from every type of supposed mass broadcast medium, there have arisen grassroots, bottom-up popular manifestations of the technology that have repurposed it for purposes of fandom, leisure, communication, and sociality. Sociality, to repurpose William Gibson's populist epithet, has its own uses for things – media included.

By the late 1990s, almost every institution was discovering its own uses for the Internet. The Internet and the World Wide Web were strange and powerful, equal parts technological, cultural, and economic. The enthusiasm about online communities was tied into a general Internet fascination, a fascination that was present as much in daily conversations and fashion trends as it was on the stock market and in intellectual circles. Former Harvard professor Timothy Leary was probably reaching as far out as anyone else regarding the mind-expanding potential of the new age of computers, creatively deploying the term 'cyberdelic' to relate online experiences to psychedelic ones. Personal Computers, PCs, were 'the LSD of the 1990s', according to Leary, who also admonished the emerging groups of bohemian net surfers to 'turn on, boot up, jack in'. And then, after the expanding dot.com balloon in the stock markets finally burst in 2000, popular and academic attention temporarily waned. It seemed, from the perspectives of the ivory tower, that the tea leaves had not settled enough for a clear reading.

But online, sociality was continuing its evolution at a breakneck pace. In fact, there were nascent varieties, and signs everywhere, of the future in the social media of the 1990s. Rheingold (1993), for instance, was already talking about social media conversations being inundated by bots. Stone (1991) and Virilio (1994) were already exploring virtual worlds and virtual reality. Politics were already on the menu when Jones (1998: 19), who was quoting David Harvey, who was following Heidegger, said that technology applied to social communication can lead to 'reactionary' impli-cations and even 'fascism'. From the point of view of the early 2000s, things online were about to get a whole lot bigger and a whole mess crazier. And then, MySpace, YouTube, Facebook, Twitter, Flickr, LinkedIn, Instagram, Snapchat, and Pinterest entered the scene.

In this chapter, we will track the development of the Age of Social Media from the early 2000s through to 2019 by describing the range of social media sites, analyzing their unique characteristics and then providing examples of netnographic research that have been conducted among them. An early wave of the Age of Social Media was initiated by the rise of blogging and dynamic webpages. This first wave provided forms of social media, such as Twitter and YouTube, that provided a type of publish-ing forum for individuals to gather audiences. Twitter, as a microblog, followed in this pattern, but so did YouTube with videos. The next wave was the ripening of social net-working sites that began with early offerings such as Friendster and brought us major mainstream sites such as Facebook and LinkedIn that are the heavyweights of this for-mat. The third wave was made up of more visual sites, led by Flickr, and represented by social media platforms such as Pinterest, Instagram, and Snapchat. Throughout this chapter, we will learn how the sociotechnical infrastructures of different platforms transform people's social experiences by offering them new social affordances such as Twitter's following and trending, or Facebook's sharing and liking. We will also discern the variety and vastness of social media experiences, with old-style formats such as those of Reddit and 4chan coexisting with aggregation services such as Tum-blr, virtual worlds, and gaming sites. We will learn how social media have advanced across the globe, with sites such as China's WeChat and QQ and Russia's VKonktake acting as hosts to hundreds of millions of members. The chapter will also overview ethnographic research conducted on Twitter, Friendster, Reddit, LinkedIn, Facebook, Flickr, YouTube, Instagram, and Snapchat. These netnographies have already taught us how social media are used in life transitions, business processes of credibility and trust formation, resistance and activism, alternate news channels, how platforms are creating new ecosystems of online entrepreneurs and influence networks and much more, as we will see. Let's continue the history lesson by moving from the blogs of last chapter to the main microblog of today's Western world: Twitter.

Twitter

Introduced in 2006, Twitter was originally devoted to a single purpose, revealed by the screenshot depicted in Figure 3.3. That goal was to have 'a global community of friends and strangers answering one simple question: what are you doing?' Of course, the platform did not end up following the path of continuous status updates for long. And, after a fairly short operational period, it offered a range of social media functions in which connectivity between network members related to short exchanges of infor-mation, opinion, and news. Twitter was originally described as a microblog, a type of

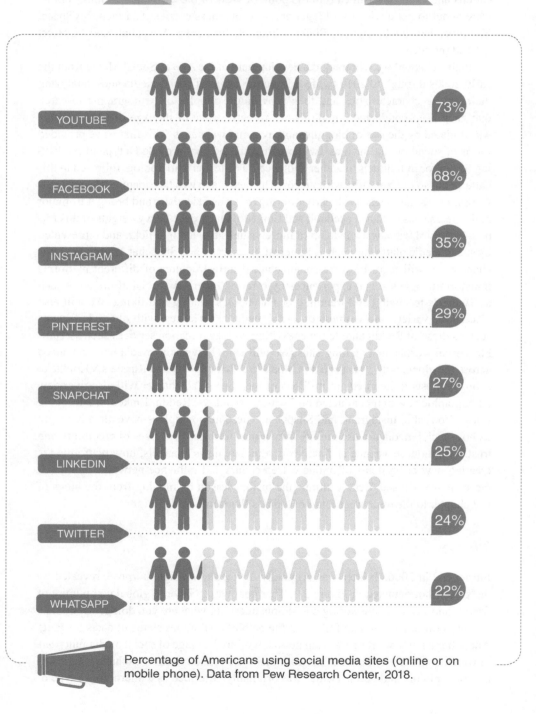

Figure 3.2 The age of social media

YOUTUBE — 73%

FACEBOOK — 68%

INSTAGRAM — 35%

PINTEREST — 29%

SNAPCHAT — 27%

LINKEDIN — 25%

TWITTER — 24%

WHATSAPP — 22%

Percentage of Americans using social media sites (online or on mobile phone). Data from Pew Research Center, 2018.

3 billion

active social media
users worldwide

42%

of the world's population
use social media

1999 ///////// FOUNDED // 2006

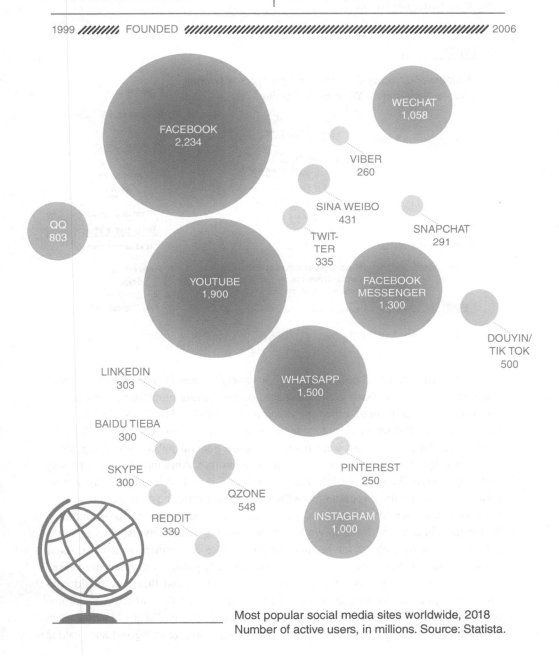

FACEBOOK
2,234

WECHAT
1,058

VIBER
260

SINA WEIBO
431

TWIT-
TER
335

SNAPCHAT
291

QQ
803

YOUTUBE
1,900

FACEBOOK
MESSENGER
1,300

DOUYIN/
TIK TOK
500

LINKEDIN
303

WHATSAPP
1,500

BAIDU TIEBA
300

SKYPE
300

QZONE
548

PINTEREST
250

REDDIT
330

INSTAGRAM
1,000

Most popular social media sites worldwide, 2018
Number of active users, in millions. Source: Statista.

blog that restricts users' posting to a prespecified and abbreviated length. Twitter was originally viewed as a microblog because it allowed users to publish on its medium, but limited their posts to 140 – and then, in 2017, to 280 – characters. Twitter was also viewed as a social network, because it allowed members to subscribe to newsfeed only from particular sources.

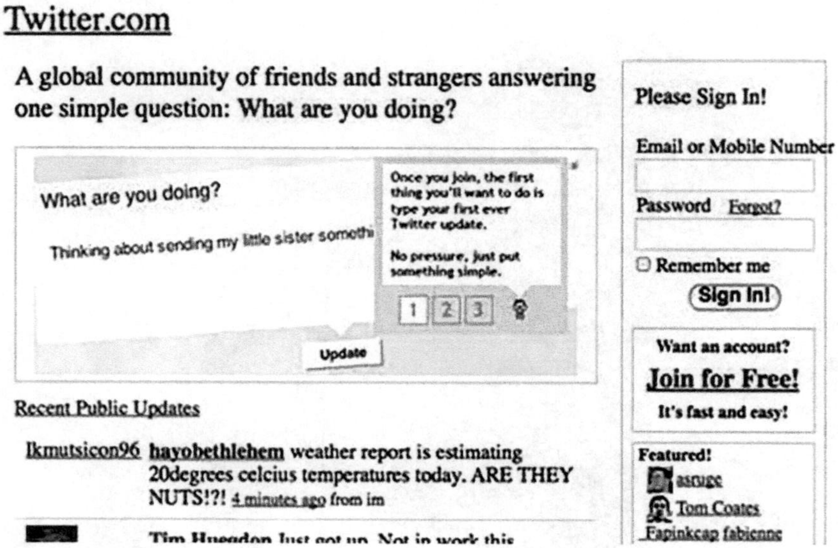

Figure 3.3 Twitter's launch page from 2006 ('What are you doing?')

On Twitter, one could post, or 'tweet', a variety of largely uncensored and open posts and images. The posts could be shared on the Twitter medium as 'retweets' in one's own feed, or through other sites such as LinkedIn or Facebook. Twitter users could also use Twitter to comment upon posts, very similar to a blog. Like blog comments, those comments were open to a more general public, including members that might have no other contact with one another. Although Twitter's brevity and megaphone-like nature might lead some to see it as less interactive than other forms of social media, this assumption does not hold. Twitter posts and their associated comments often form conversations in which users are speaking to one another. Sometimes, because of the abbreviation of the medium, these conversations assumed a form similar to a chat. But because Twitter is like an unmoderated blog, those conversations roamed far and wide, were intentionally public, and often showcased dissent and even acrimony. Twitter users also quickly found that they could continue their tweets, stringing as many of them together as they liked to overcome text limitations. The result of this was longer, deeper, tweets. Finally, Twitter users could directly message one another using direct messaging, reaching out and making contact, even if they were not otherwise connected. The lived experience of Twitter use then, was, and is potentially quite social.

Sociality Affordances Baked into the Interface

Two distinctive social features that Twitter's interface integrated were the concept of 'following' and that of 'trending' (van Dijck, 2013). The notion 'that users may subscribe to others users' tweets, and subscribers are known as followers' (van Dijck, 2013: 71) creates a metric for measuring influence and engagement. In 2008, Twitter's architecture implemented 'trending topics', a feature enabling users to group together posts by using certain words or phrases prefixed with a hashtag symbol (#). Indexed and filtered, these hashtagged topics now became subject to a rating system that provided an ongoing quantitative rating of the popular consciousness flowing through Twitter's conversational streams. And the hashtag itself, the most success-ful example we have of a 'folksonomy' (Friedman, 2005), became a household term and was widely employed on other social media platforms (such as Instagram). The platform enables something not possible before: people can build their own categori-zation schemes by 'tagging' something and naming it. People use that platform ability to build differences and similarities, to distinguish and explain, to try to have meaning both literally and culturally, denotation as well as appropriately understood, experi-ence-based connotation. The platform's ability changes in synch with users' ability to adapt to and ride those changes, then make choices between them. Platforms change collective behaviors while those collective behaviors also adapt to and then change platforms. Following and trending on Twitter is, as van Dijck (2013: 69) rightly notes, a complex cultural, communal, technological, and business activity: a way to 'enable connectedness while engineering connectivity' and to 'propagate neutrality while secreting profitability'.

Research on Twitter

ENGAGING ETHNOGRAPHICALLY WITH TWITTER

3.1

Take a look at the Twitter site and Twitter feed (you do not need to be a mem-ber to search Twitter, but if you have not joined, consider joining). What do you notice about Twitter feed as a type of data? How is it useful for research? How does it make certain kinds of research more difficult? How would you recom-mend approaching Twitter as a site to conduct netnographic research? What makes you enthusiastic about using it? What cautions would you have? As you will read in this chapter, these are important questions with which a number of netnographic researchers have grappled.

One of Twitter's most attractive elements for researchers has been the ease with which its ever-flowing textual data can be downloaded, archived, and processed. The Twitter 'firehose' has served to sate many a researcher's thirst for large amounts of tagged real-time data and has been a huge boon to social media research. Like the text from blogs, the texts (and, in some limited ways, the symbols and photo images) from these conversations have been 'mined' using automated data-collection procedures such as scraping, and then sorted and analyzed. Examining the results of netnographies that use Twitter data provides us with an overview of some of the ways that this type of social media discourse can be related to particular topics of theoretical and substantive research interest.

Because there is so much Twitter data, and Twitter is recognized as an important medium for some kinds of communications – such as customer service discussions or political conversations – the platform provides data that is often intrinsically of interest to researchers exploring particular topics. Thus, one way to use Twitter data in a netnography is to examine a specific area or aspect of Twitter behavior, and then report on it. Ahuja and Shakeel (2017), for example, were interested in how a particular airline (Jet Airways) seeks to elicit customer engagement using Twitter. The researchers collected and then content analyzed over 2,500 customer service types of interactions on Twitter and then classified the type of content that they represented, analyzing them alongside with their observations about customer engagement. Their results suggest that a more 'relational' type of content creates more 'brand resonance' than the more commercially-driven 'promotional content' (2017: 21).

Twitter also provides data that is useful for studying theoretical concepts in a social media context. Wesely (2013) used Twitter to understand how communities of practice formed, operated, and maintained themselves using contemporary communication platforms like Twitter. The article focused on how world language teachers formed a community of practice on Twitter to support their professional development. Based on over a year of participant observations in the 'hashtag chats' of #langchat, nine interviews with their Twitter participants, and a range of archival sources, Wesely (2013: 315) found that the Twitter-based 'community' of world language educators manifested the three characteristics of a community of practice (domain, community, and practice), and also that 'there was ample evidence to show that [professional development] learning was taking place'.

Because it can be easily collected and coded, but also may contain enough verbal and contextual content to be culturally informative, Twitter data has also been found useful to those researchers pursuing paths of hybridized data coding and interpretation. Whelan et al. (2016) recommend qualitative, meaning-centric approaches such as netnography are mixed with the quantitative analysis of 'big trace datasets' in order to attain heightened understanding. In an example that applies equally well to the automated quantitative analysis of any social media data, they refer to a Twitter post cited in Gaspar et al.'s (2016) mixed qualitative and quantitative study of social media reactions to the 2011 food contamination incident in Germany. Their example on Twitter follows:

My government is staying on top of things and informing me the latest on the
E. coli outbreak here in Germany. #thanks.

As Whelan et al. (2016: 9) note, human analysts will instantly recognize that, although
it is phrased positively and might seem to be expressing gratitude towards the
German government, this tweet is written in a sarcastic tone and is actually expressing
distrust and dissatisfaction. Without cultural understanding, the actual meaning and
sentiment of tweets – and any social media data – is still very difficult for machine-
based approaches to discern (ibid.).

Tumblr

The platform Tumblr's name comes from the term 'tumblelog', used to refer to a
type of abbreviated format blog where the shortened contents from a user's blog
subscriptions all appear together. The interface of the Tumblr platform is thus
focused on a tumblelog dashboard that allows users to subscribe to a feed of blog
posts and virtually any other content, and from there to comment, repost, like, or
connect their blogs to the tumbleblogs of other users on the platform, or to other
platforms such as Twitter and Facebook. Similar to sites such as Facebook, the
platform allows users to 'follow' other users' blogs – or to make their blogs private.
Tumblr is thus a combination of a microblogging and content aggregation site with
a social networking site. Tumblr was founded in 2007, and is one of the earlier
social media sites. As of 2018, the site hosted over 400 million blogs and had over
700 million unique monthly visitors.

Tumblr Netnography

Ethnographic research using Tumblr social media data is currently scarce, but there
are still some noteworthy examples. Hart (2015) conducted an examination of young
people's intimate relationships formed on Tumblr. As part of 'an ethnography into
online dating groups on Tumblr' (p. 197), the author conducted 10 'in-depth' and
'semi-structured online interviews' among a sample where 'half identified as queer,
two identified as having a fluid sexuality, and the remaining three were heterosexual'
(p. 198). Hart's results reveal that Tumblr's appeal to participants is that its groups
and affordances seem to offer them a more emotionally authentic experience than that
found on other social media platforms.

In an investigation of transgendered identity on Tumblr, Dame (2016: 28) used a
netnography-like process. He engaged in a manual search and data-collection process
of 'publicly available posts using five transgender-related tags (#transgender, #ftm,
#mtf, #trans, and #trans*) collected manually through Tumblr's public tag search
function'. His analysis concentrated on locating and identifying some of the dura-
ble social structures of Tumblr participants' language, classifying them 'line-by-line

using emergent coding' and then looking for patterns of behavior for theoretically interesting 'assemblages' and 'practices' such as 'self-identification, conflict management, and definitional policing'. Dame's findings illustrate how 'the performance of self' relies on 'the social and technical classification systems that are applied to it' (p. 35). In this case, transgender individuals navigating Tumblr's social tagging architecture:

> are expected to self-categorize, to transubstantiate their lived gender performance into a set of subcultural linguistic labels. To refuse is to become invisible; again, the database cannot make sense of that which goes unnamed ... the linguistic carries within it the unbearable weight of the self, which continually exceeds and overwhelms its capabilities.

Reddit

Launched in 2005, Reddit is a popular American social media site whose simple format makes it similar in many ways to the communications media of the bygone age of virtual community. Internet old-timers (like me!) will find Reddit still hosting many familiar formats, such as the central message or discussion boards, which on Reddit are called 'subreddits'. Subreddits are organized by theme and cover a massive variety of topics such as science, politics, news, music, fitness, travel, pets, food, hobbies, and photo-sharing. On these subreddits, members submit content such as links to other content, posts, or images. Those posts are rated by members (also called 'redditors'), and those redditors can post comments (which can also be rated), resulting in Reddit's core interactional experience being the familiar conversational social media form of message boards. Known for its open culture and lack of heavy-handed moderation, Reddit also maintains an old-style resistance to overt commercialization and advertising-serving. The official policies of the platform frown upon blatant self-promotion and try to encourage organic user participation. Finally, the site is open to the public – anyone can view it without registering, but registration is required if a user wishes to post.

Reddit can be credited with at least three sociotechnical infrastructural innovations. The first is the ability of registered members to 'vote up' or 'vote down' particular posts. The posts with the highest daily rank in each subreddit are featured at the top of that subreddit, and recent posts with the most positive up-to-down rating ratio and numbers of votes are featured on Reddit's 'front page'. Up-and-down votes lead to Reddit 'karma', a reward that users earn for posting links or comments that are up voted – and which can be lost when links and comments are down voted to a number lower than zero. Reddit's third innovation is the idea of hosting individuals, who might be famous, infamous, or simply interesting for something they do or represent, in public 'Ask Me Anything' or 'AMA' sessions. Launched in 2005, Reddit had over 230 million unique monthly users in 2018.

4chan and Forums

Reddit has a number of similarities and some important differences from the site 4chan, which is an imageboard site known for its somewhat anarchic – and highly creative – culture. Due to space constraints, I will not detail 4chan in this chapter. However, I would encourage those readers who are interested in 4chan to check them out in more detail. In addition, the interested reader might consult published netnographies of 4chan such as that of Nissenbaum and Shifman (2017), which explored 4chan's /b/board's memes as new and contested forms of cultural capital.

There are also tens of thousands of forums and bulletin boards on the global web dedicated to specific topics such as entertainment, food, cars, sports, technology, and hobbies. These forums and bulletin boards contain massive amounts of rich data focused on particular topics, and they use some of the most popular forum software platforms, including vBulletin, phpBB, and SMF. Unfortunately, there exists no good search engine or catalog of these netnographically valuable sites. Finding them is generally a matter of persistence and detective work, as search engines like Google rarely feature them among their first few results' pages. A number of netnographers have made excellent use of the information on these forums. An example is van Hout and Hearne (2016), who combined a number of specialized search terms (such as 'chlorodyne') with the term 'forum' in Google and Yahoo search engines to locate 11 websites hosting forums relating to over-the-counter use of morphine-based medicines, and then studied them for their insights into indigenous knowledge exchange about pharmaceutical opioids.

Reddit Netnography

Although one might think that Reddit, with its many topics, convenient public access, and muted commercial presence, might be a key site for locating a variety of contemporary netnographies, one would be wrong in this assumption. Ethnographies and netnographies of Reddit are still rather uncommon. However, there are some provocative studies sited on the Reddit platform that use methods similar to those of netnography. For instance, in order to understand the dynamics of selective self-disclosure on social media, Shelton and colleagues (2015: 5) interviewed 24 active redditors, and then collected a 'corpus' of Reddit posts over ten weeks which included 1,393 threads with 30,170 different topics. Their findings suggest that the use of relatively anonymous media sites such as Reddit allows people to 'compartmentalize' their participation from their social lives and activities beyond the site, creating a 'culture of disinhibition and open disclosure' (p. 10).

In a study that benefited from Reddit's disinhibited context, van der Nagel (2013) studied the subreddit 'gone wild' which is a bulletin board where users can post photographs of (presumably their own) nude or partially unclothed bodies. Van der Nagel's (2013) intriguing 'case study' discussed how algorithms, interfaces, accounts, cultural codes, and social norms interact to create an environment where many post face-less bodies, and there are clear patterns in the types of bodies appearing on the front page of the subreddit. Finally, Potts and Harrison (2013) conducted a study in which they carefully monitored, collected, and analyzed content on the Reddit and 4chan platforms immediately after the 2013 Boston Marathon bombings. They discovered that novel forms of citizen journalism spread through the two sites almost instantly, including somewhat haphazard, but also admirable, amateur detective attempts to try to identify and track down the bombers.

THE RISE OF SOCIAL NETWORKING SITES

Social Network(ing) Sites

Providing some helpful early conceptual organization, Boyd and Ellison defined 'social network sites' (without the 'ing') as:

> web-based services that allow individuals to (1) construct a public or semi-public profile within a bounded system, (2) articulate a list of other users with whom they share a connection, and (3) view and traverse their list of connec-tions and those made by others within the system. (2007: 211)

We can think of these three enabling characteristics as profile-making, linking, and searching/surfing. Prior to formulating this definition, Boyd and Heer (2006) had studied Friendster using nine-months' worth of participant observation, which included interviews, qualitative surveys, and focus groups, as well as the collection of 1.5 million member profiles. Their results, which combine cultural analysis and the interpretation of social network analysis visualization, emphasize the importance of the profile to the understanding of the social networking site. Boyd and Heer (2006: 1) note that these are changing times for online communications: 'blogs and photo sharing communities have presented new issues for thinking about conversations'. They suggest that future analysis of these online communications should holistically view conversation 'as the interplay of performance and interpretation within a medi-ating architecture ... As online sociality incorporates ever more forms of expression, the sites of digital performance – whether Profile [sic] or photo, avatar or ASCII text – remain at the heart of both context and conversation' (p. 10).

At the same time, social networking sites were the enactment of all sorts of team structures already present in gaming communities that were early pioneers of differ-ent forms of connective arrangements, such as massively multiplayer online games and local–global 'clans'. Although providing a history of online and social gaming is behind the scope of this chapter's range, I feel that it is important to note that a number of interesting netnographies have already been published about online games and game culture. For instance, in a recent study, Yi-Sheng Wang (2018) used netnography along with online interviews to explore female users' experiences of online gambling games (also see García-Álvarez et al., 2017).

Friendster and MySpace

Social networking sites as a form of social media began in the mid-1990s with classmates.com, sixdegrees.com, and arguably with dating sites such as Match.com – but the most popular and recognizably social network-based site was Friendster. Founded in 2002, Friendster was conceptualized as a way to allow users to create standardized profile-based homepages and then connect them with the profiles of their friends. This early format is captured in Figure 3.4, which shows how the prototypical social networking site format of friends, feed, and posts was already perfected in the early 2000s. This notion of building a profile and then 'connecting' it to potential and actual friends was a key infrastructural innovation that inspired rapid acceptance of the Friendster platform and became one of the bases of all social networking sites. Finding near-instant popularity, Friendster became one of the first websites to gain over a million members, eventually obtaining over 115 million. It attracted massive attention from the press and industry, and also from academics.

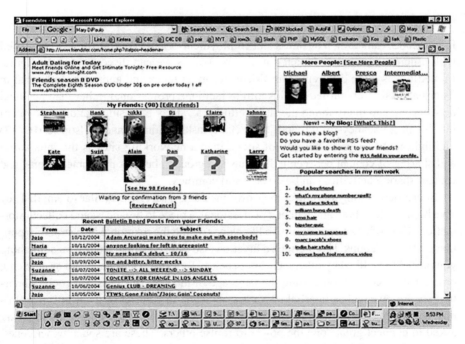

Figure 3.4   Early Friendster screenshot (using Microsoft explorer browser)

In 2003, several technology company employees with Friendster accounts saw potential in its connective features and decided to build a site that mimicked the more popular features of the website. Within 10 days, they had the first version of MySpace ready for launch, creating a powerful competitor for Friendster that would eventually attain a billion registered users and clearly usher social media into the mass audience sphere. MySpace popularized and grew the field of social networking sites, was then acquired by one of the major media conglomerates in 2005, and was ultimately overtaken by an even more powerful competitor, Facebook.

One of the first online ethnographies of a social networking site was Boyd's (2004) ethnographic examination of Friendster, in which she describes the platform as 'an online dating site utilizing social networks to encourage friend-to-friend connections' (p. 1279). Although these connections are actually not exclusive to dating sites, they were less known as technical abilities offered to the general public in open access platforms. In services like Facebook, Instagram, and Twitter, these abilities are commonplace now. Like blogs, social networks often contain copious amounts of content from the general media. They thus provide a rich media experience that combines updates from one's own personal network with targeted digital advertising, as well as almost endless servings of free news and information content. The personal profile format and its connection to other users' profiles have continued to be the core elements of these forms of communication.

LinkedIn

In late 2002, LinkedIn, a business and employment-oriented social site, was launched with a homepage that is depicted in Figure 3.5. As we can discern from the figure, LinkedIn was quite different from Friendster in its focus and approach. Industrial in its orientation, users turned to LinkedIn to facilitate professional rather than personal networking, and many found the site useful for a variety of business and employment intelligence, vacancy-filling, and job-seeking tasks. Quinton and Wilson (2016: 17) highlight that 'The core activity of social media networking sites is the interacting and sharing of content between individuals and groups', but that these interactional and content-sharing activities can be diverse and complex.

Social networking sites offer their own messaging services, similar to email. They give broadcasters, both amateur and professional, a place to broadcast and collect information. They offer an opportunity to like things, using the relational infrastructure popularized by Facebook. Having such a function also offers the opportunity for something you posted to be liked by others. On sites such as LinkedIn, one can friend or unfriend, or connect to connections, using the language of the site. Business and social opportunities are revealed as interlinked: to ask someone to connect to them in LinkedIn's business setting is also to open oneself up to the vulnerability of being refused. Being asked to connect grants one the power to refuse others. These are social experiences, moderated by the site. The sites themselves are like data-collection vacuum cleaners:

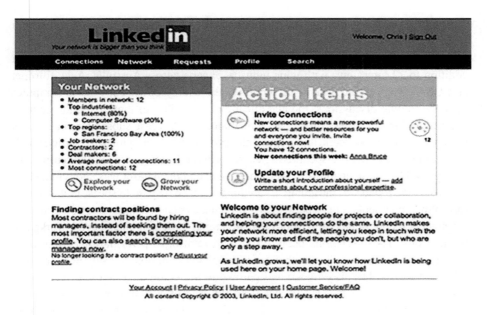

Figure 3.5 Original LinkedIn homepage

they are factories minting customer information from user data. They control the data flow between their borders. Their surveillance capitalism-based business model monetizes the data, creating value for advertisers, social commerce, and online commerce transactions, and they engage in real-time surveillance and prediction, implemented using machine learning in ever more sophisticated ways (Zuboff, 2019).

LinkedIn Netnography

LOOKING AT LINKEDIN

3.2

If you have a LinkedIn profile, go to it and take a look. If you do not have one, you might consider creating one. Write down what you like and dislike about your own profile. What does your profile communicate about you? What sort of person do you seem to be? What seems to motivate you? Now, think about the following issue. How does the form of social media direct our representations of our identities? Is this a good thing or not? Are there conditions under which it might be useful or not? These are important issues for all social media, but the link between platform and representation might be especially apparent with a platform such as LinkedIn.

Quinton and Wilson (2016: 18) conducted 'a two stage qualitative research study, encompassing netnographic research principles which involved analyzing 554 dynamic interactions between professionals on selected LinkedIn wine groups in addition to 12 interviews with wine industry experts across Australia, Asia, Europe, and USA'. Their netnography 'incorporates the use of direct copy from computer mediated online discussions, the classification and coding of these data, the contextualisation through further direct data collection, – in this case subsequent interviews with discussion group contributors, and the provision of anonymity of participants', and application of the pre-specified selection criteria. Eight groups on LinkedIn commonly used by the wine industry were identified, and the dataset was anonymized.

What they found was intriguing. Everything is not so rosy, so to speak, in the land of rosé. When they looked into the world of wine makers and business-people online, the researchers found a range of tensions that structured these combined social–workplace interactions. These tensions centered around relationship formation, credibility, authenticity, and trust – themes that are increasingly common and salient in the Age of Social Media, but also invoke and partake in the communal ethos of reciprocity and moral economies that is familiar from the Age of Virtual Community. Among these online companions, customers, capitalists, and competitors are not only those who apparently seek and offer camaraderie and also those who deal coldly and in a transactional manner. Trust is incrementally built, even online. It is the product of 'a gradual courtship' (2016: 21). Similarly, social media interaction takes a lot of time – there is no credible way to automate the building of trusting human relationships. Thus, the professionals studied by Quinton and Wilson seem to use LinkedIn to try to speed up and make more efficient the process of building trust in business–social relationships: 'Trust within potential business partners is being established via social media networks and membership of these professional networks acts as a trust filter mechanism. The development of relationships remains incremental but time has been compressed into shorter periods for relationship initiation and development.' LinkedIn is a platform where users attempt to balance their transactional and relational needs using the communicative and legitimacy-building capacities of the technology, walking a sometimes fine line between transactional and social norms.

Facebook

Publicized, politicized, and turned into a Hollywood blockbuster, the origins of Facebook are already enshrined as modern mythology. Launched in 2004 as a Harvard student website, Facebook grew organically for eight years before launching as a public company, growing into an online advertising and data sales powerhouse, gaining over two billion active monthly users worldwide, and becoming the uncontested face of the social media industry. As Figure 3.6 shows, 'Thefacebook's' initial platform was based on the same sort of 'friending' connections as Friendster, or any of the signature social networking platforms. However, Facebook perfected a vital dimension: ideology. With its fresh-faced young entrepreneurial leader, its mass popularity, and its legitimizing Harvard credibility, Zuckerberg's Facebook also became one of the key voices for the emerging – and powerful – social media industry. As van Dijck points out, Facebook's appropriation and strategic deployment of the already commonly-used term 'sharing' to describe various online activities has had major impacts not only on the influential social media industry, but on society itself:

> Changing the meaning of sharing turns out to be vital to altering legal rulings concerning privacy and to accepting new forms of monetization. Whereas the term 'privacy' commonly refers to the judicial realm, 'sharing' involves social as well as economic norms, cultural as well as legal values. (2013: 46)

Similarly, 'friending' someone on Facebook is not the result of spontaneous, human-based interactions, but instead an outcome of the 'programmed sociality' of 'People You May Know' suggestions and friend-of-a-friend algorithms (p. 51).

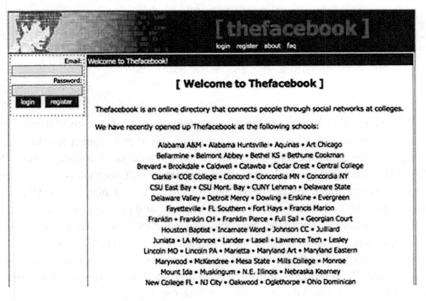

Figure 3.6 Early homepage of 'Thefacebook'

In addition to their provision of affordances that enable particular kinds of online activities under the guise of 'friending' and 'sharing', Facebook's programmers and managers introduced another important term and ability in 2010: the now-famous Like button. Liking a post, brand, or a news story provided a new way to connect.

It must have seemed to users a simple and easy way to affirm, to send a quick positive message, to instantly approve. It was, in essence, a perfect media representation of its visual representation: a digital way to tag something with your thumbs-up. But behind the scenes, 'liking' was much more than this. In fact, the Like button allowed Facebook to record any user's presence on a site, track their online movements, identify them using APIs, and then turn ostensibly private information into corporately owned data (van Dijck, 2013: 48–9).

3.3 COMPARING YOUR IMAGE ON FACEBOOK AND LINKEDIN

If you have a Facebook profile, go and look at it. (And if you are one of those rare individuals who does not have one, you might consider moving counter to the current de-Facebooking trend and creating one.) Write down what you like and dislike about your Facebook profile. What does your profile communicate about you? What sort of person do you seem to be? What seems to motivate you? These are the same questions you were asked to complete regarding your LinkedIn profile. Now, compare your answers for your Facebook and LinkedIn profiles. Did the social media platform alter your representations of identity? How? Do you think that this alteration of your public identity (if it happened) is a good thing, or not?

With new technological offerings layered one on top of the other, Facebook has become much more than just a place where people build and connect profiles. Its messaging includes chat functions and video chat for synchronous communication. With Messenger, it integrates seamlessly into phone messages. Facebook is also an archive, and its message functions can substitute for email. It is a place to host and share photographs. Its Timeline function creates intimacy and prompts memories, while its public defaults arouse suspicion and consternation. Facebook offers the ability to easily form groups or set up pages where companies or individuals can post, complain, debate, discuss, and organize in various ways around particular topics and themes. This includes the important ability to create dedicated research pages for online ethnography, which we will discuss further in Chapter 9.

Facebook is also a popular game server, hosting some of the world's most popular games, such as Bejeweled, Clash of Clans, and Candy Crush. It offers Facebook Live for live video streaming. Facebook demonstrates the immense variety of online interaction types that can be encompassed under the umbrella of what is ostensibly considered a single social media platform. As Facebook evolved and introduced these new technologies and abilities, the platform both responded to users and shaped their behaviors. Facebook's abilities include providing a number of free services that, although not essential, can certainly be useful to the conduct of netnography. Through it all, however, Facebook has been focused on establishing a branded service that served the needs of a huge base of active users while exploiting them as a resource to provide attention to advertising and ever-more-defined targeting data (van Dijck, 2013: 56). In this manner, the post-IPO Facebook truly defined the new face of online connection as a type of media business: *social media*, the media industry that develops and monetizes online sociality.

Facebook Netnographies

RESEARCH ENGAGEMENTS WITH FACEBOOK

3.4

If you are like many people, you probably spend a significant amount of time on Facebook already. However, using a social media site and conducting research on that site are two very different matters. Try taking a more objective look at the research environment that Facebook offers to qualitative researchers. How would you describe the type of opportunities for research that Facebook offers? How would you describe the type of data it provides? How might it be useful for netnography? What topics could Facebook inform well? Which types of questions would not be appropriate for a Facebook-based investigation? Do you think the site limits your research in any way? As we will learn in this chapter, Facebook has already provided netnographic researchers with the data to conduct some very interesting studies.

There have been numerous netnographies that have used Facebook, and a number of chapters and articles written specifically about conducting this type of research on the platform. Piacenti and colleagues (2014) discussed and then demonstrated the usefulness of Facebook as a site for studying migration and immigration. The authors argue that, in particular, ethnographic transnational migration and immigration research is constrained because it involves complex 'structural barriers' of geography, travel funding, travel time, and the logistics of ethnographic entrée. Referring to the first author's fieldwork in Mama, Yucatán in Mexico, the authors describe the development of local Internet and Facebook access there as the creation of 'what Appadurai (1996) calls a transnational technoscape, or that "the global configuration, also ever fluid, of technology, and the fact that technology, both high and low, both mechanical and informational, now moves at high speeds across various kinds of previously impervious boundaries" (p. 34)'.

They then discuss their study, which evolved organically from 'a chance encounter with an undergraduate student' wearing a Facebook t-shirt in 2007, to account creation, to the creation of a dedicated Facebook page for migration and immigration research among the migrant and immigrant families relating to Mama, Yucatán, whether they lived in the municipality, or in other locations such as New York City. They visited the site several times a week, posted news articles, removed non-(im)migration content, responded to commentaries and posts, and maintained the research site. Within three months, they had several hundred participants.

Interestingly, they found that, as the site developed, the role of researcher and research participants became blurred, as some participants shifted into roles more like research assistants, and some shifted the discourse of the research project. Indeed, the Facebook research page created a new ethnographic context, one where all research participants could see the participation of others, connect with them, and actively engage in the research project in a variety of ways. The authors called this 'a post-structural experience', describing it as follows:

> Dualities were blurred, if not temporarily breached, and soon disoriented by the de-anchored co-presence of multiple, transnational roles and identities. Although the Mama, Yucatán Facebook page was used as a space to focus on (im)migration issues and human rights policy, it quite unexpectedly allowed for a new social relationship marked by a more flattened hierarchy of statuses between the town citizenry and academia while allowing for a more democratic approach to information production and dissemination, as well as shifts in roles, identities, and purposes. (Piacenti et al., 2014: 13)

Facebook has also been found useful for examining life transitions among individuals. In a conceptual article that advanced from her own developing research among students undergoing educational and disciplinary transitions, Baker (2013: 134) describes how she started her research with personal interviews, 'shadowing' research participants, and archival research using documents such as students' textbooks and photographs of their 'institutional learning environments'. Eventually, she found that maintaining contact on Facebook helped to solve the challenge of how to maintain meaningful communication with her young and mobile research participants in order to conduct longitudinal qualitative research among them. She tried phoning, emailing, and texting, but none of these were satisfactory. Finally, 'Facebook emerged as a good-fit solution' to her research needs, not only because of its popularity with her participant groups' demographic, but also because of the range of communicative affordances it provided. Using Facebook as an ethnographic context, Baker (2013) asserts, provides 'a source of rich data' (p. 140) and is an 'innovative and convenient alternative to traditional conceptions of participant observation', although one which also 'presents ethical challenges' (p. 141).

Given that it is a rich, novel, popular, influential, and even controversial context for social communication in contemporary society, the Facebook context is also an important site for ethnography in its own right. Farquhar (2013: 449) conducted 'a 12-month cyber-ethnography' which involved '3–5 hours of researcher activity on Facebook' per day, mainly involving recruitment for interviews and 'guided tours' of participants' typical Facebook activities, as well as their view of their own performance of self and the performances of others. The study finds that Goffman's (1969) concepts of strategic interaction and the intentional presentation of the self, as well as the general precepts of symbolic interaction, fit well as theoretical descriptors of the social life of Facebook participants.

Facebook and other social media sites also may have important effects upon particular populations and on social behaviors. Combining three focus groups with 15 participants (males and females aged 19–23) with a netnography of alcohol-related, nightclub groups and pages, and official alcohol brand Facebook pages, Moraes and colleagues (2014) studied how the platform is used to promote drinking among young consumers. Narrowing down from thousands of drinking-related Facebook groups to eleven, the researchers kept fieldnotes on their involvement with these groups and then interpreted over 63,000 words of textual data. Their findings reveal how nightclubs and alcohol brands actively use Facebook to reinforce already existing discourses and conversations linking drinking with sociability, using the platform 'as a tool to communicate, co-produce and generate alcohol-related content with young adults, which encourages drinking' (p. 1377).

As a manifestation and indeed a force of the mass industrialization of social media, Facebook is obviously a commercial as well as a social context, one where the interests of monetization are omnipresent and thus are also accessible to investigation. Existing pages can be useful and informative contexts for this type of study. Peeroo and colleagues (2015) used a non-participative procedure to help reveal how people engage with retail sites on Facebook. Examining and analyzing the content of Tesco's and Walmart's Facebook pages over one month of data collection revealed a variety of cognitive, emotional, and behavioral forms of engagement. One of their main findings was how individuals subverted commercially-sponsored Facebook pages to engage in resistance and consumer activism:

> Customers 'mainly use the Facebook pages of grocery stores to post complaints and criticisms. Furthermore, they actively recommend customers to boycott the grocery stores and to patronise stores of competitors. Additionally, customers provide information about products and services of competitors, thus encouraging the other customers to shop in other outlets.'

Another intriguing study into how commercial interests manifest through Facebook is that of Roth-Cohen and Lahav (2018). Their study, which sampled a range of Facebook groups over a one-month period in 2016, found that small and medium enterprises sometimes 'go undercover' on Facebook, using unidentified messages to try to exploit open and closed Facebook groups while disguised as ordinary users. In doing so, these commercial actors sought to exploit through mimicry the 'sense of community, belonging, and trust' of these communicative groups in order to more effectively place their promotional business messages (p. 4).

VISUAL, VIRTUAL, AND AUDIOVISUAL SITES

Gretzel (2017a) theorized that social media have recently experienced a 'visual turn' in which the visual aspects of existing platforms have become more important and, especially, new platforms that emphasize visual elements are growing in number, popularity, and influence. Visual modes of representation and communication, she argues, are assuming 'a central rather than just supporting role' in social media experiences and platforms. Clearly, this evolution has been ongoing. As this book's history of social media attests, even early platforms such as Prodigy, CompuServe, and especially GEnie developed visual and even 3D representations to accompany their gaming services. Yet one of the earliest and most successful of the purely visual sites was clearly Flickr.

Flickr

Launched in 2004 by a Vancouver-based company and acquired one year later by Yahoo!, Flickr is a type of social networking site with user-generated pictures at the center of its experience. At its launch, Flickr differentiated itself from the inferred difficulties of digital photography, promoting itself as 'outrageously simple' and 'ridiculously easy', as captured by the screenshot presented in Figure 3.7. Flickr added strong social and online components to the photo-sharing experience. Van Dijck (2013: 91) explains that photographs were not some sort of byproduct of sociality at Flickr, instead 'online picture sharing was the core of a creative and communicative function'. To manage this function, Flickr's interface offered sophisticated privacy functions as well as 'features for posting, favoriting, distributing, curating, exhibiting, and storing photographic objects online'. These functions were not entirely novel or unique to the online environment. As van Dijck (2013: 94) notes, they build on both private rituals – such as family picture albums and photo exchanges – and professional and artistic ones, such as professional portfolios, archival collections, and photo galleries. Although it is not widely granted the status of a currently successful social media site, Flickr still has a significant, participative, and loyal user base. It reportedly has an archive of over 10 billion images, and over 90 million active monthly users sharing over 1 million images per day, as of May 2018 (Flickr Stats and Facts, 2018).

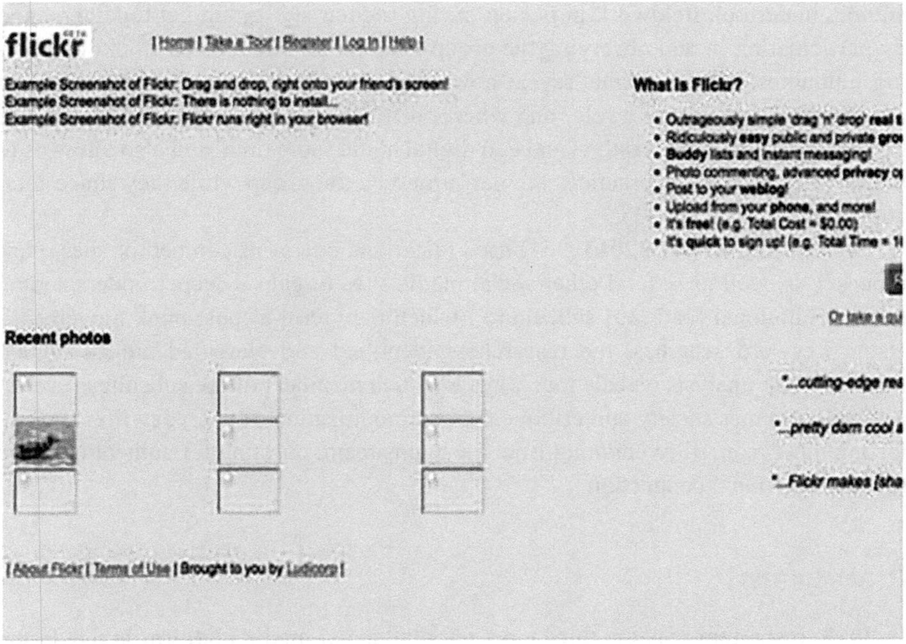

Figure 3.7 Flickr homepage at launch, circa 2004

Eiler points out some important differences between Flickr and Instagram, the platform's wildly successful successor:

> on Instagram, everything is public ... That is not the case on Flickr, where users have granular settings for changing photos to public, visible to friends, visible to family or completely private. Communities are more deliberate. Following is not an option, but joining is. What Instagram lacks, Flickr fulfills: a possibility for adjusting privacy settings so that every photo uploaded doesn't appear out there, for the entire Web to see. On Flickr, there is no such thing as social media celebrity. The public nature of Instagram makes the idea of celebrity not only normal, but encouraged. (2012: n.p.)

Several online ethnographies have been conducted which either focus on Flickr or else use it as one source of data among other sources. Providing a very interesting example of a combined traditional and online ethnography that partakes in the visual turn, photographic scholars Gómez Cruz and Ardèvol (2013) conducted fieldwork with a group of Barcelona-based photographers named 'SortidazZ' organized primarily through Flickr. Using practice theory as a theoretical frame, the authors undertook fieldwork in person during regular sub-group get togethers, and by participating in and observing the group's online interactions on Flickr and taking fieldnotes. Their findings reveal how online technologies enable photography to take on a performative role, one where 'different practices enable and enhance mediations that are material, visual and digital at the same time' and also allow us to understand 'how these practices are performed by the group while they shape their collective identity' (p. 35).

Mortara and Ironico (2013: 351) used Flickr and one of its competitor sites, Photobucket, as well as several other social media sites to gain a deeper understanding of 'the Emotional [or Emo] subculture', which they term a 'post-punk movement'. Using keyword searches, the researchers identified and classified almost 10,000 images. Their analysis reveals four ways in which members of the subculture protest against consumer society and critique the commoditization of everyday life: aestheticizing inner pain, differentiating from the mainstream, questing for authenticity, and seeking emotional connection.

Instagram

In 2018, Instagram was the third most popular social media platform in use in the United States, with 35% of all American adults responding that they use the site online or on their telephones. Like Flickr, Instagram is a visual native site built on the idea of communicating and interacting through photographs. Unlike Flickr, Instagram was created to be a mobile phone native application. As Figure 3.8 captures, Instagram's interface is highly photographic and provides the user with a lot of visual choice. However, as the above quote from Eiler (2012) indicates, the configuration of the site is much more individualistic, providing, in essence, the visual equivalent of McQuarrie et al.'s (2013) megaphone. Launched in 2010, Instagram is an application that allows users to upload photos and videos to the platform, and then offers a variety of different and easy-to-use visual filters to improve or stylize them. As well, the photographs can be classified with hashtags, comments, and location information. Instagram posts can be shared publicly, or only with a list of pre-approved 'followers'. Facebook acquired the platform in 2012 and began integrating some of the elements of the two sites together. The Instagram experience is quite social, with messaging features and comments that often lead to user interactions. In addition, it is inherently competitive, with users often competing for greater numbers of followers (and thus social and commercial influence) as well as the engagement of likes (which in this medium are heart-, rather than thumbs-up-shaped) and comments. Commercially, the site has been very successful at monetizing social activity by serving visually oriented advertising and by featuring the paid content of product endorsers, who often resemble, or even actually are, regular users of the application.

Figure 3.8 Instagram screenshots, circa 2016

Instagram Netnography

Exploring how contemporary tourist experiences link both with photographic practices as well as the sharing of travel photographs, Gretzel (2017c) conducted a netnography of 'travel selfies' in Instagram. She followed ethnographic and netnographic principles of researcher immersion, involving 'deep and long-term' engagement with the subject area:

travel photography, travel photo posting on social media, and Instagram use in particular. While the latter had been going on in systematic form since 2013, a focused observational data collection period on Instagram was conducted from August to November 2016 to specifically inform the current research.

Searching Instagram posts for those tagged with the hashtag #travelselfie and sorting organically through these posts led the researcher to capture 'up to a hundred of the most recent pictures during each engagement with the platform' (p. 5). Following 'hermeneutical cycles of reading and rereading, coding emergent themes, formatting the identification of themes with the researcher's personal experience and news articles' led to her findings. These revealed many travel selfies that capture pithy or mundane moments in buses and trains, although often using angles, filters, expression, or composition to make them more interesting. Irony and parody of classic travel selfies are also interesting twists on allegedly iconic travel photography. These Instagram selfies possess continuity with traditional travel photography, and conform to many Instagram conventions. However, Gretzel (2017c) also finds that they illustrate a strong desire to individualize and innovate.

Although she labels her writing an 'essay', Marwick's (2015) research on Instagram fame and celebrity appears to result from a deep engagement with the site as well as interviews with social actors involved with the site, such as its founding community manager. Further, she describes a 'textual and visual analysis' of 'forty public Instagram accounts with over ten thousand followers each' (p. 145) that resembles the type of data-collection procedure commonly associated with netnography. Providing an interesting spin on data analysis, she worked with undergraduate students not only to collect data, but also to taxonomize Instagram accounts and then 'try to explain why some accounts had become so popular' – a task she describes as 'especially challenging'. Her findings on the nature of fame in the age of Instagram illuminate the role of traditional celebrities such as Justin Bieber and Kim Kardashian, as well as a group of what she, using Senft's (2008) term, calls 'microcelebrities'. The microcelebrities are either those who have achieved a degree of fame on another social media platform or those who have built their own fame on Instagram and thus become 'Instafamous'.

Examining three highly-followed Instagram accounts, Marwick (2015: 155) explains how they use different 'microcelebrity techniques to achieve attention and popularity online'. Each of the three case studies 'embodies a different personal brand – all-American teenager, sexy Barbadian star, and wealthy fashionista'. Each account portrays its user in an aspirational way, 'creating content that portrays them in a high-status light, simulating the attention given to celebrities' (p. 156). The study provides a window into the marketizing of the self, with techniques of fame-building that belong to social media's wider 'online attention economy' (p. 157). This economy is 'one in which page views and clicks are synonymous with success and thus online status'. It is also one in which, I might add, large numbers of targeted fans and followers are a form of attention capital that is commercially convertible into lucrative sponsorship funding.

Snapchat

Alongside Instagram, Snapchat is another of the most popular visually-oriented messaging applications. Founded on the basic idea that a mobile phone 'snapshot' could be the basis for online 'chat' conversations that contribute to social relationships, Snapchat introduced several affordance-based innovations to social media users. First, it offered temporariness. 'Snaps' (as the photographic images are called) are only available for viewing for a short amount of time before they become inaccessible. Second, it was the first major platform to introduce 'stories' of chronological content. Third, it presented cutting-edge applications of augmented reality that, for instance, allowed people to easily create animated avatars of themselves in humorous or romantic situations with their friends' avatars (using the 'Bitmoji' application), all placed against photographic backdrops which they captured. The middle section of Figure 3.9 illustrates one such popular augmented reality filter on Snapchat, which places dog ears and tongues on the user. Launched in 2011, Snapchat had 187 million daily active users in early 2018, and is the fifth most popular social media platform in America, with 27% of American adults saying that they use the platform.

FRIENDS PAGE   **CAMERA**   **DISCOVER PAGE**

Figure 3.9   Original Snapchat screenshots from time of launch, circa 2011

Snapchat Netnography

3.6

ENGAGING ETHNOGRAPHICALLY WITH SNAPCHAT

Like Instagram and Twitter, Snapchat offers a unique type of social media experience. Using your mobile phone, take a look at Snapchat (if you have not joined, consider joining). How would you describe the platform and experience of Snapchat, in relation to some of the other social media sites you have already examined and discussed? What are the unique characteristics of Snapchat's social data? What types of topics could you study through Snapchat? Does Snapchat's format lead you to certain kinds of research? What guidelines might you offer to researchers seeking to use Snapchat as a site for conducting netnographic research?

Published online ethnographies that use Snapchat as a field site are still somewhat rare in the academic literature. Partly, this may be because Snapchat is still a relatively new social media platform. It might also be an effect of the fact that Snapchat messages are generally private rather than public, and thus are more difficult to study than, say, Twitter feed or YouTube posts that are publicly available. However, there are some useful exemplars. Clark (2016), for instance, studied how young students of color use social media such as Snapchat, Facebook, and Twitter to become politically involved in social movements and protest action. The article was based on a year-long ethnographic project involving weekly meetings, school-related activities, and a series of participant-generated videotaped interviews of one another and their peers about 'the role social media had played in how they had learned of and shared views' about recent politically charged events pertaining to #BlackLivesMatter (2016: 240). Clark's results reveal that Snapchat's ability to select recipients and share specific messages make it an 'attractive alternative' to the more public forums of Twitter and Facebook (p. 245). Similarly, and for related reasons, Snapchat was the primary platform used during actual protest events, because 'it let students instantaneously relay messages that demanded immediate attention'.

Providing another example, Wargo (2015: 53) utilized an in-depth study of the platform's use by a single, 17-year-old 'avid Snapchat user and digital composer' as part of 'a larger critical qualitative connective ethnography' (p. 52). Combining participant-observation, fieldnote taking, interviews, 'think aloud sessions', and video recordings of his participant's ephemeral productions on Snapchat, Wargo was able to 'retrace and stitch together the movement and stretches' (p. 53) of his ethnographic participant's retelling. His conclusions highlight how young people 'tell spatial stories and map nomadic narratives to explore their own embodied experiences with and through mobile media' (p. 47). In particular, Wargo used a 'multimodal' form of interaction analysis (p. 59), and the recognition that 'literacies are rhizomatic' (p. 60), to account for the ways that his research participant composed a narrative physically, 'through touch, swipe, gesture, and gaze'. This ongoing digital composition was 'not only overlapping across histories of access and participation but enfolded in space-time as new bodies emerged on the scene' (p. 59).

Pinterest

Pinterest is another highly visual social media site. It is also the fourth most popular site for American social media users, with 29% of the US population reporting that they use it (with about 67% of those users being female). Eight years after its 2010 launch, the site has over 200 million active monthly users, and is a publicly traded corporation with clear commercial interests and connections. Pinterest offers its users a way to organize, tag, and curate material from the World Wide Web. Resembling a catalog of interests, the links to customers' fascinations and their organizations of these desires show up quite readily in the visually-focused collections of the various longings of their hearts and minds. Webpages and videos become items that Pinterest users can 'pin', collecting them as a butterfly collector would pierce a prized specimen through the thorax. The end result, as shown in Figure 3.10, is a scrapbook-like visual arrangement, customized and carefully curated by the Pinterest user.

Figure 3.10 Pinterest pin board, circa 2017

'Pinning' is thus Pinterest's prime techno-infrastructural innovation. It combines saving, uploading, and tagging an item for a variety of 'sharing' options, including, most often, public. Like Facebook, the site offers sponsored pages to businesses so that they can promote their wares to the platform's users. Like Twitter, boards and users can be followed and unfollowed. Like Tumblr, Pinterest is a platform that benefits from the wide dispersal of information across the World Wide Web, allowing users to bring together and visualize information collected from that ecosystem.

Pinterest Netnography

Published ethnographic and netnographic approaches to social media research on Pinterest are surprisingly rare. I say surprising because Pinterest is such a rich source of categorized visual lifestyle information. It allows a revealing insight into the contents of people's interests, what they aspire to, what concerns them, what they are planning, and how they organize their thinking and their practices. It can even be a useful tool for netnographic researchers searching for a way to organize and represent their own far-flung online sources of high quality data.

There have been a few studies of Pinterest use already published. Pearce and Learmonth (2013), for example, used a study of Pinterest data, along with focus groups, to evaluate the way students used the platform as an educational resource in an introductory anthropology course. In order to understand the public health and health communications aspects of social media, Guidry et al. (2015) examined 800 vaccine-related pin boards. And another study by Guidry et al. (2016) looked at portrayals of depression in 800 different Pinterest posts.

Digital possession rituals and a symbolic sense of ownership were the key analytic categories developed by Schiele and Hughes (2013: 48) in their published conference paper. The authors used netnography 'to keep a record of interactions, and perform analysis on the collected data. The type of data collected includes the text that online participants type directly into "comments" sections, and observational data' that the researchers recorded in fieldnotes. One of the authors is a regular user of Pinterest, and introspected on her own subjective experiences of platform use as an element of the participant-observational element of the study. In addition, the researchers conducted 10 semi-structured interviews with female Pinterest users during which 'the participants gave the interviewers a tour of their Pinterest boards, describing images chosen and taste preferences' as well as answering open-ended questions about their Pinterest selections and arrangements. Their research discovered a range of compelling practices and rituals, including claiming, hoarding, personalizing, and sharing. They concluded that digital consumers' rituals of possession are related in many ways to traditional rituals of possession, but are also altered by the use of new software platforms. If you are interested in an example of a consumer- and advertising-centric Pinterest study, have a look at Phillips et al. (2014), an article that conducted a pictorial and textual analysis of 2,291 images found on 20 pin boards and related it to women's aspirational selves.

YouTube

In 2018, YouTube was rated the number one social media site in America, used by 73% of the adults in the country. YouTube is not merely an American, but an international, social media phenomenon. As you can see from its original launch homepage depicted in Figure 3.11, YouTube began as a fairly humble video-hosting site. Created in 2005 by three former employees of the electronic payment service PayPal, and bought the next year by Google for over a billion dollars, YouTube had long been a part of the popular consciousness of social media. YouTube is a website devoted to video sharing. The platform allows its registered users to upload an unlimited amount of their own videos, rate videos, share, subscribe to video feed 'channels', and comment on videos (and on others' comments). The videos are available for public viewing by anyone. Conversations between users occasionally occur through addressing each other in videos, but much more commonly interaction takes place through the comment sections.

Figure 3.11 YouTube homepage, after launch, circa 2005

Although there is a large amount of professionally produced content shared on YouTube by major media corporations, and much of this is among the most popular material on the site, the platform also contains a far larger number of user-generated videos on a vast range of topics. The world of video blogging, or 'vlogging', using YouTube videos is currently highly influential. Vloggers in industries such as beauty, fitness, fashion, automotive, and food command large devoted audiences and (as with Instagram) attract lucrative promotion deals from major brands and their companies. Besides its commercial characteristics, YouTube has contributed to a massive increase in the amount and availability of independent content and video programming. It has also both developed its own industrial ecosystem and democratized aspects of the talent acquisition side of entertainment, with some YouTube stars, such as Justin Bieber, Shawn Mendes, Ed Sheeran, Emily Ratajkowski, and Kate Upton going on to achieve fame in the global entertainment and music markets. YouTube has been credited with changing access to education by providing high quality programming (such as the TED talk series) to the public free of charge. Prompting user experimentation with forms of video production and collaboration, and providing exposure to new technologies such as 3D and virtual reality, YouTube is a constantly changing site that promises researchers an ever-evolving set of novel topics.

YouTube Netnography

ENGAGING ETHNOGRAPHICALLY WITH YOUTUBE

3.7

Like Snapchat, Instagram and Twitter, YouTube offers a unique type of social media experience. How would you describe the platform and experience of YouTube, in relation to some of the other social media sites you have already examined and discussed in these exercises? What are the unique characteristics of YouTube's social data? What types of research topics do you think that you could effectively investigate through YouTube? Does the format of YouTube lead you to favor conducting certain kinds of ethnographic (or other) research? What guidelines would you give to a researcher who wishes to use YouTube as the main site for his/her netnography? (Note: hold that thought, because you will begin engaging with and using YouTube data in a series of exercises beginning in Chapter 8 of this book.)

Likely due to the fact that it is such a popular and rich site of cultural information, there is a very substantial literature composed of online ethnographic and netnographic investigations sited on YouTube. In one of the earlier articles of this type, Lange (2007) investigated the formation of social networks on the site using one year of observation of YouTube videos, fieldnotes on her observations, 54 semi-structured interviews, and attendance at video-themed events in three cities. Her findings revealed a complex system in which social acts, technological abilities, and existing relationships interacted in a variety of ways: 'Posted videos and related comments create media circuits that take on a variety of different forms according to the relationships that they reflect' (p. 377). Lange's early findings among YouTube users underscore the importance of conceptions of private and public, of sharing videos, and of posting comments, in the formation of YouTube socialities.

Some researchers have studied a few of the many institutional changes that YouTube has brought to the sphere of media and communications. Sumiala and Tikka (2013) began their YouTube netnography with a major news event – the Israeli navy's interception of the flotillas headed to the Gaza region. Almost 8,000 videos on the topic were released over about a two-week period. The researchers followed certain categories and keywords such as 'Israeli flotilla', gathering and collecting data for analysis, while maintaining a participant observational research stance (p. 325). Their results study the medium of an amateur-driven online 'news culture' on YouTube, finding that it 'alters the truth claims of [official] news [organizations] and the professional hegemony of news making, [affecting] the ways in which we, as the audience, maintain relations with professional news institutions' (p. 318).

There are also a number of articles studying the evolving ecosystem of bloggers and YouTube 'influencer' entrepreneurs. Snelson (2015) investigated the former in a study of school-related vlogs, vloggers, and viewers. Over a three-month period, the researcher collected a 'purposive sample of 120 personal video blogs' (p. 321). In addition, she described her background as a YouTuber as well as a teacher and researcher of YouTube technologies, content, and community. Describing her study as ethnographic, the author explained her approach as follows: 'In the present study, the vlogger community was studied within the context of their native online habitat much like an anthropologist might go into the bush to study a remote culture' (p. 324). Findings from Snelson (2015) revealed the various contours of youth vlogging, and how rooted the practice is in notions of social connection. In another study, Ashman and colleagues (2018) studied the practice of autobiographical entrepreneurship among YouTube bloggers who seek to become monetized brands. Using online ethnography and nine face-to-face interviews with YouTube vloggers, Ashman et al. (2018) concluded that these activities on YouTube were driven by a pernicious neoliberal ethos that led not only to a naive optimism, but also to precarious work circumstances and an attention-seeking self-absorption.

Some of these darkside elements are also present in other ethnographic studies of YouTube. In a disturbing study, Veer and Barakat (2009) delved into the world of anorexia nervosa YouTube vloggers. Their netnography began with a search that yielded 212 weight loss vloggers. After refining and examining the results, they then narrowed down their dataset to five vloggers who specifically mentioned that they had been diagnosed with the disorder. Their findings showed how the 'online exhibitionism' of the medium offered anorexia sufferers not only a sense of personal catharsis and anonymous public support, but also a sense of control. As well, these vloggers often used their videos to obtain validation from a sympathetic audience and from other people with anorexia nervosa. However, Veer and Barakat (2009) provided data showing how numerous comments from viewers actually encouraged anorexia sufferers to keep fasting. At times, this anonymous audience 'validation' exaggerated the effects of the disease by reinforcing the disorder sufferer's need for control over their body and their desire to lose more weight (p. 12). Hence, the usually positive terms 'support' and 'validation' took on a new and twisted meaning in the context. As the researchers concluded in their article:

> The support rich environment offered by YouTube means that sufferers are able to be a 'validated self' and it is this 'self' that may continue to slowly kill them in the privacy of their webcams, computer screens and [in the presence of] hundreds of thousands of online voyeurs. (2009: 14)

Virtual Worlds and Games

Virtual worlds and multiplayer videogames present a somewhat unique form of sociality to online experience that arguably may not fit neatly into the existing definitions of social media. Nonetheless, because they have already served as important contexts for published netnographic work, I include them in this chapter. Virtual worlds and multiplayer videogames place their users in a computer-generated simulation which may be populated by other users. Videogames tend to have particular objectives, rules, and structures that influence the kinds of sociality their users exhibit, while virtual worlds tend to be more focused on exploration and social interaction for their own sake. Virtual worlds and some but certainly not all games are experienced by their users through re-embodiment in an avatar figure, which is the form through which users navigate, participate, and communicate. Worlds can be themed in simple or complex ways, using works of fiction, or be completely original. They can draw their rules from reality – such as limited human locomotion, or having gravity – or can be completely fantastic – such as providing winged avatars, or removing the constraints of gravity.

One of the best-known ethnographies of a virtual world is Tom Boellstorff's now-classic (2008) work *Coming of Age in Second Life: An Anthropologist Explores the Virtually Human*, in which he develops and demonstrates how ethnographic methods apply to the rich socialities of Linden Labs' Second Life environment. Other notable examples of Second Life-situated ethnography include Bardzell and Odom's (2008) study of spatial experience, Connelly's (2010) study of 'virtual Buddhist' religious practice, and Tavakoli and Mura's (2015) study of Muslim Iranian women's virtual tourism behaviors. For those attracted to virtual world and videogame ethnography, I highly recommend the useful and detailed method handbook about the conduct of ethnography in virtual worlds authored by Boellstorff et al. (2012).

For an example of an extensive videogame netnography, consider García-Álvarez et al. (2015). In work that is exemplary for its methodological detail and its researcher participation in the field site, the researchers studied Restaurant City, a game hosted on Facebook. Their article provides a contextualized, useful, and engaging description of their three-year-long netnographic fieldwork, which stretched from soon after the game's launch to its cancellation by Facebook. Also noteworthy in studies of video gaming and social media sociality is the popular live streaming gamer site Twitch.

Although it is a video site, Twitch also hosts live streaming of comments, and thus a running social interaction between active viewers. In online ethnographic dissertation work, Bingham (2017) finds a neoliberal capitalist ethos driving conceptions of professionalized content creation and community leadership on the Twitch platform.

THE GLOBAL SITUATION

There is an entire world of social media thriving outside of the North American context, apart from the dominant American Silicon Valley firms who initiated the field and its ensuing industry. Indeed, Hootsuite statistics from January 2018 indicate that there are over three billion active social media users around the globe, accounting for a worldwide penetration of about 42% of the world's population (Chaffey, 2018). They also reported an annual global growth rate of social media adoption of 13%, with the populations of Saudi Arabia, India, Indonesia, and Ghana leading all nations (ibid.).

Although Facebook (and its properties WhatsApp and Messenger) and YouTube dominate as the top four social media sites in the world, they are followed by two very important and influential Chinese sites, WeChat and QQ (Statista, 2018). As a consequence of the Chinese government's 'Great Firewall', Chinese citizens use new Chinese social media platforms, and those social media have been incredibly dynamic and innovative. WeChat, for instance, is a social media platform that combines WhatsApp-like messaging, Facebook-like status updates, voice-over IP, city services, and a mobile payment system that is widely accepted and used. QQ is software for instant messaging that also offers online social games, voice chat, music, and shopping. Qzone is a Chinese social networking and blogging platform. All of these Chinese platforms are owned by the same Chinese company, Tencent, which is one of the top technology firms in the world, as well as the largest and most valuable gaming company. Tencent does not own Sina Weibo, which is yet another successful Chinese social media platform. Sina Weibo can be described as a Twitter-like microblogging service.

Russia is also a world leader in social media sites. A good example of this is VKontakte (or VK), the Russian online social media and social networking service, which had over 500 million accounts as of 2018. Another important Russian site is Odnoklassniki (or OK.ru), a social networking platform for classmates and old friends.

Beyond China and Russia, there is a range of important and influential social media platforms operating around the world in different languages. These platforms are culturally attuned to local customs and needs, and, unfortunately, it is far outside the scope of this book to try to name and describe them all. Needless to say, it would be a highly useful contribution for researchers in any local context to study sites that are native to them and to ethnographically capture their nuance and cultures for the global scientific community. Currently, there is a dearth of netnography conducted in languages other than English, and relatively few published investigations of social media sites outside of English-speaking national contexts.

CHAPTER SUMMARY

In the wide-ranging technological headtrip that was Chapter 3, we followed the development of the Age of Social Media through three overlapping types of waves. First, initiated by the rise of blogging and dynamic webpages were forms of social media that were more individual-centered, focused on providing a type of publishing forum for solo actors to gather audiences. Twitter, as a microblog, followed in this pattern, but so did YouTube with videos. The next wave was the ripening of social networking sites that began with early offerings such as Friendster and brought social media to mainstream popularity as well as commercializing online social experiences, turning them into opportunities for serving targeted advertisements, gathering personal data about consumers, and facilitating online transactions. Facebook and LinkedIn are the obvious heavyweights of this format. The third wave is the turn to the visual, led by Flickr and represented by social media platforms such as Pinterest, Instagram, and Snapchat. Throughout the chapter, we learned how the sociotechnical infrastructures of different platforms altered the experience of sociality by offering new social affordances such as Twitter's following and trending functions, or Facebook's friending and liking. The variety of social media experiences is vast and continues to grow, with old-style formats such as those of Reddit and 4chan coexisting with aggregation services such as Tumblr, virtual worlds, and gaming sites. Globally, social media is advanced, with sites such as China's WeChat and QQ, and Russia's VKontakte acting as hosts to hundreds of millions of members. We learned how the ethnographic research conducted on these social media platforms is as complex and diverse as are the platforms themselves. The chapter overviewed a range of netnographic research on sites such as Twitter, Friendster, Reddit, LinkedIn, Facebook, Flickr, YouTube, Instagram, and Snapchat. Numerous netnographies have already shown how social media are used in life transitions, how they play a role in business processes of credibility and trust formation, how they become involved in various forms of resistance and activism, how they offer alternate news channels to the public, and how they are creating new ecosystems of online entrepreneurs and influence networks. These, and many other research findings, were presented and summarized in this concluding chapter on the history of social media.

KEY READINGS

Piacenti, David Joseph, Luis Balmore Rivas, and Josef Garrett (2014) 'Facebook ethnography: The poststructural ontology of transnational (im)migration research', *International Journal of Qualitative Methods*, 13(1): 224–36.

Quinton, Sarah and Damien Wilson (2016) 'Tensions and ties in social media networks: Towards a model of understanding business relationship development and business performance enhancement through the use of LinkedIn', *Industrial Marketing Management*, 54: 15–24.

Snelson, Chareen (2015) 'Vlogging about school on YouTube: An exploratory study', *New Media & Society*,17(3): 321–39.

Van der Nagel, Emily (2013) 'Faceless bodies: Negotiating technological and cultural codes on Reddit Gonewild', *Scan: Journal of Media Arts Culture*, 10(2): 1–10.

Van Dijck, José (2013) *The Culture of Connectivity: A Critical History of Social Media*. Oxford: Oxford University Press.

Wargo, Jon M. (2015) 'Spatial stories with nomadic narrators: Affect, Snapchat, and feeling embodiment in youth mobile composing', *Journal of Language and Literacy Education*, 11(1): 47–64.

SOCIALITIES: ALL THE WAYS WE CONNECT

CHAPTER OVERVIEW

This chapter will offer a theoretical analysis of the history of social media and social media-based ethnographic research, and conceptualize these new forms of human sociality. Some theorists, philosophers, and mystics of the past believed that social media and technology would lead to a great unification of humanity. Other researchers, particularly those working during the Age of Electronic Communication, have seen it as leading to a more cold and impersonal society. Chapter 4 investigates these claims through the lens of community, a concept whose ideological underpinnings and empirical bases will be carefully questioned. Furthermore, these predictions tend to gloss over some of the important and under-recognized links between the structure and agency effects of social media technologies on human sociality. For instance, we will see how the consocial perspective's emphasis on people's momentary decisions leads us to emphasize their human agency while we see social media as less of a structural influence on those decisions. On the other hand, numerous studies and perspectives view social media technologies and the algorithms that underscore them as forces that strongly constrain and impact people's decisions. The chapter will then examine the structure-agency dimension of social media use through the deployment of four distinct but overlapping theoretical lenses: technogenesis, affordance theory, intersectionality, and networked individualism. In the chapter's concluding section, we will consider the role of contemporary capitalism in social media. The central role of finance and marketing in the social media industry has led to a variety of production processes dedicated to monetizing the communitarian dimensions of social life online, with important attendant effects upon both society and our researching of it.

SOCIAL MEDIA: THE GREAT COMING TOGETHER – OR BREAKING APART?

In the last three chapters, we have overviewed a brief, descriptive, and analytical history that encompasses both the field of social media and the ethnographic research conducted within it. This history, which stretches back about half a century, has been offered with the express intent of helping the reader develop a deeper appreciation of the structures and institutions that underlie the contemporary world of social media. The investigations I have overviewed – which are only a small sample of the many approaches that use online communications as cultural data and online sites as qualitative research field sites – show how social media-based ethnographic research has been historically and socially attuned to social trends, historical periods, technical infrastructures, and the exigencies of marketplaces. Social media and the Internet evolved from the workplace mainframes of Hiltz and Turoff's (1987) studies, to the anomalous and nerdy pastimes of Baym's (1993) and Jenkins' (1995) users, to the market-manipulating Facebook deceptions of Roth-Cohen and Lahav's (2018) small business owners. An understanding of past research casts the present in a new light. Each and every netnography from the past is a time capsule, providing multiple snapshots of the skyline of online cities that no longer exist, but upon whose strata today's world of social media is built. Reading through past netnographies is a form of social media archaeology.

Figure 4.1 Asking Google about social media (search run, October 7, 2018)

Google Search's autocomplete makes predictions based on common and trending searches on the popular search engine. Thus, used as a research tool, the autocomplete bar can be seen as a sort of barometer of the types of queries people currently and locally using the search engine have about particular topics – and thus what they may be thinking about them. Figure 4.1 resulted from an open query that began 'does social media ... '. As you can see from the results, some of the most prominent questions people have about social media in 2018 relate to whether it isolates people and makes them less social or makes them more social. These questions are accompanied by others asking about social media's effect on mental health and well-being – depression, anxiety, and self-esteem – and ones about using it for marketing. These same types of questions about social media's effects on society and individuals are ones that researchers have struggled to answer.

In a historical overview, we can discern how theorists of the past have been interested in exploring the potential impacts of technology on sociality. Researchers have been curious and interested in the effect of technological mediation on communications and society since the radically disruptive introduction of the telegraph and, later, the telephone. Some have postulated utopian or even mystical alterations in human society. More than four decades before Facebook and Twitter, the Canadian media theorist Marshall McLuhan predicted that 'cool', participative 'nonspecialist electric technology' would 'retribalize' human society (see, for example, McLuhan, 1994, p. 24). From our current vantage point, we might question whether social media actually are participative. We might point to various examples where despots and demagogues use Twitter and Facebook as their ideological billboard and democracy-debilitating dashboard. We might wonder if the retribalization they lead to is not so much a unification, but the dangerous and anti-humanitarian divisions we saw preceding former industrialized genocides. We might even question the determinism and totalized viewpoints behind these conclusions and instead seek subtler understandings.

McLuhan considered individualizing to be a negative societal trend, initiated by the rise of the phonetic alphabet and the culture of private reading. To McLuhan, isolation, nationalism, and individualism were negative outcomes of various technologies eventually fated to become things of the past. He saw electronic retribalization as a sort of Omega Point that would rectify these problems, as technology would allow lone human beings to become part of a vast collectivity that synchronized their minds and nervous systems through integrative, interactive technologies. McLuhan's theorizing drew on a long and established philosophical base in what we might term 'technology mysticism'. From the time of the Gnostics and on into the present, seers have predicted our technologically mediated ascendance and integration. For the twentieth-century Jesuit paleontologist and mystical philosopher Pierre Teilhard de Chardin, for example, 'technologies are not simply human tools, but vessels of the expanding noosphere, the body and nervous system of a world consciousness striving to be' (Davis, 1998: 296).

Coming from a completely different worldview were researchers who felt that technological communications had deleterious effects on society. Many psychologists in the early years of electronic communication used lab studies or natural experiments to simulate elements of the online (i.e., computer-mediated) environment. Those studies tended to view computer mediation with leery suspicion. They concluded that online was not a social place, but a context that created task-oriented, 'impersonal', 'inflammatory', 'cold', and 'unsociable' interactions (Kiesler et al., 1984, 1985; Rice, 1984; Rice and Rogers, 1984; Sproull and Kiesler, 1986; Walther, 1992: 58–9, 1995). However, these early researchers may not have counted on the way that social media would be used with already existing relationships. As of 2014, '67% of [American] Internet users say their online communication with family and friends has generally strengthened those relationships, while 18% say it generally weakens those relationships'. By 2014, 'equal proportions of online men and women, young and old, rich and poor, highly educated and less-well educated, Internet veterans and relative newbies' were saying, by a margin of 3-to-1 or better, that 'online communication is a relationship enhancer, rather than a relationship detractor' (Fox and Rainie, 2014: n.p.).

As we can also see from our history, the early online ethnographers were already, by that time, discovering a range of complex and changing social relations, which included inflammatory remarks, arguments, and something else: a fleeting sense of 'communitas', the seeking and finding of 'an essential and generic human bond, without which there could be no society' (Turner, 1969: 97). The Internet, its applications, and all networked communications technology have always combined the informal with the formal, the inflammatory with the congratulatory, informational purposes with interactive ones, and mere connection with meaningful community. Media have always been as social as we are.

Ascribing Community

Although media have always been social, this does not necessarily mean that all media are communal, or that all platforms for online communications can be construed to be communities. As we learned in Chapter 3, the word 'community' became attached to platforms of online communications at some point in the term's development in the 1980s and early 1990s by a variety of authors and academics. There were three reasons for this. First, these technological developments were completely new. To comprehend them and describe them to others, people needed simple metaphors. Community served the purpose well. And in addition, for sociologists, the notions of community related to Max Weber's ideas of elective affinities and to Ferdinand Tönnies' influential notions regarding the informal (Gemeinschaft) and formal (Gesellschaft) bases for social relations. Over time, this was enough theoretical heft to raise the notion of virtual or online community from a mere context to becoming, itself, a key construct and dependent variable. It also may be worth noting that the virtual community terminology is still widely used to this date in certain fields such as health, education, and computer science.

The second reason that the community metaphor was used so much is because it seemed to fit well with some of the activities of the early users of social media's forebears such as the Arpanet, Minitel, Prodigy, and CompuServe. As we can see by reading ethnographies of early forums and message boards by authors such as Rheingold (1993), Correll (1995), and Markham (1998), the social exchanges seemed to possess a higher level of commitment and emotional investment than a typical tweet or Instagram post does today. Third, many of the early scholars and authors were a bit idealistic in their viewpoints, which was an easy perspective to adopt given the exciting zeitgeist of the age. Reflecting the rosy technophilic lenses of the times, they wanted these new spaces to be positive, democratic, communal 'places' to replace the physical locations where communal relationships used to be located.

So, what happened to that more communal version of social media? First of all, it is not necessarily gone. In various places, among various groups, committed group-ings and intimate social relationships are everywhere. Many Facebook groups have friends and family who are extremely close. Many online groups resent being studied expressly because they have created a close-knit set of relations between users and do not want to see it disrupted.

But in many ways, media changed culture. Side investments in social technologies turned into real businesses. Ostensibly communal platforms turned into media con-glomerates with user 'audiences' in the millions. Social media audiences went from being the domain of a few groups of dispersed hobbyists to become the mainstream way we all communicate. More than two decades ago, Castells (1996: 31) predicted that major social upheavals would result from the novel forms of network society, suggesting that these were 'fundamentally altering the way we are born, we live, we sleep, we produce, we consume, we dream, we fight, or we die'. In 2005, MySpace was acquired for $580 million by Fox Media, shocking the world with the valuation given to this new type of company. AOL was valued at $20 billion that same year, which would be worth over $50 billion in today's dollars. Using venture capital financing, Facebook acquired over one billion free, largely unmonetized monthly users before going public. After the IPO, Facebook became a multinational mega-corporation, a new media success story of the modern stock market, a digital advertising platform and data pioneer with 2018 profits of $22 billion and a whopping profit margin of almost 40 percent. Facebook exploited its accumulated network of free service subscribers, with the services underwritten for years by venture capital investors, into the most immense single mass market of consumer attention around the world, bar none. With wise acquisitions, it bought Instagram, Messenger, and Snapchat. With all of this data combined, it has become an unstoppable advertising, news-serving, public opinion influencing, and data warehousing behemoth. Ten years after the MySpace acquisition, it was apparent everywhere that social media were indeed changing the world.

The radical changes predicted for the network society have happened, and are still happening. For example, the way we relate to the dead is changing. Brubaker and colleagues (2013) found that the public affordances of Facebook disrupt and expand traditional practices of mourning and memorialization (see also Gustavsson, 2013). This is but one of the many ways that social media networks become plugged into extant social norms and systems that inspire trust and reinforce interpersonal connections. TripAdvisor and other online review and rating systems have altered how people make travel and other important decisions, assuming a role in decision-making that was previously accorded to institutional actors such as travel agents (Jeacle and Carter, 2011). Over the time it has taken for deaths to be memorialized on Facebook and travel decisions to be made using TripAdvisor, the characteristics that best describe and best motivate the ordinary (and extraordinary) people who use social media and mobile communications to connect with each other have changed. Those who sought purchase advice joined with those who were seeking camaraderie and connection, and were accompanied by those seeking influence, followers, and commercial sponsorships. Platforms which charged for time and provided media appropriate for intimate conversation were replaced by platforms whose business models favored offering connections for free, trafficking in private data, and using social information to serve targeted advertising. As smartphones and a variety of communication platforms became more commonplace, the information and access provided by social media grew to be viewed as more of a disposable resource – and the communal ties of gratitude and reciprocity that fueled earlier platforms were dispersed. As the mutual concept of sharing was appropriated and altered, communal elements were leached out of online communities by Facebook and the social media companies who followed its lead.

Questioning Community

But the questioning of the role of community also reflected considerable diversity and even debate in what that notion actually meant. Some of that complexity and variance had been baked into the concept over time, as Raymond Williams's (1976: 74–5) historical analysis of the term in *Keywords* makes abundantly clear. Communities are 'common people', 'the quality of holding something in common, as in a community of interests', 'a sense of common identity and characteristics', 'actual social groups', and 'a particular quality of relationships (as in communitas)'. Community could be contrasted with the more formal, abstract, and instrumental relationships of state or of society, similar to the aforementioned Gesellschaft of Tönnies (1887). As Williams notes, the term 'seems never to be used unfavorably' (1976: 75).

And yet in the decades to come, community's special status as a social scientific construct had begun to be interrogated. Although the notion of a physically grounded community had long served as an anchor, anthropologists increasingly inquired about the actual and notional stability of communities (Clifford and Marcus, 1986). Can 'the ethnographic enterprise' assume that its 'ethnographic subjects' are members of a community, or that they share a culture, when they are 'no longer fixed conveniently in singular places' such as particular time zones or physical locations (Amit and Rapport, 2002: 1)? Does the fixation on stable and committed relationships obscure important forces at work in contemporary culture and manifest through social media: dislocation, displacement, alienation, plurality, hybridization, disjuncture, compartmentalization, escape, and transgression? The anthropologist Michael Jackson (1998: 16) reminds us about the ephemeral nature of culture.

> That which we designate 'culture' ... is simply the repertoire of psychic patterns and possibilities that generally have been implemented, foregrounded, or given legitimacy in a particular place at a particular point in time. But human culture, like consciousness itself, rests on a shadowy and dissolving floe of blue ice, and this subliminal, habitual, repressed, unexpressed, and silent mass shapes and reshapes, stabilizes and destabilizes the visible surface forms.

We can therefore acknowledge that cultures and communities are 'worlds of meaning' that exist purely because of their continued adoption and use 'in the minds of their members' (Cohen, 1985: 82). Considering the different possibilities that exist for sociality to emerge through the communications and connections of social media, rather than assuming the mutually stabilizing presence of communities, cultures, and networks, should remind us that the term 'social media' does not refer to one phenomenon but to many. Social media is not some fixed, easy-to-define notion, but a set of technical platforms and possibilities that, like Facebook, are constantly developing and changing, adding features and affordances, removing others. As social media changes, and people's adoptions of it and adaptations to it alter, worlds of meaning also alter, and with them cultures. As online groupings shift and liquefy, and new configurations and networks constantly assemble and disperse, notions of community and sociality themselves are changed.

We can emphasize human agency, as Amit and Rapport (2002) do, when we conceive of the various degrees to which individuals choose their communal relations and cultural identifications online. We can try to think about how the same individuals use different kinds of social media, with a repertoire of other 'polymedia' (Madianou and Miller, 2013) to express different types of social meanings and connections. If we were to follow Amit and Rapport's (2002) approach and emphasize individual agency, we would emphasize individuals before cultures and communities, seeing the former preceding the latter both ontologically and morally. These ideas question the illusion that social media, or the social structures they promote, are solid and fixed and cast into doubt the apparent stability of the interconnections they express and reveal. From this viewpoint, the identities, communities, and cultures of social media are semi-solid, temporary, and transitional affairs.

Consociality

In contrast to the tight bonds of community or the multifarious connections of sociality, an important form of contact guiding human relations in contemporary society seems to be that of consocial relations. Coined by Austrian phenomenologist Alfred Schütz, 'consociality' refers to a state of co-presence where two or more people physically reside within the same time and space (Schütz, 1962). The anthropologist Ulf Hannerz (2016: 151) extends this notion of being physically present to a contemporary frame in which 'consociality is defined by co-presence of both – or either – physical and virtual [proximity].' In the social media environment, as we have seen, the notion of consociality includes a particular type of sociality that is contextual, temporary, bounded, and instrumental, but can also possess elements of communal feelings, affability, and social satisfaction (Dyck, 2002). Recently, Rebeca Perren and I built on these bases to define consociality as 'the physical and/or virtual co-presence of social actors in a network, providing an opportunity for social interaction between them' (Perren and Kozinets, 2018: 23). Consociality tends to be more about 'what we share', a contextual fellowship, rather than 'who we are', an ascribed identity boundary such as race, religion, ethnicity or gender. Using the term 'consocial relations' suggests a proximity between social actors. When we study sociality, one of our core concerns is what actors do with that state of co-presence.

Applying a more agentic and consocial perspective to social media phenomena might lead us to view proximal social actors' technologically-mediated socialities less as an institutional or technical arrangement, and more as an 'assemblage of individual life-projects and trajectories in momentary construction of common ground' (Amit and Rapport, 2002: 111). A historically grounded and temporal examination of personal commitments, a sense of meaning and place, hierarchies, and values would reveal their instability, as they are constantly churned by forces such as globalization, migration, politics, and technology. We might conceive of online ethnographic work that portrays individuals who are free to choose a range of identities and subject positions from inside a structuring system that pushes and pulls them in various directions. Respecting their life narratives, we might also focus on how the various elements of social media and contemporary sociality shape and direct it, and how this ancient dance of individualism, enculturation, and social pressure has been transposed onto digital times. The rapidly evolving traditions, customs, rituals, values, and institutions of people communicating and connecting on social media platforms depend upon 'the contractual adherence of interacting individuals' for their continuation, meaningfulness, maintenance and value (2002: 111). However, other approaches might be useful to emphasize the interrelated role of technological and social structures in creating, maintaining, and altering the experiences that individuals have with and through social media.

THEORIES OF SOCIALITY STRUCTURING

This book's historical overview has demonstrated how – with every new social media innovation, from friending, sharing, and liking to snapping, tweeting, and pinning – the social experience changes. Subjective experiences of sociality, perceptions of identity and meaning, and norms of behavior change as technologies change. Wherever people

use new communication technologies such as social media, 'there will be circulations, reimaginings, magnifications, deletions, translations, revisionings, and remakings of a range of cultural representations, experiences, and identities, but the precise ways that these dynamics unfold can never be fully anticipated in advance' (Coleman, 2010: 488). However, this complex, fluid, and nondeterministic quality should not prevent us from reporting upon and rigorously conceptualizing these representations, experiences, identities, and remakings, and the contextualized and often complex patternings of their ongoing dynamics.

Sociality shapes technical infrastructures as it is being shaped by them. New forms of expression and new infrastructures of intimacy are emerging rapidly, experimentally, in the supercharged petri dishes of modern social media and then evolving through a type of quasi-genetic process. The structuring power of institutions, technologies, and cultures works with the agentic acts of individuals to create the social media experience. Therefore, we must remember in our netnographies to try to understand not only the cultural experience, but also individual and collective interactions with the technical infrastructure, the system, and its 'mediating architecture', to use Boyd and Heer's (2006: 10) term, its technological affordances (a term we will develop in this chapter) that both enable and constrain users' various socialities. The insight that technology does not determine human social behaviors, but that technologies and human beings are co-determining, co-constructive agents is crucially important in science and technology studies.

In a different age, one before omnipresent CCTVs, facial recognition, government social credit systems, and airport body scans, Penley and Ross (1991: xiv) wrote in their work on the emerging world of 'technoculture', in which technological and cultural institutions blended together that:

technologies are not repressively foisted upon passive populations, any more than the power to realize their repressive potential is in the hands of a conspiring few. They are developed at any one time and place in accord with a complex set of existing rules or rational procedures, institutional histories, technical possibilities, and, last, but not least, popular desires.

We might over-emphasize individual agencies and popular desires in our conceptions of social media developments because some of their more insidious surveillance purposes are hidden from view. Nonetheless, the point remains that it would be wise to assume neither a primarily structural or a primarily agentic view on the wider phenomenon underlying social media.

Over the past three decades, there have been important transformations in the ways that human sociality is being expressed and impressed upon by technologies. Increasingly nuanced theorizing has made discernible conceptual patterns within these changes. We can view this coevolution of socialities and technologies through four very different yet overlapping theoretical lenses which are, in their own ways, intended to mitigate some of the structure–agency dilemmas of technological determinist positions, such as those assumed by Ellul (1964) and Mumford (1967). These lenses are technogenesis, affordance theory, intersectionality, and networked individualism. The four short sections that follow will overview each of these theories in turn with an eye to (1) positing how they help to overcome difficult ascriptions of technology and culture that erringly view them as dissociable, and (2) suggesting and providing examples showing how they can be applied to enhancing our understanding of social media's effects on sociality.

Technogenesis

Netnography has not, up until this point in its development, had a clear and appropriate ontological foundation. In 2015, with the publication of *Netnography: Redefined*, netnography began to align itself with technogenesis. Online sociality and consociality reveal both the 'modern' and the 'postmodern' condition: the constant appearance of flux, movement, speed, change, and progress. As social beings and cultural observers, we experience this progression as consumers and laborers, playing a part in a marketplace and an economy, one of technological change where, certainly as researchers and professionals, engineers and MBAs, accountants and lawyers, we witness and adapt to a constant dynamic remodeling. This dynamic is composed of new hardware, new software, new abilities to communicate, broadcast, listen and learn for both our professional self and our personal lives, as well as embedded in our conversations, our entertainment, our imaginations, and every other aspect of our lifeworlds.

Our lifeworld has in fact become one of never-ending adoption of new products and services. As consumers, we adapt to new products as they adapt to the marketplaces we co-create, while we adapt those products to our needs as well, producing ever-increasing rates of change. Ever-tighter integration, imbrications of machine and human intention underlie our accelerating technogenesis. Studies of online social experience reveal how our existing worlds of interpersonal relationships, work relationships and structures of power are reinforced, extended, developed, and altered in response to these new technologies and their various calculative, social control, economic, and algorithmic functions and features. Yet stepping back from the individual events and movements, and gaining a historical perspective reveals that human beings and our technologies are part of a single and interrelated system, and have been so for a very long time. Exploring the nature and implications of this interrelation is the jurisdiction of technogenesis.

Technogenesis is the correct ontological foundation for netnography. Technogenesis is apt, with an underpinning methodological assumption that the rates of change in contemporary society are speedy, but that the trained researcher has an ability to sense, record, and then analyze these cultural changes.

Technogenesis originated in the philosophy of Bernard Stiegler. Its core insight might be boiled down to the idea that human beings and our technologies coevolve. Paleoanthropologists have long accepted that early Homo sapiens coevolved with their tools. For example, Homo sapiens' bipedalism and more flexible opposable digits coevolved along with the need for stone implements and sharp bone chip-tool manufacture and transportation (Hayles, 2012: 10). That ongoing expansion of the human-technical assemblage continued through history until accelerating in fully mature consumer capitalism. Technologies are rapidly altered by contemporary environments and contemporary human beings rapidly change their social and physical environments through technology.

Technogenesis holds that our technological environment also changes us, selecting people who are more capable of succeeding within it. In netnography, this idea of technogenesis connects with ideas that young people in today's society are growing up adapted to the social, economic, and cultural elements of the social media environment that surrounds them. Those who adapt to the rapidly changing and demanding environment of social media move ahead in society more rapidly, and those with power and influence also may change the technologies to tilt them in their favor. Netnography is one methodological pathway to investigate and chronicle the unfolding of these technogenetic notions of coevolving human-technology transformation and adaptation.

Affordance Theory

A key issue in studies of technology has been the role and nature of human agency in relation to technological or material structure and, relatedly, the agency of machines. Structuration theory, which addresses the interrelation of structure and agency and focuses on human agency, does not directly address the role of a technological-material agency or the related concerns of technology researchers to attempt to understand its role (Leonardi, 2011: 154). Actor-network theories, on the other hand, tend to believe in the interchangeability and equivalence of human and technological agencies, a position that is difficult to maintain through an ethnographic study that favors a human viewpoint. An alternate approach has been to conceptualize the interweaving of human and material agencies. Taylor (2001) has named this interweaving 'imbrications', a process that maintains the distinction between human and material (or technological) agencies with respect to their intentionality, while still also recognizing that their effects in the world occur as a synergistic and nondeterministic interaction. Using such a philosophical position, we might have an AI express its own view of its social media behaviors, or interpret the unpredictable wanderings of an algorithm or a bot working its way through online webs of human longing.

Affordance theory has been adopted by many technology scholars as a way to understand how technological-material and human agencies become imbricated. The perceptual psychologist James Gibson (1986) originally developed affordance theory in order to explain how animals perceive their physical environments. A dog, for instance, might perceive the shape and then the hardness of a wooden branch on the ground as something that is good to chew. Applied to human beings, affordance theory suggests that people interact with objects because they perceive the objectives an object might be good for. The perception of what the object is good for is called its 'affordance'. Because they are just perceptions of value, affordances can vary between species or individuals. Although the material and symbolic properties of things such as technologies may be stable, the ways that people perceive them can be very different.

Gibson's affordance theory has been usefully developed in relation to discussions of technology by Norman (1990). Norman uses a design orientation to assert that technologies generally have affordances, or features, intentionally built into them. Affordances are generally signaled by their designers and thus, in Norman's formulation, by the intrinsic properties of artifacts such as technologies. Seeking a middle ground between views of affordances as based solely in people or in technologies, Hutchby (2001) emphasized how affordances are created in the interaction between the functional and material qualities of a technology and the various abilities, constraints, objectives, and contexts of a human actor, conceptualizing a locus for investigation that exists in between human and material agencies.

Thus, we can see how the different material features of various social media platforms have been promoted to people as affordances that can help them achieve their goals. Those goals could include things such as staying connected with family and friends, making new friends, managing a network of business contacts, gaining answers to questions, learning about hobbies, or discussing the news. Affordances might also include features to which people may not have previously realized they had access, such as filters for taking better selfies or providing metrics to manage one's social media audience. Perceptions of social media affordances are shaped by people's goals as well as by promotional language such as Facebook's talk of 'sharing', 'friending', and 'liking'. In fact, these particular affordances were created by Facebook as social features of its platform and in the process of imbrication a need for them was also created.

In an illustration of netnography's aptitude for handling affordance theory-derived questions, D'Ambra and colleagues (2017) examined comments by online readers to articles in the *New York Times* and *Scientific American* which could help answer their research question of 'What are the affordances of e-reading and do they enhance the reading experience?' With a relatively modest-sized dataset of only 45,000 words or so, they were able to provide some detailed analysis of the content, mostly in the form of overviews and lists of product features such as 'environmental sustainability', and in their words 'confirmed the use of affordance theory to analyse the rich data gathered in the comments made online' (p. 22).

Intersectionality

Because of its social nature, the analysis of netnographic data often reveals, and is intended to reveal, the social situation of people engaged in conversation and interaction. As one person uses social media to discourse with imagined and actual others about matters relating to them, their own unique perspectives are revealed by the particular language they use, the specific ideas they find interesting, the way they relate to other people, and many other features. The analysis of deliberately collected online traces thus opens a door into thinking about the social positioning of individuals as they communicate through social media.

The idea that every person is situated in a particular position in society at the intersection of multiple social axes, such as gender, age, race, religion, sexual preference, ethnicity, nationality, immigration status, and class, and that people interpolate these positions as their individual and shared identities, is a core foundation of the interdisciplinary field called *intersectionality*. Works in the field of intersectionality pay special attention to how people at the junctures of these intersecting social axes are subject to particular structural advantages and disadvantages by virtue of their intersectional positions. As Gopaldas and Fischer (2012: 393) tell us, 'intersectionality' is an academic concept that has been described as a 'buzzword' and 'an analytical tool', as well as a 'perspective' and even a 'paradigm'. Intersectional studies emerged from Crenshaw's (1989) and Collins's (1990) work in the field of Black feminist discourse, and spread in a relatively short time to fields such as sociology (e.g., Ritzer and Goodman, 2008), psychology (e.g., Warner, 2008) and anthropology (e.g., Boellstorff, 2007).

Palo and Manderstedt (2017) combined the concept of intersectionality with a netnographic approach. They studied *The Murderer's Ape*, a young adult novel by Swedish author Jakob Wegelius, in which the protagonist and narrator is an intelligent, literate, mute, female spy – and a gorilla. The concept of intersectionality is used to highlight the 'in-betweenness' of the humanized animal book character (p. 2). The article proceeds to use netnography to collect online discussions about the book and intersectional theory to analyze what they reveal about readers' response to its 'liminal' protagonist (p. 11). Their findings indicate a range of reader responses, such that they differentiated the more active and skilled readers, calling them 'connoisseurs', from the more unskilled and passive readers, who they called 'consumers'. Nonetheless, their analysis of social media data shows how 'those factors that Sally Jones did not choose – gender, profession, species and class – contribute to readers' image of the protagonist' (p. 14). In this case, in which people consider the adventures of an intelligent gorilla, 'readers seem to consider species as a point of departure and a backdrop to their reflections on the qualities not expected in an animal: that is her acquired training, her emotional sensibility and her moral compass. Thus, Sally Jones allows readers multiple inroads to the novel.' A different type of intersectional netnography is provided by Medrado and Muller (2018), which I discuss in Chapter 5.

Examining the role of feminist positions such as intersectionality on online research, Shaw (2013: 92–3) notes how some of the early online ethnographic work, such as Markham (1998), Hine (2000), and Turkle (1995), had a reflexive awareness of social structures that resonated well with feminist methods. In online worlds that often express the diversity of the societies they engage, the different positions with which social media posters identify are sources of both conflict and camaraderie. On social media, an intersectional frame can help reveal how people build divides or alliances across their differences, how identity categories are elided or acknowledged, or how commonalities in differences are either negated or recognized. These perspectives can assist those interested in activism and social movements and their online elements and manifestations. An intersectional approach to netnography can help researchers 'identify the effects of interlocking oppressions' (Haslanger, 2000: 36). For example, Shaw (2013: 98) studied feminist bloggers, finding a range of 'disability and anti-ableist discourses' in communications that presumably linked them to conceptions of disability and accommodation. Feminist bloggers 'inherit feminisms not only as ideology and received discourse, but also as kinship and community, and the ways in which these relations can be risky, threatening, or dangerous. Discourses become imbued with affect, both personal and shared with kin' (p. 91).

An understanding of the structural impairments and empowerments of both social media and social media posters can prove valuable to a deeper understanding of their relation with wider social movements, including feminism (Bjork-James, 2015: 98): 'These sub-community, intersectional debates are where the impetus for activism and the identification of areas for action are occurring within the community'. Thus, Shaw's research reveals how the intersection of identity positions with social media affordances and communications can result in conditions that inspire collective activism and other social actions, rather than individualistic responses. However, we still know little about how these theoretical elements relate with one another. We need to know much more about the way intersectionality, online co-presence, social affordances, and types of sociality interact. To further our understanding, we might turn to Rainie and Wellman's (2012) recounting of the rise of 'networked individualism', which the next section of the chapter will detail.

Networked Individualism

In the last chapter, we heard how the tight-knit gatherings and meaningful cultures written about in the Age of Virtual Community are not necessarily aspects of much of today's online experiences. One way to conceptualize this recognition of community's absence is through the subjective viewpoint of the individual, captured in ethnographic work through fieldnotes written from the reflexive stance of the researcher (see Chapter 10).

Another way to study and conceptualize the connections would be through an 'ego-centered' social network analysis, an analytical method that focuses on the structures and patterns of relationships between and among social actors in a network. As Rainie and Wellman (2012: 55) explain, each person is 'at the center of his or her own personal network: a solar system of one to two thousand and more people orbiting around us. Each person has become a communication and information switchboard connecting persons, networks, and institutions.'

The idea of conducting social network analysis on social media data goes back to at least 2007. Applications of social network analysis to the understanding of social collectives have led to reams of quantitative analysis that now show clear patterns widely accepted across sociology. According to Rainie and Wellman (2012: 11), networked individualism is a shift in people's social lives 'away from densely knit family, neighbourhood, and group relationships toward more far-flung, less tight-knit, more diverse personal networks'. As a combined result of the social network, Internet, and mobile 'revolutions', networked individualism means that 'people function more as connected individuals and less as embedded group members'. For instance, members of a family may now act more like participants of multiple networks – only one of which is the family – than solely or primarily as members of that family. Their home may no longer be a place where they mainly congregate together as a family and pursue common family activities. Instead, it becomes more of a base for their individual networking with the outside world, with each family member maintaining their own separate personal computer, mobile phone, set of contacts, and so on. Rainie and Wellman's results and examples illustrate a shift towards the sort of more fluid, open and individual-centered conceptions of culture and community related earlier in this chapter. They also reveal a theme connected to work life, privacy, and commercialization that we will continue to explore after this subsection (see Box 4.1).

And yet, as with all matters human and social, there is balance. Although it is extremely helpful to recognize that the rise of the network society is enabling a form of networked individualism, we still know relatively little about the communal bulwarks pushing against these processes. We also must attend to the many ways that technologies are using people to achieve corporate aims, at the same time as we account for the many ways that people are also using that same corporate technology-ideology to build new social forms of technological consumption. Our concluding sections to this chapter now proceed to develop these corporate connections in much greater depth, asking, in the chapter's final analysis, if we paved communitas only to put up another energy-guzzling underground server farm, a gigantic virtual parking lot for data.

CORPORATE CAPITALISM AND SOCIAL MEDIA

Corporate capitalism in 2018 appears to be at once here to stay, too good to be true, and definitely not built to last. The utopians of the past may not have counted on the impact of market needs and commercial structures on the socialities of the present. The history of social media recounted over the past two chapters of this book shows how commercial activity has been present throughout that history. Early records of rules for the use of the Arpanet attempted to discourage its use for individual entrepreneurial activities. Electronic communication began as a combination of public and private experiments, Arpanet, and Minitels, with major corporations like Sears, IBM, and General Electric entering those early markets, and shaping them to their own advantage. After many failed experiments in said markets, several formats stuck. In particular, the technical engineering of the Facebook interface, its use of massive infusions of venture capital to build a gigantic network of free subscribers, alongside its social engineering of a communal discourse of 'sharing', provided an important inflection point for the adoption and acceptance of the new technologies. Venture capital poured into the ecosystem, resulting in the odd mix of the competitive and communal that we know today as the social media industry. Currently, the social media industry is an oligopoly, with companies like Facebook, Google, Tencent, and a few others able to scale their processes, build sociality into economic network effects, and turn that scale into profit.

Yet some of the most intriguing effects of social media on capitalism derive not from its corporate influence but, rather, from its ability to turn private into public space. In an increasingly neoliberal global economy characterized by competitive interconnection as well as precarity, social media's commercializing affordances have been increasingly adopted by ordinary people. Early theorists of this relationship emphasized how the 'post-Fordist production process' of information economies 'directly exploits the communitarian dimension of social life' by incorporating relationship management as a critical component of contemporary brand management practices (Arvidsson, 2005: 241). Similarly, in regard to the appropriation of the creative (or, in the marketing literature, 'co-creation') skills of online consumers, many scholars have been skeptical. The 'empowered, entrepreneurial, and free consumer' who allegedly is in control of 'digital, globally networked marketplaces', creating branded content and providing market-relevant information on social media, can also be seen 'an operant resource' of contemporary production processes: 'Co-creation, as a set of organizational strategies and discursive procedures aimed at reconfiguring social relations of production, works through the freedom of the consumer subject with the objective of encouraging and capturing the know-how of this creative common' (Zwick et al., 2008: 184).

4.1

NETWORKED INDIVIDUALISM: 12 PRINCIPLES

Adapted from Rainie and Wellman (2012: 12–18)

1

Dispersed Versus Intimate Need Fulfillment: Networked individuals increasingly meet social, emotional and economic needs by tapping into dispersed networks of diverse associates instead of relying on more intimate connections with a relatively small number of core associates.

2

Partial Versus Permanent Memberships: Networked individuals maintain partial membership in many networks or social groups and rely less on permanent membership in established groups.

3

Technology Effects: Technology is accelerating the trend toward networked individualism by accelerating the growth, accessibility, and diversification of a less committed form of social interaction.

4

Internet as Neighborhood: The Internet is the new neighbourhood, increasingly containing some of the networked individual's most important social contacts.

5

Extended Audiences: Networked individuals are empowered by the Internet to project their vision and voice to extended audiences, and invite them to become a part of their social world.

6

Communication = Action. The lines between communication, information, and action have become increasingly blurred as networked individuals use the Internet, mobile phones, and social networks to instantly access information and act upon it. Think of a political leader who tweets policy changes on a cell phone while sitting on the toilet; this is the essence of online communication turned not only into action, but also institutional change.

12

Post-trust Shifts: In this new era of less hierarchy, more information, and looser relationships, there is greater uncertainty than ever before about which information sources to believe and who to trust.

11

Privacy Shifts: New expectations and realities are emerging regarding the transparency, availability, and privacy of people's data and how it is treated.

10

Breakdown of Distinction Between Private and Public: The public and private spheres of life are far more intertwined than in the past.

9

Breakdown of Distinction Between Home and Work: Home and work are far more interlinked than in the past.

8

Less Formal Work Relations: Less formal, more fluctuating, and more specialized peer-to-peer relationships are more easily sustained at work, and the benefits of hierarchical boss-subordinate relationships are less obvious

7

More Fluid Identity Construction: Networked individuals move easily between relationships and social settings to construct their own complex identities, depending on their passion, beliefs, lifestyles, professional associations, work interests, hobbies, media habits, subcultural inclinations, and other personal characteristics.

The tendency to turn consumers into co-producers of value has intensified in recent years, becoming both more pronounced and more direct. Because of its ability to allow corporations much wider access to people with varying sizes and configurations of audiences and social networks, social media enabled a new type of 'word of mouth marketing' to which both sides rapidly adopted. Kozinets et al. (2010: 83) found that word of mouth marketing actually depends upon social media actors' transformation of messages 'from persuasion-oriented, marketer-generated, sales objective-oriented "hype" to relevant, useful, communally-desirable social information that builds individual reputations and group relationships', a process that relies upon a combination of commoditization of self, quantification of network, and translation and communication of commercial message. As studies like those of McQuarrie at al. (2013) and Marwick (2015) show us, platforms such as Instagram and YouTube are increasingly serving as places where individuals can build and monetize different sorts of capital in pursuit of both the fame and money that accompany the status of 'influencer' (a marketer term) or 'creator' (what they prefer to call themselves). Kavanaugh and Patterson (2001: 507) suggest that 'the longer people are on the Internet, the more likely they are to use the Internet to engage in social-capital-building activities'. The social-capital-building activities of the social media of the past have morphed into the fame-seeking and audience-building practices of the present. Contemporary social media is a world that still includes the community-seeking and information quests of days gone by, but adds onto them a layer of the 'Instafamous' (Marwick, 2015) and YouTube 'autopreneurs' who sell their ongoing life narrative hoping to gain lucrative commercial endorsement deals (Ashman et al., 2018). These transformations have occurred as the commercial affordances of social media have become increasingly apparent to marketers, technology firms, and social media users. Social media is a communication phenomenon whose content is progressively influenced by contemporary capitalism. The result often seems as much media industry as it is social.

They Paved Communitas, Put Up a Server Farm

New York Times columnist John Herrman (2018: n.p.) uses Twitter as an example to illustrate the difference between the more communal online platforms of the past and the more individualistic social media platforms of current times: 'The internet of old – composed largely of thousands of scattered communities populated by people who shared interests, identities, causes or hatreds – has been mostly paved over by the social-media giants'. Similar to the way it was conceptualized in the age of virtual community, Herrman finds the presence of the basic foundations of community in the online platforms of the past.

Online communities in those good old days had three characteristics that helped them stay communal, according to the columnist. First, they were specialized, so people shared interests and passions from the start. Participants were all there because they cared about the same things. Second, they were voluntary, by which he seems to mean that each group controlled major elements of its own structure – and thus its rules and culture. And third, they were sometimes difficult to find, which made them more exclusive, smaller, and more intimate:

> Even the largest web forums felt vaguely subcultural, existing as they did in relative isolation from countless other communities online. They had their own rules, their own ways of enforcing them and their own reasons for being: to argue about music, to commiserate about an illness. Each forum was ultimately run by whoever owned it and moderated largely by volunteers. (Herrmann 2018: n.p.)

Core communal elements seem absent from mass audience-targeted new forms of social media such as Twitter: 'The member becomes the user; the peer becomes the follower' (Herrman, 2018). 'Unlike a smaller community, to which admission is a choice that reflects your interests or needs or personality, Twitter has no shared identity beyond "people who want to use Twitter to post"'. He sees Twitter's organizational model as similar to a crowd of people with megaphones who convene as temporary audiences and then disperse. It is this continual dispersion, this dissolving of the audience which has formed, that he finds so different from the past – and so discouraging.

Over time, a core assumption that had guided early conceptualizations – that online social platforms were a kind of community – became increasingly cast into doubt. Certainly, some of these media did foster more lasting, committed, personalized, Gemeinschaft types of relationships, and many still do, or are based on pre-existing relationships, such as Friendster, LinkedIn, or Facebook. However, the addition and development of advertising, measurement, direct marketing, web retailing, and data aggregation pushes social media into the domain of a mass medium and an economic category. As venture capital investors seek returns on their prior investments in network infrastructure and member marketing, those relationships must be monetized – friends, likes, and their content must be turned into data and transactions: ads served, e-commerce products sold, and subscriptions paid. Twitter is a more formal, distant, and individualized experience – something similar to the gathering of a traditional media audience, a community in imagination only (Anderson, 2006).

Yet it is hard to deny that some sort of connective social arrangement is forming despite Twitter's processes of dispersal, just as it does in the endless back and forth of YouTube comments and replies. For nothing in digital culture truly dissolves. Memories are formed. Identities are expressed. Data is recorded, deleted, then recovered. Tweets are retweeted and gain vast new audiences, sometimes years later. Tweets appear on other platforms, in blog posts, research, and the news. People connect things because of what they have seen, and then they shift their actions. Twitter absorbs the dissolution and broadcasts it back like television reruns. Collective and individual memory includes staccato bursts of Twitter, just as Twitter itself is fully inhabited by collective memory. Sociality and communitas are transformed by social media but, like weeds growing from the cracks of a sidewalk, they persist.

CHAPTER SUMMARY

This chapter has provided a theoretical analysis of social media and social media-based ethnographic research. In doing so, it has offered conceptualizations of new forms of sociality. Social media and technology have been considered by some theorists, philosophers, and mystics to be forces that will lead to a great unification of humanity. Others have seen them leading to a more cold and impersonal society. The chapter investigated these claims by questioning the ideological and empirical bases of claims of community, and also by examining structure-agency effects. On the one hand, a consocial perspective leads us to see social media less as a solid institutional arrangement and more as a momentary construction that assembles individual life projects and trajectories. On the other hand are theories positing more deterministic effects of technology upon individual lives and cultures. The chapter then viewed the structure–agency questions of social media technology through four distinct but overlapping theoretical lenses. First was technogenesis, a way to study how technology, culture, individual, and sociality influence one another in a process mimicking natural genetic selection. Next was affordance theory, a way to study how technological-material and human agencies become imbricated through human perceptions (and design intentions) about what particular uses things are good for. The third theoretical lens was intersectionality, a view that looks at how people at the junctures of intersecting social axes are subject to particular structures of advantages and disadvantages. The final lens was networked individualism, a perspective holding that people's use of networks is shifting from tighter and more close-knit relationships to more far-flung, expedient, and diverse personal networks. The chapter's concluding section considered the role of contemporary capitalism in social media. The central role of venture capitalism in building and maintaining the social media industry has led to platforms' post-Fordist production processes, which are dedicated to monetizing the communitarian dimensions of social life and utilizing consumers as operant resources for the production of economic value.

KEY READINGS

Bjork-James, Sophie (2015) 'Feminist ethnography in cyberspace: Imagining families in the cloud', *Sex Roles*, 73(3–4): 113–24.

D'Ambra, John, Concepcion S. Wilson, and Shahriar Akter (2017) 'Affordance theory and e-books: Evaluating the e-reading experience using netnography', *Personal and Ubiquitous Computing*, Online first 1–20. Available online at http://ro.uow.edu.au/gsbpapers/523 (last accessed 4 February 2018).

Frömming, Urte Undine, Steffen Köhn, Samantha Fox, and Mike Terry (2017) *Digital Environments: Ethnographic Perspectives Across Global Online and Offline Spaces.* Bielefeld, Germany: Transcript Verlag.

Gretzel, Ulrike (2017) 'Social media activism in tourism', *Journal of Hospitality and Tourism*, 15(2): 1–14.

Palo, Annbritt, and Lena Manderstedt (2017) 'Beyond the characters and the reader? Digital discussions on intersectionality in *The Murderer's Ape*', *Children's Literature in Education*: 1–17. Available at: https://link.springer.com/article/10.1007/s10583-017-9338-2 (last accessed 28 June 2019).

Pink, Sarah (2017) 'Foreword', in Urte Undine Frömming, Steffen Köhn, Samantha Fox, and Mike Terry (eds), *Digital Environments: Ethnographic Perspectives Across Global Online and Offline Spaces* (pp. 9–11). Bielefeld, Germany: Transcript Verlag.

Pink, Sarah, Heather Horst, John Postill, Larissa Hjorth, Tania Lewis, and Jo Tacchi (eds) (2015) *Digital Ethnography: Principles and Practice.* London: Sage.

Rainie, Lee, and Barry Wellman (2012) *Networked: The New Social Operating System*. Cambridge, MA: MIT Press.

Zwick, Detlev, Samuel K. Bonsu, and Aron Darmody (2008) 'Putting consumers to work: Co-creation and new marketing govern-mentality', *Journal of Consumer Culture*, 8(2): 163–96.

PRAXIS: INTRODUCING PRACTICES AND DATA OPERATIONS

CHAPTER OVERVIEW

The purpose of this chapter is to initiate your understanding of net-nographic praxis, the operational protocols of netnography, while also beginning your research project. We will start with a methodological overview that introduces the four elements distinguishing netnography from every other research method. These four elements are cultural focus, social media data, engagement, and netnographic praxis. The chapter will then go on to present the six movements of netnography: initiation, investigation, interaction, immersion, integration, and incarnation. These six movements each contain a range of operations within them, and transpire over four general, discrete, and sequential stages: research focus, data collection, data analysis and interpretation, and research presentation. With this initial overview in place, the chapter will move into a discussion of the first stage of the netnographic research process, initiation. The initiation stage focuses the research with a net-nographic research question. This section will teach you about the two major parts to a research question, the research topic and the angle of inquiry. Then, the chapter will explore how research questions are initiated through focusing either on an existing conceptual relationship or one that examines an empirical phenomenon. We will discover that both of these initiators are intertwined in the act of doing netnography. Through a series of exercises, the reader will then learn how concept and phenomenon are dynamically interrelated in netnographic research questions – and also about the meet-in-the-middle process. Finally, the chapter will examine and analyze a range of research questions that have been used in netnographic research, providing clear guidelines and a strong foundation for readers to move forward with their own netnographic project.

WHAT NETNOGRAPHY IS

It might be worthwhile at this early point in your learning of netnography to stop and take stock. The first four chapters have been loaded with information about digital and media anthropology, social media, its history, sociality, intersectionality, techno-genesis, and many other things. You might try to synthesize some of this knowledge now by asking yourself a basic, clarifying question: what is netnography? Without looking back at any of the material you have read in this book so far, and without looking ahead to the next few pages, simply relying on what you know so far, type or write some of the main words or phrases (I guess you could use emojis too) that come into your head when you think about netnography. Netnography is ... (you fill in the blanks).

In my 2017 netnography course at the University of Southern California's Marshall School of Business, I asked my MBA students to describe what netnography is, and I wrote their answers on the board. After we had exhausted most of the answers, the board looked something like Figure 5.1.

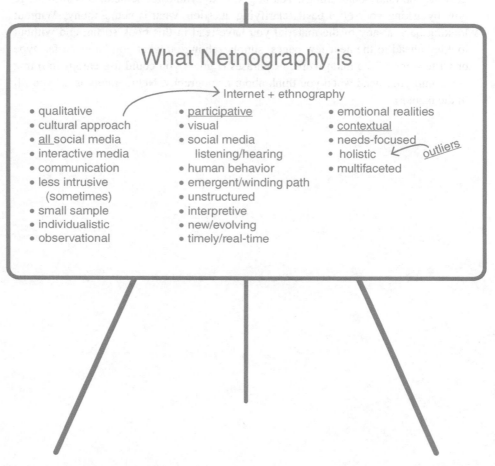

What Netnography is

→ Internet + ethnography

- qualitative
- cultural approach
- all social media
- interactive media
- communication
- less intrusive
  (sometimes)
- small sample
- individualistic
- observational

- participative
- visual
- social media
  listening/hearing
- human behavior
- emergent/winding path
- unstructured
- interpretive
- new/evolving
- timely/real-time

- emotional realities
- contextual
- needs-focused
- holistic ← outliers
- multifaceted

Figure 5.1 What Netnography Is... (adapted from a classroom blackboard exercise)

In about fifteen minutes, my students were able to derive a powerful and fairly exhaustive set of descriptors of the netnographic approach. Using my phone, I took a photograph of the whiteboard and shared it on Twitter with a #netnography hashtag. Although it is a long and informative listing, it might be a bit overwhelming. It could be inevitable that, as soon as we begin to learn about a complex approach like netnography, we begin to see connections and linkages with other areas and concepts. We begin to see contradictions and complexities. But if our purpose is to guide and clarify, perceiving those connections and complications too early on in the process can be more confusing than helpful. This chapter's purpose, then, is to simplify. And so, to begin, I will provide a few short guidelines to clear the way and enable you to start doing your own netnography. By the end of the chapter, you will not only understand what makes a netnography research project different from other projects, you will also experience how those guidelines have led you to a research question that will help guide your netnographic project.

Four Elements that Distinguish Netnography

What are the defining elements of netnography? Which particular elements separate this approach from all other ways of understanding the world? If we understand the elements that differentiate netnography, we should be able to combine netnography more effectively with other approaches, gaining in the process a more multidimensional understanding of its underlying procedures. The four distinct elements that differentiate netnography from every other investigative path are: (1) its cultural focus, (2) its use of social media data, (3) its requirement of appropriate engagement, and (4) its specification of particular procedures as a nexus of netnographic praxis. In this section, we discuss each of these briefly in turn.

Element 1: Cultural Focus

The first of netnography's four defining elements is its 'cultural focus'. Netnography is a form of ethnography. Like ethnography, it focuses on an understanding of a focal phenomenon, site, topic, or people that is attuned to difference, complexity, context, and meaning. As with anthropological studies, a netnography values an empathic sense of verstehen, it seeks explanation in cultural causality, and its perspective seeks to unite individual local beliefs and practices with wider, shared, let-us-call-them networks of knowledge, information, and institutionalized influence. If culture is socially patterned human thought and action, netnography seeks these meanings within the realms of social media, whether through:

a. the use of new language and symbols, such as novel words, acronyms, memes, fonts, or emojis, which may be created exclusively for online use, or reflected online, or

b. the expression of various online rituals, such as posting particular types of video, image, or avatar; some of these will be practices that are only possible online, or are enabled by various facets of online experience such as anonymity or partial anonymity; or

c. the adoption of new identities, expressed through role modeling and play acting, adopting new fashions, attempting new social positions (such as influencer, or activist), sometimes through aggression, and often in a dynamic manner, as if trying on new identities were a stylistic matter; or

d. the telling of stories, sharing of beliefs, passing along of powerful images and media; social media is filled with narratives whose importance requires deep analysis, identification, and (re)connection of meaning; and

e. the inculcations and reinforcement of value and value systems through the feedback reward structures of social media sharing, commenting, and liking; which is also tied into

f. relations of power, group dynamics, exclusion and inclusion, submission and domination, and hierarchies that express themselves online.

As Chapter 1 explained, these cultural elements link netnography not only with the epistemologies and other philosophical bases of established qualitative research methods, but also with newer variants such as digital anthropology, virtual ethnography, and most renditions of online ethnography.

Element 2: Social Media Data

The second element, 'social media data', distinguishes netnography from traditional ethnography. Netnographies focus primarily on social media communications. Again, social media are applications, websites, and other online technologies that enable users to easily engage in creation, distribution, commenting, and connecting activities. Research on social media use in 2018 by the Pew Research Center listed the following social media sites as the most popular ones: YouTube, Facebook, Instagram, Pinterest, Snapchat, LinkedIn, Twitter, and WhatsApp. Social media are created and accessed from a variety of different devices, from wearables like watches and glasses to tablets, omnipresent smart phones, stalwart old laptops, and desktops. In netnography, we often seek out data that seems to be created by regular, ordinary, people – as much as we can interpret who they are. The data collected in netnography can also originate in media outlets such as online news media, corporate blogs, and professional reviews. Increasingly, there is no hard line between amateur and semi-professional content creation, which creates new opportunities and challenges for netnography. Ordinary posts can go viral, attaining an impressive influence. Authentic amateurs become professionalized at a rapid pace, as oceans of money flood into social media and turn everyday conversations into advertising and public relations opportunities. The entire communication ecosystem is grist for the netnographic mill.

Element 3: Immersive Engagement

The third distinguishing element is something I term 'immersive engagement'. A key factor in netnography that I have emphasized from its inception is a reflective type of personal involvement in the focal phenomenon by the members of the research team or the individual researcher. This is the part of netnography that often creates the most confusion, and rightly so, because the word 'participation' has been used frequently to refer to this aspect. However, the word 'participation', like the words 'community' and 'culture', is both loaded and imprecise – especially when considered within the novel social media contexts in which netnography operates. Participation sounds like action to some people, and that suggests to people that posting messages is necessary. And because posting messages in every social media site you study invites a range of ethical and practical problems, people are perplexed. That confusion is why I think it is necessary and propitious to define a particular kind of engagement: immersive engagement.

In an in-the-flesh traditional ethnography, cultural participation is rather clear. I conducted field research at the Burning Man Project by repeatedly attending the organization's annual event in Black Rock City, Nevada, getting to know the people there, taking part in various theme camp activities, and generally learning about the local on-the-ground culture and acting the way that other participants do – except that my learning and actions transpired in a reflective manner that always also included my work's research objectives, resulted in me recording most of my conversations and many of my acts, and required me to write fieldnotes for one to two hours every day. My ethnographic participation with the Burning Man Project was a physical, social, and emotional engagement with the place and the people, and it happened at particular times and in specific locations. But one of the keys to my immersion was not simply that I was presently there, it was that I was learning about the place and its people by being an active, reflective learner – and that active learning and reflection was captured in my fieldnotes.

Consider the contrast with a hypothetical Burning Man netnography. If I was to have exclusively studied conversations and topics related to Burning Man that occur online, on the public-facing Burning Man website forums, on Instagram, Reddit, blogs, Facebook, Twitter, and YouTube, then my attendance at the event would not be important. The idea of participation could be transferred to a range of online sites devoted to Burning Man. What if I never attended Burning Man, never posted a single message or comment, but read and pondered the postings of event participants every day for the month prior, during, and for one month after the physical event? Would you have to consider my intellectual, cultural, and emotional engagement with the event and in particular its online manifestations to be strong? The 'field' of my involvement would change. And my ongoing, daily, immersive engagement would need to be captured somehow. That somehow is in reflective notes, what I will in this book term entries into an immersion journal (see Chapter 10 for details).

From the contrast between the examples, we can quickly see that involvement in the much more dispersed and loosely structured communications that typify social media are not exactly commensurate with traditional participant-observation. In particular, netnographic engagement does not necessarily need to involve discussion with other people, although it often does. It does not need to involve posting messages. It does not require interviews. However, it cannot also be limited to the 'download and code' of content analysis, either. Data collection and its later analysis must reflect and capture an active intellectual and emotional engagement with online sites.

Netnography thus requires a structured and disciplined approach to immersive engagement in qualitative social media research. Engagement means keeping a special type of netnographic fieldnotes in an immersion journal. Immersive engagement is a major and important topic in this Essential Guide, and we examine the topic in finer detail in an entire subsection of Chapter 10. The next section of this chapter examines netnographic praxis in finer detail.

Element 4: Netnographic Praxis

The fourth and final distinguishing element is something I term 'netnographic praxis'. With this version of the text, netnography gains an unprecedented level of operational precision, accompanied by entirely new terminology. With that precision and new terminology come a clear differentiation from other methods. A given piece of research is a netnography if it utilizes recognized and recommended netnographic research practices, and also discursively demonstrates an awareness of netnographic conventions, terminology, history, methodological perspectives, and other relevant scholarly works that might impact upon its procedures and research topic. These conventional, historical, methodological, and procedural elements are netnographic praxis, and they include elements discussed throughout this book such as following specific ethical procedures, collecting data using a netnographic research webpage, creating and using an immersion journal, using integrative analysis and interpretive techniques, and so on.

As you will read and learn in the remainder of this book, netnography replaces a range of traditional ethnographic concepts and terms with new ones more suited to the data environment and the research task at hand, that is, using social media data to develop deep cultural understanding. Table 5.1 summarizes some of these changing terms for this, the newest, most elaborate, and most up-to-date version of netnography.

Table 5.1 Changing Terms for Netnography

Traditional Ethnographic Term and Concept	Netnographic Term and Concept
Ethnography	Netnography
Field or Field site	Data site
Fieldnotes	Immersion Journal
Participation	Engagement
Observation	Data Operations
Participant-Observation (or Observer)	Engaged Data Operations (or Operator), abbreviated as EDO
Interpretation	Integration

Focus, Data, Engagement, Praxis: The Four Elements

These four elements distinguish netnography from all other methods of under-standing and provide a methodological basis for any netnographic project. Cul-tural focus links the purpose and core conceptual notions of netnography to the guiding principles of anthropology, sociology, cultural studies, and other fields that use ethnographic approaches. Social media data differentiates netnography from traditional ethnography and other methods such as surveys, focus groups, and personal in-depth interviews. Immersive engagement distinguishes netnog-raphy from more experience-distanced methods of understanding social media data such as content analysis, text mining, quantitative modeling, and big data analytics, and adds the deep human insight that comes from informed cultural reflection. Finally, netnographic praxis sets netnography apart from generic forms of online or digital ethnography, or other well-known approaches to online research such as Hine's 'virtual ethnography' (2000) or her later 'ethnographies of the Internet' (2015).

When all four elements are present together, the work can be nothing other than a netnography. If you wish to create a netnography, these four elements are your guide. First, choose a topic of study that contains a cultural focus and then find rich veins of informative cultural data in the communications of social media. Carefully design and execute your research in relation to the netnography procedures and guidelines that will rigorously structure your investigation and its scientific presentation. Engage in a relevant manner with those mediated cultural worlds. The following section expands on the relation between the procedural steps of netnography and the approach's grounding in cultural focus, social media data, participation, and netnographic praxis. After this, the chapter will proceed to explain how to begin doing netnography by choosing appropriate initial research questions.

THE SIX PROCEDURAL MOVEMENTS OF NETNOGRAPHY

Many who understand ethnographic research scoff at the idea of a simple set of steps or guidelines to describe the process. They are right to be skeptical. Ethnography is undoubtedly more complex and far more contextualized than any bare bones pro-cedural guideline can address. However, brain surgeons start out by being able to identify the parts of the brain on charts. For teaching purposes, a systematic and dis-ciplined approach is ever-important. So, what do we do?

In this version of netnography, I offer a repertoire of different operations in four general categories:

1. Interrogatory operations that help us ask better questions.

2. Data-collection operations that guide a systematic and methodically structured approach to building a dataset from a social media data site.

3. Data analysis, interpretation, and integration operations to provide a range of perspectives on findings.

4. Presentation options for conveying results, implications, and innovations.

Within these four categories are a range of more specific data operations. Using them, the researcher can construct the best netnography to suit the research question at hand. There is also a fair degree of creativity, novelty, and innovation that the big sandbox of the method invites in terms of combining elements and adapting the operations. One key element, however, where adaptation is not welcome is in bending or breaking the ethical rules of good research behavior. As you will learn in Chapter 6, you are expected to maintain a certain moral standard in netnography by following particular ethical research procedures.

Within these four general categories there are six operational sub-categories for undertaking a netnography, called movements or moves. There are six moves: initiation, investigation, immersion, interaction, integration, and incarnation. However, a netnography can also be conducted using a carefully chosen subset of them (this is explained in Chapter 7).

In the process of data collection an ethnography, perhaps more than any other method, is subject to frequent changes, revision and adaptation of research questions, shifts in focus, as well as alterations and substitutions of particular contexts and participants. Similarly, ethnographic research does not always have a clear start and end point. It is not uncommon, for instance, for a researcher to collect and analyze data, and then to reformulate the research questions and collect additional data to analyze. It is also not unusual to see your data sites as Heraclitus might, as dynamic ever-changing streams that you can engage with over decades without ever reaching some preternatural state of data saturation. Some ethnographic engagements will likely continue broadening and deepening for as long as you care to engage with them openly.

The six movements are intended as a starting point to give structure to the way we think about the conduct of netnography. They are a representational convenience that can convey a sense of the main practices one must perform when undertaking a research ethnography and how they flow together as the interconnected stages of a discrete project.

Explaining the Six Procedural Movements of Netnography

As represented in Figure 5.2, the big picture of the six movements of netnography covers: (1) initiation, (2) investigation, (3) immersion, (4) interaction, (5) integration,

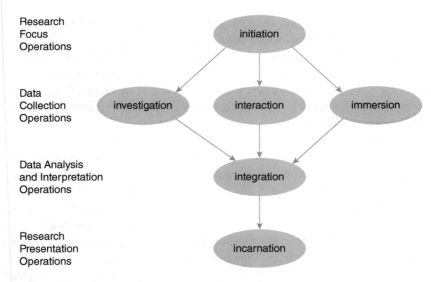

Figure 5.2 The six procedural movements of netnography

and (6) incarnation. The following sections explain the constituent parts contained in each of these six steps.

Movement 1: Initiation

The first movement of a netnography gives the project its investigatory direction. Netnography is an intentional research act, and the first movement focuses on its all-important objective. Does the research investigate a particular online site or phenomenon? Or is it drawn by a particular construct or theory of interest from past research? Is there a trend at work in the world that the researcher believes to be worth investigating? In this initial investigatory phase, the researcher is likely to think about many possible topics and approaches, and then to craft and hone the research question so that it can lead to some sort of research design that includes netnographic inquiry. In this initial movement we would also include all sorts of informational, organizational, regulatory, and administrative preparation for the act of research. These would include becoming informed about the ethical considerations and relevant research ethics procedures of the netnographic research, attaining ethics approval from requisite regulatory bodies, and planning the study so that the type of data you collect will be appropriately matched to the research questions you wish to answer.

Movement 2: Investigation

The second movement maps out the investigative space of the project. Social media is a universe unto itself. There are currently over 3 billion active social media users in the world, with each averaging about 6 social media accounts, active across at least 30 major social media platforms which account for a lion's share of global social media traffic. At current rates of global involvement, about 1.3 million new social media users join the social media party every day. The second movement of the netnography is where the researcher narrows down this expansive and expanding field of communication, treating it not just as a public forum for communication and connection, but also as a cultural research site.

The investigation movement is directed by the focus imparted to it by the research question. This phase utilizes search engines and other automated means to seek and find traces that are relevant to the research. Search engines can reveal sites as well as individual conversations, topics and sub-topics, tags such as hashtags, and visual images or other non-textual representations. In this movement you will localize, examine, and interpret these traces in order to 'site' such communicative data as clues to lead you to generative netnographic data sites. One useful practice employed in this movement is landscape mapping. A netnographic landscape map is a visual representation of sites containing communications relevant to a particular research question. Along with careful analysis and consideration, a landscape map can reveal unexpected commonalities and disjunctures that may lead to productive new paths of exploration. In this movement you will also make choices, which can always be revisited, about which sites you will focus on, and consequently which ones you are not going to study. There are concrete criteria that you will employ to help you make these decisions, and further focus your netnographic project. The result of movement 2 is a type of bounded conceptual space for your research immersion, a type of 'siting' of the project.

Movement 3: Immersion

Movement 1 directs the project by specifying its conceptual focus. Movement 2 launches into the vast universe of social media, encountering it mainly through search engines in order to map out investigative areas of interest. The third movement of netnography involves the researcher's inhabitation of the bounded conceptual space of the project. The notion of immersion is drawn from ethnographic conceptions. Anthropologists like to compare human beings living in their culture to fish inhabiting water. Like water to fish, culture is invisible and taken for granted until the fish finds itself out of water. Likewise, ethnographic immersion is a liquid metaphor intended to imply that we dive deeply into the cultural pools of others, and not merely skim along their surfaces. Because this is netnography, however, rather than ethnography, the precise practices indicating immersion are somewhat unclear and require explication and specification. What does it mean to immerse oneself in a novel online topic rather than a new national culture? What is data immersion and how does it relate to netnography?

Immersion in netnography is data-centric. Between the finding of deep data and its collection is a general encountering of gentle streams, flowing rivers, and roaring tides of data that always threaten to submerge our project's focus and intent. Despite that omnipresent threat, in the doing of netnography cultural experiences must be had. In the first section of this chapter, we learned how netnography's cultural focus encompassed: (a) the use of new language and symbols; (b) the expression of various online rituals; (c) the adoption of new identities; (d) the telling of stories, sharing of beliefs, and passing along of powerful images and media; (e) the inculcations and reinforcement of value and value systems; and (f) relations of power and group dynamics. Thus, netnographers in the course of their research may encounter new languages and rituals that need to be learned and deciphered, as well as new identities, values, stories, and hierarchies that can be identified and experienced. Exploring how any or all of these elements play out in synchronous as well as asynchronous communications constitutes an invitation to the sort of personal, intellectual, and emotional involvement that characterizes netnographic immersion.

Finally, netnographic immersion enacts data collection and indexing strategies. These ensure that large amounts of data are examined and noted in research notes that are called entries into an immersion journal. These notes can be composed of various types of data, such as textual, graphic, photographic, and audiovisual, but a key point is that the amounts of data collected in the journal are not overwhelming. The quality of the data is emphasized rather than the quantity. Much of the immersion movement is spent in a quest for elusive high quality or 'deep' data, which may carry forward into various strategies of interaction.

Movement 4: Interaction

Interaction consists of a phase with explicit questioning or research engagement with online participants. Immersion in the third movement is already a type of interaction, albeit one that is largely unobtrusive and non-invasive. The researcher is already interacting with different field sites, searching them, observing them, downloading parts of them, writing analytic and observational fieldnotes about them. And for some netnographies, this immersion will be sufficient to answer their research questions. There need not, for these netnographies, be an explicit stage of interaction with online participants. However, many netnographies will find that particular nuances or even large themes still elude them. Sometimes, particular topics that are important to the investigation are not discussed online, or they are not discussed in sufficient depth. At other times, meanings are unclear. At still other times, making a positive identification of the people behind the messages is crucial theoretically – for example, a study of Venezuelan refugees' online behavior would likely want to have some confirmatory interviews with people who are definitely Venezuelan refugees. Identification is also useful in order to gain a more holistic cultural and social understanding of the communications of particular peoples, if that is the project's theoretical focus. Clarification is often required and this is when netnographic observation usefully extends into other and related types of investigation such as online interviews. An interaction entrée strategy will help the researcher be deliberate in the way in which she enters into these more obtrusive forms of data collection. In netnography, we have several options for these interactions, including not only interviews, but also online participation, the creation of a netnographic interaction research webpage, and the use of digital diaries and mobile ethnography techniques.

Movement 5: Integration

The lines between data collection, interpretation, and analysis are amorphous in ethnography and netnography. Data is being interpreted, analyzed, and collected almost from the initiatory moment when you decide on sites or topics. That analytical and interpretive activity intensifies as you begin to investigate which sites to research and continues through the various choices, interactions, and immersions of your netnography. Ethnography and netnography are both iterative processes, where the vagaries of analysis and interpretation often necessitate return trips to both the field and the literature to collect more data and to sharpen your understanding of both the empirical field site and the theoretical literature base. In netnography, with its provision of persistent contact with field or data sites, the temptation to return can be especially strong. Nonetheless, at some point, data collection slows down considerably, even if it does not fully cease. And at that point, the integrated analysis and interpretation of the corpus of collected, co-created, and created data move center stage – and when this happens you are in netnography's fifth movement.

Integration in netnography is an ongoing process of decoding, translating, cross-translating, and code-switching between parts and wholes, between data fragments and cultural understandings. When you became immersed in online communications, you encountered many strange new cultural elements that required decipherment and holistic viewing in order to extract their meaning. These may have included translating new words, terminologies, and expressions, perhaps even new poses and types of avatar bodies or digitally augmented selfie photos. They could have included patterns of significant behavior, novel technological affordances, routines, habits, procedures, and other meaningful practices. Roles and moralities, personalities and status – all of these things once may have seemed unfamiliar, but by movement 5 they will have become recognizable, nameable, mundane, even intimate. As you relate your understanding of your findings to your research question, you will engage in acts not only of analysis (breaking down into parts) and interpretation (building and connecting wholes) but also of integration, the mutual and co-constitutive collision of perspectives that produces something new. In movement 5, the sought-after depth of cultural understanding becomes applied to the task of answering the research question. Researchers will collate data, code it, categorize it, and often wield humanistic, phenomenological, existential, discourse, and hermeneutic methods of interpretation.

There is room for a variety of approaches in this wide-ranging movement. As the integration phase encourages answers to resolve from our repeated close encounters with the data, literature, imagination, and site, we begin to build the representations that will incarnate the project and bring it to a stage of completion.

Movement 6: Incarnation

To incarnate means to put into or represent in a concrete form. In the final movement, a netnography, which began as an idea, a question about the world, finds its form as research. In order to be complete as an academic endeavour, a research project must be communicated. Incarnation is thus communication. Netnographies have become term papers and class projects, master's degree and doctoral dissertations, poster sessions in conferences, conference papers and presentations, full papers in academic proceedings, journal articles and the chapters of books. The purpose in all of them is to bring to life and also to communicate. These productions should be rigorous in that they deliberately and precisely use some of the approaches described as netnographic praxis. They should be readable, accessible, and interesting to the audiences they intend to reach. They should include clear communication of the method of netnography, the netnographic data operations, the netnographic dataset, and representation of the data. We can consider the groundedness, novelty, resonance, and perhaps above all, the usefulness of our netnographic research. Quality netnography must clearly and compellingly answer its stated research question. As a consequence, the results of the research might be trusted to inform important decisions, and inspire further work and enhanced understanding of subject topic areas.

Initiation, investigation, immersion, interaction, integration, and incarnation. These are the six movements of netnography. With a description of them concluded, we are almost ready to begin the exercises and discussions that will guide you through your own netnographic research project. The remainder of this book is structured to take you through these six research movements. In fact, after a necessary discussion about conducting netnography in teams, this chapter transitions into the first movement. As with all scientific inquiry, we will begin with a question. Will you be conducting your netnography solo, as an individual? Or will you be doing netnography, as so many people do, in coordination with others? Will you be enacting your netnography as the member of a team?

DOING NETNOGRAPHY IN TEAMS

Although considerable research has been done by individual netnographers, a lot of netnography has also been done by teams. Almost from the beginning, groups began applying the ideas of netnography in their co-conducted and co-authored research. Kozinets and Handelman's (1998) early work on boycotting and consumer activism was part of a team effort, as was Brown, Kozinets, and Sherry's (2003) netnography. So was Nelson and Otnes (2005) and Muniz and Schau (2005). From the beginning, these groups were constructing what 'team' meant when applied to netnography.

An important key to advancing social science in general is to systematize and develop its use by a range of different team forms. So much is known about teams, leadership, and teamwork from the organizational and management literatures. Yet so much is still to discover when it comes to the practices and functions of particular research teams, such as ones pursuing netnography. There are a number of lessons we can gather from some past team netnography experiences.

Division of labor can be handled in a number of different ways. You can divide by online site, by county, by netnography movements or operations, or by perspective of researcher. I've been teaching netnography to my students since 1998 and I've observed that my student teams usually split up netnographic data collection by platform. One student would run a data collection operation on Reddit, another on Instagram, and a third on Facebook. Someone would try to hunt down some useful forums. Another would take responsibility for Twitter. After several weeks of data collection, they aggregate all the results and together discuss where to focus and what to do next. One issue I have noted is that they generally find it a challenge to aggregate the data in one place where they all have access to it. Organization is key! Often, having a single online repository, with folders (like a Google Drive folder with sub-folders) is a very good idea for team work.

In team projects I have been involved in, we were often able to usefully divide tasks. I wrote Kozinets et al. (2010) with Kristine, Sarah, and Andrea. Kristine was a visiting scholar for much of the study. Sarah was a PhD student. And Andrea was a professor at a university across town. We did all our meetings in person. We were researching an online phenomenon, collecting data from 91 discrete data sites (each of them a blog created by an influencer given a free product as part of an influencer marketing campaign). We had carefully divided who would be monitoring which blogs, and over which time periods. We had frequent meetings to ensure that we were collecting data in ways that were useful to the project and the team. And we discussed the analysis a lot, in team meetings that were always respectful, but often intellectually demanding and rigorous. Each of us brought data of our own to the meeting, but we also were always trying to combine it with data from other team members. One thing we did not do, which I regret, was keep individual immersion journals and use them to discuss our different personal perspectives on the work.

Another way to run a netnography team is to set up a global network that divides tasks by nation and language. This was how I worked with eleven other researchers in Egypt, Moldova, Indonesia, Ukraine, Italy, Brazil, Uruguay, the Philippines, and India, to root out the barely hidden social media marketing practices of big global tobacco companies on a project we conducted for the Washington-based

Campaign for Tobacco-Free Kids. Each researcher conducted investigative data-collection operations leading to some personal interviews in the country whose culture they were embedded in and with which they were familiar. Rossella, Silvia, Jerome, Maribel, Abu, Eni, Ruxandra, Antonina, Mridula, Verónica, Ilona, Ulli, and I consulted frequently on procedure. We met in smaller groups over Skype several times. We also took part in ongoing conversations that involved the whole group over email. Each team member collected data from social media data sites and from a common interview guide we adapted for local purposes and different interviewee participants (usually either tobacco brand ambassadors, or media industry insiders). Just a few of the partners created advanced models with both investigative and interactive data (Maribel, Rossella, Silvia, and I). We never met in person, and most of the members I have still never met in the flesh.

Important additional clues to netnographic teamwork are provided in the article by Minowa, Visconti, and Maclaran (2012) in which they describe being a contemporary global academic team doing multi-sited cultural work and then collaborating on a finished ethnographic product. The basis of their collaborative ideal is easily understood. Meanings can be interpreted best when the interpreters are 'familiar with the historical, social, and cultural context in which they are conveyed' (p. 483). Thus, the researchers conducted 'an ethnography of desire and imagination in the transforming cities' that they each currently inhabited (New York City, Leicester, and Milan). Introspection by each researcher on the meanings associated with local cultures with which they are familiar played a large role in the data collection and interpretation which the three researchers shared with one another.

They end up deriving a name for the approach, 'xenoheteroglossic autoethnography', which they define as a form of ethnographically-driven introspection from researchers hailing from multiple countries with diverse cultural backgrounds. However, the actual autoethnography they produced was surprisingly impersonal. The product seemed as if it assumed that the naturalized and now totalized culture was something that the authors could uniquely channel without recourse to significant personal depth and intimate disclosure. We are left wondering about the role of personal factors such as socioeconomic status, occupation and educational cultures, sexual orientation, and the habituses they provide. Do these important cultural lenses not alter the way we would work in teams, and the different cities we might inhabit – and reveal? Could those individual differences and personal elements of individual interpretations be gently but firmly questioned by the interaction with other research team members, brought into the light, and further examined?

The idea of xenoheteroglossic autoethnography leads me to think about a more intersectional form of netnography where a team of researchers uses the opportunity provided by netnographic team meetings to plan data collection, discuss search, share data, plan interactional data-collection strategies, and disclose their personal reflections, as operationalized in the immersion journals each team member will be keeping (see Chapter 10). In intersectional team-based netnographies, we would expect to see cogent inclusion and analysis of the divergent perspectives of the researchers, as their research and personal experiences differentially refract the phenomenon under study. Medrado and Muller (2018), for example, provide a rich portrayal of the intersectional perspective of black Brazilian mothers represented on a feminist blog/media platform. Alongside this, they present a cultural and historical unpacking that studies the digital activism and social conflicts created when a range of feminisms intersect on the site. Using individual immersion journals to systematize a similar process, teams can build upon the strengths of personal ethnographic viewpoints to expand into multiple research perspectives.

As we have learned in this section, the organization of data by teams is important and can be facilitated by use of a central online depository. Division of labor is also important, and some alternatives that this section discusses are dividing work by online site, by county, by netnography movements or operations, or by perspective of the researcher. With this brief set of guidelines in place to help steer your team netnography, it is time to slide into the first movement of netnography, the interrogatory movement. Are you ready to start a project? Are you ready to start thinking about asking research questions?

ASKING GOOD QUESTIONS

Albert Einstein is quoted as saying that if he had an hour to solve a problem and his life depended on the solution, he would spend the first 55 minutes determining the proper question to ask, because once he knew the proper question, he could solve the problem in less than five minutes. If Einstein says that asking the right questions is so crucial that he would stake his life on it, we should probably believe it.

Because research questions are incredibly important to the success of your netnographic project, this section is dedicated to helping you construct and focus research questions appropriate for netnography. As Belk et al. (2013: 17–20) point out, 'there are two basic sources of inspiration for original, important research questions: prior research, and empirical phenomena'. Prior research can be conceptual or theoretical, but its most important aspect will be its abstractions, the constructs that it uses, and the specified relationship between them, which is theory. Empirical phenomena encompass contexts such as sites or events, types of behavior, or even types of social actors. For beginner researchers – and to be frank for seasoned professionals too – it can often be difficult to distinguish whether a conceptual research area or an empirical phenomenon has already been sufficiently understood. In order to help, this chapter has a series of exercises and guidelines to get you closer to that goal post of a thoughtful, significant, innovative, and intriguing research question.

Topics and Angles

I propose that there are two major parts to a research question. The first is the topic of the question. All research questions have a particular topic, which is its subject or focus. The topic is an answer to the question 'What exactly is the concept that you will investigate?' Topics need not be concrete, but can be abstract. You could be studying faith, sexual orientation, or cyber-bullying, or you could study a particular online site, or certain sites that foster climate denial, neoliberal beliefs, or anti-immigrant nationalism. As White (2017: 43) suggests, you could begin writing your research question topic with a single sentence. Simply fill in the blank:

I want to investigate _____.

After you decide on a topic, you can refine that topic endlessly. Topics and questions are infinitely malleable. Let us say that you started out by stating that you want to investigate the topic of cyber-bullying. Your follow-up refinement could be as follows:

I want to investigate the cyber-bullying of young Asian females by non-Asians.

Research questions also have a particular angle of inquiry or focus. This is their second part. The angle of inquiry is the answer to the question 'What do you want to know about the topic?'. The angle of inquiry provides important boundaries that define the question, fencing in what it includes and what it excludes. The more specific the angle of the question becomes, the narrower is the investigation. Being precise can be a good thing, but there are often trade-offs between being focused in your questioning, and being either overspecific or context-bound, and being interesting. Particularly with qualitative techniques like netnography, you probably are best advised to keep your questions fairly wide and open enough at the beginning to allow surprises and the opening up of unexpected but potentially fruitful new pathways to explore. Consider the following extended example, in which you would once again fill in the blanks:

I want to investigate _____ in order to learn who/what/where/when/whether/how or why they _____ so that we (as a field) can better understand _____.

Creswell (2009: 129–31) suggests that you should try using exploratory verbs such as 'discover', 'understand', 'explore', 'describe', or 'report' in your research question. As an example, we might add an angle to the more specific question about Asian female cyber-bullying as follows:

I want to investigate the cyber-bullying of young Asian females by non-Asians in order to build a contextualized understanding of the racist attitudes, roles, rituals, and identities that circulate on social media.

Risk-Free Questioning

With the fill-in-the-blanks options of the section above, you may have already begun thinking about your research question. This section offers a further set of exercises to focus on the conceptual topic of your research question. Your topical focus will inevitably be shaped by a variety of forces, not only your curiosity and idiosyncratic thirst for particular kinds of knowledge, but also the extant current of interest and thought running through your academic field, your particular academic department, and your colleagues, perhaps even something you saw recently in the media or heard in another research presentation. As well, you may be working in a team. If so, landing on a particular topic may require some advocacy, discussion, and negotiation. The topical interest you institute into your research question will direct you to locate your netnography in certain areas, and the angle of your question will cause you to look for particular kinds of data within those particular areas. In order to begin learning more about creating research questions, let us begin to practice with a no-risk exercise that focuses in on a particular theoretical or conceptual area that you are comfortable exploring.

5.1 **EXPLORING THE CONCEPTUAL BASIS OF A PRACTICE RESEARCH QUESTION (PROJECT EXERCISE)**

 Pick a Practice Research Question relating to an abstract theoretical concept in your field.

 If you can, discuss your question with a classmate. Then, together, explore that theoretical topic using a search engine such as Google Scholar. Look at a few academic articles. Track down a few references. Read a few abstracts. Try to learn, with an investment of about 15 minutes of time, what has been written about this theoretical topic. What discernible patterns exist in the literature about this topic?

What gaps do you detect in our collective knowledge? What unspoken assumptions could you challenge? Write down a summary of what you have learned.

 Based on what you have learned, refine and revise your research question into a new research question that more clearly specifies the research gap that you have identified.

(Optional): Repeat the procedure one or two times.

 Step 5: After you are done, discuss or write down, what you have discovered.

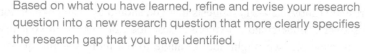

Situating Netnography in Research Traditions

In netnography, although we are using social media data, we often situate our work within particular fields such as nursing or queer studies, and within particular research traditions that are related to cultural topics and their consideration, such as hermeneutic, phenomenological, critical, or neopositivist traditions. These fields and traditions guide us to consider particular kinds of research questions, which I have called 'particular angles of inquiry'. For example, netnographic inquiry within a hermeneutic research tradition would likely consider questions regarding how cultural bases shape particular kinds of experience and behavior. Work within a phenomenological research tradition might consider questions about the essence of people's lived experiences. Work within a critical research tradition would lead us to develop questions about the factors contributing to the oppression of some marginalized group of actors, and how to alleviate those conditions. Work that comes from a neopositivist research tradition might prompt us to inquire about the factors that explain a particular phenomenon or the consequences of its occurrence (see Belk et al., 2013: 20–26). You might look back at your initial theoretically-derived research question exercises, which you may have completed above, and examine them in light of these research traditions. Do your theoretically-derived research questions resonate with any of these research traditions? Do they contain any related angles of inquiry?

Conceptual or theoretical topics are one source of inspiration and focus for your netnographic research question. Now let's turn to the other source: an empirical phenomenon. Let's begin with another exercise, one which is similar in structure, but actually quite different in focus from the one you just completed. To continue learning more about research questions, we will continue our practice with another risk-free exercise in which you now focus in on an empirical phenomenon, for example, a context such as a site, event, type of behavior, or social actor.

EXPLORING THE EMPIRICAL OR PHENOMENAL BASIS OF A PRACTICE RESEARCH QUESTION

5.2

 Step 1   Pick a Practice Research Question relating to an empirical phenomenon that you find worthy of investigation.

 Step 2   If you can, discuss your question with a classmate. Then, together, explore the empirical phenomenon using search engines such as Google and Google Scholar. What has been written about the phenomenon already? What news articles? What academic articles? Read a few abstracts and the first few paragraphs of the news stories and articles. Try to learn, with

(Continued)

an investment of about 15 minutes of time, what has been written about this empirical phenomenon. What discernible patterns exist in the literature about this topic? What gaps do you detect in our collective knowledge? What unspoken assumptions could you challenge? Next, write down a summary of what you have learned.

Step 3 Based on what you have learned, refine and revise your research question into a new research question that more clearly specifies the research gap that you have identified.

Step 4 (Optional): Repeat the process one or two times.

Step 5 After you are done, discuss or write down what you have discovered. How does it compare with the abstract conceptual exercise that you completed above? How was it similar? How did it differ?

Situating Netnography in Empirical Phenomena

A majority of netnographic research seems to begin with interest in an empirical site or actual phenomenon. This is unsurprising. Ethnographic research is empirically embedded; this is its signature element. The history and traditions of ethnographic research are located in exploration of new cultural contexts. And yet, if netnography is intended as an academic enterprise, it cannot be entirely descriptive. It must move from being an exploratory depiction of a cultural phenomenon to an explanatory one, and to do that it must invoke related concepts and theories.

In the investigatory phase, new scholars often make an obfuscating mistake. They claim exclusivity on a term, rather than seeking to embed what they know in a conceptual network. For example, if I studied how media audiences conceived of themselves, and then invented the term 'media collective' to describe them, could I rightly claim that my contribution was in revealing this new construct? The answer is no. True, you may have coined a new term. However, the concept behind it is what is important, not the term. What exactly is a media collective, and how does it relate to other, known concepts such as 'media audiences', 'fan groups', and 'imagined communities'? Sites can also, at first blush, seem highly unique. However, I advise against the type of idiosyncratic flag-raising in which a researcher lays claim to an exceptional or even one-of-a-kind concept or site, even in cases when they actually are studying an extreme case or example. If you want to make claims about how unique or unprecedented your case is, you may find that you have a very steep hill to climb. Much more advisable is to 'argue that while yours may be an extreme case, the dynamics or properties you are focusing on can indeed be found elsewhere and are therefore worth explaining' (Belk et al., 2013: 18).

All of this is to say that it is an incumbent obligation facing you as researcher to look far and wide for scholarly academic works that are related to your conceptual topic – regardless of whether the exact same terms, particular sites, or exact same framing have been used by prior scholars. Although this type of positioning is considerably more work than simple terminological territory-claiming, the advantage is that you demonstrate to readers that you are contributing to an actual field of interest, one with a literature base and perhaps some already-present confusion that your study can rectify.

When considering how to research and position a study that is inspired by a particular empirical context or phenomenon, there are several useful guidelines you can follow. The first is to ask yourself 'What the heck is going on here that I find so interesting?'. You will need to be specific about naming exactly what it is about the site that you find to be unusual, extreme, or intriguing. As you name that quality, you transition your study from the empirical realm of descriptive depiction into the world of abstract concepts. Once you have this conceptual footing, you can ask whether the abstract concept you located in your empirical context is worth investigating further. To do this, you will need to undertake a critical reading of prior literature, just as you did in the exercise above. You might ask yourself the following questions:

- Is this concept widely studied already? If so, what are the patterns in that investigation?

- If widely studied, are aspects of it already taken for granted? Is there an opportunity to explore certain overlooked elements further, in a more systematic or focused investigation?

- Are there boundary conditions that are interesting and at work in this empirical context?

- Are there related concepts present under different names? How are they similar to and different from the way this concept presents itself in this empirical setting?

- Are there processes at work in this context that have not yet been discovered? Or that may be misunderstood? Or that may vary in different contexts and settings? (See Belk et al., 2013: 17–20.)

Keeping in mind these questions, you might examine your second set of exercises, which you may have completed above. How are these concerns reflected in your empirically-derived research question? Does your answer to these questions help reveal a potentially novel contribution? How might the questions help you refine your empirically-derived research question's angles of inquiry?

Now that we have reached the end of this section, you should begin to get a sense about what is involved in constructing a research question based on two primary sources of inspiration, conceptual topics and empirical phenomena. You have gained some background information, and even some 'risk-free' practice, first in thinking about conceptual topics, and then about empirical phenomena. What is missing is some sense of how these two important elements work together. And work together they must, because as we are about to learn, their synergy is key not only to formulating effective research questions, but also to crafting viable research positioning for your entire inquiry. We turn to the next section in order to develop your understanding of the holistic nature of the research question and guide you towards its realization.

Meet-in-the-Middle

A meaningful, novel, and intriguing research question may be essential to the success of your netnographic project. But finding that research question at the very beginning of your project is probably a bit unlikely. Why? Because research questions are subject to change. They are not carved in stone! Reviewers, friendly and otherwise, suggest new research questions. Editors and associate editors offer them up. Researchers and co-authors debate them at any stage of the research project. I have sometimes performed a last-minute fine-tuning on the final research question after a submitted manuscript has been conditionally accepted for publication. My last-ditch research question revision acted as a sort of ritual tightening that assists in aligning the paper's question and findings. The reason for all this activity is because research questions are dynamic. And it is because of something that I have termed 'the meet-in-the-middle research process'.

In netnographic research, the meet-in-the-middle research process goes something like this. The researcher is inspired by a research focus, which usually derives either from a fascination with a supposed gap within an abstract, conceptual, theoretical domain, or an alleged contribution from an empirical, contextualized phenomenon. Let's say that the theoretical topic derives from something called 'the world of ideas', while the empirical phenomenon is situated in something we can call 'the world of things'. As the researcher engages in the research, the two worlds are forced into interplay. Let's assume that she is inspired by a theoretical concept such as affordance theory, the tourist gaze, or authenticity. She reads some literature, and is probably familiar with more literature, and tries to locate a particular gap in that literature, some lacuna that is unclear, problematic, contradictory, or unexplored. Then, in a difficult matching process, she tries to locate a good empirical site in order to explore that topic. In netnography, that site could be a particular communication platform such as Facebook, or part of it such as a public group, or it could range across a number of platforms, and be linked conceptually or by a classifier such as a tag or hashtag.

Now, the rubber from the world of ideas hits the road of the world of things. The researcher begins investigating the empirical phenomenon, collecting data and analyzing it. After drawing some initial conclusions, she finds many interesting things, some of which relate to the topic, and others which seem very interesting but are not as related to the topic. But often these findings will not exactly fit into the preordained gap the researcher has found. They might relate to it somehow, but not quite. At this point, what does she do? She keeps in mind her initial findings, and goes back to the theoretical literature. Delving into the literature with more focus than before, she can locate precise theoretical areas where there are (or are not) gaps that more closely fit the findings her actual empirical work reveals. Similarly, once she has a clearer focus from the theoretical fine-tuning she is now performing, she can re-encounter both her collected dataset and her ongoing fieldwork in order to focus in on specific phenomena that illuminate aspects of the new, and more refined, theoretical gap she has identified.

Eventually, over a number of iterations between the world of ideas and the world of things, the researcher identifies a specific and coherent gap in the theoretical and conceptual literature, and matches it with evidential findings drawn from the empirical phenomenal field site. The question has been polished so as to meet the redirected answer. The two worlds have met, and they meet in the middle: somewhere between theory and phenomenon, between preconceived abstract ideas and material reality, between the world of ideas and the world of things.

If you are a novice researcher, what is the bottom line on the meet-in-the-middle process? There are three takeaways, as far as I can see. The first is that you should expect research questions to come and go. Your first, second, and third iterations do not need to be perfect. Research questions are vehicles that take you on your journey. Sometimes you will ride all the way with the very first one. But other times you will switch vehicles and lines, several times, to get to your destination. The second takeaway is related to the incrementality of this change, and suggests that you should always be working with your past research question, honing it and revising it. You should never be throwing your question away! Adjust it, fine tune it, make it better. Go back to the literature. Go into your dataset. See where the two can meet. Find the question that matches the phenomenon in the literature. Find the answer that matches the question in the data. Sometimes the process will broaden your theoretical topic, while at other times it will be narrowed. Expect it to change, but start somewhere that is as close to your genuine interests as you can. This is the theoretical process you will follow in a netnography. Theory and social media data will meet in the middle. And the final takeaway is about managing your own expectations. Expect the greatness of your project to be revealed gradually and over time, rather than in an unearthly flash of indelible insight. It is totally unnecessary to begin your netnography project by driving yourself insane trying to locate that perfect, unexplored research domain, that fascinating anomalous and unique phenomenon upon which you establish your research question. Follow the process of meet-in-the-middle, be patient, be systematic, and your project's unique and important theoretical and substantive insights will undoubtedly emerge.

NETNOGRAPHIC RESEARCH QUESTIONS

Much of this chapter applies equally well to most cultural or qualitative research projects as it does to netnographic research. The importance of asking good questions is a common element. All research questions have topics and angles, and all of them have a fairly similar structure. Similarly, the researchers who initiate most qualitative research projects draw inspiration from theoretical topics and concepts, or from their own interest in an empirical context or setting. The meet-in-the-middle process, in which theories and contexts bump up against one another until a supportable and novel research positioning can be expressed in a research question, also can be widely applied.

So, we might ask, what makes a netnographic research question unique, if anything? In order to discover the answer to that important question, you must first do a bit of homework with our next exercise.

5.3

FINDING UNIQUE NETNOGRAPHIC RESEARCH QUESTIONS

1. Using a search engine such as Google Scholar, or a general repository of research such as academia.edu or researchgate.net, search for some recent publications that use netnography. Three or four articles that have been published in the last one or two years will be sufficient.

2. Skim through the articles, looking for their research question. What are the research questions that they used? Write them down.

3. Can you identify the topic in each question? Can you identify the angle of inquiry?

4. What other patterns do you notice in the research questions? How would you describe them?

Some recent research questions from netnographies that I found were:

1. How do female tourists conceive of their tourist experience and how they 'gaze' on Macao? (Zhang and Hitchcock, 2017)

2. What are the affordances of e-reading and do they enhance the reading experience? (D'Ambra et al., 2017)

3. How can we better understand orthodontic patients' decision about receiving orthodontic care by studying how people talk about their orthodontic desires and experiences online? (Pittman et al., 2017)

4. How has the merging of technology and the music industry affected how freelance female popular musicians in the United States music industry negotiate their career development? (Lorenz, 2017)

5. (i) How does the evolution of a person's identity conflict correspond with the evolution of the extended self?; (ii) What extended self strategies do people utilize to cope with their identity conflicts?; and (iii) How do social norms shape the enactment of these extended self strategies? (Ruvio and Belk, 2018)

6. In research I am currently conducting on activist discourse in social media and the conception of utopia, my research questions are these: How do social media discourses of utopianism challenge the institution of capitalism itself? What contours do these challenges assume? What type of activism or clicktivism might these discourses represent? What are its implications for developing our understanding of both utopianism and activism? (In Chapters 12 and 13, we will be working with one of the datasets from this research project.)

Patterns in Netnographic Research Questions

When I look at some of the research questions that I have asked in my own published netnographies, I see how intertwined the research question is with the theoretical positioning of the article itself. Consider first an example from the 'networked narratives' article that my co-authors and I published about 'word of mouth marketing'. This paper had its origin in an opportunity to work with a digital marketing agency on a campaign to promote a new smart phone with 91 online influencers. In 2007, when we collected this data, the term being used was 'word of mouth marketing' or 'WOMM', and this was still a fairly small and marginal practice. We currently refer to this type of promotion as 'influencer marketing', and it is currently a much more widespread and mainstream phenomenon than it was in 2007:

> Yet, despite awareness of the complexity of these communal relationships, marketers are just beginning to understand the formation, reaction, and effects of communally-based marketing promotions. This article's contribution is based on empirical inquiry that attempts to further develop the understanding already captured in the coproduction model and to answer the following three

questions: How do communities respond to community-oriented WOMM? What patterns do WOM communicator strategies assume? and Why do they assume these patterns? (Kozinets et al., 2010: 73)

Because this was a fairly new phenomenon, and we had the opportunity to study it in context, we had a range of exploratory types of questions we could explore, as well as attempting to make a fundamental theoretical contribution to our understanding about how markets and social media communities interact with one another. How do communities respond to word of mouth marketing? What patterns do communicator strategies assume? And why do they assume these patterns? The questions are 'how?' (a process-based question, requiring some description of a process), 'what?' (a structure-based question, requiring some description of communication patterns), and 'why?' (an explanatory question, requiring some description of underlying causal forces).

Although you can also see how particularly the explanatory 'why' component of the research question is part of the broader positioning of the article, you can recognize an even broader sociocultural set of questions at play in the 'networks of desire' paper, which I quote from here:

Yet, for a central concept, the term 'desire' has received relatively little reexamination and extension. In this article, we reboot the concept of desire. Updating desire, we ask how it is changed by contemporary technology. What happens to desire when consumers collectively combine and connect their cravings through technology in new and unprecedented ways? How can we bring novel understanding to bear on this new reality? (Kozinets et al., 2017: 660)

That article was initiated when Rachel Ashman took my PhD seminar on netnography and social media research, and decided to study food porn as her final project. We continued the investigatory work, added Tony Patterson to the team, and decided to look at food porn and the empirical phenomenon of food image sharing using social media as an opportunity to learn something about desire in the age of connective technology. How is desire changed by contemporary technology? This was our broad, opening question, which we positioned as a counter-opinion to longstanding opinions that technology had a dampening or muting effect on human desire. What happens when consumers combine and connect their cravings through technology in new ways? This gave us an opportunity to explore and develop our variety of observations about the food porn phenomenon. Finally, when we asked 'How can we bring a new understanding to bear on this reality?', we were opening the article up to introduce some new perspectives which included developing Deleuze and Guattari's conception of 'desiring machines' (which they later reformulated into the notion of 'agencements', or assemblages), as well as a post-human view that networked human and nonhuman together into vast and variegated 'networks of desire' with an enhanced capacity for desire.

Guidelines for Netnographic Research Questions: Phenomena, Platforms, and Sites

There are no defined limits to netnographic research questions, but a good general guideline relates them back to what makes netnography a particular form of scientific inquiry. That is, netnographic research questions tend to focus on:

- Cultural phenomena manifesting online such as:
  - new languages, changes in, or forms of symbolic, communications;
  - social media rituals, postings, poses, and practices;
  - new identities, fashions, or social roles;
  - shared stories, beliefs, passionate interests, and desires;
  - values, value systems, and their exchange;
  - group dynamics, power structures, and hierarchies.

- Social media platforms and sites, and the way that they interact with other aspects of social existence, such as:
  - how particular platforms and sites are gendered, and react to gender or sexuality;
  - how particular topics are discussed on social media;
  - how people respond online to particular kinds of organizational or interpersonal communication directed to them;
  - how particular themes or concepts are revealed through online discourse, e.g., how authenticity is discussed and negotiated on classic rock sites (Henriques and Pereira, 2018), how engagement manifests in fashion blogs (Henderson et al., 2017), or how racial exclusion is extended into online social relations (West and Thakore, 2013);
  - how various instances of online communication differ from one another;
  - how people use social media to communicate or educate one another about practices, ideologies, or information they might not gain elsewhere.

Sometimes, researchers will conduct netnographies about particular sites, such as the 'whole food plant-based Aussies Facebook group' (Chuter, 2018) or 'young women's blogs on Macao' (Zhang and Hitchcock, 2017). Studies of sites can also be used for specific purposes, such as investigating how the '411 rallies' were interpreted by studying international and national audience responses on the 'international and Indonesian YouTube community' (Setiadarma and Rizkiansyah, 2018).

As you are examining these past research questions and their angles of inquiry, it is important to consider the question words that they employ. If you are interested in locating people and topics in context, their locations in online sites, then 'where' may be an important question word. If you are interested in processes, then 'how' and 'when' may be important. If you are interested in the people who communicate through social media or discuss particular topics and their identities and roles, then 'who' may be important. Your most useful questions will often begin with 'what', as they relate to descriptions of things such as types of online stories, topics, or meanings. And despite conventional wisdom, I believe that cultural investigations can provide explanations for phenomena. Thus, although it can be a little bit tricky to deal with at times, asking 'why' a particular social or cultural process happens (but not, I should add, why someone is motivated to do something) can be useful.

A Starter Research Question

So where should you start? We have discussed quite a bit about research questions and netnographic research questions, and found that they have a particular form and a particular inclination. Further, we have learned that they are positioned in a very important place in between the empirical context and the research literature. If you are stuck, or want a recommendation for an opening, I am fond of the following 'starter' research question form found in Box 5.4.

5.4

STARTER FORM RESEARCH QUESTION (PROJECT EXERCISE)

What can we learn about _____ [abstract topic X] from an empirical study of _____ [online phenomenon Y]?

In filling in the blanks, you should have already done a bit of homework. Actually, having gone through all of the exercises in this chapter will be enormously helpful. You should have already identified the strong and recognizable presence of abstract topic X, which we want to learn about, in your empirical online phenomenon. Similarly, you should have already established that abstract topic X is interesting, has a basis in relevant literature, and is part of an established research conversation – but perhaps one that could have some gaps, inconsistencies, omissions, or other problems.

This starter question gives us some good specificity to get our project going. But it also leaves us with lots of room to circle in on aspects of topic X later on, something called the 'double-funnel effect' of netnographic search resulting from investigative data operations. The question also allows you to explore in some depth the literature surrounding both abstract topic X and phenomenon Y, including its online and perhaps other related manifestations. As you perform the netnography, immersing and participating in phenomenon Y, you will find that your analysis of the data drives you back to your research question, honing it. The gaps you identified earlier might shift or become more well-defined. The extant literature may refocus the questions.

The questions may refocus the subsequent collection of data. Each will affect the other and become more precise as they gradually meet in the middle – delineating a theoretical sweet spot for your netnography.

CHAPTER SUMMARY

In this chapter, we have transitioned from overview to how-to view. We began by gaining an understanding of cultural focus, social media data, participation, and a netnographic praxis – the four elements that distinguish netnography. Next, we learned the four operation categories (interrogatory, data collection, data analysis/interpretation, and presentation). Then, the six movements of netnography: initiation, investigation, immersion, interaction, integration, and incarnation. The chapter then offered some important practical considerations about conducting netnography as a member of a team, as so many netnographies are performed by groups of researchers. The chapter then proceeded into a discussion of the first stage of the process, initiation. We learned the two major parts to a research question, the research topic and the angle of inquiry, and then explored the initiating factors of research questions. Through a series of exercises, you discovered the relation of concept and phenomenon in netnographic research questions. Then, you were introduced to the meet-in-the-middle process and became acquainted with its implications for your own research. As the chapter drew to a close, it presented and analyzed a range of research questions. In total, the chapter provided clear guidelines concerning the basis of netnography, its six-step process, how to conduct it in teams, and how to construct and refine an appropriate netnographic research question.

KEY READINGS

Agee, Jane (2009) 'Developing qualitative research questions: A reflective process', *International Journal of Qualitative Studies in Education*, 22(4): 431–47.

Belk, Russell, Eileen Fischer, and Robert V. Kozinets (2013) *Qualitative Marketing and Consumer Research*. London: Sage.

White, Patrick (2017) *Developing Research Questions*. Basingstoke, Hampshire: Macmillan International Higher Education.

6

ETHICS: PROCEDURES AND FLOWCHARTS, UPDATES AND RULES

CHAPTER OVERVIEW

Ethical decisions will follow you throughout the process of conducting your netnography, presenting it, and perhaps even afterwards. Chapter 6 will carefully detail the need for and bases of ethical research standards in online ethnography. It will then discuss the consent gap, an important concept in which to ground your qualitative social media research practice. Following this, it will present an integrated flowchart to guide data collection and presentation procedures. The flowchart will help ensure that you understand how to make your practices comply with the current ethical standards governing online and ethnographic research. This chapter is not the end of the discussion about research ethics procedures in netnography, but the explanation of its presence throughout the range of netnographic research practices. It offers a general overview of research ethics that will set the groundwork for the inclusion of more detailed procedural treatments in later chapters on data collection and presentation.

ORIENTING TO ETHICS IN NETNOGRAPHY

Figure 6.1 Tom Bukowski, Second Life researcher; found on http://hplusmagazine. com/2011/02/21/tom-boellstorff-on-being-virtual/

In his award-winning book, Tom Boellstorff (2008) relates the ethnographic result of more than two years of fieldwork in Second Life, during which he 'lived among' and observed its residents in ways that are described as the same as the ways that anthropologists have traditionally done. As we can see from the picture in Figure 6.1, Boellstorff's ethnographic experience was a type of altered embodiment; he used a detailed, tattooed, bespectacled, stylish, and embodied virtual presence, an avatar named 'Tom Bukowski', and ethnographically investigated a number of sensitive issues in virtual sociality, including topics of sexuality, gender, race, finances, conflict, and antisocial behavior. In the interactions occurring during his online ethnography, Boellstorff/Bukowski was visible, as he is in the picture, as a social presence. However, he had to discover ways to ensure that the people he was interacting with in the virtual world were aware of his status as an online researcher and consented to being a part of his study.

During netnographic research, we are often not nearly as visible as Boellstorff was during his virtual world engagements. However, our research has the same capacity to be invasive. By observing and writing up that research, we open up the potential to expose, outrage, ridicule, and offend. Once we begin interacting with others online, we can mislead, misquote, and misrepresent. Online fieldwork is an opportunity to be a goodwill ambassador or an ignorant exploiter. With its mix of participation and observation, its sometimes uncomfortable emotional and relational closeness, and its traditions of distanced description and cultural revelation, traditional ethnographic inquiry has a long history of ethical issues in which almost every aspect of the research process has been problematized. Simply because the ethnographic researcher is physically present in social gatherings does not mean that disclosure has been full, fair, and accurate. Data gathering in ethnography has the potential to be intrusive, for example, by taking photographs and video recordings or by collecting artifacts that community members may not wish to subject to public or scientific scrutiny. Many of ethnography's ethical concerns arise from the manner in which cultures, communities, and the individuals who compose them are represented in scientific works. As Parker (2007: 2248) notes, ethical concepts such as respect, recognition, and dignity are often invoked in relation to ethnographic portrayals, and researchers' customary concept of 'negotiating' these concerns with research participants is obtuse and requires further ethical inquiry.

When we add the scale and anonymity of online experience and data to ethnography's particular thorny bramble bush, these already-difficult ethical issues become even more formidable. Online research works with the massive amounts of personal data that are inadvertently and often without their producers' volition or permission being created by people's interactions with various online platforms using their cell phones, laptops, desktops, tablets, set-top boxes, wearables, and other computing devices. These public digital signals are of great interest not only to academic researchers across the sciences, but also to technology companies such as Google and Facebook whose business models are based on advertising, and to government agencies who find in this wave of data major opportunities to enact public policies for the common good, including using them for public surveillance in the name of security. In recent years, with travesties such as the Cambridge Analytica abuse of Facebook data and social media users' goodwill, social media research and its ethical conundrums have been cast into the limelight. Data security, privacy, and confidentiality have become important matters of public concern, subject to important new legislation in the European Union.

Figure 6.2 reveals that netnography's key concerns lie squarely in between the complex ethical issues of traditional ethnography and those of social media research. At the current time, there are enough general resources available about online research ethics that we can construct a view of a specific one for netnography. Significant amounts of new research and literature have emerged in the past decade to enlighten our perspective on what constitutes ethical online research and ethical online versions of ethnography, including netnography. Although a perfect consensus on these matters will probably never exist, we currently have clear guidelines that allow netnographic research to proceed. How should you navigate research ethics questions in netnography? What concrete actions should you take? How should you represent those decisions to governing bodies? These are questions that we now have the ability to answer clearly. This chapter is therefore intended to provide you with one of the most comprehensive treatments of ethics in online ethnography available anywhere. To begin building our understanding of this sensitive topic in an empathic and personal way, try to complete the exercise in Box 6.1, which asks you to introspect about your own public social media profile, and how you would feel about other researchers using it in their investigations.

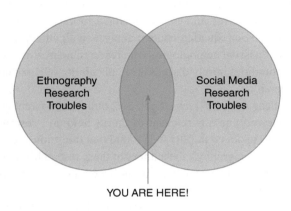

YOU ARE HERE!

Figure 6.2 Orienting to ethics in netnography

INTROSPECTING ABOUT ONLINE ETHICS

6.1

Go online and then have a look at some of your public profiles, comments, and posts on social media such as Facebook, LinkedIn, Twitter, Instagram, or YouTube. How might a researcher use your publicly-posted information in a research study? What kind of research study do you think your public profile and posts might inform?

Write out the title of the research study. Then, give it a very personal title (Your Name): Portrait of a (Description), or (Your Name): Social Media (Description).

How would you feel about seeing your name and your posts or comments used in this way? What if your name was not attached to the research, but your personal information (age, gender, interests, perhaps political affiliation or sexual orientation) was included, alongside direct quotes from your posts and comments? Would this be acceptable to you, or would it violate your trust? Can you explain your response? What issues does it raise? How does it feel to be the subject of a detailed examination of your social media traces?

The Need for Ethical Standards in Netnography

Excellent resources have been available for over two decades to help online ethnographic researchers navigate the ethical standards of their work. Yet many authors, reviewers, and editors of peer-reviewed journals seem to be ignorant or dismissive of these important resources. Costello et al. (2017: 5) looked at how other researchers had adapted the established 'netnography process', and found that a number of research studies omitted the 'ethical standards' portion. They found confusion about whether the ethical guidelines were 'inappropriately rigorous' to use as 'general guidelines' for what some researchers considered a form of 'content analysis'. They concluded that 'this logic [equating content analysis with ethnography] may explain why practitioners of passive netnography, who research nonrestricted communication within online communities, rarely discuss the applicability of Kozinets' ethical guidelines to their research'.

Tuikka and colleagues (2017) investigated 52 online ethnographies that were published in peer-reviewed journals relevant to the IS field and described their ethical practices. Although Tuikka et al. (2017: 3) found that the studies 'use research methods which resemble netnography', the authors of these research studies describe them with a variety of different names, including online ethnography, virtual ethnography, cyber-ethnography, and digital ethnography. A significant number did not name the type of research they were doing at all. Most surprising of all was the finding that the standards of ethical research practice they followed were highly variable. Tuikka et al. describe a number of journal articles that exhibited questionable ethical practices, such as violating norms of confidentiality or including direct quotes of a sensitive nature that could be traced back to original sources. Extrapolating from the study, the variety of methodological approach names may be connected to the variety of, and use of, questionable ethical research practices.

Tuikka et al.'s conclusion paints a rather dire portrait of the ethical awareness of peer-reviewed and published netnographies:

> This review has led us to find out that not many researchers seem to be all that interested in – at least disclosing their – ethical practices relating to netnography. Most (38 papers) do not seem to concern themselves with the topic at all, and we are left with only 16 papers in which the ethicality of the research is deemed of such importance that it is worth mentioning. (2017: 9)

A full 70% of the published online ethnographies examined did not offer *any* disclosure of their ethical practices! The authors resolved that 'The field of IS research is clearly in need of ethical guidelines which do not rely only on traditional ethnography inspired ethical guidelines, as the environment, especially when conducting the research on the internet typically does not seem to coincide with the kinds of closed environments often studied in traditional ethnography.'

Unfortunately, research that positions itself as an 'online ethnography' has no pre-existing standards or procedures, other than a general orientation towards cultural understanding gained through some form of participant–observation, qualitative data gathering, and interpretive analysis. 'Online ethnography' is a generic term for a general category that fails to provide a methodological framework, and particular to our purposes, *does not explain what ethical research procedures were followed in the research.* As Tuikka et al. (2017) note above, this procedural information is especially crucial in regard to matters of research ethics. With only 30% of studies mentioning their adherence to good ethical research practices, there is a major information deficit to overcome. This is a problem not only for researchers to address, but also for institutional review boards, journal reviewers, and editors. Each of these institutional players must become educated about acceptable current standards and practices. As legislation tightens, these are not simply internal matters of university business, but may also become legal concerns that expose the institution and perhaps the individual to liability for harm. By using the guidelines provided in this chapter, and by clearly citing work that illustrates and explains the ethical standards to which it complies, you not only elevate your work above that of the 70% who did not mention it, you also handle those ethical concerns appropriately and meet a higher standard.

Although this level of ethical reporting laxity seems to have been accepted by journals and reviewers in the past, it may not (and should not) continue into the future. To be ready, you might start to think about some of the important ethical questions you would need to answer when conducting and reporting findings from a netnography. The best way to understand research ethics is to understand their true nature and their origins in moral philosophies and the disgraceful history of unethical medical experimentation. To gain this understanding, you can find a summary listing some of the most important questions to consider in Box 6.2.

RELEVANT ETHICAL QUESTIONS IN NETNOGRAPHY

6.2

Conducting a netnography that is both ethical and effective is important. With Human Subjects Research reviews, Institutional Review Boards, and complex legislation like the European Union's General Data Protection Regulation (GDPR), ethics in netnography is dynamic and complex. Some of the ethical concerns that are relevant to netnographic inquiry include:

- Are online social interactions private or public?
- What roles do corporations like Facebook, Google, and Twitter play in our research? Do they have a say in what we are ethically or legally permitted to do with the data from their platforms?
- How do we gain the informed consent of people in online environments?

(Continued)

- How do we deal with information published on corporate news sites or websites, general blogs, blogs by famous people, and other online forums?
- Should we use conversations that we participate in or 'overhear' during group chats?
- Are there different ethical rules for different types and sites of online media?
- Do age and vulnerability matter online? In media in which identity is difficult to verify, how can we be sure about the age or vulnerability of research participants?
- Do international boundaries influence the way a netnographer collects data and publishes research? Do new international rules like the EU's GDPR legislation apply to netnographies conducted outside this geographical area?

These are vital questions. The answers will help you formulate guidelines for your research to keep it ethical while maintaining its accuracy and rigour. In this chapter, we will offer answers to these questions and formulate research tactics based on the latest information. However, these matters are constantly changing. Thus, you should also stay current with the latest readings on research ethics that can affect your netnography. The information and guidelines in this chapter are an excellent place to start.

Moral Roots I: Deontological Ethics

Morality is a choice of right behavior over wrong. Moral reasoning is how we come to make those choices rationally. Ethics is both the brand of knowledge that studies moral principles and those moral principles themselves. Ethics as a scientific field wraps a humanist, procedural, and calculative frame onto human behaviors. Religious teachings tell us which are right behaviors and which are wrong: those teachings tend to be deontological in their focus – they speak of absolutes, of sacred acts and objects that must never be profaned, of behaviors which are always wrong. Some examples are sacrilegiously desanctifying a holy word by taking the Lord's name in vain, failing to honor the Sabbath day, and the inability or unwillingness to love thy neighbor as thyself such as a true Christian would do. Deontologies are also ontologies, they create realities – and split them: de-ontologies. Right principle, right thinking, right action is cleaved from wrong. From a cultural perspective, we can see that deontologies are not moral absolutes, but the beliefs of certain groups, certain peoples, at certain times. They are intimately related to cultures, their customs, histories, and traditions, including research cultures.

Deontological ethical procedures prescribe the morality of an action to be right or wrong based on whether it adheres to or violates a prescribed set of rules: 'You Shall

Have No Other Gods Before Me'. This, the Judeo-Christian first commandment, is not contingent. There is no 'unless' clause which follows. No 'under these conditions you can worship human money or power, status or celebrity instead of worshipping me' section, with footnotes. The deontological view is about duty – following the rules, not calculating ways around them: 'You Shall Not Commit Adultery'. Period, full stop.

Deontological ethical systems of moral reasoning do not need to be religious. They might hold sway at a social or civic level. For instance, multiple peoples have held that committing genocide or polluting a major waterway is always wrong, regardless of the reasons. Murdering an entire religion, or an entire ethnic group, is a despicable thought and an almost unthinkable objective, one which can never, ever be justified.

We see the deontological approach in the principles-based views of research ethics, including online research ethics. For example, Morris (2016) follows this approach to provide five of the most commonly accepted guiding principles of ethical research, which follow:

- *Autonomy*: the research participant should be as aware as possible of the purpose of the research; participants should be free to agree or decline to take part in the research, or to withdraw at any time without coercion, threat, or penalty.

- *Beneficence*: the research should be beneficial, rigorously designed and conducted, and have positive effects.

- *Non-maleficence*: the researcher must make diligent efforts to avoid possible harm to participants and mitigate any unavoidable harm through precautionary measures.

- *Confidentiality*: participants' personal data must be kept private from everyone except those with a strict need to know.

- *Integrity*: the researcher must disclose any actual or potential conflicts of interest and conduct every aspect of the research using applicable and legitimate standards of research integrity.

These five 'principles' seem on the surface to be deontological. Autonomy, beneficence, non-maleficence, confidentiality, and integrity all suggest that the researcher has a clear sense that some actions are moral, and others are not.

Deontological ethics can also apply to online ethnography and its ethical practices. For example, Kantanen and Manninen (2016: 91–2) find that 'Several authors are unequivocal about identity deception, such as Kozinets (2010): "Netnographers should never, under any circumstances, engage in identity deception" (p. 147).' A deontological, or rule-bound, approach to online ethnography might hold that being deceptive about who you are or why you are communicating with someone on social media is a clear violation of research ethics, regardless of the reasons why such an action is being performed.

There are still many open questions, however, regarding whether violating someone's privacy, or going against their personal wishes about what to do with their online data, is unequivocally and always absolutely wrong. As we will see in the section following, research related to the consent gap makes it very clear that a significant number of people – very likely a majority – would prefer that researchers should not use their social media data and information in their investigations. This would suggest some moral absolutes about people's privacy when they interact online might be in effect. And in a very neoliberal sense, as more of the public become aware of and exercise more control over their own data through adjusting their (often rather hidden and complicated) privacy settings, people do take charge of their own privacy and make absolute choices which we must honor. Are these changes enough? Deontological ethics are not really our concern here, although they might become important and worth debating soon (see Box 6.3). The major concern of anyone practicing netnography today in academia is consequentialist ethics, the root and foundation of our university and legal system.

6.3 DEBATING DEONTOLOGICAL ETHICS

Ethics is a matter of beliefs. Can you think of any moral absolutes which are beyond question? What would they be? Are there no conditions under which your moral absolutes can be questioned? Are there any contingencies under which it is acceptable or even appropriate that your moral rule could be bent or broken? Please discuss with a classmate or colleague. Then report back to the class or to an ethics group (you will find more on the founding and conduct of ethics groups later in this chapter).

Moral Roots II: Consequentialist Ethics

We have seen how deontological ethics are about moral absolutes: 'Thou Shalt Not Steal'. Consequentialist ethics are far more contingent. Unlike deontological ethics, which hold that actions such as stealing can be right or wrong in themselves, consequentialist ethics judge the morality of an action based upon estimates and arguments about likely consequences. Rooted in the notion that the end justifies the means, a consequentialist view of ethics might say that stealing is okay, if it is to save someone who would otherwise die, or even yourself if you are starving. The same level of argumentation can be applied to conclude that some genocides or major pollution events are ethical if they can be shown to result in some greater good (e.g., a more healthy gene pool, major economic benefits for the area, jobs, jobs, jobs). As a more realistic example, we generally consider killing people to be wrong (which is a deontological view). However, we might conclude that it is moral to proactively go out and kill terrorists because we will save many more lives by doing so. That sense that you are saving many people by sacrificing a far fewer number is the very essence of Mill's utilitarianism, itself an excellent instance of the application of consequentialist moral thinking.

As you will see in this chapter, contemporary research ethics are based on a consequentialist view of moral reasoning. Researchers are expected to be able to estimate the harms and benefits of particular research actions, such as exposing sensitive topics, and then to act in a manner that reflects the greater good. We can see how informed consent, which is one of the foundations of ethical research practice, may seem to be a deontological principle. In other words, we might assume that individuals who post on social media must provide informed consent before we can use their data. As the research in the next section related to the consent gap makes very clear, a significant number of people – very likely a majority – would prefer that researchers did not use their social media data and information in their investigations. However, the informed consent rules that we enact are actually based upon the moral reasoning of consequentialist ethics. The duty to gather informed consent can be violated when there is a strong enough reason, such as public safety or information about an important matter. The same sorts of consequentialist arguments are routinely used to justify the use of deception in scientific experiments.

However, we know from history that simply because a consequentialist moral code is used, widespread, and convenient, this does not actually make it just. Further complicating matters, there are national and regional differences in ethics codes and regulations, and even principles. Kantanen and Manninen (2016: 91) suggest that 'in the U.S., a utilitarian stance may prevail, meaning that benefits to society are weighed against potential risks; whereas in Central and Northern Europe, a deontological or communitarian stance that does not compromise confidentiality and anonymity may be taken'. Deontological codes also tend to be associated more with religions that consider certain actions intolerably profane, and others ineffably sacred. Deontological religious legal codes such as chopping someone's hand off for stealing may not seem moral to many other ethical codes, or to consequentialist bargains such as making the punishment fit the crime.

The history of social media demonstrates how the vital and vibrant, meaningful and communal actions of people using online communications over the last fifty years have been increasingly colonized, profaned, and exploited by corporate and governmental interests and their armies of capital and labor. Consequentialist thinking applied to data-security issues may have been applied to move ethical standards such as informed consent and access to privacy settings such that they favor economic growth in the data sales sector alongside managerial convenience. As of 2019, matters regarding data ownership, public values on privacy, and data security are most definitely not settled. At some point in the future, the populist desire of the public for more control over their personal information may come to play a much greater role in the way social media data is treated by institutional actors, including social science researchers.

6.4 IDENTIFYING CONSEQUENTIALIST AND DEONTOLOGICAL THINKING

Which of the following seven statements are consequentialist, and which are deontological? Mark each one with a C or a D.

C/D

1. Deceiving research participants is sometimes necessary for a study to work. ☐

2. Informed consent forms must always be used when interviewing participants. ☐

3. Data should always be kept in a locked box, where only the researcher and her team have the key. ☐

4. Some embarrassment of community members may follow the public exposure of these crazy events that happened on their web forum; however, we can gain a lot of knowledge from them. ☐

5. Ensure than no minors under the age of 16 are included in your research. ☐

6. Naturalistic interactions should always be open, honest, and truthful. ☐

7. Having a complete set of permissions is not always possible, but that need not stop you from doing netnographic research. ☐

Answers: 1C, 2D, 3D, 4C, 5D, 6D, 7C

THE CONSENT GAP IN SOCIAL MEDIA RESEARCH

Over the years, it has become apparent to me that there is a serious problem with social media research that uses publicly available data, such as netnography. I call this problem *the consent gap*. It goes like this. In written and presented work that uses social media data, academics often insist that, when people post things on public facing web applications like Instagram or Twitter, they already know that what they are posting is public. They usually say something like, 'It's [insert year here], of course people know that the Internet is public!' Sometimes, they will compare quoting online data to quoting from a letter to the editor in a newspaper. As Zimmer (2010) notes in his examination of a careless research handling of Facebook data, many researchers simply assume that social media data is 'already public'. I would estimate that at least 90% of all social media researchers believe that the following statement is true: because almost everyone knows that social media is public, there is little need to ask social media posters' permission to use their posts.

In short, the consent gap is the difference between the ascribed and actual beliefs about social media users regarding the need for permission in the research-related use of the information they share online. It may be true at this point in history that most people do know that their online postings and information can be read in that form by members of the general public. However, the fact that people know that their postings are public does not automatically lead to the conclusion that they are also granting their automatic unspoken consent for academics and other types of researchers to use this data in any way they please. As well, we really don't know what *most* people means. If 51% of them know, that is quite different from if this was 95% of them. And it still leaves wide open the very important ethical question of consent.

The History and Present of Major Platform User Consent

In fact, research on the matters shows that the public have a long history of being displeased with this use of their data. LeBesco (2004) reported that, in a single month, eight researchers tried to gain access to a particular online community site, and all but one was rejected by the group. Bakardjieva (2005) voiced her frustration with recruiting respondents through announcements on online newsgroups, a tactic she later abandoned. In a summary, Johns et al. (2003: 159) stated that 'many list owners and newsgroup members deeply resent the presence of researchers and journalists in their groups'. And in an article pithily titled 'Go Away', Hudson and Bruckman (2004) related that people in chatrooms reacted with hostility when they were aware of being studied by researchers, and that when those people were given the opportunity to become part of the research, only four out of 766 potential participants chose to do so. Granted, this was 2004, and ancient history in terms of social media time. But it is difficult to ignore that the research opt-in rate they found was only one half of 1%! The other early studies confirm the suspicion and even outright hostility of social media users in the Age of Virtual Community.

Fortunately, we now have more recent data to examine. In an extraordinarily detailed and helpful review of 17 studies that examined the ethical concerns of social media users, Golder et al. (2017) found a range of different views expressed. Despite the variegation, their findings clearly show that social media users expected privacy in their ostensibly personal and private communications. Three studies were most salient. Although there is some variance in technique and result, in all of these studies, large percentages of social media users expressed concerns about using their social media posts as research data. The study in which participants were most forgiving was conducted among adolescent student Facebook users in a university setting using a face-to-face interview method. In that study, Moreno et al. (2012: 5) revealed that 29% said they had a neutral attitude towards the practice of being recruited using their public Facebook profile, 9% were 'uneasy', and 6% were 'concerned'. Thus, in a situation with potentially stronger demand effects, the researchers still found 44% of the students expressing various degrees of concern over the research use of their social media data.

Other studies among more general samples revealed even higher proportions of concern. In an online survey of 554 people, Williams (2015: 10) found that 46% of respondents were 'slightly concerned' with the idea of university researchers using their social media information for research purposes, 11% were 'quite concerned' and 5% were 'very concerned'. That is 62% expressing varying levels of concern. The percentage of 'very concerned' responses rose to 22% when the researcher was described as 'commercial' (p. 12) and 24% when the researcher was described as 'government' (p. 11). A full 55% agreed that they 'expected to be asked for informed consent' if their social media data was included in an academic publication (p. 13). Similarly, in their survey of 268 Twitter users, Fiedler and Proferes (2018) found that 67% expressed some degree of discomfort with the idea that their post was used in a research study without them being informed at all (with 35% saying it made them feel 'very uncomfortable').

Platform Users Think in Contingent, Consequentialist Ways as Well

In comprehensive and wide-ranging secondary and primary research, Evans et al. (2015: 5) found clear evidence 'that public perceptions of how their data should be used do not align with the [then-current, pre-GDPR] regulatory and legal frameworks'. From on 'an online quantitative survey of 1,250 adults aged 16–75 in the UK asking about people's attitudes towards possible uses of their social media data', the researchers found that only 38% of the people surveyed thought that 'sharing social media data with third parties for the purposes of research currently happened under the terms and conditions they sign up to on social media sites' (p. 6). Furthermore, a full 60% of the survey respondents believed that their social media data should not be shared for research purposes.

There is a rather startling alignment between the three studies indicating that large numbers of social media users are apprehensive about the idea of their social media data being used for research purposes. In all of them, between about 40% and 60% express various levels of concern and unease with this notion. (For a study showing the same sort of consent gap in mobile phone users and their data, see Martin and

Shilton, 2016.) As these findings already indicate, there are many contingencies and complexities involved in the situation.

Golder et al. (2017) found in their overview of 17 studies that social media users are more amenable to their traces being used in research if they are being put towards a good cause, and if the benefits outweighed the risks. Users were generally aware of those risks too, listing these as being identifiable in the research, being subject to ridicule, and taking verbal quotes out of context. They thought that vulnerable populations such as children, teenagers, people with mental health issues, those talking about sensitive topics, and the deceased all needed extra levels of protection. They favored university researchers over the research of students, government, or industry. But they also expressed a level of apathy, a feeling that they could not do much to affect the outcome of the social media research process.

Apathy is a frightening emotion, because it is the lack of enough commitment to feel a solid emotion. We might relate this sense of apathy to these people's general sense that their rights to their own information and privacy are being violated, but that they are also becoming inured to this new reality. If this is the case, then the consent gap is a powerful concept that we may need to measure more precisely (e.g., by measuring and comparing online researcher attitudes to the same social media publics they research). The consent gap might help us appreciate the way that consequentialist ethical formations are favored over deontological ones in contemporary research ethics formulations. Changes in the consent gap might signal crises in the legitimacy of research or science institutionally, or a problem with the moral codes of researchers. All of these important elements of the consent gap should probably be monitored – as a way for scientists to keep their finger on the pulse of the many social realities expressed through social media, and thus through netnography.

The Consent Gap in Netnography

As the deontological and consequentialist arguments of the prior sections suggest, the consent gap is an important concept that I believe should ground ethical practice in netnography. From the beginning, I have emphasized people's general wariness towards the use of their information: 'The consumers who originally created the data do not necessarily intend or welcome the data's use in research representations' (Kozinets, 2002a: 65). That statement seems to be just as true today as when I wrote it almost twenty years ago. The simple fact that many of the people posting on social media expect their data to be kept private is not, of course, the determinative factor in netnographic research ethics. As this chapter will explain, under the current ethical research system governing academic research, there are many other considerations that are weighted into ethical decisions and protocols, such as the potential for public benefit, and the advancement of social and scientific knowledge.

Despite all of the above, I believe that the discrepancies between the public opinion of the consent gap and our research practice will come back to haunt us. The more misaligned our assumptions are about permission and consent from those of the people whose conversations, comments, and posts we appropriate in order to study, the more due we are for some kind of regulatory or legislative correction. That is why I try to keep the consent gap in mind when making ethical discussions in my netnographic research projects. I try to err on the side of consideration by building in extra information for social media users, and extra opportunities to gather their permission and consent wherever possible. I try to think like the person whose data I am interpreting. I try to use my empathic organ, activating the mirror neurons in my head and heart. As you encounter ethical decisions in your own research, I recommend that you also keep the implications of the consent gap in mind.

AN ETHICAL PROCESS FOR DATA COLLECTION IN NETNOGRAPHIC RESEARCH

Is Netnography Human Subjects Research?

In most institutions, ethics reviews are triggered based upon whether the research is considered human subjects research, or not. Much of the debate about Internet research ethics is concerned with whether we should treat computer-mediated interactions as if they took place in either a public or a private space. This spatial metaphor is commonly applied to the Internet and seems, in fact, to be a fundamental human cognition (Munt, 2001). According to the Protection of Human Subjects, US Code of Federal Regulations Title 45, Part 46 (2009), which governs Institutional Review Boards in the United States, the following definition pertains:

> Human subjects research is research in which there is an intervention or interaction with another person for the purpose of gathering information, or in which information is recorded by a researcher in such a way that a person can be identified through it directly or indirectly. (US Department of Health & Human Services, 2009)

The complexity of both the online environment and the method is such that netnography should be treated as if it were human subjects research and should be sent out for ethical reviews as if it were. Here is the reasoning. Although social interactions as they have been captured in social media archives, such as historical Twitter feed or comments on YouTube videos that stretch back for years, do not constitute human subjects research per se, they would become human subjects research, according to Title 45, Part 46's (2009) definition, the moment that a real person could be identified through it 'directly or indirectly'. The modality of the online medium, in which people can use search engines to query verbata from public data and thus track down people's identities, creates a more demanding environment than one in which the text used derived from private archival or interview documents whose access could be controlled by the researcher. Furthermore, many netnographic research projects will expand into interaction with online participants. Netnographers do this once they make a comment, like a post, direct message or email someone they met through the research, request or conduct an interview, or through a variety of online communications that are very simple to enact (e.g., just a mouse click, or a few typed words and a smartphone's return key push), but which have major implications when considered in light of the question of human subjects research.

After considering the question, Kantanen and Manninen (2016: 90) also conclude, as I do, that most netnography is human subjects research. In a very helpful exploration of online ethnography's 'hazy ethical boundaries', the authors describe in some detail their netnographic research project on a LinkedIn group devoted to higher education, and the various steps they took to ensure that it was conducted in an ethical manner. These ethical procedures, which took them the inordinately long period of eighteen months to complete, included the following practices, among others:

- applying to their university's Committee on Research Ethics for an ethics review;

- seeking moderator approval for studying the LinkedIn group;

- seeking approval from the LinkedIn group's own Institutional Review Board (which is very unusual);

- discussing their study's informed consent procedures with forum founders, administrators, and group moderators;

- using a 'light disguise' (Bruckman, 2002) cloaking procedure to disguise poster names and identifiers (see Chapter 14 of this book for details).

In summary, if we are doing any interviewing or online interaction (e.g., asking someone some questions in a chat), the inquiry is immediately human subjects research. Posting and then replying to comments on the posts? This is human subjects research. Even making a comment or liking a comment or post conceivably moves your research from being passive and observational to being interactive. Working only with archives of past comments – this is a gray area. It is made less gray by the fact that data from those archives might be used, even indirectly, to identify the people who posted the comments. Another key consideration is impact. Published and publicized research can have an impact upon individual persons, online groups, and upon society. The published or publicized research itself then becomes a source of interaction with people, not simply the researcher conducting the research.

Because we might be contacting and conversing with individual persons in netnographic research, we need to utilize the human subjects moral reasoning framework, and pay even closer attention to whether the population is vulnerable, the data is confidential or sensitive, or whether the research reveals potentially personally identifiable information – and then take appropriate steps. The remainder of this chapter will present and explain a framework of the appropriate steps to take in order to effectively handle the ethical challenges of netnography as a form of human subjects research.

An Ethics Process for Netnography

Ethics need to follow your research project from the beginning right through to the very end. Not only do ethical concerns follow you around as you gather data from public sites and contact and interview people, they are also ever-present, involving the presentation of your data and even the way that you disclose and interpret things about the people who have posted the online comments you are citing.

In the last chapter you learned about the six stages of netnography: initiation of the project, investigation of the online sites, immersion in the data sites, interaction with conversants, integration of the analysis and interpretation of the results, and incarnation of the research presentation. Initiation and incarnation are the beginning and ending of the process, and integration works with the data. But investigation, immersion, and interaction create the dataset in a netnography, through archival downloading, immersion journal noting, and computer-mediated communications, respectively. There are three distinct kinds of netnographic data-collection procedure: (1) archival search and save, (2) the capture of your own personal notes, observations, and screen captures, and (3) direct communications with people either on a public platform or through a more private medium like direct messaging or email. These three categories of data – which I call investigative, immersive, and interactive – shape the exact ethical procedures that you would follow if you were utilizing the flowchart in Figure 6.3.

Applying the Ethics Process Flowchart

The figure's flowchart will guide your general decision making in netnography, and each general step in the ethics procedure is overviewed in an upcoming table. Following the figure's directions carefully will help you answer the important ethical questions raised in Box 6.1. Some of the aspects of these decisions will not make complete sense until you have completed working your way through this book. However, this chapter is provided at the outset of your investigation because of the importance of keeping these matters in mind throughout the process. Using a flowchart such as this one is never a linear or simple process because every netnography is different. There will undoubtedly be ad hoc decisions that will be required in the course of doing your netnographic research. But as much as possible you will want to anticipate and prepare for the issues you can handle in advance, and try to be ready for the ones that you cannot. Gaining familiarity with and consulting a flowchart

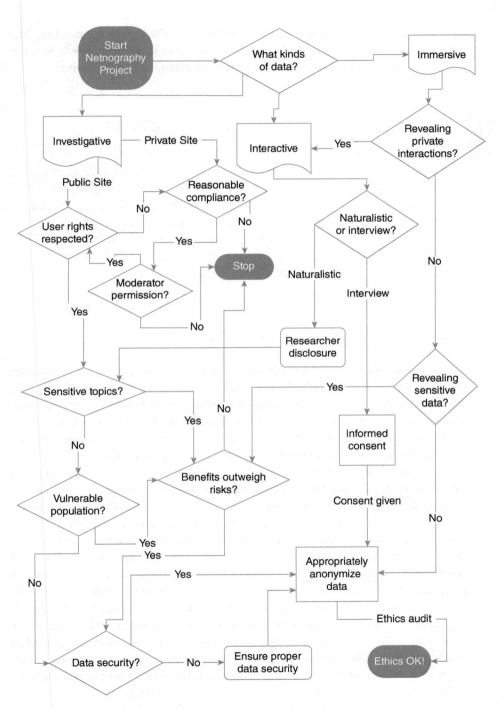

Figure 6.3 A research ethics process flowchart for netnography

such as this one allows ethical questions to be dealt with, whenever possible, in a proactive and deliberate manner. Indeed, the review processes for academic research at many institutions around the world promote an anticipatory perspective.

6.5 INITIAL ETHICAL STEPS IN YOUR NETNOGRAPHY

Using your research question as an initial guide, work your way through Figure 6.3: A research ethics process flowchart for netnography. What ethical issues can you anticipate from this flowchart? Which ones are probably not going to be relevant to your project? Write down and keep track of these initial impressions. As we progress through this book, you will likely often find yourself returning to this flowchart in order to help you structure and understand the procedural decisions you must make in the course of your netnography, and their likely ethical consequences.

Ethics in the Process of Netnography

The doing part of research ethics happens in context, as part of the enacting of research practices. That is how they will be presented throughout the remainder of this book. An ethical stance alters data collection most of all, but it also transforms sampling choices (and therefore analysis) as well as changing the way that data is presented. Therefore, the various elements of the ethics flowchart depicted in Figure 6.3 are worked into the remainder of the text as part of their respective procedures.

Once you begin your netnographic project, you will start collecting data. There are three distinct kinds of netnographic data-collection procedure, which will be covered in depth in the next four chapters of this book. The first is investigative, which involves archival search and saving or storing the results. The second is interactive, which involves direct communications, such as commenting conversationally in a thread or sending a direct message. The third is immersive, and involves the researcher's creation of personal notes that include such things as observations, budding ideas, and screen captures. In practice, all three kinds of data collection often intermingle. Some researchers will only collect investigative data, conducting what has been called the 'observational netnography' (e.g., Brown et al., 2003) without apparent immersion journal notes or interview data. Many will combine data collection from archives with some interviews and online interaction, thus using investigative and interactive data-collection procedures. Some might only reflect upon their online experiences in detailed fieldnotes and data captures, as Kozinets and Kedzior (2009) did with their Second Life netnography.

These categories of data – investigative, interactive, and immersive – shape the exact ethical procedures you need to follow depending on which of the three you are collecting at the time. However, the ethics guidelines in the flowchart are intended to be used additively. Even if the netnography is mainly investigative with only a small amount of interaction, the ethical routines for investigative as well as interactive data collection would need to be followed. They would be followed as data is collected and afterwards, when it must be interpreted. Later on, you will prepare that data for presentation. In the incarnation movement of a netnography, data is anonymized in an appropriate manner, and then an overarching ethics audit can be conducted.

Table 6.1 is presented to enable an overview and greater understanding of the separate elements of the netnography ethics flowchart depicted in Figure 6.3. Table 6.1 provides the name of the research ethics concept, its definition, some brief summary guidance regarding its application in netnography, and then a page reference to guide you to the section in this book where the ethical principle is explained in context as part of the netnography research process. As you encounter the research operation in the text and learn about how to enact it, you will also learn the appropriate ethical procedure to perform at that stage.

Combining Figure 6.3 and Table 6.1 will provide a structure to methodically guide you through each of these data-collection procedures. Before implementing any of them, you may wish to consult with the more detailed developments in the text at the pages indicated in the fourth column of Table 6.1. In the following sections, I will make some more general comments about the importance of following good ethical research practices in netnography.

ETHICS, EMPATHY, AND MORALITY

As well as invoking the humanism often found in contemporary social science, I have also drawn on a few religious metaphors and examples in this chapter in order to ground research ethics in a sense of heightened significance. To approach research ethics in a Buddhist way means remaining reflective throughout all the stages of our investigation, seeing our research work as an extension of our attempt to live a moral life. It means that we approach all things we do in the world, including and especially our careers, carefully and with rules to guide us so that we avoid causing through it the suffering of the other living beings with whom we interact. Throughout all religions, it seems that moral guidance of a deontological variety is necessary in order to avoid causing ostensibly 'necessary' (i.e., consequentialist, and usually inflicted on others) pain and suffering.

These deontological ethics continue to guide my approach to online ethnography, although the current research milieu favors – or perhaps more accurately *requires* – a more consequentialist position based on economic-style trade-offs between the projected harmful costs to individuals and benefits to society. The guidelines I offer in this chapter are certainly not the only approach to online ethnographic research ethics. In fact, it is useful for readers to be exposed to other opinions and to make informed choices of their own.

Table 6.1 Research ethics concepts applied to netnography

Research Ethics Concept	Definition	Guidance to Application in Netnography	For more detailed information, see page(s) in text
Public site	Online platform or web application that has open access to the public, does not require registration or password login, and is usually indexed by and accessible using common search engines such as Google	Public sites present public data that has been shared under conditions that do not require special ethical procedures for netnographic study	197–199
Private site	Online platform or web application that requires some kind of registration or password login, and is not indexed by and accessible using common search engines such as Google	Private sites require extra levels of ethical procedure for netnographic study, potentially including reasonable compliance with platform policies, researcher disclosure, and moderator permission	197–199
User rights	All platform and web application users have legal and ethical rights regarding research and research use of data, which are constantly changing and differ according to national law and academic custom	Netnographers should stay responsibly informed about general user rights as well as the specific rights accorded to platforms and web applications used in the research project	198–199, 219
Reasonable compliance	Specific procedures negotiated with authorities in charge of the data on private platforms	When using private sites, netnographers must negotiate the procedures that constitute reasonable compliance with the site's policies prior to engaging in study	198–201
Moderator permission	Permission to study a private data site, granted by an authority or official of the data site	When using private sites, netnographers must gain moderator permission in writing prior to engaging in the study	198–201
Sensitive topics	Discussion topics, texts, images, or other data that reveal personally sensitive information such as stigmatized behaviors, images of the body, illegal acts, and sexual behaviors	The use of netnographic data that depict sensitive topics must be justified by an initial assessment of benefits versus risks, and then handled in special ways, including providing extra levels of data security and anonymizing the data and site	232, 303–304

Research Ethics Concept	Definition	Guidance to Application in Netnography	For more detailed information, see page(s) in text
Vulnerable population	Populations who are unable to give full consent, such as children, teenagers, people with mental health issues, and the deceased	The use of netnographic data from vulnerable populations must be justified by an initial assessment of benefits versus risks, and then handled in special ways, including gathering an extra level of informed consent, providing extra levels of data security, and anonymizing the data and site	232–233, 303–304
Data security	The steps taken to ensure that only appropriate individuals involved in the research project have access to its sensitive or confidential data	Depending upon the sensitivity of the data and the need to protect participant and informant identities, data-security operations can include password protection, encryption, and sensitive data storage on a dedicated external hard-drive which is kept in a locked location	235–236
Benefits	An assessment, performed by the researcher, of the potential benefits to participants, science, and society accruing from conduct and completion of the research project	Benefits assessment in netnography is a consequentialist ethics-based procedure that often attempts to describe the public benefits from a greater understanding of online behaviors, specific groups, and their particulars	234–235
Risks	An assessment, performed by the researcher, of the potential risks, mostly to participants, perhaps to the research platform, and sometimes to future researchers, accruing from conduct and completion of the research project	Risk assessment in netnography is a consequentialist ethics-based procedure that should attempt to understand, value, and describe potential personal and datasite disclosure and its impact on particular people and specific groups	234–235
Researcher disclosure	The public disclosure of the identity and presence of a researcher studying a particular online site, usually accompanied by a general description of the purpose and possible value of the research	Researcher disclosure is necessary when interacting in any way with other persons online (e.g., liking a comment, replying, posting); disclosure often occurs through a post combined with sending people to a more detailed profile or separate web-page	199–201

(Continued)

Table 6.1 (Continued)

Research Ethics Concept	Definition	Guidance to Application in Netnography	For more detailed information, see page(s) in text
Informed consent	The granting of knowledgeable permission to be researched by those who are being researched, the acceptance of the terms of the research engagement by someone who is fully apprized by the researcher about those terms	Permission is usually not necessary when dealing with publicly available data; informed consent is essential whenever there will be direct personal interaction between researcher and participant, as with an interview or in situ engagement	268–275
Anonymizing data	Providing pseudonymous new names for people who are cited in research so that their identity is not exposed and cannot be determined from the data by a reasonably motivated individual	Quoted public online data can easily be backtraced from a netnography using a search engine; additional safeguards may be required to change the name of online sites, as well as altering data so that it is no longer traceable to original quotes	396–403
Uncloaked data	No changes made to the presented identity of social media posters, other research participants, and the precise contents of their traces	Where risks are minimal or the quoted information is from a public figure, the online pseudonym or the real name of the poster or participant is revealed in the research representation and their data is presented intact and unchanged	398–399
Cloaked data	Reasonable safeguards taken to conceal the presented identity of social media posters, other research participants, and the precise contents of their traces	Where risks are low to moderate (a situation that will cover the vast majority of cases), the social media site of the traces is mentioned, but actual names, pseudonyms, identifiers, and verbata are altered to prevent identification	399–400
Highly cloaked data	Strong efforts made to conceal the presented identity of social media posters, other research participants, and the precise contents of their traces	Where risks are high, social media site, actual names, and pseudonyms are all altered before being presented, verbatim quotes are either changed or not used, and fabrication strategies may be employed	399–403

YOUR RESPONSIBILITY IN NETNOGRAPHY FOR ETHICS

Regarding a more general principle of qualitative inquiry, a netnography should try to sensitively reflect a concern for the perspective of those it seeks to understand. I have always recommended taking the ethical high road in research even if that means, in the early years, taking positions on research procedures that might seem overly restrictive by today's standards (or, as recent GDPR rules, and the public sentiment of the consent gap indicate, perhaps not). It is important to follow the ethical guidelines of netnography rigorously, and not to pick and choose particular references where you might find them convenient. Calling your work a netnography and citing methodological guides to netnography such as this book means that you believe this is the correct stance to take as well.

In the past, some authors have published work that recommended revisiting netnography's allegedly over-restrictive ethical guidelines. One article, which I will not spotlight with a mention, has been very influential, even though it inaccurately casts netnography as a form of covert content analysis, and negates the researchers' need to pay special consideration to sensitive research topics, vulnerable populations, and data-security concerns. My stance on the matter is this. The guidelines in this book are up-to-date and relevant. The moral concerns behind them are timeless. I emphatically believe that there are no conditions under which it is acceptable to disregard the concerns of sensitive populations, or to publish things that mock, name, and shame the people you are ostensibly trying to understand (as that article-which-shall-remain-unnamed unfortunately does). Doing so in the name of netnographic research damages netnography and it also harms social media research in general. It creates future problems for all researchers who will come after you.

Thus, I must make a request. If you want to follow guidelines that revisit netnography's ethical rules and empathic stance on the study of sensitive research topics, then please *do not call your work a netnography*. Because netnography is defined by its adherence to general and agreed-upon procedures, a netnography revisited in this manner *is definitely not a netnography*. It is something else entirely.

Ethical procedures are at the very heart of what a netnography is and what it does. When you think about online ethnography, or traditional ethnography, and ethics, I would prefer that you think first and foremost of empathy. Perhaps empathy, putting ourselves in the shoes of the other, seeking to glimpse in some detail, emotionally, and with genuinely heartfelt compassion what it might be like to sense what they sense, to think what they think, to travel their path, perhaps this is the true essence of contextual inquiry. I believe that its ability to help us peek in a structured way behind life's intersubjective barriers and gain a phenomenological insight into the human worlds of other living beings may be the main reason we do qualitative research.

When we deal with any group of people, but perhaps particularly when we are seeking to understand sensitive topics or vulnerable populations, we want to expend extra effort to envision the perspectives of the human beings who stand behind the various posts and comments we will collect and hoard as data. We want to try to see across the consent gap to those who mistrust us, our cryptic language, and our hidden motives. We want to ensure as much as we possibly can that we are not doing things that might bring harm or embarrassment to them, and disgrace upon ourselves, our work, and our institutions. We want to handle their identities with the utmost of concern, never carelessly. We must try to always respect their rights and use good practices of data security. When we speak to them or interact with them, we need to disclose ourselves, and gain their informed consent about the project they are contributing towards, and where it will go. We have a moral, legal, and ethical obligation to treat the persons behind the data with dignity and to handle their data with respect. Keeping accuracy and truth always in mind, we also want to publish and present works that beneficently portray our participants in as positive and pseudonymous a light as possible.

Beyond and throughout all of this, we should seek empathy in the conduct of our research, empathy in our interpretations, and empathy in the presentation of our research results. Empathy is ultimately what powers a good netnography. As we will learn in this book's closing chapters, what separates netnographies from other forms of social media research is the outcome of empathy. Following ethical research practices thus is not just good hygiene, not merely some time-consuming bureaucratic procedure that must be dutifully followed. It is an assurance and set of structured ways to encourage us to think about the others whose worlds our research intersects and affects. Ethical practice, in itself, can also be a methodology. Rigorously following research ethics procedures then becomes a very deliberate way to initiate, systematize, and maintain a practice of empathy throughout the entire netnographic research project.

CHAPTER SUMMARY

Ethical decisions are central to netnography. In this chapter, you learned the fundamental principles behind research ethics, and in particular how netnography follows standards that are adjusted for the current realities of both ethnographic and online research. The chapter discussed the fact that one study found approximately 70% of recent online ethnographies published did not offer any ethical guidelines or standards. Then, the chapter presented the two main moral philosophy stances: deontological and consequentialist. It applied these moral stances to the question of online ethnography ethics. It also related the consent gap in which as many as 60% of the public does not want their social media data to be used in any research investigation. The chapter then presented an integrated flowchart to guide data collection and presentation procedures. Following the flowchart presented in Figure 6.3 will ensure that your practices comply with many of the current ethical standards governing online and ethnographic research. Finally, the chapter reflected on the underlying morality of research ethics and the need for human empathy. In all, the chapter offered a general overview of this ethically attuned data collection and presentation process that sets the stage for the more detailed treatment of these topics in the chapters which follow.

KEY READINGS

Golder, Su, Shahd Ahmed, Gill Norman, and Andrew Booth (2017) 'Attitudes toward the ethics of research using social media: A systematic review', *Journal of Medical Internet Research* 19(6). Available at: www.ncbi.nlm.nih.gov/pmc/articles/PMC5478799/ (last accessed 30 April 2019).

Kantanen, Helena, and Jyri Manninen (2016) 'Hazy boundaries: Virtual communities and research ethics', *Media and Communication*, 4(4): 86–96.

Tucker, Anne-Marie, Chau Nguyen, and Kai K. Kimppa (2017) 'Ethical questions related to using netnography as research method', *ORBIT Journal*, 1(2).

DATA: THE METHODOLOGY OF NETNOGRAPHIC DATA COLLECTION

CHAPTER OVERVIEW

Chapter 7 will explore the methodology and implications of netnographic data collection in general, with a specific focus on investigative operations and sampling issues. The chapter will begin by explaining what the terms 'data' and 'data collection' mean in relation to the practice of netnography. It will then explore the implications of observer choice on the creation of data from social media traces, interactions, interviews, and researcher experiences. Then, the three main data-collection operations will be overviewed. Investigative, interactive, and immersive data-collection operations can be used together, in combination, or separately in qualitative social media research. Which operation(s) is/ are used must be determined in deference to the research question and other elements of the research context. The chapter will continue to develop the ideas from Chapter 6 and will explore ethics in investigative data operations, including the right to use public versus private sites and data in research, and the need for and forms of researcher disclosure. Some of the practical elements regarding sampling and dealing with data in which message posters are anonymous or pseudonymous will then be discussed. The final subsection will foreshadow the way in which the netnographic procedures of the next three chapters will build on the base of a data-oriented methodology developed in this chapter.

UNDERSTANDING DATA

What Exactly are Data?

Data collection is a term closely related to the operations of networked computing and, as such, the meaning of the term 'data' is not obviously related to a qualitative research procedure and product. So it makes sense to begin this chapter by explaining what the terms 'data' and 'data collection' mean in relation to the practice of netnography.

Data are trustworthy pieces of information, things known or assumed to be factual, evidential, and reliable. In research, data are the informational raw materials that are selectively either co-created (e.g., through a procedure such as an experiment), observed (e.g., by an animal behaviorist observing interspecies bird sociality), or collected (e.g., by a chemist collecting samples from different points in a city's water system). The term 'selectively' is important because the act of collecting data happens as particular pieces of information are chosen to be part of a project, and then processed in the act of interpretation during the attempt to build knowledge and uncover scientific truths. As Quinton and Reynolds (2018: xvii) assert, data is central to every element of research in the digital age:

> working with digital data necessitates reflection on the ethics surrounding ownership, sharing and use of digital data, which is connected to the expectations of the researcher, the participant and the reader, which is in turn connected to the expertise required of the researcher to successfully navigate those data.

Netnographic Observer Effecting

In netnography, there will be no data before a scientific observer effects their research project by classifying some form of information – usually a set of social media postings, a comment, some messages, a conversation or a thread – as data. Before classifying them as part of the project, there are only those posts and comments, messages and characters, photographs, hashtags, pinboards, pages, and online interactions. But also there are other types of information. There are the researchers' own experiences and recordings of experiences, as well as researchers' expansive observations of others' social media-related experiences with notes and reflections. And also very often there is data intentionally collected from interaction and interviews. All of these forms of information are to be considered nothing but information until they are collected. They are not yet data.

7.1

QUANTUM PHYSICS AND NETNOGRAPHY

Netnographers need to deal with the choice among ever-present options for data collection, and the way that their actions and choices shape the dataset they will use to answer their research question. The field of quantum physics has had a long philosophical connection to similar questions, calling such measurement options and their effect upon physical data collection 'observer effects'.

For this exercise, do some reading about the famous Double Slit Experiment in physics. What are the implications of this experiment for how we might understand netnography and the choices we make when doing it? Is it fair to compare conclusions from physics with those of qualitative social media research? What might we learn from such strange new worlds that can help us become better observers of social belief and behavior?

Autogenesis Prohibited

It is important to realize that data do not create themselves in some mythical act of autogenesis. Regarding facticity, Sherry said in Sherry and Kozinets (2001: 166), that 'the theory-ladenness of facts is a qualitative preoccupation'. We might similarly consider that the method-ladenness of data is a netnographic preoccupation. Information does not exist in a pristine form 'out there' as data any more than facts do, and by collecting them, we turn traces of information into data and then into facts. Facts must be gathered and measured, whether by man or machine. Facts must be observed. Data must be sampled and its rules uncovered. It has to be tested on the path to discovering something meaningful, but the complex processes of discovery that bring particular data into being are important events through which those disclosures must be interpreted.

What is data selection in science? Whether buried in rock created hundreds of millions of years ago in a geological event that is then sampled by a geologist, or locked in the genetic code of an altered fruit fly whose progeny are sampled by a geneticist, information of various types must be chosen as part of a research study to become data. As a result of their choosing, data will bear the mark of the methods, choices, and hands that chose them.

- Experimental data bears the marks of the experiment and the experimenter.

- Survey data reflects the quality of the survey questions, the sampling procedure, and the actual sample obtained.

- The sketches of birds in the wild drawn by a biologist reflect the eyes and artistic skills of their maker.

- The fieldnotes of an ethnographer studying an Amazonian tribe reflect the perspective, interests, and education of that researcher.

Every method colors the information it collects and co-creates in the act of turning it into data. Data in netnography are produced by three general types of procedural operations – investigative, interactive, and immersive – and each of them tints data into particular hues. We will briefly discuss each of these sets of procedural operations in turn.

INTRODUCING THE THREE DATA-COLLECTION OPERATIONS

Investigative Data Operations: An Introduction

Investigative operations are selective, they chose from among the vast and ever-increasing wealth of informational traces created in the act of communications between people on social media platforms, and saved in archives and real-time recordings of social media interaction. Investigative data are not directly created by the researcher's questions or writing but, instead, are created by generally unknown others and selected for various reasons by the netnographic researcher to include in the project. Often, to enable and facilitate different types of analysis, the amounts of information collected can be relatively large, and various elements of the context of their social media surroundings will be reduced or removed. Although they may have originally been written for reasons other than as a response to the particular research study, the traces that are chosen to become investigative data are shaped by the netnographer's decisions, interests, perspectives, and observer effects, and can never be completely free of them.

Interactive Data Operations: An Introduction

The second type of data operation is interactive. Distinct from investigative operations, interactive operations are the result of some sort of researcher interference, questioning, or prodding using social media or some other online or offline interrogatory tool. Interactive operations include but are certainly not limited to online interviewing, posting a public question, commenting with a query, asking via email or direct messaging, conducting mobile ethnography, using a digital diary, or utilizing a research webpage. The informational traces collected as a result of these interrogatory operations are interactive data, and they carry all the traces of the question and the questioner that we might expect of other question-based methods, such as surveys and other interviews.

Immersive Data Operations: An Introduction

Immersive operations bear the mark of their creator in an even more overt manner. Like the other operations, immersive operations evaluate and filter what is to become netnographic data from among the vast amount of social media information flowing through public and private online communications. However, immersive operations manifest a more selective set of choices. The act of collecting information for immersion tends to be much more focused on rich or 'deep' data, extensively descriptive or informative data. Immersive operations attempt to preserve as much of the original context of that data as possible. This is done through recording detailed descriptions and explanations in the netnographer's immersion journal (the netnographic equivalent of the ethnographer's fieldnotes). The data contained in the immersion journal also reflects the process of doing the research, including the various social media sites visited, clues followed, paths taken and not taken, ideas explored, original thoughts, and so on. Immersive operations are reflective and contextual, capturing the experience of doing the research, as well as attempting to preserve and curate some of its richest examples.

Qualitative Social Media Data-collection Guidelines and Examples

In general, these three different forms of operation are used either separately or together in netnography, depending upon the research question and the research conditions considered. Often, they will overlap in content and in time. For example, the immersion journal should reflect upon and explain the major data-collection choices, providing some sense of context and background missing from the investigative dataset itself. Similarly, the immersion journal would contain reflections on interviews conducted, perhaps containing personal comments and asides regarding the process of the interview and explaining the unexpected turns it may have taken. Other times, a few choice statistical analyses will be brought in as the data is calibrated. Samples are surveyed, words are processed, networks are mapped, and interesting characteristics calculated out and reported. At other times, these operations can be quite distinct.

There have been a large number of so-called 'observational netnographies' (in future, let's just call them netnographies), in which investigative data operations are the sole type of data collection utilized in the research. I have always been a big proponent of unobtrusive online observation, and often use it myself (almost always in the contexts of wider investigations that include interviews, and immersive journaling, covered in Chapters 9 and 10, respectively). One example of the 'observational' type of netnography that focuses primarily on investigative data-collection operations is Schuman et al.'s (2018: 357–8) article that seeks to understand the health issues of combat-related trauma and, in particular, to explore 'how socially disconnected

Iraq and Afghanistan combat veterans communicate narratives of their combat-related experiences' using social media. Because the purpose of the research is to understand the trauma-related themes that emerge across the military video blogs of those combat veterans, the content of these video blogs is entirely sufficient to address the guiding question. The researcher could have asked veterans why they created the videos, or why they used a particular video method rather than another, but this would only be required to answer a different question – one about each veteran's intention or motivation. Because Schuman et al. (2018) were interested in the end result, the communicative narratives and their trauma-related themes, the videos themselves provide all the data that is required. No evidence of immersive or interactive data operations is present in these observational netnographies, and as this example shows, none may be requited. However, as explained in Chapter 10, even with an ostensibly observational netnography, immersive journaling practices offer a useful procedure for saving particularly choice specimens of data, reflecting upon them, and conducting the early analysis and interpretation that will assist you as you move through your data-collection process towards research communication.

Other netnographies are far more focused on interactive or immersive data. For example, Diniz et al. (2018) wanted to study how Brazilian patients with gestational trophoblastic disease (nonviable pregnancies which are highly curable, but worrisome to patients because of the potential for malignancy) used a dedicated Facebook page headed by a physician who specialized in the disease. For this study, the researchers combined observation of the online site with an interactive and survey-based research page method. The goal of the research was to explore the way that a social media site affected perception of doctor–patient relationship and emotional well-being and to understand it in relation to patients'/social media network site users' socioeconomic profile.

More reflective netnographies, such as the autonetnography of Muslim female virtual tourist experiences conducted by Rokhshad Tavakoli (2016), rely mainly on immersive data operations, and provide lengthy and meticulous autobiographical and introspective detail with little emphasis on investigative operations. Again, these are completely appropriate choices given the applicable research questions and data site contexts. Diniz et al. (2018) wanted to gain an understanding of patients' sense of their relationships with doctors, and inner phenomenological states, as well as how patients at different ages, from different regions, and with different education levels might respond differently. To accomplish these objectives, interaction was required, and to achieve it ethically, informed consent procedures were necessary. Similarly, in order to understand the intersection of female identity, religious (observant Muslim) identity, and virtual tourist identity, plunging into Second Life and recording that dive through immersive operations was an appropriate methodological choice for Tavakoli (2016). Her autonetnography of the touristic virtual journeys she personally experienced was centered upon an immersion journal-type of data collection, and did not require further investigative or interactive sorts of operations.

THE CENTRALITY OF THE RESEARCH QUESTION

As these examples attest, it makes good sense to let the type of research question you are considering dictate the relative predominance of the data operation you will use. Generally speaking, most published netnographies use investigative operations to select and filter social media data. A good number of these publications will also add interactive operations of various sorts to product data through interrogatory principles. In the past, and likely because of confusion over the role of 'fieldnotes' (a term I recommend replacing in this edition of the book), only small numbers of scholars have communicated their reflective and curatorial processes. However, immersive journaling may be good research practice to keep your data collection organized and to continuously reflect upon, analyze, and interpret particularly insightful fragments of data.

The exact approach you use for your netnography – i.e., which of the 25 different research practices you will use, in what order, and how you will combine them – should of course fit the research question asked. However, the immersion journal is there to assist you with the entire process, including your investigative and interactive data-collection operations. If there is a good reason not to disrupt an ongoing community, or if it is already providing a rich data source that can answer the stated research question – as in the example of Schuman et al. (2018) above – then investigative operations may be perfectly sufficient. If the research objective requires more phenomenological or reflective accounts, then relying solely upon interactive or immersive operations might do well enough. However, to benefit from the full range of data-collection possibilities of an ethnographic toolkit, unless there are good reasons to exclude particular kinds of data, I recommend utilizing at least two (immersive + investigative or immersive + interactive) if not all three types of data operations in your netnography.

DATA ETHICS

Ethics in Investigative Data Operations

Because investigation is the most unobtrusive and surreptitious means of collecting data in netnography, performing it ethically requires a range of understandings and informed decisions about social media user rights, data rights, reasonable compliance with platform policies, permissions from moderators, sensitive topics, vulnerable populations, data security, anonymization, and risk mitigation. These ethical elements are woven into data collection and communication operations throughout this book. In this chapter, we will begin to engage with these topics more specifically, beginning with the right to use public versus private sites and data in research, and the need for and forms of researcher disclosure. The remainder of the topics from Chapter 6's ethical online ethnographic research flowchart (in Figure 6.3, a visualization to which this text will often refer) will be peppered throughout the remaining chapters of the book.

Public versus Private Sites and Data

Whether the site is public or private will influence the ethical procedures we should follow. Investigative data can be drawn either from a public site or a private one. Public sites should be considered to have public data, and private sites offer private data. The difference between them is as follows. In general, a private site requires registration and a log on with a password in order to access information. A public site, in contrast, is open to any browser, and does not require registration and a log on with a password. Most blogs and forums are public sites. The publicly available areas of YouTube and Reddit are public sites. The content of public sites is usually indexed by and accessible using common search engines such as Google, Yahoo!, and DuckDuckGo. Private sites might be searchable using their own proprietary search engines, but would normally require you to be logged on as a member first, before you could use their search engine.

However, as with many things in social media, there are shades of gray. For example, although it might seem that I need to be a member to search for Twitter, LinkedIn or Facebook posts, this is not so. If I want to search the public posts of Twitter, for instance, I can do so without joining the site or logging on simply by using https://twitter.com/search-home. In fact, if someone has blocked me from seeing their public Twitter feed, I can view it simply by logging off the public search and using the Twitter search function instead. Similarly, public profiles and posts on Facebook or LinkedIn can be searched with a number of different search engines. Therefore, public information posted on these sites and searchable using general search engines should be considered public information and these areas of the specific sites themselves can be considered public sites.

As Moreno et al. (2013: 710) have explained, United States court law has already 'examined Facebook's privacy policy and determined that individuals do not have a reasonable expectation of privacy in information they post on their Facebook pages'. The same is very likely true for their posts on any social media site. Individuals have a reasonable expectation of privacy within their homes. So, for example, someone peeking in your windows in the evening is a clear breach of that privacy. However, when an individual knowingly exposes information to the public, by posting a photo, video, or comment, there is no reasonable expectation of privacy.

Just because a site is public, however, does not mean that using data from it is ethically unproblematic. Although they may be posting publicly, the users of such sites might have some reasonable expectations of privacy (even if the courts say these expectations are not legally enforceable). As we saw from the research presented in Chapter 6 supporting the consent gap, there is considerable variety in these expectations. However, what is important for you to recognize is that you will generally see data as public when people's privacy settings are set that way. Privacy settings being set to public has been treated as a type of proxy for the granting of consent for others to see and for researchers to use their data, presumably for good causes.

The Right to Use Public Data in Research

The second data rights consideration is concerned about whether researchers have the rights to use this mostly-public data. Is the use of social media data similar to the 'fair use' or 'fair dealing' of copyright materials in the USA and UK, respectively? That is, is it subject to certain restrictions, but otherwise effectively waived as far as research purposes are concerned (Walther, 2002)? Some of these fair use exemptions are not in effect in international law, making matters a bit more complicated. However, the European Union's GDPR (short for 'General Data Protection Regulation') legislation, which is the strictest and most elaborate general set of rules currently governing data creators' rights, is likely to be (at least for a time) the new default standard governing global research ethics.

Under GDPR, which is a complex set of regulations, research occupies a privileged position. For example, restrictions on data use and even on important ethical categories such as sensitive topics may be overridden by researchers and research organizations that implement appropriate safeguards. We will discuss those safeguards in a later section, but the key point here is that the GDPR permits the collection of public data for research purposes by legitimate research actors who are processing data for purposes that are in the public interest, including scientific and historical research purposes, as long as the researcher (or 'data controller') acts in keeping with the recognized standards for scientific research. In all, these legal guidelines strongly suggest that public data can be used by social media researchers, as long as they take appropriate safeguards. Those specific safeguards, including the most up-to-date GDPR safeguards, are baked into the process for netnography research ethics depicted in Figure 6.3 and discussed in these sections.

The Right to Use Private Data in Research

Private data is found on private sites which require registration and a log-on with a password in order to access them. Private data is usually not indexed by and accessible using common search engines such as Google, but many of the sites have their own search functions or search engines that can be accessed once a user is logged on and operating behind its firewall. Private sites are generally restricted. However, they are not completely off limits to netnographic research.

There are a number of conditions under which data can be collected from private sites and used in netnographic research. There are two important steps in this. First, the researcher must ensure reasonable compliance with the terms related by the platform, as well as the specific site where the social interactions are occurring (e.g., a particular topic-dedicated group within Facebook or LinkedIn). Second, the researcher must gain written permission from appropriate bodies that govern the social media site.

Reasonable compliance will need to be negotiated with the platform and with relevant moderators. Numerous published netnographies talk about their research on closed groups and the efforts they made to ensure reasonable compliance. A good example is Kantanen and Manninen (2016) whose procedure took a full year and half (this is atypically long). If it is a small website or message board, such as a corporate or organizational site, compliance would likely include gaining the permission of the platform owners. Reasonable compliance may mean that the researcher must post a notice to participants on the group about the research and its purpose, how the data will be used, how privacy will be maintained, and where the final research will appear. Compliance might also mean disclosure of the researcher and their affiliations. It might mean posting a listing of verbata (i.e., quotations drawn from social media data) that you intend to publish in the research, and allowing the people who are quoted or cited in the research to opt-out if they do not wish their posts to be used in this manner. It may not be realistic to expect Facebook or LinkedIn to grant you explicit written permission – in fact, this is highly unlikely. That does make your request to do research illegal or wrong. Your educated and informed expectations for what is reasonable are important, and you may need to justify these to further regulatory bodies. To do so intelligently, researchers are advised not only to consider these guidelines, but also to check on the relevant laws, regulations, and institutions pertaining to their countries and governing institutions.

In the second and interrelated step, the researcher must explicitly ask for and gain permission in writing from any moderators or relevant administrators of the group to gather data. There may be several moderators. If possible, you should try to determine which one, or ones, are in charge. If there is any doubt, contact all of them. Note that, in these ideal cases, the data is purely investigative; the researchers are not interacting in any way with online participants, and disclosure to the general group of social media users may be optional. Once interaction is going to occur, as it often does in netnography, the researchers also have to invoke the data ethics rules that pertain to the use of interactive data.

Researcher Disclosure

When a netnographer reaches out, projecting their voice across the digital chasm in search of other human voices, and another voice answers, then complete honesty and disclosure must prevail. It has already been said, but I want to emphasize it again, in the present: there is no prevarication in reasoning why a netnographer would want to deceive online. If you are doing research, you must disclose that activity, along with your real identity (i.e., the one on your birth certificate or driver's license).

In a comprehensive and current evaluation of the use of netnography in hospitality and tourism research, Whalen (2018: 3427) found that only 11% of published netnographic studies explicitly mentioned disclosure and/or consent, while 35% explicitly mentioned that they did not disclose their presence and 54% did not mention the topic at all.

In those cases of human contact, whether with an identified online site of social interaction, with individuals across many sites bound by similar topics, or with particular profiles of particular individuals, the netnographer should always fully disclose their presence, affiliations and intentions during any research interactions, which is especially important in the first few interactions as they established the social arrangement. During reflexive fieldnote writing and subsequent construction of the netnographic representation, the researcher has a responsibility to record those instances of disclosure and, if possible, follow them with questions of consent for the person who is the subject of the interaction. Honest researcher disclosure, without hesitation, obfuscation or deception, is the edifice upon which the research relationships in netnography are built.

If you talk to people as a part of your research, you should never, under any circumstances, engage in identity deception. Every member of your team must use their real name and disclose their actual affiliations and purpose. Tolerate in your team and yourself absolutely no deception about why you are interacting with someone or what you are doing online if you say that you are doing netnography. Even if the practice of identity play, gender mixing, and other types of altered representation is common on the site, researchers are bound by codes of research ethics that necessitate behaviors different from the norm and are compelled to disclose themselves accurately.

Disclosure and Your Profile

In the flowchart of the netnographic research ethic process shown in Figure 6.3, if you are using YouTube, Facebook, Twitter, Snapchat, WeChat, Instagram, Pinterest, Reddit, LinkedIn or some other common social media platform in order to do at least some of your netnographic fieldwork – and if your netnographic fieldwork is going to involve you communicating with other people – then I highly recommend that the fact that you are conducting research while interacting on those sites should appear prominently in your personal or user profile, and probably should also appear at regular intervals in your status updates.

In forums or more traditional online sites, the same advice about user profiles applies. In emails, your researcher status might appear in your signature line. Another possibility would be to visually communicate your different status by wearing a t-shirt or a large button, or just digitally manufacture what is needed, and have that shout out your researcher credentials in your profile picture.

Think of ethical challenges in netnography as interesting mental experiments that reveal intriguing new things about our contemporary social media consumer-entrepreneur culture. How would you gain permission to study the profiles of dead people on Facebook or LinkedIn? How would you ethically study a community of people who discuss how they relate to dead people's social media profiles? In ethnography, it has always been a huge challenge to keep the research dance separate from the rest of the researcher's life. Ethnographers regularly marry members of the culture they study. They are accepted in many different cultures because in the embodied physical world we often encounter people who are kind, accepting, and compassionate – this seems to be one of the bases of our collective humanity. In netnography, we often see a darker and more funhouse mirror-exaggerated reflection. In a way, all communications are artifacts – real or potential. When we send messages to each other, we are dancing with ghosts. In netnography, we must deal with these facts by realizing that we are also ghosts in this space, and that others may be dancing with us.

Disclosure and Cultural Entrée

If you are going to be engaging in an online conversation, this enlisting is completely analogous to joining a physical culture or conversation. Disclosure, simplicity, and clear communication are key: 'Hi, I am a researcher at XYZ University in Cityville, and I'm interested in how Moms connect on Facebook. Can I interview you about this topic on Skype or FaceTime?' The description of research can and should be a satisfying handshake. It can be a type of ethnographic entrée and ethics combined.

It is also highly desirable for the netnographer to offer some more detailed explanation about themselves while they are introducing people to the research study, beyond simply that they are a researcher conducting a study. Providing this information is relatively simple in social networking sites such as Facebook and LinkedIn. A single post can offer plenty of detail. That link can easily be sent in an email or direct message in an app. A well-written bio will bring you and your interests to life, making you a more three-dimensional figure, rather than a cartoon image of a lab-coated online researcher holding a tablet clipboard.

So, from the beginning of the research through to its end, good research ethics dictate that the netnographic researcher: (1) openly and accurately identifies themselves when contacting and communicating directly with actual human beings, avoiding all deception; (2) openly and accurately describes their research purpose for interacting with people online; and (3) provides an accessible, relevant and accurate description of their research focus and interests, preferably with some links to some official-looking webpages somewhere which are entirely legitimate, and with more links that allow people to read your bio and learn more about you and your interests.

THE PRAGMATICS OF ANONYMOUS DATA

This subsection will discuss some of the practical elements of dealing with data in which the posters of messages are anonymous or only pseudonymously identified. We will begin by discussing an interactionist approach that has guided netnographic research from its beginning. We will then extend the discussion into a more developed consideration of sampling issues. Finally, the last subsection will provide examples from published research and guidelines regarding the use of samples and other triangulation strategies for ascertaining or estimating the social membership categories of people who post online.

As sociologists like Zygmunt Bauman (2013) remind us, contemporary social situations and their networks are increasingly liquid, slippery, and dynamic. So too are contemporary identities that express through them. We are constantly constructing and reconstructing ourselves through context-specific social acts of display, which include posting and replying on social media sites and through software applications. The study of participants' online personas, and the fact that they are different from the personas they use in other social contexts, is about as problematic as saying that a photo of you in your story with a Snapchat filter on it is not the real you. The reason it is not problematic is because alterations of identity, like Snapchat filter photos, are a natural consequence of our contemporary social life everywhere. These changes are not simply some idiosyncratic tendency manifesting itself on social media (although maybe the Snapchat filter is; however, there is a trend of people having plastic surgery to look more like their Snapchat selves – more grist for the netnographic idea mill).

In 1998 I wrote, 'The same freedom which inspires people to mischievously construct deliberate falsehoods about themselves and their opinions also allows them and others the freedom to express aspects of themselves, their ambitions and inner conflicts, that they would otherwise keep deeply hidden' (Kozinets, 1998: 369). As we begin this section on anonymous and pseudonymous data, we should not overlook its strength. Often, people are more honest when they are anonymous and shielded in this way from the more uncontrollable social consequences of sharing their opinions, fears, and inner worlds. We might keep in mind what sorts of data we wish to explore. If we are interested in sensitive matters, in people discussing unsavory, illegitimate, or stigmatic things, then we might turn more towards anonymous public sites such as Reddit, YouTube, Twitter, and various forums, rather than to the sites which require identity validation such as Facebook and Instagram.

Taking an Interactionist Approach

In George Herbert Mead's (1934) interactionist approach, the unit of analysis is not the person, but the behavior, the speech act, or, as he called, it 'the utterance'. Netnography is all about utterances. Twitter provides 500 million utterances per day (that's 6,000 per second). YouTube offers up 432,000 new hours of utterance-and-social-act-filled video every day (that's 300 new hours of video-utterance every minute).

Many netnographies are focused on these social acts and utterances. They are not disguised elements of something else, but social facts in themselves. If we want to understand the communicative strategies that Indian beauty influencers use on YouTube, we don't need to know the real names of those beauty influencers. All the data we need is contained in the utterances of the YouTube videos. For example, my co-authors and I identified four distinct types of social media narrative strategies employed by early influencers using blogs – evaluation, embracing, endorsement, and explanation (Kozinets et al., 2010). It was unnecessary to distinguish the real names of the bloggers using these strategies; the point was that they were being used. When you start working with the practice dataset of YouTube commenters discussing utopian themes in Chapter 8, you will find that the identities of the message posters are similarly unimportant to your research conclusions.

What is important is that each photograph, each video, each tag, each comment, each posting of text is an utterance, a speech act, a social act that someone (or perhaps some thing, such as a bot or a smart home device) has taken. These elements 'pose interpretive puzzles for the ethnographers' (Garcia et al., 2009: 61), but the puzzles are based on realities, real actions and behaviors – not fictions!

Even though personal data on people's identities is increasingly easy to find, and rather straightforward to incorporate into our analysis and interpretation, many inquiries using netnography will be focused on utterances rather than utterers. Following the pragmatics of interactionist principles means we focus on what is said, the interaction captured on social media, rather than needing to know exactly who is saying such things. However, that is most certainly not always the case.

SAMPLING ISSUES WITH INVESTIGATIVE NETNOGRAPHIC DATA

Survey researchers are rightly concerned with non-response bias. Surveys try to draw conclusions about general populations from particular samples drawn from that universe. However, because people choose whether to respond to a survey or not, a researcher must be careful to assess the chance that the difference between those who responded to the questionnaire and those who did not will bias the results. If, for example, survey respondents tend to need the money that the survey pays, then the sample might under-represent higher income groups.

In netnography, we encounter a parallel problem to the survey non-response bias when we assume that the sample of message posts we find in social media adequately represents some sort of general or mainstream thinking or group identity. This discrepancy occurs because of several well-known differences between those who post on social media and those who do not. We know that the characteristics of the people who post and respond to messages in public sites such as Twitter and Reddit, or on the public parts of more private sites such as Facebook and LinkedIn, are not exactly the same as those of the people who read those sites, but do not post, or who do not post as frequently or as much, or who do not read them or post at all. For one thing, people who post tend to be more polarized and more extreme in their opinions and expression than those who do not. On Twitter and YouTube we might hear from people who feel passionately about particular topics, either loving or hating them, with a big middle ground of largely ambivalent people generally unmotivated to expostulate to the same length about their ambivalence. People who post anonymously also tend to be more reactive and more opinionated. Those who post publicly using their given names tend to be motivated by attention-seeking, for one reason or another.

These issues are likely exacerbated when the netnography focuses only on public posts. If we favor collecting information from message posters who do not maximize their privacy setting but instead share their data publicly, we must realize that these people have particular motivations for sharing their data publicly that may not represent those who choose to keep their data private. People who blog, tweet, seek Instagram fame and run Facebook groups are utilizing social media as their own personal 'megaphones'; they use public settings to build audiences for various reasons, many of them financial, some of them social, others political. If we restrict ourselves to this group then we restrict ourselves to a sample of exhibitionists and activists, those who want to be seen by, sell to, affect, or change the world. Social media celebrities are analogous to opinion makers in traditional media. Studying them can be important and fascinating. Their actions may well influence or reflect the mainstream. But we should not confuse the studying of celebrity social media posters with a representative sampling of the mainstream. That is why it can often be useful in netnography to also sample private data or to extend our investigation to interactive data collection conducted with carefully chosen participants.

In sum, the people who post publicly on social media may be more extreme, opinionated, attention-seeking, and self-promotional than those who do not. It is important for us to understand that when we draw data from the conversations and other information posted publicly on social media sites, we are not dealing with a representative sample of the public, or even of some particular group drawn from that public. Like survey researchers trying to assess non-response bias in a survey sample, as netnographers we must keep in mind the differences of those whose posts we turn into data for our research projects. Like those same survey researchers, we must try to compensate for the effects of this bias in our analysis and on our asserted findings. There is no doubt that we can learn much about what is going on in the world by studying the many communications available to us through social media. But particularly when we use investigative data operations, we must be careful that our analytic conclusions are appropriate. Those conclusions should refer to the computer-mediated social medium, the preselections and predispositions of those who use it, and its potential distortions on those communications and deviations from relevant norms. Anthropology, qualitative sociology, and cultural studies tend to be sciences of contexts and specifics. And good social science does not mistake the characteristics of particular samples for those of more general populations.

Sampling and Ascertaining the Identity of Anonymous Online Content Creators

What if your research interest is in investigating a particular group or type of people, such as Portuguese women or Finnish Millennials? Following investigative research operations, how would you know for certain exactly who is posting to a particular social media site? Even if you were to sample an ongoing and long-standing Portuguese site dedicated to women's issues, could you ever assert with certainty, for example, that you had sampled conversational online data from a group of Portuguese women? Or consider another question. Would it be accurate of you to cite one of the posts you found on that Portuguese women's issues group, in which the poster says that she is a 32-year-old mother with two children from Lisbon, and then analyze it as representing this type of person?

The answer to both of these sampling questions is no. At least, not without some further validation or triangulation. You could not say with certainty that you had sampled Portuguese women unless you have reliable, confirmed information regarding exactly who is posting to the group. For instance, an online site where Portuguese speakers communicate might also attract many individuals from Brazil, Mozambique, Angola, East Timor, and a range of other countries and regions besides Portugal that all share the same language. Similarly, a site that discusses issues related to women might also attract attention and comments from other genders. Thus, even though a person claimed to be a member of a certain group (and in all likelihood, probably actually is a member of that group), it would be remiss to simply take their statement of identity as a social fact without further supporting evidence. This sort of skepticism towards online personal data is the application of critical thinking to the production of good social science.

It is true that we do not ever know for certain exactly who is posting in platforms where anonymity and pseudonymity prevail. This could be a different matter on platforms such as Facebook, Instagram, and LinkedIn that have encouraged people to forsake their anonymity for the convenience of both promoting themselves and being available to people and companies. However, just as survey results must rely on the honestly of self-reports, we can also never be entirely certain that people are who they represent themselves to be online. Even on census forms, people lie.

One strategy for addressing this ambiguity is to consider the platform to be the level of analysis. Thus, instead of saying that its focus is a study of Portuguese women, the netnography would be more accurate if it was to state that it is a study of online sites where Portuguese speakers (who may be from Brazil, Mozambique, or other Portuguese-speaking countries) discuss issues related to women. The act of defining the site helps pinpoint the sorts of knowledge claims that can be made (such as that the posters communicated in the Portuguese language about issues pertaining to women) and also that cannot be made (such as that these are women of a certain age or who live in a particular region). As investigative data is collected from such a site, the netnographer can become increasingly specific about various elements of it. For example, certain posters might mention the Algarve region or the challenges of finding management positions in Portugal. That these things are mentioned on the site are social facts – and thus trustworthy data. As data, they are no truer or falser than any retrospective recounted in interviews or any answers given to a questionnaire, and they must be treated with the same analytical care. But, like surveys, interviews, and experimental questionnaire results, the contents of such statements can never themselves be treated as matters of fact. In netnography, the uncertainty extends not only to the statement, but also to the identity of the statement maker.

Another strategy for ameliorating this uncertainty about the identity of the social media content creators whose information we use to inform our studies is to cross-validate the data we collect using investigative procedures with interactive operations. One way to do this is to interview message posters whose data you have already collected using investigative operations. This is commonly used to validate netnographic findings obtained through investigative operations when making knowledge claims about group membership or identity is important to the research conclusions. Another way to pursue a valid link between netnographic data and group membership is to reverse the order and first interview members of a particular chosen group, such as Portuguese women, and then ask about their social media activities, following them online with investigative operations. One example of this is Teresa Davis's (2010) sociological study of migrant identity as it is expressed through online social experiences. In this case, the author was a member of a group of South Indian university friends who, twenty years after their graduation, formed an online group to discuss their experiences and keep in touch. Because Davis knew exactly who was involved in the group personally, her confidence in the reliability of the data as able to speak about actual Indian migrant experience was very high.

Another way to validate the group membership and identity of message posters is to evaluate how similar are the topics, language, and knowledge discussed and shared between message posters to those of known members of the group. Olga Isupova (2011) wrote about the lived experience of Russian women undergoing fertility assistance treatment by joining a Russian forum dedicated to the topic, www.probirka.ru. Because the author was involved as a participant not only in the community but also in fertility assistance, her intellectual and emotional proximity to the topic, as well as her prolonged engagement of five years interacting through the site, served as a close check on the validity of the data she was collecting through investigative operations.

Keen attention to sampling was also important to Berdychevsky and Nimrod's (2015) study of the way seniors use online platforms to discuss sex and sexuality. In that example, the researchers triangulated facts about the sites with other research on the membership of these online communities in order to reach conclusions about who was represented in the 2,534 posts they collected as their dataset. The communities were named to serve adults 50 years old and over, all but one of them targeted a global audience, and a recent survey had revealed that most community members were between 55 and 75 years old with a mean of 64.7 years. Berdychevsky and Nimrod provide us with a valuable example revealing how particular social media sites are sampled (ones named and related to elderly people), with particular social groups (seniors, who are validated with a triangulation methodology and argument), alongside a particular topic (sexuality). Investigating this type of intersection of social media site, social group, and particular topic is one of the more useful and common applications of netnography.

Group member identification in netnography means associating the information collected from investigative data operations with particular sorts of membership beyond its social media context. For instance, if you wish to study how members of the Millennial generation in Finland talk about politics and political activism, it is not enough to sample data from a Finnish social media site targeted to members of that generation. More validation will be required, and a careful delimiting of knowledge claims produced, before data collected using the investigative operations of netnography can reliably make statements about that generation's general political conversations and activist leanings. Why? Because Finnish Millennials on social media do not speak for all Finnish Millennials. In general, where group membership identification is important to your research question, the three membership validation strategies mentioned in this section become important procedures to ensure that your knowledge claims are based on more than self-reports and assumed identities.

THE FOLLOWING THREE CHAPTERS

Method follows methodology. With the exception of a few subsections in Chapter 5, these first seven chapters of the book have been largely conceptual, theoretical, historical, and abstract. In the following three chapters, the problematization of some key conceptual elements of traditional ethnography will lead to the procedural development of netnographic praxis: the 25 different netnographic data practices that, perhaps along with co-researchers and co-authors, you will apply to create a netnography.

This chapter began with an investigation of the notion of 'data' and discussed concepts of choice, decision-making, and observer effects. These conceptual explorations are important methodological elements driving the development from research question to the searching, scouting, selecting, and saving operations that will create the netnographic dataset during the investigative data-collection operations explained in Chapter 8. Chapter 9 will begin with a philosophically-driven interrogation of the idea of 'participation', and concludes that engagement is a more appropriate feature of interaction and that engaged research operations are the epistemological requirement of this stage of netnographic data collection. In Chapter 10, which will begin with a discussion of the possibility of a 'field site' in social media ethnography, we will learn how concepts of motion, mobility, and interconnection are important elements driving immersive operations.

There are 17 exercises in total over the next three chapters that will guide you through the data-collection procedures and allow you to collect the dataset that will form the backbone of your project. As this one did, each of these three chapters will be paying careful attention to the ethical challenges faced by the data-collection procedures of investigation, interaction, and immersion. Ethics is not confined to a single chapter of this book, but pervades its entirety, forming content in every operational and theoretical chapter. Each of the following three chapters is cast at a workbench level in order to offer pragmatic guidelines and directive advice. They are filled with numerous examples drawn from the extant interdisciplinary literature on netnography. Regardless of whether you have already done numerous online ethnographies, or are about to write your very first one, the knowledge in these chapters will help guide you through the conduct of your netnographic research project, and also help you ensure an organized process leading to high-quality outcomes.

CHAPTER SUMMARY

In this chapter, we explored the methodology and general implications of netnographic data collection while focusing on ethics in investigative operations as well as data sampling issues and strategies to address them. The chapter explained and defined the term 'data' as the informational raw materials that are selectively either co-created, observed, or collected. The term 'selectively' is important to the definition, and the chapter proceeded to explore the implications of observer choice on the creation of data from social media traces, interactions, interviews, and researcher experiences. Investigative, interactive, and immersive data-collection operations are the three main data-collection operations in netnographic social media research. They can be used together, in combination, or separately. Which operations are used must be determined by referring to the research question and other elements of the research context. The chapter also explored ethics in investigative data operations, and the practical elements of sampling and dealing with anonymous online data.

KEY READINGS

Bauman, Zygmunt (2013) *Liquid Modernity*. New York: Wiley.

Moreno, Megan A., Alison Grant, Lauren Kacvinsky, Peter Moreno, and Michael Fleming (2012) 'Older adolescents' views regarding participation in facebook research', *Journal of Adolescent Health*, 51(5): 439–44.

Quinton, Sarah and Nina Reynolds (2018) *Understanding Research in the Digital Age*. London: Sage.

Whalen, Elizabeth A. (2018) 'Understanding a shifting methodology: A content analysis of the use of netnography in hospitality and tourism research', *International Journal of Contemporary Hospitality Management*, 30(11): 3423–41.

8

INVESTIGATING: FIVE STEPS TO SOCIAL MEDIA DATA COLLECTION

CHAPTER OVERVIEW

The focus on data collection continues in Chapter 8 with a full description and development of investigative operations. In netnography, investigative data is searched, filtered, and then collected in a process that focuses on selection. Building upon Chapter 7's reorientation of the notion of data, this chapter will outline the specific investigative operation practices of simplifying, searching, scouting, selecting, and saving in netnography. Simplifying translates research questions and focus into a consistent set of search terms or keywords. Searching involves the entry of keywords, search terms, hashtags, trends, and their variations into search functions and engines. Scouting operations provide the initial filter that narrows down the choice set from which you will select your data sites. Selection is the judgment process whereby you apply specific relevant criteria in order to decide which data sites to choose for your dataset. Selection also involves data ethics concerns such as sensitive topics, vulnerable populations, and weighing benefits against risks. Saving operations including capture, cut and paste, and scraping, and are also implicated in ethical procedures of data security. Saving operations include saving data from mobile phones. This chapter will describe, illustrate, and provide numerous examples to help you learn about these five practices that, together, constitute the process of investigative data-collection operations in netnography.

THE INVESTIGATION PROCESS DEPICTED IN THIS CHAPTER

In this chapter, we home in on investigative qualitative social media data-collection operations. You will learn about how to perform these in an ethical manner, and their methodological justification. As the remainder of this chapter will explain, investigative data operations take place as an underdetermined set of procedures that:

- begin with the *simplification* operations that translate research questions into searchable search terms, and then move to

- *search* operations that uncover options for further exploration, and then require

- *scouting* operations that reconnoiter various potential 'sites' of data, interaction, and experience.

The data operations for investigation then involve:

- the careful decision-making and scrutinizing required in *selecting* which data will become part of the netnography's dataset, and finally,

- the *saving* of the data in one particular form through capture, cut and paste, or scrape.

The next subsection of this chapter discusses the development from research question to the five core investigative data operations: simplification, search, scouting, selecting, and saving.

From Question to Dataset: Understanding the Range of Investigative Operations in Netnographic Data Collection

In netnography, investigative data operations offer a structured approach to the conduct of search processes that replace the inscription of fieldnotes in traditional ethnography. Instead of field sites, netnography has data sites. And these data sites are located through a series of processes of searching and filtering, which in practice often operate as a type of double-funnel operation, as pictured in Figure 8.1.

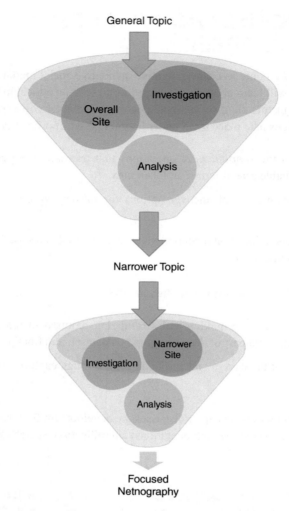

Figure 8.1 The double-funnel process of netnographic investigation

The idea behind the double-funnel process of netnographic investigation is as follows. The initial review and data collection look at the overall general site of investigation, exploring terms such as 'environmental activism', 'domestic abuse', or 'bargain shopping'. After this initial stage of investigation, the findings can then lead to a narrower and more specific topic. This topic then becomes the site for a more detailed investigation, which can finally narrow in on the specific topic, developing it in a rich and thorough way.

The Five Operations in Brief

So how will you start collecting the dataset you will analyze and interpret in order to answer your research question and incarnate your netnography? The initiation of the netnography is in the research question. The initial stage of investigation operations focuses the research on the question it seeks to answer. The five operations can work in sequence or out of sequence. Like netnography itself, investigative data collection is an iterative process, nondeterministic, flexible, and adaptable to research needs and contexts. Some research projects will require very limited simplification and only a few searches. Some will begin with search in order to then find additional terms to simplify. After noting that deviations from the norm are probably normative, for general purposes it makes sense to present these five operations in the following order.

First, simplify. Render the key elements of your research question and research focus. Translate them into a consistent set of search terms or keywords you can enter into a variety of search engines. Simplification operations provide the terms of your search.

Second, search. Enter the keywords, search terms, hashtags, trends, and their variations you have developed into every kind of social media site search function and data search engine you might find useful. Searching operations provide the sites for your scouting.

Third, scout. Click, follow, enter, read, watch, listen, and reconnoiter the sites, threads, images, podcasts, videos, and other content that will spill from the search engines as you tilt the great information horn of plenty. Scouting operations provide the initial filter that helps narrow down the choice set from which you will select your data sites.

Fourth, select. This is the time of judgment for your data sites. You cannot and should not collect everything that pours out of your searches. In fact, you want to be judicious in what you do decide to select. The selection stage is where you make those evaluations. Selection operations provide the data you will save into your investigative dataset.

Fifth, save. You must now save the data you have selected. You have several options for this, including capture, cut and paste, and scraping. The data you save in this way will constitute the investigative dataset of your netnography. That data will then be studied and interoperated in integrative data analysis operations.

These are the five investigative data-collection operations in brief. There is enough guidance in this short summary for you to start on your journey. You may wish to try them out now. Or, you may wish to read the following sections first, which provide additional detail and exercises that will guide you step by step.

SIMPLIFYING

Simplifying Data Operations: Turning Research Questions into Searchable Search Terms

Simplifying or simplification data operations are a way to examine, consider, and then render the key elements of your research question and research focus into terms that can be used for search in search engines that classify social media. Simplifying is actually more challenging than it sounds, because it means translating the abstract reality of your research question into a viable set of more concrete search terms or keywords, where viability is partly a function of the context you are searching. Abstractions can be difficult to translate into concretizations, exactly because concrete elements of the social world are enmeshed in associations and contain rich cultural connections full of meaning and language. This is why we do qualitative research such as netnography. But the methodological consequence of these challenges is that, when you begin your inventive work for your netnography, you may not know at first exactly what you are searching for, or which terms are going to yield the best results.

8.1 SIMPLIFICATION EXAMPLE 1: TRANSLATING IDENTITY CONFLICT INTO MAKEUP TIPS

Consider, as an example, one of the published netnography research questions that we looked at in Chapter 5. Ruvio and Belk (2018) were interested in 'identity conflict' and the way that they decided to study this abstract conception was to study 'transpeople', who they defined as 'individuals who experience a lack of congruence between their gender identity and their biological sex, resulting in a conflict between desired and socially acceptable performance of gender identity' (p. 102). Their set of three research questions is stated in the abstract:

> 1) How does the evolution of a person's identity conflict correspond with the evolution of the extended self? 2) What extended self strategies do people utilize to cope with their identity conflicts? and, 3) How do social norms shape the enactment of these extended self strategies? (2018: 103)

Think about what you would do if you were given this research question. Where would you start to simplify it? What search terms, keywords, and hashtags would you convert it into? Would the term 'identity' get you anywhere? How about 'extended self strategies'? 'Social norms'? 'Enactment'? Obviously, you would find these terms difficult to work with. In order to simplify you need to get closer to the phenomenon. Abstract research questions such as this one are likely the result of a process of analysis and interpretation, as the researchers try to link their findings with the nomological network of extant theory. In order to start collecting data to build those findings, a netnography and its research question need to be positioned much closer to a particular phenomenon.

So how did Ruvio and Belk (2018) translate their interest in transpeople into search terms? They focused on 11 online public forums that were known to be targeted at or used by transpeople. Although the data they decided to include in their investigative dataset included some general discussion platforms, they also queried for and found 'sub-forums on specific topics such as coming out, passing, makeup tips, M2F [male to female transgender], F2M [female to male transgender], relationships, legal advice and medical issues' (p. 104). Once they had located these topics, they honed in on what they called 'identity-related discourses' occurring within them.

SIMPLIFICATION EXAMPLE 2: TRANSLATING SENIOR'S DISCUSSION OUTLETS INTO LUST

8.2

Let's ponder one more example of simplification in a published netnography. For many online ethnographies, researchers are interested in the intersection of social media, social groups, and particular topics. For example, consider a topic such as how elderly people might use social media to try to understand and cope with the challenges of geriatric sexuality. Although they do not phrase it explicitly as a research question in their article, I will rephrase their research focus as a question here.

What is the role of senior-focused online communities as a sphere for discussing sex-related issues? Do these communities compensate for the information and connection that society and particularly healthcare professionals currently fail to provide? (See Berdychevsky and Nimrod, 2015: 470).

In their investigation, Berdychevsky and Nimrod (2015) followed an observational method that used only investigative data operations. They found that most seniors' online communities did not have special sections dedicated to sex, and sex-related discussion threads were instead scattered through various sections such as health, family/relationships, and general discussions. They therefore adopted a general collection strategy that then filtered out the topics of interest to their study. They used 'an existing dataset that included 686,283 messages posted by 79,665 members of 14 leading English language-based communities during one full year', and then filtered out posts 'that included keywords related to sex (e.g., sex and its derivatives, intimacy, libido, romance, love, lust, etc.)' (p. 471).

(Continued)

We can see from this example and the one in Box 8.1 that the four data operations of simplifying, searching, scouting, and selecting are somewhat fluid and iterative. Researchers in both of these examples seem to have begun with an interest in particular social groups (transpeople, seniors), and then investigated platforms and sites targeted towards those social groups. After investigating those platforms and sites, the researchers then experimented with various search terms related to their research questions. Based on the results, they chose particular data to save and include in their dataset.

8.3 TRANSLATING YOUR RESEARCH QUESTIONS INTO SIMPLIFIED SEARCH QUERY TERMS (PROJECT EXERCISE)

Are you ready to begin the investigative data operations for your research project? Once you are sure you have honed and focused your research question (from Chapter 5) as much as you can, then write your Refined Research Question from Chapter 5 here (it might be nice to use your best and most creative handwriting too, to spur some of that right-brained creativity!):

....
....
....
....
....
....
....

Now, using any search engine you like, start thinking about which search terms might be helpful. These can be keywords, hashtags, trends, or other search terms. Think about variations of them. Use a thesaurus. Try misspellings or alternate spellings. If you have already done some fieldwork or reading, bring that in. What acronyms or insider terms have you encountered?

List them here (and keep on listing and revising throughout your project's data-collection operations):

....
....
....

....
....
....
....
....

SEARCHING

Data Rights and Social Media Users' Rights

One of the first questions we might ask about search is 'Is it right to use this data in our research?' Although we dealt with this issue in Chapter 6, particularly in the section about 'the consent gap', it is important when searching data to keep in mind the rights of social media users. That is the purpose of this section.

When users join social media platforms and share content on them, they are partaking in a contractual relationship between themselves and the platform. Creating the account requires agreement to Terms of Use, Terms of Service, End User Licensing Agreements or other types of servicing agreements, which are legal contracts. For most of the major platforms, like Facebook, Twitter, LinkedIn, Snapchat, and Instagram, the agreement states that users retain ownership of the content that they share. They also grant the platform a non-exclusive, royalty-free, transferable, sub-licensable worldwide license to use the content that they create and share. What this means, effectively, is that although users continue to own their content, in actuality they lose control over it.

Because content creation on the Internet is very much a cut-and-paste type affair, copyright infringement is rampant. People copy others' quotes when they retweet them. They copy and quote each other automatically in many message thread programs (and emails). Although technically these are all legal violations, enforcing copyright on social media posts is almost impossible in practice. As soon as someone posts something on social media, they have lost control of that content. This is not to say that we as researchers can do anything we like with this data. We most certainly cannot and should not! However, research is a legitimate and legally recognized use of social media. As the individuals charged with building knowledge about and for society, we have some privileges granted to us. One of those is the privilege to use social media data for research purposes.

Searching for Sites

Netnographic data search will not be unfamiliar to you in terms of its operations, but it should feel novel in terms of its commitment. The structure and intention are unlike the casual sorts of searches you are probably performing habitually, almost unconsciously, throughout the day as you navigate your way online and search for tidbits of information to answer the questions that pop up. When you begin your netnographic investigation, you may feel like you are a panner seeking gold. At other times you might feel like you are looking for a particular book in an explosive library, trying not to touch anything overly incendiary. At others, like a detective following a trail of keywords that could quickly go cold. At others, like a judge, sentencing some once-promising pools of data to exile from your research project.

You will use the output of the simplification stage as your starting point. You will enter the keywords, search terms, hashtags, trending words, and their variations into any social media site search function and data search engine you might find useful. The choice of search engine is, of course, important. You want to use search engines and platform searches that are appropriate to your research focus, question, and terms. If you are trying to understand how adults play, for example, you might look for sites or areas of sites related to games. If you are studying politically-stratified dating, you would look for sites where this occurs or is discussed.

There are many general level search engines available to you: Google and Bing, Yahoo! and DuckDuckGo, Ask.com and Baidu, and WolframAlpha. I also like to use visual search engines such as Google images. With a visual search, you can click on particular images and then choose 'visit' (or whatever other term for it your browser is using). Doing this will take you to the original site where the image of interest was posted. This simple strategy has often led me to interesting material (visual as well as textual) that I would otherwise have missed.

As well, and importantly, many if not all social media sites, such as YouTube, Facebook, Instagram, Twitter, blogs, and forums will have their own search operations. You can use those functions to search for groups, pages, message boards, and discussion forums that deal with particular topics that interest you. You might also use them to reveal particular messages, which will lead you to particular threads. Audio, video, and images can also be searched. You will likely be relying quite closely on these types of searches in your initial stages of investigation.

Try to extend your search vocabulary and begin to develop your search skills with some advanced search operations. Include some new search engines you may have not tried before, such as WolframAlpha and Ask.com. Then, for the main part of your investigation, start entering your search terms into the specialized search engines you know, such as Facebook, Instagram, YouTube, and any other relevant ones you are able to identify, such as Wikis, TripAdvisor entries, *New York Times* article discussions, Yelp reviews, Amazon reviews, and so on.

The point in the search stage is not to be comprehensive, but to be thorough. You are not trying to enact a social listening or big data-type strategy of including everything online related to your search terms. Your goal is to find high-quality data that you can investigate further. Search is the most inclusive stage of a data-collection operation. However, you still want to be fairly judicious in what you decide to examine or scout. You also want to be vigilant about the ethical obligations that will follow from pursuing particular sites rather than others.

STARTING AND DEVELOPING YOUR SEARCH (PROJECT EXERCISE)

8.4

What are some of the good search engines you plan to use to investigate your research question? Write them here. Note that search engines such as Google might take you to specific sites – or messages on specific sites – which themselves can then be searched further. The process is a bit like a random walk. No two people will end up searching exactly the same. There is an emergent, unexpected characteristic to search. As its name suggests, search is an exciting journey of discovery.

....
....
....
....
....
....
....

Now, go to those search engines, and enter your search terms from Box 8.3. What are the results? How do you judge them? Which ones do you 'naturally' start to explore further? Make a note of your decisions in a dedicated notebook or file, as these choices will be enhanced and developed in the next set of data operations, which deal with the scouting of the platforms and data sites your search turns up.

Finally, consider the ethical guidelines presented in this chapter. In your search, are there any sites and platforms you find that are private? Do they require you to join as a member, and create a password in order to access their information?

Search Example 1: Finding Images of Nursing-related Tattoos

In their analysis of the cultural themes present in tattoos related to nursing, and the way these themes reflect upon popular culture images of nursing as well as professional nursing culture, Eriksson et al. (2014) needed to locate images of nursing tattoos to include in their dataset. They describe their search procedure as follows: 'Having defined the research topic, the first step was to locate the fields that were relevant for gathering data, in this case where we would find bodily inscriptions being communicated.' Their task of finding tattoo images that reflect general cultural and professional understandings was fairly straightforward, and so they chose Google, which they describe as 'the most commonly used search engine on the Internet' (p. 320). They seem to have used Google Images. They say that the search terms they used were 'tattoo' and 'nurse'. The article includes a link to the 'tattoo nurse' Google Image search that still works in 2019 (the article was published in 2014), but it now includes many images that were posted after the article was written. The article's authors state that they 'filtered for images, with safe search deactivated' (p. 320). They decided to include only 'the first 400 pictures', a somewhat random choice that relies solely upon Google's algorithm for image inclusion. They are delimiting their dataset so that they can use the smaller number of images to engage in deep cultural analysis.

If a larger dataset had been required, they might have expanded it by playing with various search term combinations in Google Images, such as 'nursing', 'tattoos', 'tattoos of nurses', 'nurse with tattoo', and so on. They might have also used the visual function of other search engines such as Bing, and then moved to specific tattoo-themed website forums, nursing blogs, Instagram hashtags, or Pinterest boards. In the case of Eriksson et al.'s (2014) article, however, because of the way they constructed their study, the search operations do not proceed to scouting or selecting, but instead advance directly to saving.

It seems that because these researchers were interested in a wider, cultural mainstream type of phenomenon, they used a public search engine – Google – which indexes other public sites. Thus, the information that they revealed through these photographs can be considered public data. When the individuals uploaded and made particular tattoo images available online, and their privacy selections allowed them to be indexed as a part of Google's public search, they can be considered to have been aware that they had transferred and lost some rights to the images. They were no longer private images. However, the images may have constituted sensitive topics. Exposed body parts may have the potential for embarrassment or worse. In their discussion of research ethics, the authors suggest that they considered the risks of harm due to exposure, arguing 'that none of the tattooed people would be harmed due to our study as no one was exposed' (p. 321). In the representation stage of their research, when writing their article, they thus took the extra precaution of only using written descriptions of the images and limiting direct reference to them. They did this in order to anonymize the data and separate it from any personal identifiers.

Search Example 2: Finding Forums with Specific Banned Psychoactive Substance Discussions

The next example is a bit more extensive. Van Hout and Hearne (2015) explored the recreational use of 'methylhexanamine' or DMAA, a banned psychoactive substance originally patented for use as a nasal decongestant. In order to do so, they described their deployment of a two-stage search process. In the first stage of the process they conducted a systematic search of social media using three search engines: Google Insights for Search, Google, and Yahoo!. They were looking for online forums in particular (I assume), because they usually offer a rich source of data, they allow anonymous posting and information exchange, and they are difficult to trace. Dedicated forums thus provide a highly appropriate social media site for the type of sensitive topics and information about illegal substance use that Van Hout and Hearne were looking for.

The search terms that they had simplified from their research focus or question were the following: 'DMAA', 'Dimethylamylamine', 'Methylhexanamine', 'Methylhexaneamine', and 'Geranamine', searched in combination with the word 'forum' (p. 1279). These initial searches originally generated a total of 254,860 results, the number which the search engines offer (all of these results, it should be noted, are not viewable using the search engine). The researchers then examined only 'the first 20 hits of each of these five search combinations', subjecting them to 'inclusion criteria relating to drug user fora activity, use of DMAA on its own, and use for intoxication purposes as opposed to sport or weight loss supplementation' – criteria relating to the relevance of the information to the focus of their particular study.

Because this study dealt with a sensitive topic (illegal substance use), and also with a vulnerable population (people who were ostensibly breaking the law, and also using an illegal substance which could harm them), research ethics considerations were paramount. The authors did not discuss the private or public status of the websites forums they had sampled and used. Google and Yahoo! will return general results that direct the searcher to either type of site. The authors mention that they 'searched internally using the website internal search engines' as a 'second stage' step. However, we do not know if these were private sites requiring the authors to register and log into them separately (in which case they were under an obligation to disclose themselves to users and ask for permission from relevant site personnel) or not. Assuming that the data was public and came from a public site, their guarantee of anonymity that they 'ensure by removal of screen pseudonyms' and the lack of site and forum names or URLs is a helpful way to ameliorate some of the concerns over the sensitive topics and vulnerable population. As well, the authors should probably consider strong data-security measures to keep their dataset safe, and probably anonymize all of the collected data so that it cannot be traced back to original pseudonyms or sites.

SCOUTING

Scouting Data Sites

Scouting is a relatively easy data operation to describe. It involves reading through your search results, following them, and exploring the general sets of sites returned by your search. Because these operations are also iterative, scouting may lead to more searching on the internal search engine of particular sites, blogs, and platforms. The things you learn while scouting the data sites from your results may inform your knowledge of the topic and introduce new search terms to help you translate your research focus into more effective search terms. In some rare cases, the information you learn while performing scouting operations might even redefine or shift your research question.

The rationale behind scouting is twofold. It is both instrumental and also a goal in itself. First, scouting is exploration and learning. It is netnography in action. It might not seem so, but most of your time in the investigative stage of data collection is probably going to be spent on scouting. Scouting requires you to read data in real time. To inspect it. To scrutinize it. To seek a deeper cultural understanding. Scouting is one of the places where you begin to build the emotional and intellectual engagement with your data sites that is so important to netnographic integrity and praxis. You will record the scouting expedition resulting from your search results in your immersion journal (the form and function of the immersion journal will be explained in detail in Chapter 10).

The second rationale behind scouting is to begin the filtering and selection process. To reconnoiter means to examine or survey a particular region or area for purposes relating to engineering, geological, or for other reasons. You are reconnoitering social media data sites in order to look for viable data. Netnography works with smaller and more focused datasets than big data analytic-type analyses of social media. You will already have some sense of the kind of data you might be looking for (but that doesn't mean that you cannot still be very surprised by what it turns up!). However, ethnographic work allows several degrees of freedom in terms of locating data and changing focus. Even when being instrumental in scouting, you are always on a journey to uncover new and interesting cultural matters. Although following every new path can potentially take you down a theoretical reformulation rabbit hole, the judicious use of scouting for discovery might help you find your own Wonderland.

In scouting, you are looking for specific social media platforms, specific sections of social media platforms, and specific social media conversations and posts that can help you answer your question. Once you find these platforms, sections of platforms, and conversations that are of interest to your project, clearly record their locations and outline their general content in your immersion journal.

Be sure to keep good records of your scouting operations. Record what you found when you checked out each site as you would in a diary journal. Was it promising as a site for further investigation? Was it interesting? Was it relevant? Bookmark the ones you would like to go back to and explore further. Screenshot them if you like. Make notes about the searches you conducted, the results you found, the data sites you scouted, your initial impressions, and your conclusions. Feel free to filter out sites that you think are lower potential. For the higher potential ones, do not forget their locations or any details. You will perform additional selection operations upon them next.

SCOUTING YOUR SEARCH RESULTS (PROJECT EXERCISE)

8.5

From the project exercise captured in Box 8.4, you have already located a number of potential data sites containing information that might be relevant to your research question and focus. Turn to that box and investigate the first three sites you have written down.

Make sure you have a place to start recording the results of your scouting operations. What sort of data did you find in the data site? Did you find it novel or intriguing? Did it help you answer your research question? Did it illuminate or nuance your research question? Did it help you gain an appreciation for the lived experience related to the cultural understanding your netnography wishes to pursue?

Record the answers to these questions – and any other observations, impressions, thoughts, or plans that might occur to you as you explore these sites. You will use your answers for the next project exercise, in which you will start to apply selection operations.

Scouting Examples: Exploring Far and Near

Scouting is an organic process that develops rather naturally from searching operations and is driven by the focus of the research question. Some research questions are very broad, and deal with entire topics or phenomenon. Perren and Kozinets (2018), for example, sought to conceptualize the domain of peer-to-peer markets in order to define them and specify their general principles and underlying characteristics. To do so, they undertook a multisited investigation that included participant observation, interviews, and netnography. Working from an initial set of 193 cases, the researchers initially searched for and then scouted various websites, focusing on peer-to-peer marketing platforms. After this, they broadened their scouting to examine a wider range of sites and platforms, ranging from websites and social networking sites to blogs and the online public comments from new stories. Finally, they engaged intensively with a subset of 31 platforms. This is an example of a wide-ranging scouting operation that took several years to complete.

Most scouting operations are more constrained, because their initial focus is considerably narrower than investigating an entire phenomenon. An example of a more tractable focus is Holden and Spallek's (2018) article that asks if Australian dental practices' Facebook pages comply with Australian regulations. Using geographically-delimited search on Facebook, and a relatively limited amount of scouting, the researchers were able to identity 266 relevant pages to include in their dataset.

Another example is the article by Saboia et al. (2018), in which the authors are interested in the way that online health-related opinion leaders influence the food-related behaviors of their followers on social networks. After what I must assume was a thorough scouting operation, they decided to focus on the use of the Instagram platform because it was 'popular' and in wide use, and used in an 'emotional support context' as well as a location for posting recipes and 'monitoring healthy eating' behaviors (p. 98). The study focused on Portuguese speakers from Portugal and Brazil. After using Google to search for Instagram, food, and diet (in Portuguese), the authors then scouted the results to find profiles with a large number of followers. This yielded 24 Instagram profiles. The researchers then broadened their search by looking at traditional profiles and suggested profiles provided on those 24 Instagram profiles, which brought their total to 3,480 profiles. From there, they narrowed again with keywords, finally ending up with 33 Instagram profiles from which they began collecting 'the first 30 posts of the day' (pp. 98–9).

A final example of scouting is the work of Litchman et al. (2018), who sought to understand patient-driven innovation in diabetes management. In particular, the authors were interested in people with Type 1 diabetes who built and shared knowledge of open source artificial pancreas systems (OpenAPS). The authors focused on Twitter and particularly the #OpenAPS Twitter hashtag, which was the subject of their search. As they followed these posts (apparently in real time), they 'became involved and familiarized themselves' with the 'OpenASP community' (p. 2). Reading these posts and following them led the research team to other data sites, such as news reports, blogs, and press articles. As well, scouting the Twitter data propelled them to engage in a range of other interactive activities, including conferences and meet-up groups, as well as informing their written fieldnotes.

SELECTING

Selection Criteria for Investigative Filtering

Selecting operations apply criteria in order to filter the results from data site searches and scouting. Selecting is about limiting the amount of data in the dataset to maintain a balance between a thorough and expansive look at a particular phenomenon, and the ability of researchers to go into sufficient depth with a particular amount of data. As Kozinets (2002a, 64) notes, 'although researchers might include all the data in a first pass or "grand tour" interpretation, they will generally want to save their most intense analytical efforts for the primarily informational and on-topic messages'. Kozinets also provided a set of guidelines for selecting operations that included focus and relevance, higher traffic of postings, larger numbers of discrete message poster, more detailed or rich data, and more interactions. These criteria have found wide use in the field, and I am hesitant to alter them much. However, they can be polished further and made clearer.

There are five criteria to utilize in data-selection operations: relevance, activity, interactivity, diversity, and richness. Relevance, activity, interactivity, and richness are based upon criteria published in Kozinets (2002a). Diversity was introduced in Kozinets (2010: 89) as a 'heterogeneous' criterion. I removed substantiality as a criterion to reflect the facts that (1) it is largely covered by the activity criterion, and (2) individual data sites do not, themselves, need to have large numbers of posts. Saving a single post from a particular site is perfectly fine if that post meets other criteria. The entire dataset will usually have large numbers of posts, but even this is not necessary. So, I removed any hint of a data quantity over quality judgment.

It is productive to note that ethical decision-making provides its own sources of selection criteria in investigative operations, operating on what we might conceive of as a parallel, but equally important (if not more important) track. If particular sites are private, for example, or focus on more vulnerable populations, then ethical considerations might make those sites less attractive, and your decision-making for moving ahead with data-saving operations should reflect this reality. In the following paragraphs, I briefly detail each of the five criteria.

Relevance

Relevance is the single more important of the selection criteria. It is likely to be one that you have been working with throughout the scouting stage as you have been deciding which sites to explore, not to explore, to explore in depth or superficially, to record or not record. Without relevance, you are collecting and studying data that is, well, irrelevant.

Relevant data sites mean sites of information which meaningfully bear upon or are connected with the research question and research focus. Judging relevance is obviously a somewhat imprecise act, requiring human judgment. The simple presence of keywords would not necessarily indicate relevance. Instagram posters might be sharing photos with very different hashtags than their images, or message posters on Reddit might be talking about an abstract topic such as 'government' or 'fatherhood' without ever mentioning that particular word. Similarly, relevant data does not necessarily answer the research question directly. Instead, the data source should at minimum provide some sense of understanding relating to the question. To nuance or inform it. That is why we need to scout our data sites carefully. Otherwise, our judgments of relevance are not as informed as they could be. Published netnographies often include explanatory statements relating the choice of particular sites to relevance criteria, relating them through search terms and scouting reports.

Activity

Activity is related to the recency and regularity of the flow of information on the social media data site. Again, 'recency' and 'regularity' are terms which need to be concretized in relation to your own study. Unless this is a historical or archival study, you are situating it in the present. Netnography is about contemporary cultural worlds. Thus, you want to favor data sites where there is a significant amount of information that is recent. Watching a data site can help you determine how active it is. As you spend a week or two following a particular Facebook group, subreddit, or Twitter hashtag, for example, you will gain a sense of how popular it is. For example, if the blog you are interested in has its last post and comment in 2009, it is not active and of only historical interest. For most purposes, you do not need a massive amount of posts. Five or ten per day will often suffice. But there should be some regular and recent activity, and the potential for more activity when new topics rouse the attention of the people who use the site. That makes it worth following. I have seen a number of netnographies that begin when an event happens – a movie is released, a protest is launched, a political decision is announced. This topicality makes data collection much easier because a lot of social media activity happens in response to these types of newsworthy events. In published netnographies, authors often relate how many messages per day the data site or sites had during the timespan of the investigative data collection operations.

Interactivity

Because we are studying social media, the interactions between people are important to our data collection. Many blogs and vlogs are more like soapboxes than conversations. The people on these sites have the microphone or megaphone and the audience listens. Those types of sites are generally poor locations for netnography, which is interested in people's dynamic social media conversations. Although blogs and vlogs can provide important information to inform our studies, the posts, comments, and replies on these blogs and vlogs tend to be of greater interest. In addition, many blogs, vlogs, Instagram pages and other platforms have been professionalized, so that they are more like a type of broadcast media than social media. Interaction is the essence of social media. When there is two-or-more-way communication, there is interaction, language, cultural exchange, emotion, and the potential for communal types of relations. These are the sorts of meaningful phenomenon that netnography studies. Published netnographies will often quote conversational interactive exchanges between message posters as evidence that the site and data were interactive.

Diversity

Diversity reflects the need for the data site to contain the expression of different types of perspectives. If the data is dominated by a single voice, such as the owner and moderator of a message board or site, then it may not be a good reflection of the sort of multiperspectival and public type of opinion that many netnographies seek. If one particular type of voice is sought, such as transpersons, then providing diversity in this sense would not be an important criterion. However, there is usually much diversity within apparently homogeneous groups. Transpersons, for example, constitute a diverse set of voices and viewpoints. Oftentimes, netnographic researchers will report the number of different user names included in the dataset as evidence that the data collected likely represented a number of different viewpoints. For example, in their study of recreational DMAA users, Van Hout and Hearne (2015) reported that a total of 169 distinct fora user pseudonyms were included in their final dataset (p. 1280).

Richness

Richness is a very important criterion relating to the presence of detail, description, emotion, and interconnection in the data site or data. Rich data is also called deep data. Rich data reveals human cultural realities. It is like a picture – worth (and often using) a thousand words or more. Short textual statements, such as one would find on a corporate Facebook page, are usually not rich or deep. Short tweets, by themselves, are not very rich or deep. Detailed stories and descriptions are some of the best kinds of rich data. Because it is descriptive, anecdotal, and often well crafted, rich data contains a lot of context – links to particular social, cultural, and physical environments and identities. These contexts reveal connections that can be further explored by the researcher during analysis and interpretation. Photographs, videos, and podcasts can be rich sources of data, especially when accompanied by detailed textual descriptions that link to them. Rich or deep data also represent opinions and perspectives that may be widely held among other posters, but they are expressed in a more evocative and eloquent way than is usual. This type of data is therefore rare and important. It is curated as exemplary because it is also explanatory. For these reasons, rich or deep data often forms the centerpieces of published netnographies.

Applying the Five Criteria in Practice

In general, applying the criteria means that social media data sites should be favored that contain data that is deemed to be relatively more relevant, active, interactive, diverse, and rich. How you evaluate the sites on these criteria is entirely up to you. For some researchers, making these judgments might be a relatively simple matter. For others, they may wish to use methods such as the one I have previously recommended of weighting the criteria and then rating each data site on a ten-point scale for each of the five criteria. This can be done in a simple matrix-like table. If you are working in a team, like many netnographers, it can also be done in a spreadsheet, with each person ranking each data site under consideration. These are also not the only criteria possible. If useful, researchers should inventively create and add criteria of their own.

Because the application of these criteria is so fundamental, widespread, and easy to communicate, there may be no need to provide extensive examples. Above, we used Berdychevsky and Nimrod's (2015) netnographic investigation of the way seniors use online platforms to discuss issues of sexuality as an example to understand how to turn a research focus into keywords. The researchers looked at 14 senior-related platforms and sites, and then used a dataset drawn from it of 686,283 messages posted by 79,665 members. After filtering out posts that included relevant sex-related keywords, they were left with a 'preliminary dataset of 6,712 posts' which the researchers then 'read and sorted based on content into relevant and irrelevant categories' (p. 471) following, I assume, the netnographic principle of selecting based on relevance to the research question. The final dataset was composed of 2,534 relevant posts. If you want further examples of the criteria's application, I direct you to look up some recent published netnographies and examine how they are applied in them.

It can make good sense to focus only upon certain criteria, or to trade off one or more criteria against others, depending upon your own research focus. If you are studying influential video bloggers, for example, then perhaps interactivity is irrelevant to you. Or if you are going to aggregate a lot of short Twitter posts, perhaps you are not as interested in richness. At this stage, you want to winnow down your dataset so that you can handle it in a reasonable manner, but you also do not want to eliminate good data. You want there to be enough data so that clear patterns can emerge during analysis and interpretation, and that you can test and refine your comprehension of those patterns with your dataset (or you might collect additional data to test and refine). The one criterion you should never sacrifice is relevance. The data you collect must be relevant to your research question.

In addition, the data sites you select should be guided by your consideration of research ethics guidelines regarding sensitive topics and vulnerable populations. We will discuss these guidelines in the section which follows the selection project exercises in Box 8.6.

8.6 APPLYING SELECTION CRITERIA (PROJECT EXERCISE)

In the project exercise captured in Boxes 8.4 and 8.5, you located and then wrote scouting reports on three data sites that were potentially useful for informing your research question and focus. In this exercise, you will gain some practice applying the five selection criteria.

For each of the three data sites (more, if you like), rate the site from 0 (very weak presence of this criterion in the data on the site) to 100 (very strong presence of this criterion in the data on the site) on each of the following five criteria. You might also enter these into a spreadsheet to facilitate a rapid and easy calculation.

Relevance: data on the site relates to my research focus and question(s)

Data Site 1 rating: ....

Data Site 2 rating: ....

Data Site 3 rating: ....

Activity: data on the site is recent and regular

Data Site 1 rating: ....

Data Site 2 rating: ....

Data Site 3 rating: ....

Interactivity: data on the site reveals two-way or multi-way communications between participants

Data Site 1 rating: ....

Data Site 2 rating: ....

Data Site 3 rating: ....

Diversity: data on the site reveals different perspectives and different socio-cultural viewpoints

Data Site 1 rating: ....

Data Site 2 rating: ....

Data Site 3 rating: ....

Richness: data on the site is detailed and descriptive, providing deep con-textual information

Data Site 1 rating: ....

Data Site 2 rating: ....

Data Site 3 rating: ....

Now that you have finished rating your three (or more) sites on these criteria, add up the scores. Which site is your 'best' according to your ratings? You can take this site to be your key data site. In the next subsection, you will focus on this key data site and then start saving data from it.

ETHICAL CONCERNS IN SELECTING/ INVESTIGATING

Sensitive Topics

Alongside the five selection criteria of relevance, activity, interactivity, diversity, and richness, we must also recognize research ethics concerns in our site choices. In particular, this section considers the research and collection of data about sensitive topics.

Because people have a decades-long history of using electronic communications to talk to other people about personal issues, and because of its long history of the use of unsolicited data, netnography has been a popular way that people use to study sensitive social topics. A quick examination of published netnographies reveals a panoply of sensitive issues, such as studying social media communications about psychedelic drug use (Hearne and van Hout, 2016; Orsolini et al., 2015), terrorism (Bertram and Ellison, 2014; Rhazzali, 2015), sexual violence (Yeager, 2012), teen binge drinking (Pettigrew et al., 2013), the use of targeted messages on Facebook to promote drinking among young people (Moraes et al., 2014), poaching (Büscher, 2016), bullying and school shootings (Raitanen et al., 2017), and cryptomarkets and illicit drugs (Moeller et al., 2017).

These topics and many others can be considered to be sensitive because they deal with matters that can be controversial and emotionally sensitive, such as people's sexual choices. Many of them are also illegal, such as illicit drug use, terrorism, and violence. Studying online discussions relating to these controversial and illegal activities can provide us with valuable insights as social scientists, and help us understand these phenomena in a way that can advise policy based on empirically-derived objective fact. Sensitive data which is 'manifestly made public by the data subject' seems to be permitted under Article 9 (2) of the GDPR rules. However, the use of sensitive data which is private (i.e., posted on a private site and/or with a personal privacy setting) is forbidden under the GDPR.

As we will see in the next section, sensitive topics are closely related to vulnerable populations because in both of these cases the data is considered to be a special category of data that requires special treatment (data security) and a consequentialist determination about whether the benefits of the research outweigh its risks.

Vulnerable Populations

Customarily, vulnerable populations are those who lack the ability to make informed choices. In research, prisoners, people who are ill, and children are common categories of groups of people with this diminished or disempowered capacity to make choices. Just as they do when topics are sensitive, under conditions where people are vulnerable, the researcher has a heightened responsibility to respect the 'fundamental human rights of human dignity, autonomy, protection, safety, maximization of benefits and minimizations of harms, or, in the most recent accepted phrasing, respect for persons, justice, and beneficence' (Association of Internet Researchers Ethics Working Group, 2012: 4).

Online, certain groups relate around topics that make their data sensitive. For example, if you are studying sites that feature marital infidelity, criminal activity or other illegal or stigmatized behaviors, the participants on those sites cannot be construed to be minimal risk. In fact, as Stephens-Davidowitz (2017) shows in *Everybody Lies*, there are large numbers of people using online social experiences to explore ideas, interests, and tastes that would very likely surprise some of the people who are closest to them. Almost everyone explores some sensitive topics, some of the time, and the threat of public exposure of those explorations makes them vulnerable.

Matters become considerably more complicated, however, when we are dealing with populations such as children. If we consider, as the section on private versus public data above suggests, that a given user's selection of public as a privacy setting for their social media account is a type of proxy for informed consent to use their data in a research study, then there are two important problems that accompany making this assumption for children. First, children may not even be able to legally make those decisions. YouTube requires account holders to be 18 years old, but allows 13-year-olds to sign up with parental permission. Facebook, TikTok, Instagram, and Snapchat have a minimum account opening age of thirteen. Second, children may be unable to properly make the decision required. Younger children are likely to lack the conceptual ability to assess complex risks, such as having yourself depicted in a study on social media in a way that could become publicized and inspire negative responses for a long time. The same issues arise when considering those with cognitive or emotional disabilities that might impair their abilities to evaluate personal risks. Because comprehension is important, we should also include that researchers must communicate in an appropriate manner and language. These concerns should lead researchers to take special care to ensure that the data from vulnerable populations and sensitive topics data is treated according to the accepted practices of ethical research.

The reality that large numbers of children possess and are using social media accounts is a matter of social and public concern. A recent survey by knowthenet. org.uk called The Social Age Study suggested that 59% of children have already used social media by the time they turned 10 years old. Given that these children are active online, that technology use may involve negative consequences as well as benefits. Companies that possess their data are using it for their own purposes. As a society, we would likely benefit from closer research examining the social media practices of children that is conducted in the public interest by academics, rather than by corporate marketing departments. To do this type of research on a vulnerable population will require the research team to apply consequentialist ethics to determine whether the benefits of such research will outweigh the risks.

Weighing Benefits Against Risks

In order to be able to make the consequentialist tradeoffs that guide ethical research decisions, especially under conditions where we are working with sensitive data and vulnerable populations, we work with the terms 'benefits' and 'risks'. In netnography, risks are a bit more complicated and in many ways more important than benefits, so I discuss benefits first.

The benefits of conducting social science research are relatively easy to frame. Often, they do not benefit individual participants directly, especially participants such as the creators of messages that may have been sitting in online archives for weeks, months, or years. In an interview situation, a participant might gain some knowledge or a degree of self-awareness. In a netnography working only with investigative data, this is not going to happen. The most important benefits come from increasing our scientific understanding of important social phenomena, such as the way people use social media, the effects of social media on children, the consequences of increasing commercialization in the social media sphere, the illicit uses of online spaces, and so on. There is scientific benefit that comes from building an enhanced understanding of these phenomena. Often, research might be conducted to enhance our understanding of the use of technology or the needs of particular groups, and this research could have the benefit of helping to inform the production of innovative solutions and products. Finally, there are important social and public benefits to research that can guide policy-making and regulation in the public interest.

For example, with an eleven-person international team of netnographers, I conducted a research project for the Campaign for Tobacco-Free Kids that examined how tobacco companies were using social media platforms to promote their combustible products to young people in ten countries. The work was featured in a story in the *New York Times* (Kaplan, 2018) and also in a complaint filed with the United States Federal Trade Commission along with nine leading public health and medical groups as signatory co-complainants (Tobacco-Free Kids, 2018). Although there were risks involved in the research (e.g., it was difficult to know exactly how old some of the young people who were posting photographs of themselves smoking were), I adamantly believe that the public benefits of reducing this indirect form of tobacco advertising to young people outweigh these risks.

Embarrassment, shame, and even censure are some of the sources of quicksand public relations disaster potentials for harm in ethnographic work. We need only point to the controversy surrounding Laud Humphrey's Tearoom Trade to understand how disclosure of hidden behaviors can be harmful to the people whose actions are disclosed (Babbie, 2004). The same potential for embarrassment is one of the chief risks of netnographic research. Consider Tiidenberg's (2014) online fieldwork studying self-shooters who expose themselves in sexy exhibitionistic photos online. This is a popular behavior, one that has had numerous impacts upon public images and political careers, and we still know very little about it. Her visual analysis of these sexy selfies included visual images of the photographs, but took various precautions to help minimize the risk of harm.

A less common, but more important risk is the possibility that illegal behavior is exposed, and that this then exposes the research participant (who, in investigative research, may be an unwilling participant) to legal risk. Although I have never heard of it reaching this point, it is theoretically possible that a netnographic researcher's records might be subpoenaed and the research could become evidence in a criminal case. This scenario, unlikely as it might be, is the maximal risk situation for a netnography. Studying a topic such as terrorism, the dark web, domestic violence, or illegal drug use using netnography does expose one's participants to these risks. Also, because this research is inductive, the possibility for harm might shift as you move through your project. You may be studying a site related to African tourism and discover a large and active area detailing how to illegally import poached items made from endangered animal species (this actually happened to a netnographer, who related the story to me in person).

Most of the time, however, netnographic projects will be dealing with situations of minimal risk. The US Federal Code Title 45 regulations define minimal risk as meaning that 'the probability and magnitude of harm or discomfort anticipated in the research are not greater in and of themselves than those ordinarily encountered in daily life or during the performance of routine physical or psychological examinations or tests' (Protection of Human Subjects, 2018). This definition is obviously tailored to a world of physical medical experimentation, not ethnographic exploration, but in the past I have linked the idea of exposing one's social media comments to public scrutiny, such as being highlighted and featured on the top page of a social or traditional media article, for example, having your tweet published on the Fox News site or in the Huffington Post (as often happens with a very small proportion of the tweets of ordinary people).

Assessing the potential for harm and the probable benefits of your study is not a simple matter, but because of the consequentialist system of ethics that guides scientific research today, it needs to be done. Listing and counterbalancing benefits against risks is a procedure that is not solely limited to investigative data collection in netnography, it is also involved in interactive as well as some kinds of immersive data collection. It is a central element of consent forms, and often becomes a subject discussed in research disclosures. Moreover, it is a key part of any research ethics review.

Data Security

Before we discuss and think about saving and storing raw data, we need to think about what happens to that stored and saved information-stuff: that which is 'chosen-as-data' and 'saved'. Hence, the final ethical procedure in this chapter is data security. Regardless of contingency, and regardless of whether data has been collected using investigation, interaction, or immersion, data security is important as long as there is information through which social media participants' identities can be linked to their data. In particular, this is most important when there is the potential for harm – such as when the topic is sensitive or member(s) of a population are vulnerable. If you have only immersive data in which you capture and reflect upon your own experiences, with hardly any information that involves other people, or identifies them by name or online pseudonym, or poses minimal risk for harm, then data security is less relevant. For many researchers, however, it will be important.

Researchers use a variety of methods to store the electronic data that results from online data practices. Taking your research and your research ethics seriously means that you must follow good data-security practices. These procedures are widely practiced throughout mid-sized and larger organizations and companies, and if you are in a university setting your school's technology department can probably update you on the latest accepted practices at your institution. For the purposes of this chapter, however, I want to overview some good data-security practices.

Research data should always be saved and stored in a secure manner. The more sensitive the data, or vulnerable the population studied, the more potential for harm should the data be used improperly, then the more advanced security protocols are required. A private laptop, protected by a simple password, is probably not secure enough for this type of sensitive data. Most institutions do not consider public cloud storage-type applications, such as Dropbox or Google documents, to have adequate security. Some very reputable academic institutions consider Microsoft OneDrive to be a secure application for file and application storage and transmission. Encrypting data with an encryption program such as AxCrypt or CryptoExpert might be advisable if your netnography deals with sensitive topics, such as potentially illegal matters, and contains possibly identifiable information. For very sensitive data, keeping the data physically separate, such as on its own hard drive, as well as encrypted, might be advisable. The hard drive should then be stored in a locked box or file cabinet of some kind, where the principal investigator of the research is in charge of who has the key to the cabinet, and thus has control over the data.

SAVING

Saving Data

Saving data operations are procedures to preserve viewed social media information and store them in a more long-lasting form as a part of an organized set of data in a netnographic research project. According to the definition of data given at the beginning of this chapter, it is during the saving operations that information from social media sites is actually transformed into the data that becomes the most important part of your research project. Arguably, that data moves from one type of experience (captured in the immersion journal of the individual researchers doing the research data capture) to another (the observations, communications, and interactions of the research participants in the netnography study).

Although everyone with a computer knows how to store data, there are some specific procedural elements that require some explanation when we want to understand how to save data in netnography. This section explains at a very fundamental level what is required. Without becoming overly technical, it will set out the four general choices we have to store data, when they are appropriate, and how to use your computer's or mobile phone's capabilities to complete them.

There are four basic data operations to choose from in netnography: capture, save and print, copy and paste, and scraping. The four different operations result in a bitmap (or pixel map) image file, text files, and a spreadsheet file. All four file types are searchable, although images are still difficult and characters in the bitmap images and print files may require a round of optical character recognition (or OCR) before they can be searched. The following four short sections succinctly describe what you need to know about capturing information from your data site using capture, save and print, copy and paste, and scraping. In them, I assume that you have a reasonable level of familiarity with the functions on your computer and mobile phone, and can use a search engine to fill in what knowledge you do not currently possess.

Screenshots

A screenshot, which is also called a screen grab, is a file that captures or digitally photographs the image that is currently visible on a computer monitor, phone screen, or other visual output device. All operating systems have screenshot programs and functions, such as Windows' Snipping Tool and macOS's Grab. Android phones and iPhones take screenshots when particular buttons are pressed simultaneously (e.g., home and power). The oldest (but still reliable!) way to take a screenshot is to take a photograph of your screen as you are using your social media account.

Screenshots are useful for preserving the full visual context of the social media experience available to you. When you capture a screenshot, you can capture images, text, font, colors, URL, other windows on your computer, your desktop, and anything that you can see on your screen. Having this kind of context can be very useful when you are trying to remember aspects of your online experience, such as the details about why you liked a particular site. What we are truly missing in netnography is more variety in the way social media is described by people. For example, for the blind. How do those without sight perform netnography? What does it mean to them?

Unless you are expert with computers and files, screenshots are still the main way that you can move data from your mobile phone to your computer. Using a mobile-native program such as Instagram or Snapchat for your netnographic data collection will probably require you to take a number of screenshots and then move these to your computer or a hard drive, or some other secure data location. In general, screenshots are useful for mobile phone, visual, and small amounts of rich data, but they are time-consuming, inefficient, and difficult to work with. They are an excellent way to annotate and preserve data in context and are very applicable for use in your immersion journals. But screenshots are ineffective for capturing larger amounts of data. The process can be, and needs to be, more automated and accessible. Computer scientists can no doubt help here. Human–computer interface and interaction experts as well.

Print and Save

All web browsers have the ability to save and print the files they are currently reading. Usually this function is accessible as a simple command from the browser. Saving from Firefox gives me a choice between: (a) saving the entire webpage, complete with images, texts, and html codes (hypertext markup language) in a file that can be read by any browser; (b) saving the html portion of the webpage only; (c) saving only the text files; or (d) saving all of the files. Printing from Safari, for example, opens a dialog box that allows you to save as a PDF (Adobe Portable Document Format) file. Saving and printing in this way saves the entire file you are viewing, which means that the program is preserving not just what you can see in your window, but also what is in the entire document or image, scrolled down completely to the bottom. Although frequently convenient, the problem with the Print File function is that it rarely prints everything, and it often distorts formatting. In addition, both printing and saving functions limit you to single page views, and thus are inefficient and time-consuming if, for example, you wish to save an entire subreddit, or the 2,000+ posts in a single thread of a forum. However, when you are dealing with image files such as Instagram posts, audio files such as podcasts, or video files such as YouTube, you may want to save the actual files from your browser, and there are still few widely available and cost-free choices available for doing this. For some of these saving functions, third-party software or sites may be required.

Copy and Paste

Copy and Paste is the familiar control-C, control-V, or hold and drag with a mouse-type function that you use to move text within word-processing applications. The advantage of copy-and-paste operations is that (1) you can select only which data you wish to save, and (2) the data can be saved in a text format that is easy to search and to work with. The disadvantage with copy and paste is that, like the other two methods above, it tends to be a time-consuming and inefficient way to get larger amounts of data preserved as part of your dataset. Unlike screenshot and save and print, however, you lose context by saving. Fonts, colors, and often images will disappear. Copy and paste can be effective to preserve small amounts of textual data in document or spreadsheet files, but it is also difficult to work with.

Scraping

Scraping is a procedure whereby a computer program automatically saves social media data from a website and puts it into a particular format. For example, scraping programs can read an entire subreddit and then put the data into a spreadsheet-readable file in which each separate post, comment, and reply is located in a separate row of the spreadsheet. Most scraping programs only scrape text (as in this Reddit example), but some will scrape images, and others can scrape both text and images. Scraping is useful for saving large amounts of specific data because it automates and streamlines the burdensome processes of capturing data through methods like print, screenshots, or cut and paste. There are several open source options for scraping different kinds of social media data sites. A number of these are available as extensions in popular browsers such as Chrome, Firefox, and Safari. Others are available through online sites which automatically download the information from particular sites and save them to your hard drive. However, finding good scraping programs can still be difficult. Depending on how much data you have to collect, and how difficult it is going to be to collect and handle it manually, it may be worthwhile to consult with computing professionals to understand the options you have for buying an off-the-shelf program or, until there are better options, even building a customized program that will satisfy your needs.

SAVING YOUR DATA (PROJECT EXERCISE)

8.7

In Box 8.6, you rated three or more potential data sites on the five netnographic criteria. From those ratings, you should have one data site that is of particular interest.

Write that data site's name and location here: _____

_____

Now, it is time to capture that data. In this subsection of the chapter, you learned about four possible options for saving the data from your data site: screenshots, print and save, copy and paste, and scraping.

For this exercise, try to apply each type of saving operation to your data site. Using your computer, tablet, or mobile phone, take a few screenshots. Using your laptop, mobile, tablet, or desktop computer, try the print and save (as a

(Continued)

PDF format file, and with separate files for images and text), and copy and paste functions (copying the information into a word-processing document or a spreadsheet file such as DOC or XLS). Then, try to find a scraping extension or application that will work on the data site you have chosen. Save your scraped data in a spreadsheet-readable file such as the CSV file format.

What did you think of the various ways to save data? Which ones did you find easier? Which were more meaningful sources of experience for you? Which ones were more natural? How did the different types of data-saving procedure affect your closeness to the data, and your sense of interaction with the data site and the people whose communications and perspectives are represented on it? Did one or the other appeal to you more?

INTELLIGENT OTHERTHINGS IN NETNOGRAPHY

The Internet of Things is turning into a hive of artificially Intelligent Otherthings. Another emergent trend is body integrations, from wearable extra-brains to implantable computing smart tattoos, perhaps heralding a more transhumanist world. Augmented reality is mapping onto physical reality, changing the way we navigate (think Google Maps) and communicate (think Snapchat). We are surrounded by a wealth of data. However, at this point in time netnographers are locked into a world of smartphones, laptops, desktops, and tablets, and the data that can be efficaciously extracted from them. All of these devices can provide useful data for netnography. We seek a human-level experience, and that means experiencing a significant amount of social media data collection in real time: taking screen shots.

And that's okay. Because even with netnography in the age of smartphones, we are still limited to screenshots because this is how we can fully experience our passionate connection to the temporal frame of a human information consumer, not only a researcher: a reflexive researcher-consumer. Then we must transfer the screenshots of data from our mobile phones to our computers for central processing and data-security lockdown. Mobile phones are a messy way to do netnographic data collection. But in today's world, they are also one of the most realistic contexts for our research. If you are really into your topic, if you are deep into your social site (which is, ultimately, an imaginary, a set of connections between abstract ideas, actual social media data, and actual linkages to a variety of corporate, governmental, and other institutional players and their very real material and economic resources focused by your research question), then you will quite probably be using your mobile phone for your research. Your phone will be a perfect vehicle through which to experience your netnography. It will most likely, until there are better ways, feed your investigation with saved screenshots.

CHAPTER SUMMARY

This chapter focused on investigative data-collection operations (but immersion operations intruded quite frequently, and interaction more than a few times). In netnography, data is searched, filtered, and then collected in a research movement called *investigation* that focuses on selection. Building upon the prior chapter's conceptualization of data as an enacted decision to turn some information or experiential realization into recorded observation, this chapter outlines the specific investigative operation practices of simplifying questions, and searching, scouting, selecting, and saving data in netnography. Simplifying translates research questions and focus into a consistent set of search terms or keywords. Search involves the entry of keywords, search terms, hashtags, trends, and their variations into search function and engines. Scouting operations examine data sites in order to understand them and narrow the choice set from which you will select your final dataset. Selection is the judgment process whereby you apply specific relevant criteria in order to decide which data sites to choose. The subprocesses surrounding selection include data ethics concerns such as sensitive topics, vulnerable populations, and weighing benefits against risks. Saving operations include capture, cut and paste, and scraping, and are also implicated in ethical procedures of data security. The chapter contained multiple ideas about making sure that your data is saved in a way that is safe and secure. Saving operations include saving data from mobile phones, and they dictate the form your netnography's investigative dataset will take. In total, the five practices described in this chapter of simplifying, searching, scouting, selecting, and saving constitute the process of investigative data-collection operations in netnography.

KEY READINGS

Berdychevsky, Liza, and Galit Nimrod (2015) '"Let's talk about sex": Discussions in seniors' online communities', *Journal of Leisure Research*, 47(4): 467–84.

Eriksson, Henrik, Mats Christiansen, Jessica Holmgren, Annica Engström, and Martin Salzmann-Erikson (2014) 'Nursing under the skin: A netnographic study of metaphors and meanings in nursing tattoos', *Nursing Inquiry*, 21(4): 318–26.

Litchman, Michelle L., Dana Lewis, Lesly A. Kelly, and Perry M. Gee (2018) 'Twitter analysis of #OpenAPS DIY artificial pancreas technology use suggests improved A1C and quality of life', *Journal of Diabetes Science and Technology*. 1932296818795705.

Protection of Human Subjects, US Federal Code Title 46, Section 46 (2018) Available at www.ecfr.gov/cgi-bin/retrieveECFR?gp=&SID=83cd09e1c0f5c6937cd9d7513160f-c3f&pitd=20180719&n=pt45.1.46&r=PART&ty=HTML (last accessed 31 January 2019).

Van Hout, Marie Claire, and Evelyn Hearne (2016) 'Confessions of contemporary English opium-eaters: A netnographic study of consumer negotiation of over-the-counter morphine for misuse', *Journal of Substance Use*, 21(2): 141–52.

INTERACTING: TURNING CONNECTION AND COMMUNICATION INTO RESEARCH DATA

CHAPTER OVERVIEW

Chapter 9 will focus on interactive data-collection operations. Interactive data is co-produced and elicited, rather than simply observed and recorded. Before detailing the elements of interactive data collection, the chapter will consider the nature of online engagement as the appropriate frame for ethnography, replacing the more perplexing former term drawn from traditional ethnography, 'participation'. The chapter will then present procedural operations under the general categories of interview, involvement, innovations, and informed consent. The appropriate way to conduct interviews will be covered, focusing especially on online interviews. After that, the chapter will discuss, describe, and provide examples of involvements, or naturalistic immersive interactions. Then, under the general name of innovative research approaches to interaction, it will discuss the use of research webpages, digital diaries, and mobile ethnography. The chapter's final section will provide the reader with a more exhaustive treatment of informed consent procedures in netnography.

INTERACTIVE DATA

Interactive data is co-produced or elicited, rather than simply observed and recorded. It is the product or artifact of some kind of deliberate interaction between the researcher, or research team, and someone or something else. Interactive data usually involves capturing the traces and recordings of that exchange, and there are specific procedural operations and ethical rules governing those exchanges.

Interactive data can be co-produced in one of three main ways. First, they can be the result of a capture of a naturalistic process which occurs in the context of a social media site. The second way you can co-produce interactive data is by asking questions of people in a formal interview situation that happens outside of the field context. There are also blended types of interaction data-collection operations that are both naturalistic and structured. These methods include the interactive research webpage, digital diaries, and mobile ethnography. As well, screen-sharing during interviews can also provide the combination of a structured but naturalistic questioning frame.

This chapter will distinguish between interviews, immersive interactions, and ostensibly innovative approaches such as research webpages, digital diaries, and mobile ethnographies. All of these techniques – interacting naturalistically on social media platforms, interviewing people, and gathering data from a customized research webpage – are more intrusive than investigative methods. Thus, they require additional levels of ethical assurance. In particular, they require the addition of procedures of researcher disclosure and the gathering of informed consent. The gaining of informed consent is included in this chapter, with an example of an informed consent form included for your convenience.

The chapter is organized into five discrete sections. The first section considers the nature of online engagement. Participation has been one of the core principles of ethnography, and yet its execution in netnography's data operations comes with a whole heap of confusion. By considering netnographic engagement as the appropriate frame, rather than ethnographic participation, this first section clarifies one of the approach's most vexing and contested procedural foundations. The next four sections consider elements of interactive data-collection operations. These procedural operations are considered under the general categories of interview, involvement, innovations, and informed consent. The next section of this chapter will overview the use of interview approaches to data-collection operations, emphasizing online interviews. After that, involvements, or naturalistic immersive interactions, will be considered. The chapter will then present innovative research approaches such as using research webpages, employing digital diaries, and using mobile ethnography. The final section offers a detailed look at informed consent procedures in netnography.

Overviewing Participation in Netnography

If netnography, like ethnography, is about participation as well as observation, then what is the right kind and amount of participation? This is one of the biggest questions and biggest debates within netnography. Providing a clear and comprehensive answer to this question, which is central to the pursuit of interactive data operations, is the topic of the next two subsections of this chapter.

First, we should have some background. Participation in ethnography is embodied, immediate, geographic, temporal, and intersubjective. In netnography, much of this involves working with communication technologies, and using their archival functions (in investigative operations) and connective ones (in interactive operation). As we will note in a section of a future chapter, terms like 'field site' have considerably less meaning in netnography than they do in ethnography. Data may be dispersed among many such sites, and thus the term 'data site', or 'data sites', may be more useful than thinking about a single field site. Observations in ethnography are usually completed in person and recounted later in fieldnotes, but in netnography they become more like data operations. People posting on Twitter, TikTok, or publicly on Pinterest, for example, may be more like a public than a community. They do not necessarily interact meaningfully with one another, but some players in the attention game will distribute their materials to a wide audience. These examples show how social media and online communities are not synonymous. Online gatherings such as the Whole Earth 'Lectronic Link, alt.coffee, MacRumors, and OpenAPS have existed, and some of them exist still. These online gatherings permit a type of communicative participation in a group that a number of online ethnographies have hailed as the essential condition of the work being ethnographic.

Thus, it should come as no surprise that netnographic research varies widely in terms of the way it defines and uses the practice of 'participation'. Costello et al. (2017) are probably the most thorough and focused in charting the shift from what they call 'human presence in netnographic studies' to 'non participatory (passive) approaches' (p. 1), or 'active versus passive netnography' (p. 6). Costello et al. (2017) are correct to point out that the justifications some researchers give for their approach are misguided. Arguing that not participating or mingling with people online somehow frees a netnography from bias is inaccurate – interaction is not a bias, it is a choice of data collection procedure. As a procedural choice, it comes with its own set of advantages and limitations. I completely agree with Costello et al. (2017: 7) that researchers' active online participation 'is admittedly neither always easy nor appropriate'.

In a comprehensive content analysis, Whalen (2018) found that a full 84% of all netnographies published in hospitality and tourism research used 'non-participative' methods, as opposed to 14% who used participant observational methods (with one study, constituting 1.6% of the sample of 63 articles, deemed an experiment). Although they did not perform a count, in their overview of the marketing literature on netnography,

Heinonen and Medberg (2018) noted that 'the vast majority of netnographic marketing studies adopt a passive observer position. This may not come as a surprise, as this position is the simplest, most convenient and most unobtrusive netnographic research approach.'

It seems then, that there is a spectrum of participation and observation that researchers regularly negotiate, and that much of the time in netnography this negotiation results in a type of engagement where direct communicative interaction with people is limited or non-existent. The majority of the netnographies studied in the above-mentioned overviews focus mainly or exclusively on investigative data-collection operations. A simple but urgent question then remains.

If participation is critical to ethnography, what is so ethnographic about a passive, lurking, observational netnography? The next two sections attempt to provide a complete answer to this question.

From Participation to Engagement

Participation means to take part and to share in. If we think about the online context as a community or a 'local' manifestation of a particular online (or cyber) culture, the siting of a field behind a screen, then participation would logically infer engagement in that particular context. To call something an ethnography, we would need to engage with people directly, in the interactive manner of an interview or online interaction. But what happens when the field site is a data site that intersects 14 different social media sites? What does participation mean in this context? What exactly are the researchers taking part and sharing in?

Engagement is a subtler concept. One can engage with an object or a person, occupying their attention or efforts. Engagement can also happen without an object or person. One can occupy oneself or become involved in an activity or a field. Gambetti and Graffigna (2010: 820) called this the 'co-creational, social sharing, interactive, collaborative and participative dimensions' of the concept of engagement. What does it mean to occupy oneself with data or a site of data? What are the fields that one becomes involved in? How would the researcher want to affect the field they are studying? Would it be enough to preoccupy or absorb the site fully, envelop it, concern oneself with interrelated interests, emotions, and commitments? Is it enough to engage only with the traces of people, rather than people themselves, for the sake of your netnography?

In ethnography, participation is important because it helps develop understanding that leads to better translation and more informed meaning-making. If ethnographers are expected to participate so that they can gain familiarity with the historical, social, and cultural contexts that they wish to understand and communicate, then it is those goals which matter most – and not the particular means used to arrive at them. Participation in ethnography leads to emic appreciation – an understanding of the contextualized subjective and intersubjective experience of particular groups of persons. The terms 'emic' and 'etic' were proposed by a linguist to denote the difference between the way native speakers use their own language (phonemic) and the way outside researchers conceptualize that same language, as a phonetic construction (Franklin, 1996).

There is a long, rich history of nonparticipant observation in ethnographic fieldwork: 'In nonparticipant observation, the researcher observes and records naturalistic behavior but does not become a part of unfolding events' (Arnould and Wallendorf, 1994: 487). Where the researcher decides that introducing novice participants or new voices would be disruptive to focal aspects of cultural scripts, or detract from the quality of the data collected, then nonparticipant observation is preferred to participation. These concerns are exceptionally important in netnography, as past recounting of my own online entrée antics has emphasized (Kozinets, 2010: 75–9). There is, in fact, a long history of ethnographers recording trace processes (Webb et al., 1966) and using mechanical recordings of cultural behaviors, such as photographs and videotapes, as data (Worth and Adair, 1972).

There is a range of membership roles available to an ethnographer within a conceptual spectrum of full participation to complete nonparticipation. In netnography, these positions may not be as important as they are in traditional face-to-face ethnographies. That is because nonparticipant data tend to provide less access to participants' perceptions, values, internal states, and beliefs in ethnography. However, in netnography we are often dealing with the first-person expression of detailed expositions and even confessions. Ethnographers are concerned about maintaining an appropriate distance from cultural phenomena so that they can attend to actions and explanations that cultural natives take for granted (Wirth, 1964). But in netnography, because we are dealing with social media interactions, the types of phenomena studied tend to be less all-consuming and pervasive. The biggest common problems relating to nonparticipation in netnography and ethnography are related to the risks of 'describing surface similarities rather than accounting for cultural variation' (Arnould and Wallendorf, 1994: 489). These are problems of limited breadth that can be partially overcome by 'careful sampling and interpretation building' that aims for 'interpretive depth regarding sociocultural patterns of action' in both ethnography and netnography. The next section of this chapter provides some general guidelines.

Five Types of Netnographic Engagement

Netnography is more like a repertoire than a method: a list of skills, techniques, and devices that are employable for answering particular kinds of questions about technoculture, where we can think of technoculture as 'the various identities, practices, values, rituals, hierarchies, and other sources and structures of meanings that are influenced, created by, or expressed through technology consumption' (Kozinets, 2019b: xx). Netnography provides a set of procedural operations larger than anyone needs for any particular project. It is a toolkit of methodological appliances from which you can pick and choose a range of appropriate research designs for different research problems.

Engagement strategies sit alongside interaction data-collection operations as an essential part of the netnographic toolkit. They represent qualitative choices along a spectrum of being highly involved with various aspects of the research, the site, and the participants, to being relatively less involved.

Before I describe the five forms of engagement, I want to position the question of netnographic engagement in relation to the extant literature. In their welcome problematizing of the question of participation, Costello et al. (2017: 6) term Alang and Fomotar's (2015) approach 'a passive stance' to netnography, noting that the authors 'describe their netnographic technique as "purely observational"'. However, we must also note that, beyond their methodological self-description, one of the authors 'accessed the forum on a daily basis over a three-month period to read messages and follow message threads. Observing online communication and interactions as they unfolded provided a deeper understanding of the purpose and content of the communication and informed the content analysis' (p. 24).

The everyday engagement for ninety days related by Alang and Fomotar is, in my view, a form of engagement or involvement. Reading messages in real time and following message threads is also an active type of engagement with the site and its messages. Seeking an understanding of purpose and content, as well as context, shows a similar commitment to an active stance. The results of their study bear the marks of these commitments. For this is no mere distanced content analysis of a forum, but a sensitive and emotionally moving portrayal of the intimate concerns and worries, the comings and goings, of lesbian mothers who are dealing with the challenges of postpartum depression. Intimate topics that the authors present and discuss include participants' suicidal thoughts, treating their babies aggressively when they cry, dealing with other mental health conditions such as anxiety, the medications they are taking, the stigma of their sexuality and mental illness, and their reluctance to seek treatment. It seems unnecessary for the authors to participate as lesbians, mothers, and postpartum depression sufferers – this is an unnecessarily restrictive standard. Similarly, the insights gained from observation possess sufficient breadth and depth to provide a compelling look at the phenomenon of interest: understanding the role of an online forum in postpartum depression, and investigating how the experiences that lesbian birth mothers share on the forum might help to inform practice, particularly that which focuses on gay and lesbian mental health issues.

In this section, I suggest five different types of engagement strategies that involve researchers' interactions with data, data sites, and people. These strategies help to ameliorate some of the concerns listed above about the possible superficiality and lack of interpretive depth of netnographic research. They also avoid the shallow usage of the term 'participation' to refer to posting potentially unwelcome, obstructive, and ethically dubious 'I'm a researcher who wants to ask some questions' messages on public social media sites. The five types of engagement strategies are intellectual, cultural, historical, emotional, and social. In the points that follow, I briefly explain and develop these types of strategy.

- *Intellectual engagement strategies* involve a deliberate effort to gain a deeper conceptual understanding of relevant interests and information. This is a common form of scholarly engagement and could include questioning the meanings of particular ideas, the mapping of structures or relations, or the seeking of a more holistic understanding of information that others take for granted.

- *Cultural engagement strategies* are ways to attend to specific practices, such as the use of particular linguistic terms, symbols, rituals, and acronyms. Cultural engagement strategies quest for deeper understanding of those terms and symbols. These forms of engagement might be more than mental understandings. They could also include such things as preparing one's own food, if one was studying a foodie-based online phenomenon, or going to particular restaurants that one had read about online.

- *Historical engagement strategies* consider past trajectories, customs, traditions, myths, narratives, and even people involved with a particular topic, idea, platform, or group. Historical engagement means delving into the past of particular groups, platforms, sites, or phenomena, to understand why it is the way it is, the forces that constructed it, and where it might be going in the future.

- *Emotional engagement strategies* relate to a type of involvement in which the researcher attends to the feelings of those whose worlds and words are being investigated. Emotional involvement in a research project means that the researcher is also moved by the phenomenon and that she seeks to share this personal feeling. Just as one can be moved deeply by a book or film, reading the words and images of people on social media can be a deeply evocative experience.

- *Social engagement strategies* are the most obvious and direct form of strategy, and the closest to what is meant by participation in traditional ethnography. Social engagement means being involved in some way with the people, platform, and groups you are investigating. It means that you communicate with them, interact with them, and openly and ethically exchange ideas.

What you should take away from these three sections dedicated to the topic is the idea that engagement in netnography is a series of choices and matters of degrees, a placement of the researcher and their focus and attention along a spectrum of various forms of intellectual, social, and emotional involvement, rather than a unidimensional choice about posting to this or that social media platform or not. Understanding the multidimensionality of these choices is important, because they indicate you can conduct a highly engaged netnography using only investigative data. However, should you choose to invoke social engagement strategies, and connect directly with research participants for the purposes of eliciting data, then you would be engaging in interaction data-collection operations that require additional ethical procedure safeguards. Those operations, their modalities, uses, and how to approach them are the focus of the rest of this chapter.

In the remainder of this chapter, we distinguish between interviews, immersive interactions, and ostensibly innovative approaches such as research webpages, digital diaries, and mobile ethnographies. All of these approaches are intrusive and thus require informed consent from participants. The next section of this chapter will overview the use of interview approaches to data-collection operations, emphasizing online interviews. After that, immersive interactions will be considered, then innovative research approaches, and finally, informed consent procedures.

INTERVIEW DATA-COLLECTION PROCEDURES

Interviews in Netnography

One of the goals of a netnography can be to provide access to participants' perceptions, values, internal states, and beliefs. We may need this insight in order to fully understand a particular cultural phenomenon. Perhaps there are particularly difficult-to-decipher terms, images, or stories that are clearly of importance to discussions online, but the key to fully decoding them remains elusive to us after months of investigative downloading. Or perhaps we find that we are creating a full description of a phenomenon, but believe that we are not yet able to sufficiently account for the complexity and dynamism of the various cultural worlds behind them as they are phenomenologically experienced by different types of people. Chapter 7 explained that for some purposes it is important to be able to choose, or to confirm with certainty, exactly whose perspectives are being represented on particular sites. For all of these reasons, interviews have been found to be a useful part of the netnographic inquiry process.

Heinonen and Medberg (2018) found that published netnographies often contain interactive, question-asking data-collection methods such as interviews, surveys, experiments, or diaries. Although we currently lack a published account that looks at the question, a content analysis that I conducted indicated that almost 60% of published netnographies combine investigative data collection operations with other qualitative or quantitative data collection methods. Of those that combine methods, 52% combined investigation with some form of interview.

Interviews in netnography can take place online through a synchronous video teleconferencing program like Skype, Google Hangouts, or FaceTime. They can occur using VOIP in voice-only form, like a phone call. They can also happen in person, asynchronously through email, through posting to a forum or webpage, or through other means. You can choose to interview a person of interest that you may have already met through social media as part of a research project. Alternatively, you might interview someone who you choose for their group membership or identity characteristics, and then ask them about their social media views, preferences, habits, and stories. Interviews conducted in person or with video aid (such as screen sharing) can also involve select persons who then guide the researcher in an accompanied manner into their personal neighborhood of online spaces.

Interviews in netnography can be group-based or individual, formal or informal, structured or unstructured. You also have your choice of multiple formats to conduct the interview. Synchronous interviewing online tends to follow a pattern that is familiar to in-person interviews. Asynchronous interviews are more like open-ended surveys. The remainder of this section offers some general guidelines for conducting online interviews. This short but wide-ranging section will be covering research focus, rigour, interview length, sampling, insider/outsider status, structured/unstructured interview forms, text versus spoken-word interviews, synchronous and asynchronous interviews, using visuals, screen-sharing, and recording and saving data.

Conducting Online Interviews

Salmons (2011: 5) defines online interviews or 'e-interviews' as 'in-depth interviews conducted using CMC [computer-mediated communication]'. Online interviewing has much in common with interviewing in general. It involves formally approaching a participant, suggesting an interview, and conducting a conversation from the frame of an interview, where the researcher's role is primarily that of the asker of questions (see Gubrium and Holstein, 2001). Online interviews are a form of primary, original, data gathering. They must be conducted in accordance with accepted ethical research guidelines. In them, verifiable research participants provide informed consent before participating in the interview. And, as Salmons (2011) notes, they should be conducted rigorously in relation to a research focus and question. You should try to match the objectives of the interview to the interviewee and the online platform (if you are using one). Interviews should also be pursued with some consistency in regard to execution. For instance, if you decide to conduct online interviews via a teleconferencing program such as Skype, it can be important for you to conduct all similar interviews this way in order to maximize comparability. You need not turn perfectly consistent interviews into a hobgoblin; just keep in mind that as you change contexts (e.g., more or less visual and personal) you also may be altering the kind of interview data you elicit or fail to elicit.

Long interviews might be difficult to obtain within certain sites, such as social networking sites or virtual worlds, where culture members are too busy to stop for one or two hours to be interviewed. That length of interview can be difficult even for motivated and compensated online participants. If your informational needs are focused, shorter interviews of ten to thirty minutes can be effective. Sometimes, a quick exchange of information may suffice to inform your research question and focus.

Because interviews and other interactive data-collection methods are often used to overcome some of the challenges of anonymous, pseudonymous, or dubious online identities, sampling concerns can be paramount. Salmons (2009) discusses two sample frames for online interview research. In nomination, the identity and appropriateness of potential interview participants is verified by someone who knows them and who the researcher deems dependable. Using existing sampling frames, such as administrative records or membership lists, relies on verification by membership of a particular group (such as an online Facebook group, for example) or organization (e.g., the moderator or administrator of a particular YouTube channel).

Researchers can position themselves either as insiders or outsiders in relation to the online phenomenon they are studying. The choice of position depends upon the nature of engagement in the project, as well as the type of information that the researcher hopes to gather in the interview. For example, if the researcher is interested in deciphering already-discovered insider languages and meanings, then they would likely be positioned as an insider. If the researcher is still mapping out the general contours of the phenomenon of interest with the aid of the interview participant, then they would position themselves in the interview as an outsider.

There is also a broad range of positions that the researcher can position the interview along in relation to how structured versus unstructured it is. It can be useful to think in advance about how the technical medium of the interview changes the flow and opens up new interrogatory opportunities (or not, in the case of in-person interviews). The interview can be a wide-open conversation, a series of questions with limited choice answers (like a survey), open-ended questions that are asked of everyone in the same sequence, using similar prompts, with varied sequences, using original and impromptu prompts, or be run as an overview in which the interviewer suggests broad themes but the actual sequence is largely determined by the interviewee. Any of these are possible, but the more unstructured and free-flowing the interview, the more a richer media technology, like video teleconferencing, will be required to maximize comprehension and effectiveness. More limited media, like text chats, might be more effective when there is a limited range and focus of questions and answers. Similarly, real-time exchanges are more effective if the interviewer hopes for spontaneous moments of revelation, whereas the answers in asynchronous interviews tend to be more deliberate and calculated. The more structured the approach to the interview, the more important it is for you to use a carefully constructed, pretested, and revised interview guide (which is often called a 'discussion guide').

Text interviews tend to be different in many ways from spoken-word interviews – and current text affordance such as emojis offer a range of new expression modalities. In fact, because the online environment is such a visual medium, using visual images in your netnographic interviews is encouraged. You can try showing your participant a meme that is popular on their platform, and ask them to explain it. Show them someone's avatar, or a recent Instagram post. You can also ask them to express an idea visually. Have them choose a particular kind of image, or sketch something to represent a specific idea, and then send it to you. Visual or graphical exchanges can offer participants a type of projective that helps them express a tacit and unspoken level of understanding. Receiving and decoding such non-textual information can enable the researcher to access knowledge and feelings that participants may find difficult or awkward to articulate verbally.

Online interviews can also include screen sharing, which opens up another world of possibilities. Through sharing their screens, interview participants will be able to show the researcher activities online, rather than merely relating these verbally. You might want to have participants go to a particular online platform and do something specific, in order to show you the behavior with all of its nuance. Then, you can employ a type of verbal protocol to have them explain what they are doing, and explain or translate it for you. You may also want to observe them as they are performing online actions, such as installing a new application or using an unfamiliar webpage or program. Body language and facial expressions might be helpful observations for you to collect as they provide their narration or explanation.

Saving the data from an interview can happen in many ways. Skype and some of the other video teleconferencing programs now allow you to save your conversations, which is an enormous benefit. You can also record your online interviews with a voice recorder (or the voice recorder function of your mobile phone). Taking notes is always a good idea to capture your own fleeting impressions and visual observations, as well as to capture future questions you may want to ask without interrupting the current flow. A screen-recording program like Camtasia, for example, captures Skype or Google Hangout interviews effortlessly. This means that the researcher can be freed from routine note-taking or transcription concerns to concentrate fully upon the interview and rapport.

These are some general guidelines to conducting online interviews, covering topics such as focus, rigour, length, sampling, insider/outsider, structured/unstructured, text/spoken word, synchronous/asynchronous, visuals, screen-sharing, the format of the interview, and recording and saving data. At this point in your thinking, you might consider some of your options and begin to plan your interactive data collection. Box 9.1 can help you build that interview blueprint. The section following continues the discussion, offering additional guidelines regarding asking questions in interviews.

PLANNING YOUR INTERVIEW (PROJECT EXERCISE)

9.1

When planning your interview, you have a range of questions to consider about your approach and sampling before you begin to refine and develop your set of interview questions (which Box 9.2 will guide you through).

First, think about your RESEARCH FOCUS. What, in particular, do you want to discover from your interviews? You might write your answer here:

....

....

Next, think about your SAMPLING FRAME. Who, exactly, do you want to interview? How will you recruit the right people for your study?

....

....

Next, consider the FORMAT of your interview. Will it be structured or semi-structured? If semi-structured, exactly what will that mean?

....

....

Will this interview be online or in person? ....

Will the interview be textual or videoconference? ....

Synchronous or asynchronous? ....

Will you adopt an insider or an outsider position? ....

Will the interview use projectives and
screen-sharing? ....

What will the approximate LENGTH (in time) of
the interview be? ....

How will you RECORD the interview? ....

Answering these initial questions will provide an excellent first draft of a plan you can continue to think about, revise, and polish as you begin working on your interview guide.

Asking Good Interview Questions (and Giving Good Prompts)

Good interviews always have an opening, a set of questions, and then a closing. The opening to the interview should explain the study, its focus and purpose, establish the procedures for the interview, and try to gain some rapport with the participant. Questions in the interview can be broad or narrow, and often are both. Broad questions help the researcher to identify and scope out relevant issues and their various dimensions. Probes are used to explore detail and help the researcher gain a fuller description of interesting phenomena.

Several kinds of interview questions are described by Patton (2002):

- Background questions (which are good for openings). For example, 'Can you tell me a bit about yourself? Where did you grow up?'

- Sensory questions. For example, 'How would you describe your typical experience on Facebook? What do you look for? What do you notice?'

- Opinion and values questions. For example, 'What do you think about Facebook as a corporation? Is Facebook a good company or a bad one?'

- Knowledge questions. For example, 'What do you know about the recent security breach that happened at Facebook?'

- Feeling questions. For example, 'How do you feel about Facebook's privacy policies? What is your reaction to the latest news about Facebook's privacy breach?'

- Demographic questions (usually asked when closing the interview). For example, 'What is your age? What is your occupation?'

Patton (2002: 372) also suggests several prompts (also called probes) that ask for details as follow-up queries to the overall questions you ask. These prompts include the following who, what, where, when, and how types of question:

- Who else was on Facebook that time?
- What were you posting?
- Where did you see that meme?
- When did you start going to that website?
- How did that big flame war start?

Useful throughout the interview are summary or reflective statements that overview the main points of the interview as you see them, and then ask the interviewee if they agree with your summary or reflections, and also if they would like to add additional points to them. The interview should be closed by transitioning out of interview mode with questions such as 'for the final question ...'. Here is some important advice. Don't stop recording until the window on your screen closes, the interviewee hangs up, or your participant physically leaves the room. Often, some of the best material is provided after the participant starts to relax as the interview is ending, but before it is actually over. As the interview is closing, I like to ask participants whether they have any questions for me. Because the interview has already been conducted, the researcher can be more forthright at that point about the focus of the research project, and sometimes this leads to further productive discussion.

Using these guidelines, you can construct your own interview guide. The project-based exercise you will find in Box 9.2 will guide you through the sections and steps of the process. Remember that throughout the depth interview, the astute and effective interviewer will be paying close attention, prompting for more information, volunteering some information to gain rapport and create a conversation tone, and asking clarifying questions. The interviewer is building rapport as well as collecting information, hoping for genuine disclosure, and – if the interview is semistructured – remaining aware of and open to pursuing segues and elaborations.

WRITING YOUR INTERVIEW GUIDE (PROJECT EXERCISE)

9.2

Thinking about the foci and formats you have decided to use in your interviews, apply the suggestions in this chapter to design a draft interview guide.

A. The Opening. The interview opening will happen after you go through the informed consent form with the interviewee, and the interviewee reads and signs the form. The interview guide opens with a section that explains your study, telling about its general focus and purpose. It also tells the interviewee how the interview will run. Finally, it may try to gain some rapport with the participant, perhaps by linking up the research to something personal, or by reassuring the interviewee that there are no wrong answers and what you are looking for in the interview is merely their opinions or impressions.

Try writing your interview opening here:

....
....
....

(Continued)

....

....

....

B. The Questions. The question section is the heart of your interview. Depth interviews (which often run two or three hours in length) often start with a grand tour question such as 'tell me about yourself'. They then proceed to ask a number of questions about the topic of interest. Avoid complex or double-barreled questions. Be very clear what you are asking. Keep the questions open-ended – not yes or no. Having a nice natural flow between the questions is important. You do not want to write an interview guide that requires the participant to jarringly move backwards and forwards in time, or to consider a major issue, then a minor one, then back to the same major issue. Related topics should go together. Usually, the interview will begin with macro topics (such as asking about online habits), then become narrower (such as asking about which social networking sites are used) and then narrow into even finer topics (such as asking about Facebook and Facebook's privacy rules). Usually prompts or probes are included (often in brackets). Prompts are used to gain additional elaboration of answers.

Keeping in mind the many decisions you have made when you planned your interview in Box 9.1, write out the series of questions you will ask in the interview. It usually takes some careful thought and even more careful revision to get a smoothly flowing set of questions. After you have the questions, write out some probes to make sure you get good data for your most important questions.

Try writing your interview questions here:

....

....

....

....

....

C. The Closing. The closing of the interview transitions the participant back to the non-interview social world. You might think about how to word some of your summary or reflective statements. You also might include in the closing any demographic types of questions that you may wish to ask, such as about age or socioeconomic class. Finally, it is customary to ask the interviewee if they would like to add, elaborate upon, or share anything that they believe is relevant to the topic of the interview. You might also ask them if they want to know anything else about how their interview will be used, or how the information from the interview will be handled.

Try writing your interview closing here:

....

....

....

....

....

INVOLVEMENT DATA-COLLECTION PROCEDURES

Explaining Involvement

Interviews are useful, but they are also intrusive and elicited. They remove participants from a naturalistic context in order to question them. They provide an artificial situation, a social script called 'an interview' with a questioner and an answerer. In attendance with this interview script are all sorts of expectations, assumptions, and behavioral subroutines (Alvesson, 2003). However, interviews are not the only operation we have to capture interactive data in netnography. A more in situ (in context) way to capture interactive data is to do so as part of an immersive interaction, which I term here an 'involvement'.

An involvement is a data capture of the researcher interacting online, in the social media field site, in as natural a manner as possible. As we observe online sites, we see that questioning and clarifying activities are commonplace. People are naturally curious and others helpful. They frequently ask each other what something means or what someone does. They share problems and ask what to do. Asking questions and gaining answers online is a normal part of online behavior, and thus can seem fairly unobtrusive. As you conduct your netnography on a site such as Facebook, YouTube, Reddit, or Pinterest, you will find many opportunities to interact with the system, and with other people and agents using that system. You can comment on a post, or post something yourself and wait for comments. When you save those comments and posts, those 'involvements', they become interactive data.

What happens when a researcher posts a question online as a part of their netnography? This is an involvement and is also a form of intentional intrusion. That researcher interaction is, however well-intentional and justified, a subversion of the ongoing flow of the conversation of that group of people using the media. As such, it may not always be welcome. It may seem natural and be very much in the flow of the regular question and answer of the platform. But because you are a researcher, and you are asking these questions not only for yourself, but also for the purposes of research which you hope to publish and publicize later, it is not actually natural. It falls under a different set of rules.

Chapter 7's section about researcher disclosure is very clear. If you are interacting in a social media context for purposes relating to data gathering for your research project, you must disclose your identity, affiliation, and purpose. If you have been spending significant time doing the deep hanging out that characterizes ethnography, and feel like you are actually a cultural insider, you might be tempted to hide your researcher identity and simply squeeze in a few questions. However, that would be an ethical breach.

Thus, disclosing your identity as a researcher is *de rigueur* when you undertake involvement-based data-collection operations. That disclosure inevitably changes things. In that particular conversation or thread, or for that particular group, this is no longer a group of people (and those inevitably playing the troll role) who are communicating for reasons of interest and passion. When you enter as a researcher, this has become your workplace. And those people have become your experimental subjects. Or, as one ethnographic participant once called himself to me, your 'guinea pig'. That places your questions and your presence in a precarious and unnatural position. It also creates a range of quandaries regarding the answers you might gather.

Reading the extant netnography literature, I rarely find involvement-based data being shared in final reports. Researchers often indicate that they have participated in the ongoing events of particular sites and platforms. However, when they have questions and answers with people, these are usually reported as interviews of one kind or another. I suspect that one of the reasons for this absence is that involvement operations are most commonly used to solicit interviews. I fairly frequently see researchers posting messages on social media sites saying something like 'My name is Jim Wilson from [something-something] University in Cityville and I'm researching cat memes. I want you to do an interview with me and answer these seventeen questions ... .' Although this sort of post overtly violates no ethical rules (we can see it involves researcher disclosure and at least approaches informed consent), it is disruptive to the normal business of the people using these sites, offers them very little in return for their time and effort and, in my experience, is rarely successful.

Involvement data-collection operations are best used judiciously, cautiously, or, my preference, rarely if ever. They seem to fit best with certain kinds of netnography projects, ones where the data site is more like an ethnographic field, where there are communal sorts of ties and boundaries. In that case, if the researcher takes the time to get closely involved with the ongoing interactions in the site and is, as Davis (2010) was with her Indian migrant online group, a recognized and respected member, then considering posting some questions or initiating a deeper discussion in an organic way might be a useful data-gathering option. This is, as you may notice, a long-term immersive strategy that fits with a more communal social media atmosphere. For most data-gathering needs, however, a shorter-term procedure such as interviewing might be more efficient. For those that require a more contextualized consideration, one that can both question and have the participant consider their online behaviors and feeling in context, there are what I call 'innovative interaction-based operations'. Although there are conceivably many of these types of novel operations, this chapter considers three of them: research webpages, digital diaries, and mobile ethnography. These will be considered in turn in the following sections.

INNOVATIVE DATA-COLLECTION PROCEDURES

Just about every year, the word 'innovation' appears at the top of the list of various magazines' most overused business buzzwords. In research, as in business, novelty is perennially and simultaneously both celebrated and despised. As an ostensibly novel method, netnography has gotten its share of applause and rotten tomatoes by its neologistic links to innovation. Yet it would be difficult to deny that newness is valuable in research. Replication research, which is highly necessary to the progress of knowledge, is consistently missing in action. Researchers are required to prove the novelty of their contribution through their sophisticated positioning of ever-advancing theory. And especially in digital research which is, by its nature, often dealing with new platforms, programs, and modes of data collection, much of what we are creating and trying to apply is actually new to the world.

Thus it is with awareness both of the connotative and denotative aspects of the term, along with a slight congenital tendency to hyperbolize, that I term these interactive procedures for collecting data in netnography 'innovative'. Although I recognize that all three of them are based on established approaches, they are each still very new and have been used by relatively few researchers. Each of them can also be an entire research method or procedure in and of itself (the same is of course true of interviews). These are intentionally short introduction and overview sections, and are not intended as comprehensive procedural guides (like much of the rest of this book). They contain a few citations that will help the interested researcher find their bearings in relation to the topic. The following sections cover in turn research webpages, digital diaries, and mobile ethnography.

Research Webpages

A research webpage (or research website) is a dedicated online page or site that provides a select set of people with a set of questions or a research focus for the purpose of collecting data about a particular topic. The impetus for creating a research webpage is that it contains the following properties which, considered in their entirety, are unique to this modality:

1. It is an online site and can blend into the 'natural' environment of online discourse and sites.

2. It does not interfere with the conversation on other domains or sites.

3. It offers an opportunity to invite particular people on interest to participate in greater detail in the research project.

4. It provides a dedicated online format to ask questions and elicit responses.

5. It gives clear information about the researcher and research project, thus satisfying ethical requirements for disclosure and informed consent.

6. It can present information and images that are interesting, useful, and/or amusing to research participants, thus giving something potentially mean-ingful back to them, or paying their contributions forward.

Although I have created and utilized research webpages for some of my own past research projects (for example, Kozinets, 2001; Kozinets et al., 2017), such use is still rather infrequent among extant netnography-based publications. The reason for this may be that people prefer other methods. Most seem to opt for more investigative modes of data collection, rather than involve any interactive data operations. Or it could also be that people do not realize how simple they now are to create, or how powerful they can be as a way to broaden your netnography.

Some simple guidelines follow. The site's landing page can introduce the research team, or individual researcher, as well as the research project itself. As you would expect, those introductions should always be completely open and honest in their disclosures of identity, affiliation (e.g., your university), and the purpose of your research. However, as with your introduction of the research project and purpose in any interactive operation (such as an interview), this preface need not be so detailed in its explanations that it divulges precisely what you seek to find out. That would be poor technique.

You can steer people to the site through invitation. These invitations can be very politely worded, apologetic-for-the-interruption, relevant, and public posts on sites that interest you. They can be direct messages or posts to people you would like to reach. You could make a YouTube video or meme about the site and then circulate it. You could even purchase advertising promoting your research website and targeting it at the right kind of person, if you wish. There are numerous ways that you can pub-licize the site to relevant individuals. I would expect that the number of participants who would organically respond (i.e., without advertising prompts or compensation of any kind) to a typical research webpage would compare to the typical lower end of the total number of participants you would seek in-depth interviews. These unpromoted pages would likely gather varying amounts of more detailed data from ten to thirty different individuals, and usually not much more than that. With advertising and payment, I would expect that these numbers could rise to survey-like numbers, but the quality of some of the data would likely decline.

I like the idea of using the research webpage as an opportunity to give something back. If this is a relatively cohesive group, like a fan group, aficionados, or technology enthusiasts, you might consider providing some unique images or overviews that should interest the people you are trying to reach. For example, you could provide past research on the topic (i.e., the interesting parts of your lit review, reworded to be generally readable). You could offer entry to a lottery with a prize for those who contribute, or contribute 'meaningfully', to the site.

Then, the page should ask its questions. Because you are not going to be present as you would be in an interview to elaborate or explain these when they are confusing, you should ensure that the questions you provide are worded in the clearest manner possible. You may want to pretest them with real people (rather than fellow academics or students). You must then offer a way for participants to respond. Responses often come through filling in boxes on the webpage. But they could also come via email, through scheduling an interview using a video teleconferencing platform, or as social media direct message responses. A very nice feature of the research webpage is that it persists. You can comment right on the page, asking for additional detail, clarifying misconceptions, or extending new questions. I will note here, and have noted before, that Facebook offers very convenient pages that easily handle all of these tasks. Box 9.3 guides you through the creation of a Facebook-based research webpage.

CREATING A RESEARCH WEBPAGE ON FACEBOOK (PROJECT EXERCISE)

9.3

Fortunately for netnographers working today, creating a research webpage on Facebook is a rather simple matter of pressing a few buttons and filling in a few forms. However, what you choose to say and who you choose to invite to your research webpage can prove a much more complex matter. In this project exercise, I will only deal with the technical aspects of creating the page. Those other more contingent and complex matters of research disclosure and sampling are covered in other sections in this book.

1. After first logging into Facebook, you will see a menu running vertically along the left-hand side of your browser (beneath the f-logo and the search bar). Under the category named 'Explore' is another category named 'Groups'. Click that category.

(Continued)

2. Once you are in the Groups section of Facebook, you will see your pending group invitations, and as you scroll down, your favorites and the groups you manage. At the top of this screen, just below the level of the search bar and on your right-hand side, you should see a green button that invites you to '+Create Group'. Click that green button.

3. A new box will open called 'Create New Group'. First, it asks you to name your group. So go ahead and name it. Then, it asks you to add some people. If you know who you want to add, then add them. You must add at least one person, so consider adding a friend or family member who won't mind being the first member of your group. The box also prompts you to select a privacy setting. The default is closed. You might also decide to make the group public, or secret. After completing your settings, click the 'Create' button on the bottom right.

4. Fill in your introduction. Find some nice image for your header to convey the feeling you would like to communicate. And then you are ready to start inviting participants, asking them questions, following up, and holding back-and-forth research-focused conversations with them as you like. It will take you only a few minutes (thank you Facebook), and your page should look something like the image I share below of the one I just created.

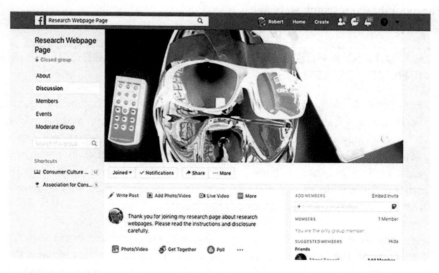

Figure 9.1 My Facebook research webpage

As Box 9.3 demonstrates, creating a Facebook-based research webpage is a fairly quick and easy matter. It can also provide viable data from a few dozen or so people with a minimum of effort. However, what if you want to do something more with the opportunity to create a research webpage? What if you aspire to create an entire site that not only helps you gather data for your research project, but is also a topically-focused, functioning, and viable conversational space for hundreds of even thousands of people? Wallace et al. (2018) went to elaborate lengths to create a website and an online community of practice to support healthy eating practices in early childhood education and care. They called it Supporting Nutrition for Australian Children, or SNAC for short. The site was both research webpage and action research enacted in the sphere of social media. Their insightful article provides a wealth of information to guide future researchers who want to use a full-on and sophisticated research webpage method in netnography. The authors found that initial recruitment, member engagement, and ongoing participation were challenges that they had to meet. Their contribution of the notion of 'netnographic slog' represents a term for the challenges they faced to recruit participants and enhance participation. Advanced knowledge of these challenges, and the viable solutions they devised to face them, is a very useful contribution that can assist anyone interested in building and using a research webpage in their netnography.

Digital Diaries

Another of the approaches most commonly combined with netnography in extant studies is the use of diary methods (Heinonen and Medberg, 2018). Diary methods, in which participants are asked to keep regular (usually daily) journals of their experiences as a means for collecting data, have a long history as useful tools of qualitative research. As Biraghi and Gambetti (2018) note, these diaries are often used as a complement to other techniques 'with the aim of getting a deeper glance into participants' daily practices and inner experience and to integrate and corroborate the thick descriptions' gained through the use of other methods such as interviews or ethnography.

In their study of the online postings of an influential group of Chinese tourists who use recreational vehicles to travel through Australia, Wu and Pearce (2014: 26) followed 22 Chinese blogs. Because these blogs tended to unfold temporally, the authors considered them to be like a 'digital diary'. The information provided in these digital diary-like social media posts was rich, and included:

> all aspects of travelling e.g., visa application, tickets booking, accommodation booking, car or RV renting, best restaurants, must see sights, must do activities, and many other issues. The blogs usually contain thousands of words and are accompanied by dozens, sometimes hundreds of photos.

Similarly, Leipämaa-Leskinen (2011) used a 'web diary' method to investigate how the web of cultural meanings surrounding and linking the body and identity is constructed and negotiated in social interaction when dieting. Purposively sampling three diet-themed diary format blogs, the author conducted a netnography based solely on this dataset. The video blogs of combat veterans studied by Schuman et al. (2018) might also be similar, in that they studied posts in which specific people shared detailed information about aspects of their lives. These uses of blogs and vlogs as diary methods is especially interesting because it provides unsolicited data that is nonetheless relevant to the researchers' research questions. It combines the unobtrusiveness of investigative operations with the detail and direction of interactive procedures.

Diary methods can also be elicited and, in fact, this is how they are most commonly used. For example, in a study of the user experiences of female online gamblers, Wang (2018: 777) employed an online diary method which 'asked 101 players to submit online diary reports by LINE [a freeware communications application for smartphones, tablets, and computers] or email every week to make further observations'. The netnographer also participated in the PokerStars online game as a player (immersive engagement), interviewed participants, and did investigation-style data collection operations.

Digital diaries can use a variety of online platforms and devices. The core idea of a digital diary method is that the researcher either gathers naturally occurring and relevant diaries, or prompts particular participants to keep a diary on a particular topic of interest and that diary is shared online in a digital format. These diaries can include a variety of materials, such as photographs, video recordings, and sound files, as well as text. Biraghi and Gambetti (2018: 117) explain that they asked participants 'to share narratives about their individual experience and realities', and then those participants enthusiastically took control of the diary-writing process 'in terms of the type of data and contents they produced, contextualization of their stories and hypertextual connection with their social media'. The authors also crafted a 'diary guide' for participants similar to the interview guide in the prior section. However, they included a number of projective tasks designed to 'engage participants' storytelling impulse'. These tasks included collage creation, drawing, and structured fantasy exercises. At times, the authors describe the results as resembling 'sophisticated graphic novels'.

Like mobile ethnography (which will be discussed in the next section of this chapter), the digital diary affords participants a large degree of creativity and control over what they wish to represent and how they wish to represent it. Words, photographs, scanned images, memes, video recordings, transcripts of conversations, posts, links, and attachments are all options for self-expression. Also, like mobile ethnography, the diary unfolds temporally and locates the participant in space. If investigative data collection lacks a penetrating look into the inner world of the participant, and if that look is needed for deeper understanding of your research topic, digital diaries are an interactive data-collection operation that you might consider including in your study.

MOBILE ETHNOGRAPHY

In recent years, marketing research agencies and bloggers have begun talking about an allegedly new form of ethnography called mobile ethnography. Mobile ethnography is a form of research based on the use of mobile smartphones. Several new abilities are provided by the accessibility of smartphones, the camera on the phone, and the immediacy and telepresence of the research tasks. At the most basic level, mobile ethnography allows researchers to conduct interviews with participants using their mobile phone. These interviews can be synchronous, but more commonly they are textual or videotaped questions provided to the interviewee for them to answer on their own time.

Mobile ethnography tasks are used to provide a glimpse into research participants' lives, homes, workplaces, behaviors, and experiences. A mobile task might ask an informant to photograph the walls of their bedroom, their desk at work or school, or their bookshelf. Mobile tasks can also ask people to record themselves doing something. For example, a task can ask someone to record themselves driving a car or eating in a restaurant. In this way, the method allows for the collection of a type of observational data. The resulting recording becomes a product of the researchers' presence moving along with people in their lives. This opportunity can feel quite ethnographic – and rather extraordinary.

Capturing live feed from the screen of the mobile phone is also achievable. Therefore, direct observation of online behaviors becomes possible. Informants might be asked to view their Instagram feed as they normally would, or to sift through their Instagram feed as if they were looking for advice on dating. The traces of everything that they see on the screen and hear from the speaker would be recorded and thus captured as interactive data. This type of data can also be useful for understanding how people install and use new applications and other software, for purposes of hardware or software design or human–computer interaction theory.

Another type of mobile ethnography task might have the researcher ask informants to capture their reflections on a particular kind of experience as soon as possible after its occurrence. For instance, informants could be asked to record when their gender felt salient in the workplace. After a workplace incident happened in which they felt their gender was salient, would be required to record a short video report about that incident, perhaps with attention both to external occurrences (events, people involved) as well as internal ones (thoughts and feelings). These sorts of critical incident technique-based methods have a long history in qualitative research methods. What mobile ethnography adds is that it leverages the practical ubiquity of smartphones to give easy assess to large numbers of people and the details and convenience of both still photography and audiovisual recording. The result is research studies that can combine the depth of qualitative methods with significant numbers of informants and control over sample selection.

Accessibility, immediacy, and audiovisual presence are strengths of mobile ethnography data-collection operations. Its limitations tend to be similar to those of interviews and other interaction methods. Combined with other data-collection operations, mobile ethnography, like the other interactive data-collection procedures outlined in this chapter, holds the promise of enhancing netnographies with the voice of informants, enriching the study with a deeper phenomenological sense of the inner world of persons and their perspectives, as well as their physical surroundings, experiences and events, habits, and favored locations.

There are a number of different companies providing convenient and user-friendly platforms for hosting mobile ethnographies, such as Indeemo, Dscout, Mindswarms, and Over the Shoulder. Most of these companies also provide technical support as well as advice about which research procedures, as well as what types of questions and tasks may be more effective using the technique. With the three innovation operations now explained, we turn in the next section to a more detailed explanation of informed consent procedures in netnography.

WRITTEN CONSENT FOR INTERVIEWS AND OTHER INTERACTIONS

In this chapter, we have covered a range of interactive data-collection operations. In each of these operations – whether interview, involvement in social media conversations, or using a research webpage, digital diaries, or mobile ethnography – the participant is being asked to personally contribute data to the study. These interactions all clearly and directly meet the definition of human subjects research. As such, they are governed by the ethical rules of informed consent.

There is no need to debate whether it is ethical or even legal to record real-time interactions such as a chat interview without permission – the answer is no, it is immoral and unethical and may be illegal depending upon where and how it is done. Recording an interaction without participant permission and without researcher disclosure is completely unacceptable.

Interviews, whether conducted online or off, clearly fall into the area of an interaction and thus require informed consent. Interviews, whether conducted on your own site, group, or page, or through those of another, require clear informed consent that reveals the researcher, the research study, informs the participant about the use of their information, and asks about the level of protection desired. Interactions on a research webpage are similar, as are questions asked through digital diary or mobile ethnography formats.

Three questions are important:

1. Are the intended participants in the interview adults?

2. Are the intended research participants members of a vulnerable population?

3. Should the research be considered to have a higher-than-minimal risk of harming participants in some way?

If the research participants are children or vulnerable populations, special additional levels of assurance are required, just as they would be in person. If the research has some risks, perhaps because it seeks to expose some immoral or illegal behaviors, then additional information and assurances may be required. The starting point for all of these ethics procedures is the Informed Consent document.

The Reality of Gaining Consent

The simple reality of gaining consent, which I can also call a 'consent language game', is that online data structures do not work this way. Companies gain consent to host data. Some people never realize that their social media account settings are set by default to public. Many others want to compete in the social media ecosystem for followers and influence, a type of gamification. Shopping and the gamification of followers are ways that mobile phone technology has become indispensable to a new generation. As researchers, our studies focus mainly on those who share their data publicly. Some go private, which is a riskier and much more delicate data-collection operation, but often worthwhile.

Diminishing Possibility of Informed Consent

In a departure from traditional face-to-face methods like ethnography, focus groups, or personal interviews, investigative data collection in netnography uses cultural information that is not given specifically, in confidence, to the researcher. However, using this data comes with some ethical questions. In the early days of Internet research and Internet-based ethnographies, King (1996) recommended gaining additional informed consent from all online research participants. However, imagine trying to achieve that level of consent for the Twitter of today – it is impossible. That sort of advice is a relic of the bygone Age of Virtual Community in the 1990s, when King was writing, as Sugiura et al. (2017) note. Now, in the age of social media, there is absolutely no possibility that even a large and dedicated team of researchers could possibly get consent, for example, for all of the Twitter posters using the hashtag '#metoo'. Having to meet that impossible standard would shut down netnography and all social media research entirely.

Ethical Cultural Participants

When they interact and co-create social media data, netnographers are cultural participants. Perhaps the closest analogue to traditional ethnography that we find online, with its exotic locations and others, is the virtual world ethnography. Writing about the ethics of virtual world ethnography, 'we are obligated to do as much as possible to reveal to our informants the nature and purpose of our studies' and also to keep them informed about the research as 'an ongoing imperative' (Boellstorff et al., 2012: 133). Yet exposing yourself as a netnographer can be a risky business, and may help account for the distancing drift of netnography away from more participative styles. Disclosure is difficult and intrusive and, especially in more localized and communal types of online settings, it changes the atmospherics of the research. If you act in a manner found to be irresponsible and disrespectful, that could lead to your public exposure and censure, and might even invite legal sanction.

Consent is a Liquid Concept

Informed consent for online work is one of the most vexing problems facing social media researchers, according to Sugiura et al. (2017). Zimmer (2010) analyzes the use of Facebook data in a multi-year, IRB-approved, NSF-funded study of a cohort of 1,700 university students. The author finds that the notion of what constitutes 'consent' within the context of divulging personal information in social networking spaces must be further explored. Consent needs to be reconsidered in light of the contextualized understanding of norms of information flow within specific spheres, which also reveals that we still have not learned the lessons of the AOL data release and similar instances where presumed anonymous datasets have been re-identified (Zimmer, 2010: 323). When we know that data can be traced, we are obligated to gain informed consent and to also attempt to make the data truly untraceable, if that is possible.

The Consent Form

Sometimes, online ethnographers have gone out of their way to ask for participants' informed consent to use their data. In a virtual world setting, one researcher approached participants asking for their 'blessing' for her project, and then presented them with links, an email, and a posting to a description of her research and an online consent form. Another researcher placed a halo over the head of her avatar to designate her role as an ethnographer (Boellstorff et al., 2012: 133–5).

A further way that consent can occur over the Internet is when research consent-related information is presented to the prospective research participant in some unobtrusive, electronic form. The participant might signal their consent by agreeing to continue in the study after reading a form or the text on a pop-up message and then clicking an 'accept' button on a webpage and/or by providing basic data such as their name and/or email. Salmons (2017) offers a number of useful examples of practical research suggestions for gaining informed consent that are based on contemporary practices. What is most important about these procedures is that there must be some clearly defined activity that the participant must perform in order to signal that they understand and accept the terms of consent. It is common in netnography for the researcher of a particular community to post information about their status as a researcher and the purpose of their study on their profile and often on forum boards. This is not consent – this is disclosure. Simply posting a document and expecting that this grants you informed consent is, as Salmons (2017) underscores, insufficient.

We usually think about the consent process occurring at the beginning of a study, perhaps as we first begin to collect data. We might need to gain consent from companies, from moderators, from online system administrators, groups, individuals, or from parents or guardians of minors or other ostensibly vulnerable persons. There are many ways to obtain consent from participants, including print or digital signatures, virtual consent tokens, or click boxes. Buchanan and colleagues (2010) usefully contextualize the consent process by suggesting that, 'Sometimes it may be more ethical to get informed consent at the end when you want to present a specific case study or quote an individual or focus on a particular element. Therefore, informed consent should be always an inductive process.' This is excellent advice, but information online can be delicately ephemeral. If you wait until you are ready to present the work, in public or in an article, and then go back and talk to who you quoted, and ask them to make an informed consent decision, the link to them could already be dead. In academia, the publication time lags are sometimes not only measured in months, but in years. There may also be constraints that could render written consent impractical or even harmful. All of these contingencies should be considered.

Although questions have been raised about whether an informed consent approach can be valid without certain knowledge of the competency, comprehension, and even the age of the research participant, Walther (2002: 213) notes that many traditionally accepted methods such as mail and telephone surveys deal with the same sort of uncertain knowledge about whether people are actually who they say they are. In fact, there is no clear, indisputable link between face-to-face research and judgments of research participant competency and comprehension. Similarly, the fact that we have no steadfast guarantees that we can truly inform our participants about study risks should not deter us from doing our best to follow the required procedures.

Looking at the sample informed consent form presented in Box 9.4, you should be able to see many of the elements of the range of ethical procedures discussed thus far in this book, from disclosure to consent, risks, benefits, confidentiality, the rights of research participants, and data security. Using the sample informed consent form as a basic format, you might now try to fashion one of your own. If you work in a country and institution that require ethics approval, you should probably start that process sooner rather than later.

9.4 SAMPLE INFORMED CONSENT FORM

Letterhead: Your school. Or company, non-profit organization, or research agency. Full name of organization and address with phone number.

Research Project Title: Netnography of online utopian discourse (for example)

Principal Investigator: Dr. Robert V. Kozinets

Online Research Consent Form

You are being asked to be a participant/volunteer in a research study.

Purpose

The purpose of this research study is to examine the online experiences of utopian conversationalists. We hope to learn more about the experiences of people who participate in discussions on utopian videos as well as those who wish to participate in them, and to better understand the role of online interaction in social experiences and intentions. A research webpage has been constructed to inform people about the research and is available at www. youtubeutopianism.com/notyet/.

Procedures

If you decide to be part of this study, your participation will involve:

- Consenting to an interview to be conducted live by one of the principal researchers on Apple FaceTime.
- The interview will take approximately ninety minutes.
- The interview will focus on your activities on YouTube comments around particular videos, and some of your other related online and personal experiences.
- You will receive $250 in compensation for your time, and your results will be fully anonymized two years after first publication of the results.
- In the case of a face-to-face interview, the session will be audiotaped; telephone interviews will be audiotaped; online and email interviews will be saved for future reference. Data will be transcribed and may be quoted as text, with you assigned a pseudonym, in academic publications such as conference proceedings and peer-reviewed articles.
- After the two-year waiting period, there will be no way to link anything you say in the research to who you are. Even your demographic information can be hidden, if you like. All personal identifiers will be permanently deleted two years from the date of publication.

- Optionally, you consent to having your interview information appear in a table, anonymized, with your gender, age, and profession stated. Journal reviewers and editors will have access to the full original data digital files to review, but your name will be anonymized and the data will not link to your real identity.

Risks

The following risks may occur as a result of your participation in this study:

There are no foreseeable risks or discomforts in this study. The risk involved is no greater than those involved in daily activities such as speaking on the telephone or using email. Because some of the topic matter related to utopia may be sensitive, there is a chance that your recollections may become personal and emotional. This is all very useful as data, and so any shared reaction is a useful one.

Benefits

The following benefits to you are possible as a result of participating in the study:

You will gain $250 in cash payment. That is the main benefit. In addition, your participation in the study will contribute to our understanding of utopia and of online experience with utopias in social media.

Compensation

There is a $250 compensation for your participation in this research. It will be deposited into your account via Venmo, Paypal, or direct deposit.

Confidentiality

The following procedures will be followed in order to keep your personal information confidential:

To protect your confidentiality, your name will not appear in any publications. You will be assigned a pseudonym (a fake name) that will be used instead of your name to disguise your participation. In the case of quotes of things you have done online (such as posts on newsgroups or forums, blog entries or comments), we will change your quotes so that they are not vulnerable to being reverse-searched and identified.

We do not anticipate uncovering sensitive information about you in this research, but there will be a discussion of politics.

(Continued)

The data that we collect about you will be kept private to the fullest extent allowed by law. We are keeping all of this data on a single hard drive locked away in a secure location. To make sure that this research is being conducted in the proper way, the Human Research Ethics committee, or the GDPR compliance group, or the University or College IRB may have access to the research records.

In the case of electronic communications pertaining to online consent, you should be aware that this form is not being run from a remote 'secure' https server, such as the kind used to handle credit card transactions. There is therefore a small possibility that responses could be viewed by unauthorized individuals or parties, such as computer hackers.

Costs to You

Research participants should incur no cost as a result of consenting to be interviewed. You will gain $250 compensation.

Participant Rights

- Your participation in this study is voluntary. You are under no obligation to participate in the study.
- You have the right to change your mind and leave the study at any time without giving any reason and without any penalty. Either party can end the interview at any time. If we end before the interview is complete, you will be paid for the time up until the interview is ended, pro-rated for a 90-minute interview.
- Any new information that might make you change your mind about being in the study will be provided to you.
- You will be given a copy of this consent form to keep.
- You do not waive any of your legal rights by signing or agreeing to this consent form.

Questions about the study or your rights as a research participant

- If you have any questions about this research study, you may contact Dr. Robert Kozinets at +1 (XXX) XXX–XXXX
- If you have any questions about your rights as a research subject, you may contact Mr. Ricky Bobby, USC's IRB Co-ordinator at +1 (XXX) XXX–XXXX

Have you read the information on this page and do you agree to participate?

(Select one)

☐   I have read and understand this information and agree to participate.
☐   I do not want to participate.

Do you consent to having your anonymous (no name, no link to you) age, gender, profession, and income information shared in a table in the final document? Yes / No

Email address: [   ]

(required to confirm identity)

[SUBMIT]

....

THE ETHICS AUDIT

The idea of overview is important to ethical research. Even if it is simply to one's peers, the ethical procedures you follow for any particular project should be subject to your own summary presentation at regular stages that can be dictated roughly by the six movements and should be reviewed by others, whether on your team or people you find online for this purpose in different groups. The ethics audit can be quite formal, as in asking a peer group or institution to conduct a peer review of a research ethics plan or statement. The ethics audit is also a chance for decentralized peer networks to meet and organize using tools like LinkedIn and Facebook groups, and share their ethics plans for netnographies. This will be helpful for grad students and other students, especially as they learn netnography and develop it as a science customized to their fields, abilities, and interests. It is also a way to test new ideas and plans before the high-stakes process of the research review boards.

As you undertake this movement of your netnography, try to remember the key to interaction, which is the fusion of the horizons of people: cultures, groups, social media sites, groups of friends and families, romantic dyads of all sorts, shapes, sizes, and ages. This is the way Hermes comes: from the depths of our interactions, our activities, with verstehen, with understanding.

CHAPTER SUMMARY

In Chapter 9, you were taught about interactive data-collection operations. Interactive data is co-produced and elicited between two or more people, rather than simply observed and recorded. Before detailing the elements of interactive data collection, Chapter 9 considered the nature of online engagement as the appropriate frame for netnography, replacing the more perplexing term, 'participation'. Engagement runs the gamut from purely intellectual through to fully social and experiential.

Interaction has four categories within it: a) interview, b) involvement, c) innovations, and d) informed consent. How do you conduct interviews, especially online interviews? This chapter provides the answers. Next, involvements, which are naturalistic embedded interactions, were described. Then, 'innovative' research approaches to interaction: research webpages, digital diaries, and mobile ethnography. The chapter's final section offers a sample consent form. There will be more related material after you read about the final data collection movement in netnography, immersion.

KEY READINGS

Costello, Leesa, Marie-Louise McDermott, and Ruth Wallace (2017) 'Netnography: Range of practices, misperceptions, and missed opportunities', *International Journal of Qualitative Methods*, 16(1). 1609406917700647.

Salmons, Janet (2014) *Qualitative Online Interviews: Strategies, Design, and Skills*. London: Sage

Salmons, Janet (2017) 'Getting to yes: Informed consent in qualitative social media research', in Kandy Woodfield (ed.), *The Ethics of Online Research* (Advances in Research Ethics and Integrity, Volume 2) (pp. 109–34). Bingley: Emerald.

Wallace, Ruth, Leesa Costello, and Amanda Devine (2018) 'Netnographic slog: Creative elicitation strategies to encourage participation in an online community of practice for Early Education and Care', *International Journal of Qualitative Methods*, 17(1). 1609406918797796.

IMMERSING: JOURNALING AND ORGANIZING A REFLECTIVE CURATION

CHAPTER OVERVIEW

This is Chapter 10. This is the chapter that goes inside the reflective and introspective heart of netnography. This chapter teaches you about the nature and practice of immersive data operations in netnography. It takes a zen look at the social media universe, the ecosphere, the topology, the assemblage network actor system structure. It opens with an inquiry about the lasting applicability of the ethnographic notion of the stable and unified, or even normally multi-sited field and field site in the face of the instability of the massively-expanding social media realm. This critique will reveal that the concept of a field site is so destabilized by the nature of social media that it fails as a useful term. If we don't have a field, we have networks, and if we don't have field sites, we have data sites. Instead of fieldwork we have experiential encounters with these ecosystem-like networks. With no field site, and immersion, it wouldn't make sense to have fieldnotes. Instead, we have an immersion journal to capture those encounters.

The four core immersive operations in netnography are: (1) reconnoitering, (2) recording, (3) researching, and (4) reflecting. Reconnoitering is a type of orienting towards data sites, guided by the metaphor of the netnographer's focus alternately employing a telescope and microscope. In reconnoitering operations, the netnographer seeks deep data that is resonant, reveals lead users, provides exceptions to the rule, or reveals the macro inherent in the micro. Recording is the detailed, specific chronicling of the netnographer doing the research. Researching requires the netnographer to deliberately reveal, systematize, and evaluate the theoretical viewpoints they consciously and unconsciously impress upon the data during its inscription and analysis. And reflecting operations encourage netnographers to develop self-awareness, emotionality, and empathy, completing the set of ethnographic immersion operations. The final subsection of the chapter provides more research ethics advice, because what you inscribe in your immersive journal still has research ethics implications.

IMMERSIVE DATA
Sit(uat)ing Online Ethnography

Traditional and emplaced ethnographies are conducted in regions, among ethnic groups, on street corners, during festivals, and among such allegedly fixed places, peoples, and times. Fieldwork, the 'attempt to view other systems from the ground level' is considered by some to be 'anthropology's distinctive contribution to the human sciences' (Ortner, 1984: 143). Yet since its crisis of representation, anthropologists have been challenging traditional notions of long-term immersive fieldwork conducted in particular bounded sites. Multi-sited ethnography and studies of transnationalism explore the relationships between ostensibly different cultural elements and thus decenter the notion of a concretized actual 'field site' as well as the traditional ethnography practices of fieldwork that accompany it. An example of such a multi-sited ethnography is James Clifford's (1997) *Routes*, a study of travel in the late twentieth century that draws connections between museum exhibits, art shows, conferences, tourist sites, and other phenomena in various parts of the United States and Europe (Wogan, 2004: 129). Marcus (1995: 100) asserts that such studies emphasize something that is currently more central and important to contemporary ethnography than bounded sites and long-term immersion, namely 'the function of translation from one cultural idiom or language to another'. Geertz (1998: 72), however, is unconvinced, and calls the approach 'hit-and-run ethnography', 'drifting, freestyle anthropology', and 'ephemeral'.

The challenges of decentering become even more pronounced when the concept of ethnography is exported into social media communications. With online ethnography, the concept of 'a' field, as a singular site in space and time becomes ever more fluid and diffuse. In the past, ethnographers of the Internet have considered it useful, perhaps even necessary, to suggest that online ethnography takes place in a location that is analogous in significant ways to the particular physical locations in which traditional ethnographies transpire among particular embodied human participants. For instance, Correll's (1995) study of one particular bulletin board system on a major online service focused on an exploration of the linkages between the geographic location of an ethnographic field site, and the way that an online group's 'sense of common reality' could 'maintain a community' function similar to that of 'geographically anchored communities'.

However, as Hine (2015: 23) notes, even the notion of studying 'online cultures and communities' assumes in some way that these things 'are coherently bounded and pre-exist the interests of the ethnographer' – charges that could also be levied against the specifics of any ethnographic (or sampling) choices. As dedicated methodological inquiries into online ethnographic work progress, many of its practitioners express deep unease with the forced equivalence between the physical field sites of anthropologists and the communicative media of the new social platforms. They seek to develop alternative conceptions as well as new procedures for addressing what

Markham (1998: 114) struggles with as an experience that combines 'an embodied sense of self' in a 'place', a 'potential way of being', and a 'simulation via a machine'.

SEEING FIELD SITES WITH CLEAR EYES

Does netnography need a 'field site' in the same sense that ethnography does? What would it mean for netnographic research to consider the notion of the site? Thinking about some of the examples in this book that you have read about thus far, and perhaps extending those examples with some research of your own, come up with two examples of a traditional ethnography and its field site, and match those with two examples of an online ethnography and its field site. How is the notion of a field site different when you compare traditional and online ethnography? How is it the same? Discuss among yourselves in any way you like.

Traversing Destabilized Fields

At what point will online ethnography finally surrender traditional notions of fields and field sites as unwieldy and unhelpful forced equivalencies between two very different approaches?

Figure 10.1 Cartoon about netnography and digital fieldwork

The cartoon in Figure 10.1 mocks the idea of digital fieldwork in netnography. With an enthusiastic 'huzzah', the main character, 'Gabe', demonstrates his ability to be 'a part of this digital community' simply by typing in a few words: 'it's me again!' He is soundly rejected by 'Barfyman' who tells him in no uncertain terms that he is 'an outsider and unwelcome': 'gtfo' should need no translation. The cartoon draws its humor from the tensions about what constitutes fieldwork in online ethnography. The idea that a researcher can claim to have joined an online group simply by typing a few words on a keyboard, and then proceed to ignore the response of members of that group, is revealed as a research-enabled form of ignorance.

But if simply typing a hello to the group is not fieldwork in netnography, then what is? Hine (2000: 39) saw the early Internet as having the qualities both of 'a discursively performed culture' and 'a cultural artifact' or 'technology text'. Her conception of online ethnography was that it 'involves embracing ethnography as a textual practice and a lived craft and destabilizes the ethnographic reliance on sustained presence in a found field site' (p. 43). Forsaking the notion that 'ethnography of the internet' was bounded or fixed to a particular site, she emphasized mobility and hyperlinks as well as crossings between online and offline worlds. Postill and Pink (2012: 126) extended Hine's conceptions, viewing the Internet as 'a messy fieldwork environment' for ethnographers, one that 'is connected and constituted through the ethnographer's narrative'.

Postill and Pink (2012: 127) also made two noteworthy additional points about the translocation of the ethnographic field site in the age of social media. First, they see the shift to 'more transient encounters and co-routes through the internet and offline' as heralding a movement in ethnographic analysis away from virtual or online communities towards 'digital socialities'. Additionally, they build on Cresswell's (2002: 26) notions of place as being 'in a constant sense of becoming through practice and practical knowledge' to highlight that social media ethnography should be involved in 'understanding social media practices as part of, and as producing, place' (Postill and Pink, 2012: 127). The result of these ideas is an online ethnography that conceptualizes its field in a much more fluid fashion than traditional, and even perhaps than multi-sited, ethnography. As ethnography becomes native to online worlds, concrete field and demarcated cultural boundaries dissolve into movements, socialities, and practices.

Culture was once thought to be more or less emplaced, confined to particular peoples in particular places. Balinese culture. Ojibwe culture. Highland culture. But today, culture is complexified, borne out through human beings and their communications, and these people, their customs, their lifeways and information, are ever-increasingly more mobile, interwoven, and dynamic. Electrified, digitized, desire-magnifying media unleash global and local imaginariums, liquefying the localities of culture and turning them into intermingling streams, as Appadurai (1990) theorized, unleashing rushing planetary cultural flows of ethnoscapes, mediascapes, technoscapes, financescapes, and ideoscapes.

In netnography, we immerse ourselves in the destabilized and destabilizing cultural flows of social mediascapes. With the notion of a stable field dissolving into a set of charged conceptual particles, notions of fieldwork are thoroughly disrupted. The waves of flows become particles. The ethnographic field changes from a stable and singular type of arrangement, the people of an isolatable region, to a conceptual and multiplicitous one, such as a magnetic field, where the interests of the research, researcher, and network constantly reterritorialize in a complex dance of attraction. In these flows, field sites become data sites in an instant, not just multi-sited but multitudinously-sited. As we will learn in this chapter, instead of fieldnotes, the netnographer will create a journal of their immersion in these destabilized online fields, using the full articulative capacity of the contemporary human academic mind. The immersion journal charts and records their glorious connections and the constant nagging disjunctures between them all.

Immersive Data Operations

Ethnography in all its forms is emergent and inductive. The consequence of this is that we do not know beforehand exactly what we should notice. Although our research questions and topics certainly guide us, and Chapter 8 in this book is full of suggestions, the emergent qualities of netnography are assisted by the immersion journal, which acts as a reflective, catalytic, and analytic guide to help netnographers find their way through the emanant process of research, and research decision making.

As the remainder of this chapter will explain, immersive data operations take place as an underdetermined set of procedures that combine: (a) the reconnoitering of fields, sites, social scenes and entire scapes, guided by a curatorial propensity to find black swans and lead users, and perhaps to build a phenomena-based science; (b) the recording of the process of questioning, immersion, search, investigation, and interaction, as experienced and understood by the research team, researcher, or unstable network of researchers; (c) the ongoing collision of research theories, conceptual fields, extant researchers, sampled sites and populations, and collected data in the quest for new and meaningful patterns and principles; and (d) the personal reflections and meta-level concerns of a cultural researcher seeking understanding from within a deterritorializing field of theoretical, professional, professorial, personal, and socioeconomic knowledges. In practice, these procedures overlap one another, but contain elements distinct enough to outline and explain. Adding a final subsection that will reflect upon the ethical procedures that need to be observed in this stage, the following sections of the chapter will explore each of these operational elements in turn.

FOUR IMMERSIVE OPERATIONS

Four essences of data operations that immerse are (1) reconnoitering, (2) recording, (3) researching, and (4) reflecting. Whereas data operations in investigative and interactive movements are about *collection*, data operations in the immersive mode are about the *writing* and *curation* of data; this chapter is particular because journaling is all about good writing, evidential writing, theoretical and introspective writing. The 'data' in immersive operations is a novel you are writing about yourself doing this research, a non-fiction novel. In that novel, entire research fields are wakening from their big data dreams to discover human social science, qualitative social media research methods applied to mapping, making records, assuming research perspectives, and contemplating the act of doing research.

Immersive journals can be written individually, or they can be created by research teams in various ways. They can be combined as live online documents, started in meetings, and/or distributed once particular stages of the research are complete. Even though data onscreen is easily captured, and in fact, you might contain in your immersion journal the collective portrayal of many kinds of visual and video data as well as text, the immersion journal is a true journal. It is a personal record, a temporal narrative, a wide-ranging diary that can also include dreams, reactions, feelings, readings, as well as ideas and sections of what you hope might become the final text for the document you will write and submit. Indeed, I think that good immersion journal excepts will make up some of the most compelling data presentations in netnographies of the future.

One of the method-related pieces of advice that Emerson et al. (2011: 1–2) baked into their definition of fieldnotes is the regularity and systematic nature of a researcher writing down (i.e., recording) 'what she observes and learns while participating in the daily rounds of the lives of others'. Being regular and being systematic – both are important. Having a regular schedule of contact in ethnographic research allows you to be structured and consistent in how you collect your data. Such immersive operations might seem to be chronicling the research journey, the route to a knowledge destination. But the act of writing the immersion journal is actually carving out the path as much as following it. There is room in immersion to record the playfulness, spontaneity, and serendipity that take place in the enacting of social science research, as well as the self-doubt, moments of elation, and chasms of frustration. Immersion allows us to capture, as the human sciences and the humanities do, both the relational and expressive qualities of the act of seeking understanding.

Using the immersion journal, netnographers will practice four methical sets of skills of immersing in the social media experience as a process for the creation of research data. These are (1) reconnoitering, (2) recording, (3) researching, and (4) reflecting. They are explained as follows:

1. Reconnoitering is the act of mapping out the territory. This mapping function can be conceptualized in precise words and visualized in concept maps drawn from your own understanding and ongoing analysis. Reconnoitering requires you to continually assess what you are looking for, as you seek to evaluate the research value of what you have found. You are scouting for deep data that is resonant and builds empathy, is richly visual or visceral, and reveals lead users and exceptions to the rule. Immersion is soaking in the social media substrate, finding pathways through the living pools of the ecosystem in which you are swimming.

2. Recording is the chronicling in the immersion journal of the questioner's quest for answers. Recording includes overviews and details as needed about each encounter with the data site, data site locations, impressions, events, decisions about data collection, and screenshots, particularly of data you consider to be deep data. There are many choices in recording, such as how to record, what to record, and how much (if any) of the immersion journal to share publicly. Immersion is submersion in the facts you are observing, and recording is the capturing of the facts of their observation.

3. Researching is the deployment of past theories and conceptual frames in the ongoing act of sense-making you capture in the immersion journal. The researcher comes to data sites with particular interests. These interests are research-related. Information encountered on social media data sites speaks to extant constructs, abstractions, theories, sites, authors, methods, samples, and other elements of research that can also be conceptualized as data. The immersion journal captures this play of ideas as the researcher juxtaposes and compares these abstractions and other research-related data with the emerging empirical dataset drawn from the data sites. Immersion is a plunge into the social media data lagoon wearing research-colored swim goggles.

4. Reflecting is first-person and introspective. Just as an ethnographer captures their experience of encountering and learning a new culture through their fieldnotes, it is through reflective data-writing operation that the netnographer captures their own experiences of the particularities of a social media ecosystem. Reflective notes capture your own construction of theory from the observations you notice, your attempts to detect what is going on, what is connected, what is new, what is meaningful. Beyond this, the reflexive act causes you to question why you are detecting what you are, why you see this connection and not that one, why you believe this to be new or that to have deeper meanings. Seized in the moment of thought, written as you think it, your reflective operations catch the human

story of your ongoing explanatory quest. Immersion is a deep-water dive into the cavernous expanse of human understanding.

Keep these four operations in mind. This chapter will develop your understanding of reconnoitering, recording, researching, and reflecting. But first, you should be sure you have already started your immersion journal. The exercise in Box 10.2 does not leave you with any choice. Once you read this exercise you *must* begin your immersion journal – with no excuses!

STARTING YOUR IMMERSION JOURNAL

10.2

Begin keeping your immersion journal. You actually should have done this as soon as you started collecting data. So you might think you did it wrong, but ... don't worry. You will know for next time. Netnography is full of choices, and no two netnographies will ever be exactly the same. This variety is the eventful expression of the idea of infinite beauty in unceasing diversity.

Find a notebook. Buy one at the store for a small amount of money. Something with 100 or more pages that you can write in and keep afterwards. Start a blog. Open a pinboard. In order to create good notes in your journal, all that matters is that they are based on immersion, returning to social media platforms repeatedly over the time period of the netnography. Your engagement with data sites and the collected dataset will occur in real time, spreading over weeks, months, over perhaps years – even if your main data downloads transpire over much shorter time horizons. Record the happenings on that real-time research beat as best you can. Not trying to find one particular theory or another for now. Just letting the phenomenon speak to you. Immersion is deep engagement, where you are reading, thinking, and absorbing a great deal of social and cultural information from hanging out on particular social media platforms; you might see the same people, or these might be completely new people, or people might be irrelevant, and it is just content, wherever it comes from.

You have been stretching and twisting your research question since Chapter 5. Immersion is theory-building that happens the minute you commit to your research project with a defined question.

Now, it is time to apply that question.

Write the date on the top right corner of the first page. Or somewhere else you prefer. Write your research question. Start investigating. Write what happens. Wash. Rinse. Repeat.

(Continued)

You are creating a one-of-a-kind document. It is a type of very personal art. Netnography has always aspired to a combined written/visual quality. My immersion journal was often the source of some of the actual writing that I then lifted and used in the written manuscript submitted. If you are careful, and take pride in it, keeping the immersion journal can be the most useful thing you do in a netnography.

RECONNOITERING

Why Reconnoitering Stands Apart

Reconnoitering is a completely separate function from the other three writing operations. Sense-making, mapmaking, and wayfinding are continuous in netnographic data site work, and they rely on a type of visual, imagistic, verbal, linguistic, and desire-focused navigation-based sense. An observation is recorded. A datum is snipped from context, screen-shotted, printed, and taped to a journal page. As you scratch a theoretical frame into its empirical flesh, infecting its concrete phrases with the virus of abstract constructs, you are reflecting the reality that theories are technologies, representations that contaminate and disseminate meaning. You or your colleagues reflect on why you have written this theory and not another. You open up to the possibility that perhaps you have been mistranslating things all along. You question your own thinking, or the thinking of your research partner, and your doubt leads you in a different direction, one that seems new and might even be productive.

You are recording, researching, and reflecting work in combination – and capturing this iterative process in your journal. So, unlike investigation, where the sub-steps are called 'operations' and where you could do them, if you wish, in sequence, immersion operations are more simultaneous. Recording, reflecting, and researching writing operations overlap in time. Just as the investigation, interaction, and immersion data operations can and should overlap in the overall netnography, the writing of the immersion journal is a combination of these three operations that I have explained as discrete operations of recording, researching, and reflecting. They are in the doing often partially or wholly combined. You cannot record something without recording it from a particular perspective. And as a researcher directed by a research question, your data collection is always going to be a bit selective, and based upon your empirical questing pre-criteria. This is true whether you are conducting an experiment, doing a survey, or writing ethnographic fieldnotes. The words and photos in the immersion journal reflect you, record you, and provide research insights into the researcher. Recording, research, and reflection are writing operations that overlap and intertwine, as accuracy, theorizing, and self-critical thinking twist around each other.

But reconnoitering adds an orienteering and visualizing element to it, more like the questing of geocachers or the surveying of cartographic artists than the careful surveying of scientists during a psychological experiment. Reconnoitering can be done at the beginning, the middle, or the end of any netnography – or it could be done continuously throughout the process of the research inquiry.

The Telescope and the Microscope

Reconnoitering is intended to indicate practices of inspecting, observing, examining, and surveying in every possible sense. The netnographer must be like a cartographer with a telescope in one hand and a microscope in the other. When reconnoitering, the eye of the netnographer is on the wider view, scoping the horizon of social media. Reconnoitering requires you to continually assess what you are looking for, where to find it, and to what is it connected, as you seek to construct from the current datascape what you have already found. What is out there, conceptually? Theoretically? How does it relate in a sophisticated fashion to your own research questions, and the ones that your scientific field requires that you ask?

Alternating the telescope and the microscope, again and again. As the paths open up before you and you take your first steps on them, reconnoitering is the act of mapping out the territory. This mapping function should be visualized in concept maps drawn from your own understanding, and as much qualitative and quantitative analysis as you can bring to bear on cultural types of theories – explanations that deal with interactions between small groups and larger institutions, individuals, systems, cultures, societies. Literal maps might be a part of your online fieldwork. For example, game players might make sketches, maps, or diagrams that relate to quests, raids, or solving puzzles.

What are you reconnoitering for? One thing you are looking for is the broad insight of deep data. Deep data is resonant and empathic. It is also lead user revealing. It can be strongly visual or strongly visceral. It can also look like a black swan. Resonant data, lead user data, exceptions to the rule, and micrological data are all manifestations of deep data.

MAPPING DATA SITES (PROJECT EXERCISE)

As you enter and move through your data sites, try to capture in your immersion journal your sense of the relation between its various elements. What is the topography of these online 'spaces'? What platforms, sites, threads, forums, and so on does it encompass? List these elements in your journal. Then, try to draw out their interrelation. How would you group them? Which ones are larger than others? Which are smaller? Which are close, and which are distant?

The following subsections detail these reconnoitering-related aspects of the immersive quest captured in the immersion journal.

Seeking Resonant Data

Part of what we are searching for in our reconnoitering is resonant data. We seek traces that will be emotionally and intraceptively appealing, subjectively import- ant and imaginatively productive. Powerful and cultural. We ask of resonant data first whether it speaks to us and second whether we believe it will speak to our intended audience. Is it visceral? Does is induce particular moods or emotional states? Does it relate, as the anthropologist Ruth Behar (1996) emphasizes, to our vulnerability as engaged observers? Does it, in some sense, break our heart? Does it lead to an intuitive grasping of the reality of another real-seeming person? With resonance, we are working with a more ephemeral and phenomenological set of criteria. Resonant data are sometimes immediately evocative in a visual, auditory, or video sense. They are also sometimes dramatic and powerful narratives, longer tales that draw us deeper into the world of the messengers or the unfolding of the conversational message.

Seeking Lead User Data

According to Eric von Hippel's (1986: 791) founding definition, which was based on Everett Rogers' (1962) paradigm-setting work on innovation adoption, lead users are voices from the future: 'Lead users are users whose present strong needs will become general' in times to come. Because lead users are familiar with condi- tions that lie in the future, scientists believe that they can usefully serve as a type of window into what will happen next. Although von Hippel devised his term to talk about customers and marketplaces, his concept is applicable to other social situations. We might look for situations, events, conversations, groups, and people who are pushing the envelope of what is possible, those who are driven by strong needs for the next stage of a particular development. For example, we might find that the political conversations of engaged groups of social media posters end up becoming mainstream conversations afterwards. Or that alternative non-commercial social media sites that offer privacy but are only used by marginal groups of sophis- ticated users might serve as models for a type of new site that will one day gain many more users. The idea of lead users – or lead situations, conversations, platforms, or events – draws our attention to the ends of distributions, rather than their means. Many of the most interesting occurrences in social worlds happen on the margins, in the in-between spaces and weedy cracks of society. From its early days, netnography was a place to identify such unusual and important things – the lead users and their 'enthusiasm, knowledge, and experimentation' (Kozinets, 2002a: 66). The idea of lead users can direct you to important new questions and findings. What sorts of canaries can you find in online coalmines?

Exceptions to the Rule

We can draw some insight into the nature of curation from the famous black swan fallacy. This notion demonstrates the falsifiability of induction and, indeed, of all universalizing scientific research – perhaps even of generalist universalized knowledge itself! Originally, it seems that the term 'black swan' was used like the term 'flying pigs' is today, to refer to something impossible. The second-century Roman poet Juvenal wrote about what a rare bird a black swan would be. However, in 1697, Dutch explorers actually saw black swans in Western Australia. The impossible was actually real.

The black swan fallacy is derived from these facts. If all you have ever observed in your research are white swans, you might be tempted to conclude that all swans are white. However, all it takes is one black swan to falsify the general statement about the universality of white swans. Accommodating black swan evidence leads to much more interesting and elaborate scientific theories that use boundary conditions and contingencies. For example, consider the revised rule that all native European swans are white. Black swans are often difficult to find and in the search for them context is all-important. While we are sorting, categorizing and classifying, we must remember and be attuned to the exceptions to the rule, expressed in the uniqueness of individuals, interactions, experiences, and moments. There are times when a thorough ideographic study of the exceptionality of the single case becomes a very important contribution that moves our understanding forward (Edgar and Billingsley, 1974).

Micrological Data

The deep data we seek in immersive reconnoitering operations can also be composed of exceptions to the rule. We can understand this idea of exceptional deep data by referring to the micrological and macrological analyses of Walter Benjamin. The remainder of this section explains Walter Benjamin's significance to netnographic immersion and our understanding of reconnoitering for data that provides exceptions to the rule.

Benjamin recommended something he called 'micrological' thinking for empirical field research, in which the researcher tried to recognize the general shapes recurring within the entire image – the repetitive fractal pattern within the chaos (Eiland, 2014). He liked to look at particular instances, at the fragment, the one powerful quotation, the sign in the park, the singular artwork, the nondescript thing or overlooked object. Taking the frame of a social scientist, Benjamin would examine that fragment, finally, with a view to generalizing it to something else, something larger that it explained. This could also be what legendary science fiction author

Philip K. Dick meant when he proclaimed that 'the symbols of the divine initially show up at the trash stratum'.

When it came to science, Benjamin was seeking a type of generalization, taking the small data analysis of a cultural artefact and unpacking it to reveal the larger-scale, universally applicable, 'macrological' secrets that lay within it (Eiland, 2014). If we translate Benjamin's macrological thinking into the world of immersive data-collection operations in netnography, he is referring to a search for deep data: individual pieces of data that capture bigger truths about the larger cultural phenomenon they represent.

The reconnoitering quest for insight and understanding is captured in the immersion journal. It manifests as a search for resonant data, lead user data, exceptions to the rule, and micrological data. In prior sections, we learned how these types of data are all manifestations of the deep data whose quest the immersion journal chronicles. In the following section, we move to a consideration of the recording procedures of immersion.

RECORDING

Your immersion journal is your chronicle and your record. Recording is your attempt to accurately represent what happened during your research: the doing of the research. Recording is the chronicling of the questioner's quest for answers. If reconnoitering occurs in a networked place, as a mapping thing, then recording takes place in time, as a pastward-looking historical endeavor. Recording is what happens to observational fieldnotes when they become immersive data operations. As you take notes, you express them in your immersion journal. This journal is written in your voice, as your story. It is the tale of your research project. It is not only your voice and your recollection, but also your collection and curation. Recording captures screenshots, particularly of data you consider to be deep and rich.

Immersive Recording and Traditional Fieldnotes

Recording in the immersion journal in netnography is related to writing fieldnotes in traditional ethnography. In an attempt to relate changes in fieldnote practice in American anthropology over the past thirty years, Jackson (2016) found a variety of different perspectives. There were many views, even on what constituted a fieldnote. To some, fieldnotes had to be physical, like a fetish; they get wrinkled and have coffee stains on them. To others, they were mystery, art, and experience. They evoked the time and the place when and where the ethnographer performed the actual fieldwork. They were an index of the time spent doing the research. They were also the raw ingredients that needed to be cooked later. Fieldnotes for others were the main labor of ethnography: 'gathering data is like gathering fruits and vegetables, it feels like you're accomplishing something' (Jackson, 2016: 48).

In a significant number of published netnographies, researchers mention their fieldnotes. For example, Kulavuz-Onal and Vàsquez (2013: 230–4) capture interactive conversations, technical details, and the temporal unfolding of their research practice in their noting, but their emotional engagement is not conveyed (at least, not in the notes they decided to place in their publication). Wei et al. (2011: 26) reported making extensive use of 200 pages of fieldnotes while observing participant behaviors as they occurred, and consulted these notes when drafting their journal article. Similarly, the netnography conducted by Aitamurto (2013) also recorded participant observations and interactions within the online community, amassing a significant amount of data in 16 weekly memos. Likewise, Gurrieri and Cherrier (2013) made reflective fieldnotes on their observation of blogs over a period of more than two months. Yet, unlike the many opinions of fieldnotes captured by Jackson (2016), these collections were in addition to the data collected during investigative operations in netnography.

When fieldnotes are used in ethnography, the regular activity of writing and reflecting becomes 'an indistinguishable part of the experience of doing fieldwork', just as Jackson (2016: 53) says, as 'the mode of inscribing establishes the mode of legitimacy'. As well, 'anthropologists now regularly download newspaper articles, NGO bulletins, and other media traces concerning their research community or institutions and events that impact it' (pp. 58–9). Jackson points out that computers regularly accompany the contemporary ethnographer, and that notes are regularly taken, stored, and sent in digital formats. In traditional ethnography, the fieldnotes are the main source of data that capture cultural interactions. In netnography, however, this is not the case.

Yet Jackson (2016: 59) is uncertain about whether these 'electronic documents (or notes taken while perusing them)' are fieldnotes or not, and leaves deciding this matter to 'the researcher's own definition'. This is the typical ethnography-without-a-recipe methodology, and although I admire its openness, I know firsthand the confusion it causes. So the recipes for conducting a netnography are more specific.

eFieldnotes

The various chapters and authors in Sanjek and Tratner's (2016) volume, entitled *eFieldnotes: The Making of Anthropology in the Digital World*, are similarly unspecific and noncommittal about the relation of fieldnotes to the capturing of social media data. Tratner (2016), for instance, describes a method that seems based on traditional ethnographic fieldnoting practices. In it, the fieldnotes are Microsoft Word document files containing 'many complete thread posts' (p. 184). Additionally, in the files, she describes and illustrates the threads and their content, and indicates the reason why she collects a thread, providing some context, some initial analysis, and some preliminary connection to larger themes she has identified (pp. 182–3). Then, to organize her work, she creates a new Word document for each theme or topic, combining the downloaded posts of that topic with scratch notes, links, descriptions, and reflections from headnotes (p. 184). Tratner's (2016) experimentations seem to produce many big, complex, interspersed documents that are too unwieldy to be a useful role model.

Tratner's method is similar to that of many of the other authors in the *eFieldnotes* volume, one of whom describes fieldnotes as things that 'write themselves' (Nardi, 2016). Others include transcripts of downloaded conversations in fieldnotes. They confuse online data collection in general with fieldnotes. They even confuse online texts with fieldnotes. Nardi (2016: 207) describes her eFieldnotes as 'a mélange of natively produced/automatically recorded notes and the usual handcrafted "personal, parochial, subjective" fieldnotes of traditional ethnography'. If the researcher can construe anything found online to be an eFieldnote, then the distinctive meaning of fieldnotes would seem to be lost. It seems unnecessary to consider any type of online data as potentially a fieldnote or journal entry. In practice, this just makes for messy netnographies of multiple documents that each serve many purposes, like the mélanges of Nardi and Tratner. That is not the purpose of the immersion journal in netnography. The idea of separating investigative, interactive, and immersive data-collection operations is to avoid this sort of confusion of source and intent. The next section explains the recording facet of those immersive data-writing operations.

What and Why to Record

'If access and transcriptions are no longer unique things that the [online] ethnographer has to offer, what then is the contribution [of the fieldnotes]?' (Beaulieu, 2004: 155). Beaulieu's question suggests the rationale for an immersion journal in netnography: methodologically and conceptually, we have an opportunity to differentiate archives from inscription. The act of inscription in netnography provides an opportunity for the researcher to engage in the set of practices that preserve the first-person element of ethnographic storytelling, but do so without needing to be burdened with the act of recording observational data.

What do the recorded aspects of the immersion journal record? The immersion journal will contain descriptions that are a combination of what is seen on the screen and what the researcher experiences. Although many of the on-screen manifestations of the 'events' that transpire through online interaction can be collected through screen captures and data downloads, your immersion journal is the place to record your own impressions, the subjective meanings of interactions and events as you experience them materializing over time. They 'allow the ethnographer to keep a record of what happens and how it feels', enabling them to document 'provisional thoughts about what these observations may mean', 'ideas about what to look at next', and concerns about puzzling aspects (Hine, 2015: 74).

The recording-based focus in the immersion journal is on dates, doings, data, and decisions. What you encountered, how you evaluated it, what you decided not to collect, what you collected. It can be useful to take notes on many types of online social experiences: platforms encountered, searches run, memes posted, events and resources encountered. Where online experiences occur in the form of audio, photographs, graphics or video, it is important to save these in the form in which they were experienced, as well as to record one's own personal introspective observations about them as soon as possible after having processed them.

What you write in the journal is the practice of your doing of the research, with justifications provided so that you can backtrack and see both the road taken and the branches of the paths not followed. At the same time, you will record sites and data, especially what strikes you as deep data: the record of your reconnoitering for resonant, lead user exceptions to the rule, and the micrological fragments that reveal macrocosmic cultural insights. These will be contained in the entries you write in your immersion journal as you provide overviews and details about each encounter you have of every kind with the data site. Whether you are reading scraped archives in a spreadsheet, going online to scan for new data, organizing files on your smartphone, or interviewing a participant using mobile ethnography, all these research practices must be noted and recorded in your immersion journal.

The journal itself is a recording, and should be dated and timestamped. Entering data into that journal is an act of recording similar to an experimental observation. As Costello et al. (2017) discovered, fieldnoting practices are only mentioned in a minority of published netnographic articles. This may be because, as Hine (2015: 74) notes, the volume of data in online ethnography 'can become overwhelming', and the ability to record and store data for review at a later date can be 'all too tempting'. Yet keeping an immersion journal provokes a systematic engagement with the topic at hand, one that is regular and extended in time. An immersion, similar in meaning to traditional ethnographic immersion. Download and code is not ethnography, it is content analysis – what is missing is the provocation of consistent reflection on meaning and pattern as well as netnographic engagement in the various online trace pools. The length of time one keeps the immersion journal is therefore a key indicator of immersive data intensity and quality. The length of pages indicates commitment to the topic and the procedures of ethnography. Keeping an immersion journal helps the netnographer guard against a passive research presence, focus on present moments of experience, and analyze and encounter data coincident with the act of collection, rather than, as Hine points out, in some 'solitary future moment' at a distance from data sites.

How to Record

In the writing of your immersion journal, you have a range of choices. You choose what to include and not include. You choose how descriptive you want to be. You choose whether to link or not link to your other sources of data. You choose whether to include some of them, or not. You also have choices about what medium to use to record your immersion journal. Will you use a physical notebook, save it on social media, or combine methods? You also have the choice of whether or not to make some or all of your immersion journal publicly available, and whether or not to invite comments. This section overviews and details these choices.

As you inscribe, write descriptively. Description in ethnography 'calls for concrete details rather than abstract generalizations, for sensory imagery rather than evaluative labels, and for immediacy through details presented at close range' (Emerson et al., 1995: 69), and the same is true in netnographic recording. Cultural research guides you to be mindful of the details, especially the one you would normally naturalize and find invisible. Descriptive recording in netnographic immersion journals will cause you to consider with new eyes the images, colors, fonts, backgrounds, avatars, symbols, brands, shapes, design elements, and other elements of the highly visual and often visceral online experience. With this sort of descriptive attention, netnography shades easily into semiotic research. Semiotic studies of the many visual design features apparent on the Internet and in social media, used as messaging communications, as alphabets, and as signs are key to understanding the many intersecting languages of people, tribes, and the media they make and which simultaneously makes them.

It can also be valuable to record observational notes that link to downloaded data, elaborating upon subtleties noticed at the time that were not captured in the data itself. These margin notes are valuable, and likely are what led to some of the large and messy fieldnote files that combined data and eFieldnotes, as mentioned in the section above. Observational margin notes offer details about the social and interactional processes that constitute online experience. Writing immersion notes as soon as possible after you work on your netnography is important because localized processes of learning, socialization, and acculturation are subtle and our recollection of them becomes diffuse over time. That is why I like to keep a physical book next to me when I am doing my netnographic research, so that I can quickly write down what I notice and what I think it means. Boellstorff et al. (2012: 82–5) build on video game culture and recommend using a 'two-boxing' approach of keeping two computer windows open simultaneously; on one screen the netnographic engagement unfolds, while on the other screen you write your immersion journal notes in real time. Whichever method you choose, be sure that you have immediate access to write down the things that you think are important as they occur to you in your encounters with sites, traces, and data.

You might consider using social media as a way to create, record, and save your immersive netnographic data. For instance, you might use Pinterest pinboards to save sites you have visited and conversations you have saved, as well as your own online posts that describe the doing of your research. The immersion journal can become your digital diary, online, saved and stored. Of course, you have other options. You might keep your journal on paper, in a bound notebook (as I do), with printed out sections taped on its pages, highlighted, with scrawled notes beside it. I like to keep my immersion journal small enough that it can be held in a few thick bound-book volumes. You can tape or glue any kind of printout in there, including any kind of printed image. By writing on paper and including scraps and remnants of real things, perhaps we pay homage to the analog roots of our discipline. We will be creating a singular book, something unreplicable, a physical artifact that can show the same wear and tear and coffee stains of its traditional fieldnote journal forebears. Amalgamations of online/offline are also possible, such as keeping both a physical journal and a Pinterest pinboard with links to your Facebook research webpage.

There are choices, too, in terms of whether and how much of your immersion journal will be visible to others. Perhaps you are the only one who can see your fieldnotes, which is far and away the most popular choice for ethnographers. In fact, Khan (2018) writes a moving and informative account about the subpoena of his ethnographic fieldnotes that could be read as a cautionary tale about assuming that your fieldnotes and immersion journal data will always stay private.

Ethnography Matters (2012) describes the need for what they call 'live fieldnotes' – and demonstrates their sharing online. Their points are well taken about the diverse format for online ethnography fieldnotes (e.g., iPhone, multiple smartphone apps, notebook, audio recorder, camera, and sticky notes) and the simplicity of a single online place to locate them. You might also wish to share your immersion journal with participants (or the general public), ask for their comments or invite their participation. Ethnography Matters (2012) combines this idea of 'open ethnography' with the conception of 'live fieldnotes', noting how the latter facilitate the former. All sorts of arrangements are possible. These include the traditional 'member checks' (Lincoln and Guba, 1985) where participants (or the public) read and comment on the ethnographic work. They also encompass more collaborative arrangements that could include having participants add margin notes to your ethnography, contribute their own thoughts to the analysis, write in authored sections of their own, or rewrite your text, perhaps in crowdsourced fashion.

Recording Summary

The sections above have detailed the process of recording data in the immersion journal and distinguished it from both traditional fieldnote practices and newer variants such as eFieldnotes. Other subsections have described what to record, why to record, and how to record in the journal. As was noted earlier in the chapter, the acts of researching and reflecting are interwoven into the practices of recording. In the next section of this chapter, we turn to a discussion of researching practices in immersion.

RESEARCHING

Researching Data Operations

Data sites are not voids encountered by tabula rasa objective operands. Instead, data sites are platforms and especially parts of platforms that hold the interest of the researcher who has particular research interests. The reason for this interest lies

10.4 RECORDING DATA IN YOUR IMMERSION JOURNAL (PROJECT EXERCISE)

Time to try your hand at recording some immersion journal notes. During your next session of data gathering or engagement (why not right now?), write recording style notes in your immersion journal. Follow the principles described in this subsection.

Record the date first. Then the time. Then the doing of your research. An overview of the data you collected from traces. And some description of the decisions you made. What did you encounter in the data site or dataset? How did you evaluate it? Why did you decide to collect what you collected, and not to collect what you did not? Record as many elements of your online experience as you can: platforms encountered, searches run, pages read, memes laughed at, events streamed, resources encountered, and so on. Save things like audio, photographs, graphics, or video, and note in your immersion journal where they are saved. Include a few screenshots for good measure.

in the way particular data seem to fit, or fail to fit, in recognizable ways with the research aims of the scientists and the project. Information encountered on social media data sites speaks to extant constructs, abstractions, theories, sites, authors, methods, samples, and other elements of research that can also be conceptualized as data. Research theories, sites, authors, methods, constructs, samples, and articles can all be treated as a type of data that can be elaborated and expanded upon in immersion journal writings. The netnographer regularly captures in their immersion journal their own deployment of past theories and conceptual frames in the ongoing act of sensemaking. In this way, the writing in the immersion journal acts as a play of concepts that the researcher juxtaposes and compares with the emerging dataset from the datasites.

Being able to objectify those conceptual acts as inscriptions in a journal is an important distancing step in the analytic process. Not only does it begin the act of analysis, it also makes the act itself available to scrutiny. Keeping conceptual notes alongside observational immersion notes that capture your own impressions, you automatically begin a process of abstraction, taking the world of almost infinite variables and turning it into a fixed and tractable set of written concepts. The key to this distancing process is to understand that what you are seeing and doing is highly bound up with your own experience, readings, intent, and past. Immersive entries are the start of data analysis and interpretation. They help the netnographer decipher, while it is still fresh and new and unfolding, the postulated reasons behind cultural actions, rather than offering a mere recording, capture, or description of them.

Especially in netnography, research is bound to search. As we search for data in netnography, we also search for traces that fit theories, break them, expand or inform them. Our searches for data and theory occur iteratively, a form of highly (inter)active re-searching. Immersive researching is thus a highly engaged act, and three of the key purposes of the immersion journal are to make visible that act, to systematize it as part of the ongoing process of data collection, and to facilitate it. One further way to conceptualize this is by reference to magical positivism.

RESEARCHING DATA OPERATIONS (PROJECT EXERCISE)

10.5

Use this exercise to practice making your research thinking a regular part of writing in your immersion journal. During your next session of data gathering or immersive social media engagement, be explicit about the research frames you are inserting onto your data. Follow the principles described in this subsection.

Clearly state the theoretical viewpoint or viewpoints you are using to make sense of the data you just collected. Consider carefully what that viewpoint reveals and what it keeps hidden. Where is its emphasis? Try this for at least three different research viewpoints (i.e., where viewpoints are theoretical perspectives).

If you are working in a research team, share these results with your colleagues. Have them try applying the same three theoretical viewpoints to the same  dataset as you. Then have them try it using three different theoretical viewpoints. Compare what you found. What do you learn from this exercise? Write it in your immersion journal – as another insight to develop and explore.

Researching and Magical Positivism

The section on reconnoitering operations discussed Walter Benjamin's use of a micrological approach, one where he searched for interesting fragments and used them to explore larger cultural truths. In this book, I link the notion of micrological analysis to the search for deep data in netnography. But Benjamin's micrological approach was also tied to his research scholarship as well as to his larger methodological techniques of immanent criticism and magical positivism, which also have possible roles in the immersion journal.

Benjamin was a wide reader who liked Marxian critical theory as well as Weber's sociology. Although he mistrusted capitalism, he adored consumption, at least as a topic of study (Eiland, 2014). Methodologically, Benjamin was similar to a multi-sited ethnographer. He combined archival work with observation, as well as observation of his own participation. He took careful journal notes on his immersion, like a netnographer. He read widely, like a scholar of days gone by. As a result of his eclectic and autodidactic tendencies, he ended up as a bridge-builder between disciplines. His work is a type of hybrid scholarly-spiritual philosophy that melds a primitivist celebration of metaphysics and a messianic theology with commercial cultural theory, art history, and cutting-edge dialectical materialism (ibid.).

Finding the deep cultural data he loved to translate was predicated on a type of immersive operation that Benjamin called 'immanent criticism' (ibid.). Immanent criticism seems like a naive gesture, but it is intended as an intent rather than an actually realized possibility. It means seeing data authentically: for what they actually are, what you think they are, rather than what someone else says they think they are. He termed the entire research perspective a methodology of 'magical positivism' (ibid.), a decidedly unorthodox name that upholds the customs and standards of literary criticism.

Applying Immanent Criticism in Netnography

In the attempt to see something as it actually is, as what you genuinely think it is, you must first go through all of the preconceptions, the preunderstanding and prejudgments about what is unconsciously influencing you to think it otherwise. This type of thinking also informs Gadamer's (2006) version of hermeneutic interpretation. As we exchange one set of theory-colored research lenses for another, we gradually (it is hoped) get a sense of the true colors behind their various color distortions of the different optics of empirical perception. And so, in pointed contrast to the precepts of traditional qualitative inquiry, in which key concepts and theoretical relationships are supposed to emerge in an inductive process during the research process, in magical positivism the research begins with a stated theoretical viewpoint. That viewpoint could be Foucauldian, neo-Marxist, Lacanian, Deleuzian, New Critical, or any theory your heart desires. But it is studiously applied to the collected data that is being investigated.

We can see how feminist literary critics expose androcentrism in the texts that they scrutinize, and post-colonialists similarly expose Western cultural imperialism. These literary methods are not necessarily rigid or doctrinaire. They do not necessarily try to stuff particular texts into pre-existing frameworks. Rather, the process involves an iterative back and forth conversation between the data and the stated theoretical position. An overriding principle in the process is flexibility.

Yet this reflective magical positivism must be balanced by our attempts to try to understand the language and meanings of messages as they were intended by their message posters. As Bakhtin (1981: 294) notes, 'Language is not a neutral medium that passes freely and easily into the private property of the speaker's intention. It is populated – overpopulated with the intentions of others. Expropriating it, forcing it to submit to one's own intentions and accents, is a difficult and complicated task.' Bakhtin's thoughts about language help us realize that by making our own reflections visible in the immersion journal, we open them to another layer of critical examination – both by ourselves at a later date and by others such as co-researchers, co-authors, and editors. We can see our own initial understandings, and try to consciously link them to our pre-judgments and pre-understandings (Gadamer, 2006). As we apply further interpretive analysis to our entire dataset, this concretizing of our initial flashes of understanding can contribute to learning what we don't know about language, meaning, and culture, and from there lead to further inquiry into transcending superficial interpretations of cultural messages.

Applied to netnography, magical positivism and immanent criticism suggest a conscious and deliberate use of particular theoretical frames. Research notes in your immersion journal would openly state the theoretical viewpoint (preferably viewpoints) that they are using both to choose and make sense of the data you are collecting. Then, they can document the iterative to-ing and fro-ing of research theory and embedded empirical positions. What is lost or hidden when data is fitted into this framework? What is gained or made visible? Doing this with several theoretical frameworks, among several data sites, and perhaps across the work of several different researchers (who later share and carefully compare their work), will likely lead to a richer understanding and more complex explanation of the phenomenon under study. With these ideas about researching in immersion operations now completed, we can turn to the final section of immersive operations, which discusses the procedures of reflecting.

REFLECTING

Reflective noting in the immersion journal is where the netnographer considers their role in the ongoing, unfolding human experience of being-in-the-network for the purpose of answering a research question. Reflection is introspective and reflects a first-person perspective. Just as an ethnographer captures their experiences with a new culture through their fieldnotes, it is through a reflective data-writing operation that the netnographer captures their own experience of encountering and learning about the specific particularities of an online social environment.

Producing Reflective Data

Reflective journals are used often in counseling psychology as well as in religious and spiritual pursuits. However, there is a sparse and fragmented theoretical literature supporting their use. One interesting intersection is with Mezirow's (2000: 7–8) transformative learning theory, which considers 'the process by which we transform our taken-for-granted frames of reference (meaning, perspectives, habits of mind, mind sets), to make them more inclusive, discriminating, open, emotionally capable of change and reflective so that they may generate beliefs and opinions that will prove more true or justified to guide action.' Reflective journal writing can provide a means for illuminating habits of mind and automatic ways of thinking.

Hubbs and Brand (2005) explore the use of reflective journals in higher education, artfully terming them a 'paper mirror'. In netnography, this mirror can reflect the researcher's inner worlds and their making of meaning. In a team netnography context, it can provide a situation for research collaborators to share their own reflections and budding ideas, resulting in an opportunity for feedback, professional and personal growth, and development of the project. Hubbs and Brand usefully provide a typology of journal entries that arranges them along two continua. The first examines whether the entry is focused outwards at content or inwards on process. The second evaluates whether the entry is a superficial reflection or a deep critical reflection. These reflective categories can usefully be applied to evaluate the reflective quality of one's own writing in their immersion journal, or the writing of fellow research team members. Journal writing and its evaluation connect the internal processes of reflective thinking and conceptual theorizing with the external realities of empirical data and literature streams. The process of connecting inner and outer realms demands self-awareness as well as a degree of empirical distancing, traits which are valuable to qualitative research and analysis.

Reflection in Netnography

In reflective immersion notes, netnographers record their own observations regarding subtexts, pretexts, contingencies, conditions, and personal emotions occurring during their time online, and relating to their online interactions and experiences. Through these written reflections, the netnographer records their learning of languages, rituals, sites, information, people, topics and practices, as well as their involvement in a social web of technologies, practices, meanings, and personalities. The immersion journal exists to provide key insights into how online social interactions function and transpire.

Your initial impressions of platforms, groups, and messages are important, as are what seem to be key events or incidents. Record those impressions in your immersion journal. Use contemplation to increase your sensitivity to the experiences of others. If you feel shocked at a particularly questionable posting, why do you feel that way? Do others seem to feel this way as well, or are they reacting to other aspects of the post? 'The ethnographer is concerned not with members' indigenous meanings simply as static categories but with how members of settings invoke those meanings in specific relations and interactions' (Emerson et al., 1995: 28). Because the when, where, and who questions of context are usually automatically recorded in investigative data operations, what is even more important to capture in your immersion journal is your own subjective impressions and expectations about more profound cultural explanations.

When writing in your immersion journal, try to let the multiple realities of the ethnographic task mirror back to you through your reflective noting of whatever it is you choose to record: the message, your reception of its meaning, your questioning of your reception, your search for the message sender's intention, the constraints upon your search for this intention, and so on. Reflective writing encourages the netnographer to gain both closeness and distance from the people and the technologies they are using as they are using them, realizing the profundity of multi-sited ethnography by translating 'one cultural idiom or language to another' (Marcus, 1995).

The Personal Nature of Reflective Writing

You should write in the immersion journal as you would in a diary. Try not to censor your recording of online events, experiences, interactions, and your own internal reactions. As much as possible, let your emotions and perceptions flow naturally, as if you are writing to yourself, for yourself (even though you may be sharing it online, with your research team, or even with the public). Your internal human reality is a key element to netnography, and the most direct way that it enters into your datastream is through inscription in your immersion journal. As well, supposedly small things can later become very important and may even be, or lead to, those elusive black swans. Beyond this, the reflexive act causes you to question why you are detecting what you are, why you see this connection and not that one, why you believe this to be new or that to have deeper meanings.

The notes in your immersion journal are personal. Some of the journal notes you write may even make their way into print, and through them you might attempt to convey something resonant about the experience of your research to your readers. But, more likely, the vast majority of reflective immersion notes will capture the awkward striving of your own construction of theory from the observations you notice, your attempts to detect what is going on, what is connected, what is new, what is meaningful.

Ultimately, those reflective notes are what will allow the story of your own vulnerable humanity to suffuse your work. The insights of your own reflection on your work and its meanings will allow your engagements, be they intellectual, cultural, historical, emotional, or social, to shine forth from within your data-collection procedures. Seized in the moment of thought, written as you think it, your reflective operations catch the human story of your ongoing explanation, your ever-flowering and ever-wilting series of hypotheses, your increasing pile of discarded interpretations. In the end, and largely because of your reflective writing, the immersion journal becomes a tale of intellectual, emotional, social, and cultural wandering through the mindspace of social media.

An Immersion Journal Example

In research I undertook on the utopianist online activism (or 'clicktivism') of comments and replies to utopian YouTube videos, I use my fieldnotes to capture my own emotional reactions to a hope-filled and heart-breaking topic – the future of humanity. Here is an edited excerpt from my immersion journal that reveals the raw nature of the emotional experiences I attempt to convey:

> After this pondering of The Venus Project's data site, I can't help but note the emotional ambivalence I feel. I get swept up at times in the energy of what seems to be a new global online movement. The most emotionally engaged I feel is when I see these many simple statements, such as 'What can I do to help?', 'I'm so sad because I want to live in the depicted future, but I don't have enough faith in humanity to believe this is ever going to happen'. And perhaps even more revealing: 'Thank you for letting me dream and be part of it. Awesome utopia.' It seems hopeful at the start, but most of the time when I am doing this work for a while, I find myself feeling a bit sad and poignant. If this is the public, they seem to feel so disempowered. Repeatedly, people express how their governments have failed them. Many of their voices seem filled with a paradoxical hopefulness-helplessness-hopelessness that I understand, sense, and share. It is also disheartening to observe so much bickering and in-fighting, with so many trolls and conspiracy theorists, consistently interrupting only to tell us that the Earth is actually flat, that NASA faked everything, that climate change is a scam. (edited immersion journal entry after engaging with 'The Choice is Ours' YouTube video and comments for 3.25 hours, February 6, 2018)

Writing in my immersion journal, I record the range of emotions I experienced during this encounter with The Venus Project's utopian YouTube-based data site, from ambivalence to sadness, hopelessness to aggravation. I record the rise and fall of feeling energized and activated, as well as enervated by the disheartening exchanges I find. In your journal writing, you will similarly find narratives, stories, your lines of flight, and these will be the personal voice of the tale that you can call your own. To do reflection well is to discover and question the value-laden morality within your scientific inquiry. Why are you involved in this inquiry? In the fieldnote excerpt above, I recognize myself in the exchanges of pseudonymous online others, my hopes, my dreams, my own mixed-up sense of helplessness and hopefulness. This kind of reflection is based at least in part upon exploring and discovering your own ideology, your personal sense of right and wrong as you play the role of the protagonist in a scientific morality tale that unfolds throughout the enactment of this particular project.

With these reflections on the features of reflective writing in immersive data operations, the chapter moves to its final section, which overviews the ethical concerns that accompany immersion in netnography.

REFLECTING IN/ON YOUR IMMERSION JOURNAL (PROJECT EXERCISE)

Use this exercise to add reflective depth to your netnography. During your next session of data gathering or engagement, try to be mindful of your own inner states, moods, emotions, expectations, and reactions. Record these while they are still fresh in your mind and body. Follow the principles described in this subsection to explore the reflective elements of immersion journal writing.

If you are working in a research team, share your reflective writing with your colleagues. What do you learn from their reflective writing? Try this using different datasets and the same ones. How are your reactions different from theirs?  How are they similar? Does the exercise lead to an increase in your own self-awareness? Does it provide additional understanding of your research partner(s)? Does it contribute added empathy for the people who are posting data on your data site? What do you learn from this exercise? Write your answers in your immersion journal. Once written, your journal becomes more grist for the netnographic mill to grind.

THE ETHICS OF IMMERSION

Regarding immersive data operations, from an ethics perspective the researcher will need to be cautious about two particular elements. First, what do your immersion notes, screenshots, and other material reveal about other people? Are these sensitive topics or vulnerable populations that you reveal in your journal? If so, how much of those identities can you cloak right away, even as you record it in your journal? How much can you meaningfully abstract out of the context of your empirical site? Can you do this in a way so that the cultural data remains intact but the exact cultural and social contexts become blurred out? If your work were subpoenaed by a court, like the ethnographic fieldnotes of Khan (2018) were, what would they reveal that might cause harm to those inadvertently involved in your research?

If your immersion journal includes or refers to interactions where you share names or personal data, anything that can be used to identify someone, then you will need to follow the ethical research rules for interactions. If the recordings and reflections you gather in your immersion journal involve observations about individual people, such as profiles of them, you need to follow the appropriate ethical guidelines. You may want to edit and clean these at a later date, but they should be pretty raw, like anthropologists' have always been. In cases where the writing in your immersion journal reveals sensitive information, such as the identities of vulnerable or compromised populations, then they will need to go through the same inclusion routines as data in your investigative dataset and be subject to calculations that weigh the benefits against likely harm. Given the reality of today's legal system, it makes some sense to assume that fieldnotes or the writings you make in your immersion journal could, at some future date, become public, and to proceed accordingly.

CHAPTER SUMMARY

This chapter discussed the role and practice of immersive data operations in netnography. It began with a critical examination of the ethnographic concepts of fields and field sites, revealing how destabilized the notion becomes in netnography. It then turned to the four core immersive operations: reconnoitering, recording, researching, and reflecting. Reconnoitering is mapmaking based on wayfinding, guided by the image of the researcher, alternately employing a metaphorical research focus telescope and microscope. In reconnoitering operations, the researcher seeks deep data that is resonant, reveals lead users, provides exceptions to the rule, or reveals the macro inherent in the micro. Recording operations are related to, but distinct from, the descriptive operations of traditional fieldnotes, as well as newer conceptions such as eFieldnotes. The researcher's use of particular theoretical viewpoints is revealed, systematized, and scrutinized by researching operations. And reflecting operations require mindfulness and encourage self-awareness, emotionality, and empathy. The final subsection of the chapter provided an overview of the research ethics implications of immersive data operations.

KEY READINGS

Hine, Christine (2015) *Ethnography for the Internet: Embedded, Embodied and Everyday.* London: Bloomsbury.

Hubbs, Delaura L. and Charles F. Brand (2005) 'The paper mirror: Understanding reflective journaling', *Journal of Experiential Education*, 28(1): 60–71.

Jackson, Jean E. (2016) 'Changes in fieldnote practice over the past thirty years in U.S. anthropology', in Roger Sanjek and Susan W. Tratner (eds), *eFieldnotes: The*

Makings of Anthropology in the Digital World (pp. 42–64). Philadelphia, PA: University of Pennsylvania Press.

Postill, John and Sarah Pink (2012) 'Social media ethnography: The digital researcher in a messy web', *Media International Australia*, 145(1): 123–34.

Sanjek, Roger and Susan W. Tratner (eds) (2016) *eFieldnotes: The Makings of Anthropology in the Digital World*. Philadelphia, PA: University of Pennsylvania Press.

INTEGRATING: COMBINING TELESCOPIC AND MICROSCOPIC UNDERSTANDINGS

CHAPTER OVERVIEW

This short chapter will introduce integration as a combination of analytic and interpretive data operations in a pragmatic quest to answer research questions in netnography. Chapter 11 will open with a metaphor in the form of a short science fiction story that illustrates a key problem with analysis in modern scientific inquiry. After that, analysis will be defined as a process of breaking a phenomenon down into its component parts in order to study and understand it, and interpretation as a process of connecting holistic social concepts. These two processes interrelate in integration, and this chapter's examination of netnographic research questions will demonstrate two different ways in which this occurs. You will then learn how deductive, inductive, and abductive approaches to research apply to the operations of integration. The notion of immanent integration will be developed and its application discussed, before explaining the analysis and interpretation exercises contained in later chapters. The chapter's final sections will detail the choices of data-processing tools available to netnographers, comparing and discussing approaches based on printing hardcopies, using word-processing programs, spreadsheets, and qualitative data-analysis programs.

UNDERSTANDING INTEGRATION

Preparing for the Chapter

This chapter is intended as an introduction to the integration stage and preparation for the two chapters following, which will provide hands-on instruction and workbench-level exercises to demonstrate and develop separately the operations of data analysis and interpretation. First, something a little bit different: a parable to introduce the overall perspective. You may not find this in a typical methods book, but the parable form can help us succinctly think through some of the bigger picture issues regarding the differences of analytical and interpretive approaches to data collection and analysis. Sometimes, we are so close to our own work and contexts that we fail to see the bigger picture. In this case, the following short story shows how an analytical approach begins by taking things apart into discrete elements, examining their structure, and attempting to understand how the pieces fit together. However, without meaningful clues about the significance of the relationships between the context being investigated and the one it is being applied to understand, there are elements of the analysis that will always remain mysterious to the analytic approach.

A Metaphor for Integration

Once upon a time, approximately 5,103,491 years from today, a vast and advanced alien civilization will enter a solar system near our own and find a single space capsule with a single human being in it. A woman, a far-future astronaut named Mishu who explored deep space. She died during extravehicular activities about 550 years in our future. At the time, Mishu will be the only evidence left that humanity ever existed.

The aliens are dextrous, and have even more dextrous machines. They look like large insects, with many legs and all sorts of modular mechanical insectoid body parts that they rapidly slip into and out of. In a single gigantic space vehicle, the aliens will direct an operation where they disassemble the small one-person space cruiser containing things such as superlight composite metal stone plates, wires, computer chips, memory devices with massive amounts of information on them, communications devices, food replicators, 3D printers, and so on.

The woman will have been freeze-dried by space, her cells blown apart and body ravaged by solar winds and micro particle hits. But there will still be plenty of her body left. The aliens will carefully dissect Mishu's remains, remove her head from her body, her eyes from her head, take out her brain, separate different parts of it, and then slice those parts into very thin cell slivers. The eyes will be separated into many pieces. The mouth as well, and ears, and throat. And all of the various sections of the body, right down to her toe joints, toeprints, and toenail parts. All will be cut, divided, catalogued, filed away, cultured, and preserved, with their exact location and condition carefully noted.

The alien scientists will send the various samples, several million in total, to researchers and laboratories in cities on over 1,200 different inhabited worlds, space stations, and large ships.

Finally, after about 50 years of intense study, they will know a lot about the technology of people 550 years in our future. They will also knew a lot about the human body, having studied Mishu's various cells, tissues, and organs, what they specialized in, how they differed.

At the equivalent of one of their academic conferences, presenting some of the most comprehensive information on this one specimen of a long-dead early interplanetary civilization, one question, however, will ring out above all.

During the intergalactic conference, a very tall, very mantis-like scientist will conclude the third presentation on the specimen. She will express this key question in ultrasonic chirping sounds that can be translated as follows:

> We know much about these various elements, the space hull and propulsion system, energy components, communication and computer devices, the functions of brains and eyes, respiratory, circulatory, locomotive and digestive systems.

> But what we can't really figure out is...

> What do these things actually *mean* to us? What were they actually saying, thinking, feeling? What can they tell us about ourselves, about our lives, our worlds?

The insectoid aliens, the T'k'lzt-p!, we can call them, had a variety of complex, hive-like societies, which were inherently networked and modular. They combined their physical and social being with artificial intelligence, robotics, genetics, and many other sciences in very careful and deliberate ways, with wisdom configured and aggregated over countless millennia and through joining thousands of civilizations together.

Going through the data, they found very little that was familiar about the people of Earth. There were large amounts of traces available but all of these lacked context. They had the human body completely figured out. But they knew almost nothing of humanity. The T'k'lzt-p! had their own conceptual categories and language systems, but the human one was very different – they could not understand it. No translation seemed possible. The T'k'lzt-p! had a variety of beliefs, institutions, and ideologies, and still they could find almost nothing to match up to human society as it was represented by the small spacecraft and by the body floating battered in space. Only small amounts of symbolic information could be painstakingly extracted from the human-made computer chips because they were using a completely different system.

> 'We lack the conceptual keys. The decoding cues. There simply is not enough detailed data to allow us to proceed further than this.'

'Perhaps we need to try harder', a colleague said.

'Or collect more data', another offered.

The mantis-like T'k'lzt-p! being nodded her regal, organic, and mechanically-encrusted antennae head in agreement – a shared gesture with humans that the aliens had immediately picked up on from holovideos they had downloaded from the spacecraft, communicated widely, and liked. But, unfortunately, without more complex situational translations the human remained an analytic subject, distant and divorced from the vibrant living reality of T'k'lzt-p! culture. No one could really say what human things meant. What their significance was to the people who lived then and there or how it might relate to the T'k'lzt-p! who now lived and explored the galaxy. The meaning of space exploration, of being a human being, of losing a planet and searching, alone and in space, for a new home. None of these things were familiar to the vast T'k'lzt-p! civilization, and there was little poetry composed about the lost races to match the piling up of isolated biological and genetic facts.

Interest in the new species languished over the next few centuries as other and much better preserved and annotated civilizations were discovered.

Integration, Meaning, and Themes

As illustrated by this short story, interpretation provides the key links between situations that contribute to a deeper level of understanding. Those key links are composed of meaning. Without interpretation, the T'k'lzt-p! analysis cannot be fully translated into terms that bring their subjects vividly to life. In the science fiction story, the stakes of this understanding and translation are very high, for they involve the far-future understanding of the significance of a lost human race.

The story leads us to seek out an understanding of how we use netnography to understand ourselves. It turns out that we do so thematically, through a quest for the meanings inherent in themes. We can think of themes as unifying ideas or particular subjects of discussion. Artworks have themes, as do novels, poems, and research studies. In a comprehensive and current evaluation of the use of netnography in hospitality and tourism research, Whalen (2018) finds a variety of broadly construed data analysis techniques, but also finds 'thematic analysis dominant among them' at 46% of publications in the field. Following that is content analysis at 11%, discourse analysis and textual analysis both at 8%, mapping and grounded theory both at 6%, and 14% unspecified. She finds that 24% of the 63 published netnographies mention some named qualitative data analysis package (NVivo being the most common), 10% mentioned that coding was manual, and a full 67% do not describe the type of coding performed at all. Thematic analysis, the quest for overriding and unifying ideas to guide the discussion, fits well with the interpretation of qualitative social media data. This is why thematic analyses have been such a popular technique.

Contrasting Analysis and Interpretation

Appreciating that there are different forms of understanding leaves us empowered to build our skills as scientists and interpreters, revealers of phenomena similar in this way to the T'k'lzt-p! of our opening story, seekers of social clues and cues, comprehenders of both social structure and cultural nuance. Just as in the story of the T'k'lzt-p! encountering lost humanity, so too does all understanding in the social sciences often come as a result of both analysis and interpretation.

Analysis is related to Miles et al.'s (2014: 10) 'quest for lawful relationships' in qualitative data. In its simplest sense, analysis involves breaking down a phenomenon into its component parts in order to study and understand it, just as the T'k'lzt-p! broke down the body and spaceship of Mishu, the far-future space explorer. Generally, analysis works through an atomistic conception of the understanding of higher structures, functions, or processes. Analysis breaks down complex processes into the independent processes and the elements comprising them, and then specifies their relationships. As a result, analysis in social science research is about 'presenting higher processes in a certain way as a sum of associated simpler elements' (Rieber and Robinson, 2013: 65–6). To a large extent, analysis comprises theory as we know it. It takes the world of phenomena, focuses on a part of it, categorizes the particular elements of that part, attempts to measure and/or manipulate those elements, and theorizes about the strength, nature, boundary conditions, and other qualities of the associative ties between those elements.

Interpretation is quite different. Interpretation is a holistic link, something Miles et al. (2014: 10) call a 'search for essences'. We can think of those essences as resembling themes, unifying ideas or discourses. Generally, the interpretation of qualitative data will conceive of these ideas as wholes rather than parts, and will seek to connect these conceptual wholes, both with the contexts from which they were wrested in the act of data collection, with the institutionalized meaning systems that give them their significance, to the people living with them, and to those who seek to understand them. In the short story that opens this chapter, the T'k'lzt-p! are unable to understand humanity because they are unable to conceptualize the links between our future successor's meaning systems and their own. They are unable, in some sense, to connect the parts of their analysis into a unifying whole, and to link that whole with the substance of their own culture.

Interpretation has been described as a gestalt shift in perspective, a synthesizing realization, or an illuminative grasp of meaning. However, it need not be defined so mysteriously. Interpretation is an attempt to elaborate or explain meaning through an association of one intact element with another, for example, by creating an equivalence of one particular text to another, or one word to another, as in categorizing terms or translating language. As another example, the meaning of a phrase can be discerned and developed using interpretation by tracking that intact phrase to its first historical usage, and then linking it to higher-order concepts such as particular social groups living in specific locations. Or interpretation can take a critical, questioning tone. Interpretation is critical thinking. It is making use of the evidence from analysis, finding out what it is trying to tell us, using the parts of it to tell a whole story and then providing an entire, more or less satisfying answer.

Triangulation and Mixed Methods

Combining methods to study the same phenomenon is called 'triangulation' (Denzin, 2012). Triangulation can deploy a 'within methods' technique to use multiple techniques within a given methodological system to collect and interpret data (Jick, 1979: 602–3). This definitely includes using investigation, interactive, and immersive data collection operations in netnography. The data must be triangulated and combined in the final sets of operations to build understanding and prepare the theoretical structure and research arguments for presentation and/or publication.

Jick (1979: 603) argues persuasively that triangulation can 'capture a more complete, holistic, and contextual portrayal' of phenomena. The core thread in triangulation Jick identified with the 'artful researcher', the role of qualitative data analysis as 'the glue that cements the interpretation of multimethod results', 'holistic work', and 'thick description' (p. 609). Using these sorts of approaches together, to specify things precisely, count them up, relate them statistically to each other, and then explain their meaning, their institutionalized networks of relationships, the way their meanings are experienced, what they signify to the people who use them: therein lies great unexplored value and promise.

In a related consideration of mixed methods approaches, Cresswell (2009) discussed processes of data transformation. In what he calls a type of 'concurrent strategy', such as where qualitative and quantitative data is gathered at the same time, researchers might quantify qualitative data (p. 218). This would involve creating codes or themes, then counting the number of times they occur in a text, or quantifying the percentage or extent of certain topics or ideas. Cresswell also discusses the alternate, where a researcher qualifies quantitative data. The example he provides is to create factors or themes from a quantitative factor analysis using qualitative information from a related database.

These transformations of qualitative and quantitative data into one another suggest that the operations of analysis and interpretation are often not completely separate in practice. Interpretations sometimes must break down wholes into constituent elements first in order to ascertain which part of the whole will be the focus. The conceptual terms of an analysis must be defined using translation. Assigning categories wisely to concepts and constructs requires interpretation, and often further adaptation based on emergent findings. The modalities of qualitative and quantitative, and analysis and interpretation, are not competitive but complementary. Integration is a stage that explicitly recognizes this complementarity.

Integration combines analytic and interpretive data operations in a pragmatic quest for answers to research questions. Integration is a way to consolidate the dataset that has been collected in the netnography into a coherent research finding for presentation. Analysis involves breaking something down into its component parts in order to understand it. Interpretation is about translating, classifying, elaborating, explaining, or revealing the meaning of some whole in relation to other wholes. Data is broken down in analysis into its constituent parts, and it is classified, associated, and evaluated during interpretation. Both analysis and interpretation are focused on connections and understanding. However, the types of connections and the means of discovery differ. The following sections will examine netnographic research questions, reexamine scientific reasoning styles, and suggest a couple of theoretical perspectives to help you organize the process of combining these differing means of discovering findings in data.

CONCEPTUAL STRATEGIES FOR INTEGRATION

Deriving Integration from Research Questions

When we consider the types of research questions that netnographies answer, some patterns emerge. Chapter 5 presented several research questions from published netnographies. Some of those questions attempted to develop extant theory through data. For example, asking about 'the affordances of e-reading' and whether they enhance reading experiences (D'Ambra et al., 2017), requires that the researcher understands the theory behind affordances in order to classify the affordances of e-reading, identify them in the dataset, and then provide some sort of organized and evidentially-informed description and evaluation of them. Asking about how 'female tourists conceive of their tourist experience and how they "gaze" on Macao' (Zhang and Hitchcock, 2017) requires that the researchers be knowledgeable about the literature regarding the tourist gaze, and then apply it to the netnographic dataset of female conversations about Macao.

In both of these examples, the categories and concepts of particular extant theory (affordance theory or the tourist gaze) are set. They break down single concepts, such as reading affordances, into their elemental component parts. The categories of these concepts guide the collection of particular netnographic data and are also used to sort it. An evaluation or interpretation of data both at the collection and processing stages must occur in order to categorize a particular trace or datum as a member of one of these extant theoretical categories. Working with research questions that develop, illustrate, or refine existing theory in particular contexts thus combines processes of analysis and interpretation under conditions that are generally deductive. They operate under a deductive stance similar to the one that guides Benjamin's process of immanent criticism and which holds many similarities to other forms of literary criticism. In these types of netnography, researchers translate research questions into search terms, traces are evaluated for their fit with extant theoretical concepts, and extant theoretical concepts may also be evaluated for their fit with collected data.

Other netnographic research questions focus primarily on particular phenomena, without mentioning which theory will be used to fit them. Looking at word-of-mouth marketing (which later came to be known as influencer marketing), Kozinets et al. (2010: 73) asked how people on social media were responding to it, 'what patterns' these influencers assumed in their communications, and why those patterns developed. Studying a new phenomenon, influencer marketing, the netnography sought to describe it, categorize it, link those categories to the categories of extant theory, present varying patterns of responses to it, and then explain these patterns in relation to both extant and new theoretical relations. Kozinets et al. (2017: 660) took a look at a very old phenomenon, desire, in a new context, the social realm presented by contemporary technology: 'What happens to desire when consumers collectively combine and connect their cravings through technology in new and unprecedented ways? How can we bring novel understanding to bear on this new reality?' In both of these examples, the netnography focuses on a phenomenon first (the concrete world of influencer marketing or the abstract notion of technologically-mediated desire), and then seeks to explain it through the data – making linkages to extant theory along the way. In order to enact such inquiries, a range of evaluative judgments is required. For example, what phenomena will be considered influencer marketing, and which will not? Which traces will be viewed as exhibiting the state-of-the-art in technologized desire? As the entire phenomenon is studied, it is also broken down into its conceptual elements (e.g., through a typology, continua, or description of parts or stages). These conceptual elements, identified in the phenomenon, are then connected to existing theory that has also used them. These connections, which are present in both types of netnographic research questions, and which combine analytic and interpretive operations, illumine the stage of integration.

Connecting Data to Theory with Deductive, Inductive, and Abductive Reasoning

Netnographic integration can combine three types of disciplined thought, or scientific reasoning styles – deduction, induction, and abduction. Deductive research begins with theoretical concepts turned into hypotheses, looks for ways to test these conjectures using data and observation in the phenomenal world, and confirms or rejects them in a top-down process (see Figure 11.1). Inductive research begins with empirical data from the world of phenomena, seeks patterns within it, and then uses those regularities to generate theory from the bottom up (see Figure 11.2).

Abductive research focuses on anomalies, puzzles, or surprises in the data, seeking to explain them (see Figure 11.3).

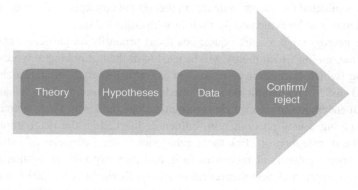

Figure 11.1 Deductive research approach

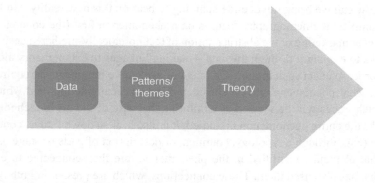

Figure 11.2 Inductive research approach

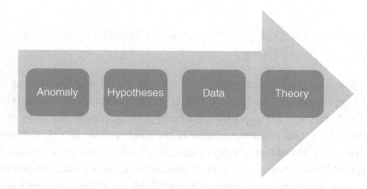

Figure 11.3 Abductive research approach

It should be apparent that abductive research must start with an existing frame of what is usual or understood in order to find data that is puzzling or anomalous. However, unlike deduction, which would use anomalous data to reject extant theory, abductive research uses it to modify or develop new theory. Abduction is the act of thinking that finds the connection between two seemingly disparate points – a simultaneous act of perception and interpretation. In this way, abduction becomes a type of middle-ground process that attunes the researcher to potentially anomalous data, which can then be subject to inductive principles of data collection, pattern recognition, and additional rounds of theoretical development and/or refinement.

Deduction, Induction, and Abduction in Netnography

Netnographic research combines all three ideal forms. Some netnographies will focus upon theoretical concepts, searching for ways to confirm, enrich, broaden, or otherwise develop the extant relations that have been proposed between constructs. Deductive processes are in some sense baked into the investigative data operations that simplify research questions into search terms, use those search terms to find traces, and then select those which fit with the established conceptual terrain. Other netnographies will try to build relatively novel understandings of existing phenomena. Often, because netnography is positioned in the universe of social media, which is a fairly new and dynamic social world, studies will make contributions by defining, describing, and detailing new elements of that universe, examining its novel aspects, revealing its structures, exposing its constituent parts, or building other inductive types of understanding. My co-authored examination of consumer desire in the age of networked communications did not begin as a study of desire, as a matter of fact. It started out as an investigation (by then Ph.D. student Rachel Ashman) into the phenomenon of food porn and the related sharing of food images.

Reichertz (2007) explains that Pierce's use of the term 'abduction' reveals that it has a certain serendipitous and mysterious quality that makes it difficult if not impossible to systematize into a logical research process. A particular conventional view exists which is transgressed by abduction when 'something unintelligible is discovered in the data' and the researcher must take certain risks in order to create 'a new idea' (p. 219): 'Abduction is therefore a cerebral process, an intellectual act, a mental leap, that brings together things which one had never associated with one another' (p. 220). This is a process of insight generation that goes beyond logic, and which Pierce and Reichertz compare to the chance happening of a lightning strike.

The operations of netnographic research, situated in the writing of the immersion journal, may encourage the researcher to note findings that are, in relation to certain theories, anomalous and puzzling. An abductive procedure can then follow in which, faced with these surprising facts, the researcher begins to look for rules, for an explanation that might fit the facts and make them unsurprising. That hypothesis would become the starting point of a multi-stage process of verification.

The researcher would need to devise some predictions from the hypothesis, as they would in a deductive research process. Then, they would begin searching for facts that further expand and fully develop the assumptions, which is inductive. This is the type of 'three-stage discovery procedure consisting of abduction, deduction, and induction' that Pierce designed (Reichertz, 2007: 222).

Abduction and Immanent Criticism

Perhaps

it is as arbitrary to say where

mathematics turns into stories,

as meaningless to identify the process

that assigns numerical codes to feelings,

as it is to mark the moment

when the narrator turns her story into data

and her data into story.

But all of them happen.

All of them are true.

There are no lies here.

What would it mean to look upon your data's story with authentic eyes?

Without a viewpoint? With different types of lens?

What would it take? The removal of all lenses?

Or only their presence in your awareness?

Abductive theory building is like waiting for lightning to strike, according to its most prominent advocate, the founder of pragmatism and co-founder of semiotics, Charles Sanders Pierce. As an insight-gathering process it is certainly valuable. However, there is definitely a degree of chance involved. However, because chance favors the prepared netnographer, we might be able to build and erect a few lightning rods. One of these is the deep data practice of scouting for interesting or 'deep' data such as black swans, lead users or uses, or exceptions to the rule. These techniques encourage you to seek out anomalous or puzzling data and focus on it. Another framework that might help attract those lightning bolts could be to build on Walter Benjamin's theory of immanent criticism to assist you in seeing the data in a new way. Benjamin used an immersive type of operation he called 'immanent criticism' whose goal was to experience data authentically, rather than clouded in other perspectives (as presented in Chapter 10). We can relate this operation to integration.

Can we see our data without the benefit of our own conceptual-theoretical filters? Or must we only move from one filter to another? Might we be limited only to be successively more aware of those filters, how they differ, and how we move between them as analysts and interpreters of data in research settings? The approach might lead us to want to hybridize and blend the breaking-down and coding methods of analysis with the micrological and cultural approaches of hermeneutic interpretation.

Applying Immanent Integration

What if we were to call this perspective *immanent integration*? To apply immanent integration in netnography is to become more aware of our own initial filters in a systematic manner. We would begin by examining, as we do in immersion, our starting point. No one goes into a data site without some expectations, assumptions, or filters. Once we are reflexively aware of the effects of these filters, we can try applying other theoretical perspectives to our data sites and datasets, successively, with methodical care and discernment, noting the various differences in what they allow us to perceive and what they block.

A similar type of sensibility is deployed by Priyadharshini and Pressland (2018) using the term 'analysis as assemblage'. The authors explain that they use the term 'assemblage' 'in the sense of a "working arrangement" (Buchanan, 2015), a conscious invitation to different theoretical–political stances from which to analyze the text' (p. 436). Their goal was to use this integrative approach in order 'to make better sense of polysemous, ambiguous media texts' (p. 437) – which would likely include social media datasets such as those encountered regularly in netnography. Priyadharshini and Pressland (2018: 436) find that 'it is the intersection of perspectives that makes the arrangement/assemblage work as analysis', facilitating the expansion of 'critical political, methodological, or theoretical inclinations' by researchers working in the complexity of the 'contemporary mediascape' (p. 437).

The key movements in the intersections of an immanent integrationist approach would be between methods that use a variety of analysis operations and those that employ several interpretive operations to seek their understanding. As well as mixing methods such as content analysis, social network analysis, thematic analysis, and hermeneutic part-whole comparison, the researcher using immanent integration can try to use different kinds of conceptual/interpretive frames (as in Priyadharshini and Pressland's 2018 'analysis as assemblage' method), research foci, or dependent variables. The members of a research team can experiment with different kinds of samples, controls, and boundary conditions. They can try relating different concepts and different independent variables to focal concepts. They might explain why one particular concept is especially important, what ideologies and intellectual histories underlie its sources of value. They might unpack its linguistic meanings, explore the personal identities that populate it, and spin a narrative about the way it anchors local rituals and the practices they assume.

An immanent integrationist approach would hybridize and blend the breaking-down and coding methods of analysis with the micrological and cultural approaches of hermeneutic interpretation using both serendipitous experimentation and serious intent. The net result of the combination and recombination of these data-processing procedures would be the development of a qualitative social media research process that combines:

- an analytic process that examines the structural elements and operations of a particular social scientific phenomenon; answering questions through an informed selection of collating, coding, combining, counting, and charting data analysis operations; and

- an interpretation process that describes, translates, catalogs, and defines the significance and meaning of that same particular social scientific phenomenon; this process would answer questions through a selection of theming, talenting, totalizing, translating, turtling, and troublemaking operations.

Like the other elements of the netnography repertoire described in this book, these various data operations of analysis and interpretation can be mixed and matched at will. Word clouds can lead to critical theory and deconstruction, or analytic coding can lead to a historical analysis. There are no rote procedural guidelines to follow. The more unexpected and intriguing the combination, the more techniques one deploys, the more lightning rods you are erecting. The more rods in place, the more favorable become the odds of the chance lightning strike carrying an astonishing abductive insight.

Integrating Analysis and Interpretation: Your Netnographic Example

The two chapters that follow will present, define, and explain the constituent elements of the two data-processing operations, analysis and interpretation. In addition, starting with Box 12.1, we will be working with a dataset (provided online) which I used for a study on utopianism and online activism. The practice exercises contained in the chapters will guide you to analyze and then interpret this dataset, providing hands-on experience at such things as data cleaning, coding, comparing, translating, and theming. I encourage you to do as many of the practice exercises as you can. Once you have completed the exercises, you can compare, contrast, and combine the various results. This will provide you with important experience in integration: the combination of analysis and interpretation to answer research questions in netnography. As well as these practice exercises, Chapters 12 and 13 will also feature project exercises that continue the project-based work you began in Chapter 5 and that intensified as you collected data in Chapters 8, 9, and 10. Following those exercises will help lead you through your netnography project to get it ready for completion in Chapter 14. Before proceeding to the next chapter, the following section will consider the practical matter of data-processing tools.

TOOLBOXES: INTEGRATION AT THE WORKBENCH LEVEL

Fitting the Tools to the Job

When I make presentations about netnography, one of the questions I am most commonly asked is 'What tools do you use?' Unfortunately, at this time, there are no good all-in-one solutions for the conduct of netnography, only a series of choices and a variety of makeshift adaptations. Those choices are guided by questions that include the following ones. Should you print your data on paper, and then work with it? Should you keep all of your data in different themed document files as Tratner (2016) did? Should you use spreadsheets? Should you share it online with your work team? Should you invest in a qualitative data-analysis program, or use a free version of one online?

Prior editions of this book have gone into considerable amounts of detail regarding the nuts-and-bolt choices involved in the physical conduct of data-processing procedures. As I have noted previously, those choices hinge on several factors, including the sheer amount of data and the presence of different kinds of information (e.g., videos, podcasts, photos), the use of different platforms and web applications (e.g., Snapchat, Facebook, Reddit), and forms of files (screenshot images, text files, scraped data). These decisions should not depend upon the fallacious notion that using qualitative data analysis software (or QDAS) necessarily distances the researcher from their dataset. Jackson and colleagues (2018) call this one of the 'unsubstantiated criticisms' or 'deterministic denunciations' of QDAS. They list four unsubstantiated and untested criticisms of QDAS: (1) a separation/distancing criticism in which the software creates a barrier between researcher and data; (2) a homogenization/standardization criticism in which software homogenizes research methods; (3) a mechanization/dehumanization criticism in which researchers mistake routinized tasks for research rigor; and (4) a quantification/decontextualizing criticism in which computers encourage quantified methods at the expense of interpretation and theory-building.

Although Jackson et al. (2018) are dismissive of these critiques, a knowledge of software history and of affordance theory might suggest that criticisms 2, 3, and 4 should not be dismissed outright. Point 4, in particular, is treated as a mystification by Jackson et al. (2018). Yet programs which automatically code and quantify qualitative data are already available, and there is little doubt that they do decontextualize data in ways that have little if nothing to do with researcher intent or insight-building. The authors' main point, however, is worthwhile: that software tools like QDAS do not determine researchers' data-processing practices, but are there to assist them. The employment of analytic tools must be guided not by the capabilities of a software product, but by the interpretive plans and directions of the researcher. It may not be necessary to use QDAS in all cases to analyze netnographic data. However, as the following sections will discuss, QDAS is the best solution for projects with larger-sized datasets – and this will include many, if not most contemporary netnographies.

Because they use qualitative data and favor deep cultural readings, many netnographies use fairly small amounts of data. For example, Eriksson et al. (2014) used only 400 images. However, the amount of data included in the average published netnography seems to be rising. Many netnographies now collect social media text that amount to between 100,000 and 500,000 words (or between 250 and 1,000 single-spaced pages when downloaded into standard-sized word-processing documents). This rise is likely attributable to several factors: (1) there is a lot more social media data available today than in the recent past; (2) data is easier to find; (3) automated data-collection techniques such as data scraping are more available today; and (4) more and better programs for data processing are available. Contemporary netnographies, then, often work with substantial amounts of data, but not voluminous amounts. I could see how a team of netnographers could handle something in the order of 1,000,000 words and a few hundred other documents such as photographs, images, screenshots, and videos. However, I would think that dealing with much more than this would become unwieldy without some sort of QDAS or a good spreadsheet approach. Selective sampling of the dataset might be necessary because of its size. The more the data is not directly engaged but processed through machine coding or machine recognition means, the less likely would be the meaningful engagement that is the hallmark of quality netnography.

The challenge with all of these approaches is not only in what tool to use to process the data (e.g., code, comment on, aggregate, search), but also in how to keep your dataset organized and available so that you can check, cross-reference, and make important connections between its elements. Keeping your files in smaller chunks, descriptively named, in neatly categorized folders and sub-folders is very helpful. When the amount of data is relatively small, you have more latitude to use more time-consuming, but data-close, techniques. When you are working with larger amounts of netnographic data that need to be analyzed, some methods (such as QDAS) have clear advantages over others.

The following guidelines, then, may help inform your workbench-level decisions about data-processing approaches.

Hardcopy Approaches

If you have a relatively small dataset, then printout-based approaches to data processing might be adequate for your needs. Hardcopy approaches involve the download
and storage of data on a computer and then printing some or all of the data on paper
in order to analyze and interpret it by hand. Categorization and coding can take place
by writing on the hardcopies. With a small amount of data, you could sort pages by
hand, draw links on them in similar colors, and store them in physical files. This sort
of manual data-processing system can work effectively when the researcher is familiar with the data, organized, has a good paper filing system, and prefers to work this
way. Using such a system can be an effective way for the netnographer to feel close
to the data, and to feel aesthetically close to the curatorial act of analysis and interpretation. Researchers who prefer and are competent with a hardcopy approach should
use it. There is nothing wrong with keeping things simple and comfortable. For most
netnographies and netnographers, however, using a paper-based printout method will
be cumbersome.

Word-Processing Approaches

With a small to medium-sized dataset (probably not more than 200,000 words or
so if using text), and with a strong emphasis on interpretation rather than coding
and analysis, you could effectively perform your data-processing operations using
search, cut and paste, highlighting, commenting, and other functions contained in
every word-processing program. A word processing-based system can work effectively when the researcher is familiar with the data, has a good file-naming and
storage system, and prefers working this way. With a refined word processor-based
system, the researcher can have a good sense of closeness to the data. However,
with larger datasets, the coding, searching, and aggregating functions of word-
processing programs are ungainly and inefficient. If analysis (rather than interpretation) is going to be an important part of the netnography's integration stage, then
word-processing programs are not the best choice.

Spreadsheet and QDA Program Approaches

Spreadsheets and qualitative data analysis (or QDA) programs are useful for handling mid- to large-sized datasets. Spreadsheet programs keep datasets organized by
separating rows of data into different cells and allowing its classification to occur in
different columns. Spreadsheets therefore can handle the functions required for data
analysis. However, they are not designed specifically for qualitative data analysis and
need to be somewhat jury-rigged to do the job. The result is never completely perfect,
but usually adequate for the task at hand, even with large datasets. When you are

working with a small number of fairly large datasets, the spreadsheet method can be completely satisfactory.

Qualitative Data Analysis (or QDA) software has been created specifically to help you manage qualitative datasets and for the categorizing, counting, and comparative analysis of qualitative data. Most of these programs are agnostic as to the type of data, and can handle photographs, sound files, and videos as well as text. Some are developing networked functions for sharing files between teams, which can be helpful. As a bonus, most of them are quite good at helping you organize your large, sprawling, diverse datasets. Almost all of them will produce word clouds on command. Some have advanced visualization capabilities which, in themselves, can potentially contribute entirely new insights to your data processing. There is a learning curve with QDA software, however. And because there are several competing products in the marketplace, formats differ. Therefore, learning one QDA program does not necessarily help you use a different program. You may not be able to import your dataset from one QDA program into another (a problem you will generally not have with a spreadsheet or word-processing programs). QDA programs can also be expensive to buy, and many have moved to expensive subscription models that hold the user hostage for updates.

QDA Programs with ADA and NLP Capabilities

Netnographic researchers producing work for fields that affirm the value of statistical evaluations and structural accounts of data sites may benefit from the automated coding algorithms and natural language-processing capabilities of some of the latest qualitative data analysis software. Netnography is gaining in popularity in computer science fields, and many business research applications also use these techniques. Many of the current programs come pre-installed with automated or so-called 'natural' language-processing functions, which recognize and pre-code certain words or phrases. Sentiment analysis functions may be offered which automatically code text into categories such as positive, negative, and neutral (and usually, in my experience, with a lot of errors). The drawback with having these functions available is that they can tempt the researcher to substitute the programming of an algorithm for the careful ingenuity of a skilled cultural analyst. Some aspects of analysis can be handled by automated programs, but they need to be critically reviewed and carefully audited. At least at the current time, algorithms cannot interpret data in the sense that is required for quality netnographic research. Artificial intelligence programs require large amounts of data and strong patterns within them, and are incapable of finding subtle differences or black swans in small amounts of data, such as those dealt with in netnography. Interpretation, insightful analysis, and their skillful integration require human intelligence, effort, and understanding – as well as the procedural operations that the next two chapters will elaborate.

CHAPTER SUMMARY

Integration is a combination of analytic and interpretive data operations in a pragmatic quest to answer research questions in netnography. This chapter began with a short science fiction story that analogized a key shortfall in social scientific analysis. From there, integration, analysis, and interpretation were defined and explained, and their relation to netnographic research, research questions, deductive, inductive, and abductive approaches to research was explored and discussed. An adaptation of Benjamin's immanent criticism was developed and its application explained, as were the analysis and interpretation exercises of upcoming chapters. There are several data-processing tools available to netnographers, including printed hardcopies, word processors, spreadsheets, and qualitative data analysis software. These options were compared and discussed to close the chapter and prepare the reader for the next two chapters, in which data analysis and interpretation exercises are provided.

KEY READINGS

Cresswell, John (2009), *Research Design: Qualitative, Quantitative, and Mixed Methods Approaches,* 3rd edn. London: Sage.

Jackson, Kristi, Trena Paulus, and Nicholas H. Woolf (2018) 'The Walking Dead genealogy: Unsubstantiated criticisms of qualitative data analysis software (QDAS) and the failure to put them to rest', *The Qualitative Report*, 23(13): 74–91.

Miles, Matthew B., A. Michael Huberman, and Johnny Saldaña (2014) *Qualitative Data Analysis: A Methods Sourcebook.* London: Sage.

Reichertz, Jo (2007) 'Abduction: The logic of discovery of grounded theory', in Anthony Bryant and Kathy Charmaz (eds), *The SAGE Handbook of Grounded Theory* (pp. 214–28). London: Sage.

Silver, Christina and Ann Lewins (2014) *Using Software in Qualitative Research: A Step-by-Step Guide*, 2nd edn. London: Sage.

ANALYZING: ELEMENTAL DATA TRANSFORMATION OPERATIONS

CHAPTER OVERVIEW

Data analysis is a research process in which a particular phenomenon is broken down into component parts in order to study and understand it. The various subsections of this chapter break down analysis into five component operations. First, the decisions involved in analysis will be discussed. Levels of analysis will be related to researchers' decisions about what is to be treated as a whole or a part. Analysis and its outcomes will also be related to sociologies of knowledge in which extant theory frames are adopted or new ones are made. The basic principles of qualitative data analysis will be overviewed. Following that, this book's more specific focus on data-analysis operations for netnography will be introduced, detailed, and illustrated using examples and practice exercises. First, collating operations will be discussed as the preparation of data for coding. Second, coding operations, which lie at the heart of data analysis, are detailed as initiations into the processes of abstraction and reflection that lead to theory development. Third, combining operations unite conceptually related codes to form new, higher-order elements called pattern codes – and thus reveal more abstract structures and patterns. Fourth, counting operations are a quantifying procedure that allows researchers to more precisely compare various elements in qualitative data. Fifth and finally, charting operations create and use visualizations, maps, graphs, tables, and other display of data. Researchers today have many tools for grasping a holistic sense of the data, as well as a sense of its component parts and how they fit together. This subsection will consider maps, network graphs, and word clouds. Together, collating, coding, combining, counting, and charting form the constituent elements of the analytic process advanced in this chapter.

UNDERSTANDING ANALYSIS
Assembling and Disassembling Levels of Analysis

As the last chapter discussed, analysis is a process in which a particular phenomenon is broken down into component parts in order to study and understand it. Think of it as a little like particle physics, which smashes substances into their smallest particles in order to understand the nature of physical reality. Analysis proceeds on an atomistic conception in which it is necessary to disassemble larger or more macro structures, functions, or processes into their elemental parts, just as the alien T'k'lzt-p! scientists of the last chapter cut the human astronaut Mishu's remains into tiny pieces in order to study it, separating organs from one another and slicing tissue and cell samples. Translated into social science research, analysis looks at particular social phenomena and seeks understanding by seeing them as 'a sum of associated simpler elements' with a structure of particular 'associative ties' governing the ostensible 'independent relationships' (Rieber and Robinson, 2013: 65–6).

Theories such as Deleuze and Guattari's assemblage theory (DeLanda, 2016) and Koestler's (1967) theory of holarchies draw our attention to the relationship between wholes and parts, a theme to which we will return. Wholeness is a matter of interpretation (and, in assemblage theory, a dynamic matter as well). What is considered to be whole, and thus of focal interest, determines a study's level of analysis.

Consider how some psychologists study the human mind. For some, the mind is a matter of brain functioning, and the brain is separated into many parts which work together: the hippocampus, the anterior lobe, the corpus callosum, and so on. Each of these parts can, itself, be separated into other parts or aspects, such as tissue, neurons, and dendrites. Together, they form a brain. Understanding the parts of the brain and the way they all function together ostensibly allows us to understand the human mind. However, we can of course question a conception of the human mind that ends at an individual's head. Minds are filled with language, images, and meanings which are transmitted through culture. People are part of families, workplaces, neighborhoods, regions, nations, religions, and cultures. Perhaps the human mind is an organizational concept, or a cultural one – a collective concept.

How does this apply to the analysis of data in netnography? Because analysis requires that we break down or classify our dataset according to some set of constituent elements, the relationship between parts and whole is salient. The example is intended to demonstrate that determining what is the part and what is the whole is a somewhat arbitrary process. Cells are wholes, as are organs, organisms, families, farms, offices, regions, governments, species, and cities. Each is complete and unique. Yet some individual elements may be connected into higher-order wholes with different properties and capacities. And the behavior of one whole may be governed by different sets of rules than those which govern another whole. The prevailing lesson from this is that the choices we make to break down our datasets can both reveal as well as obscure important aspects of our focal phenomenon.

Analysis as Social Frame Building

We might gain useful insights into the wider role of analysis by pausing to consider the role of data analysts in other functions. Beunza and Garud (2007) studied securities analysts, who were largely assumed to be mere calculators of value, and found instead that the acts of calculation they performed were highly social. One school of thought, neo-institutional sociology, found that securities analysts tend to herd together like 'lemmings' and imitate one another, because 'the search for legitimacy among analysts promotes imitation and conformity' (2007: 17). However, some analysts stood out and became stars. Given the conditions of uncertainty under which they worked, some securities analysts broke into high-ranking positions by providing a new calculative frame based upon an original interpretation of stock market facts. Analysts in Beunza and Garud's (2007) formulation are conceived as 'frame-makers', and their analytic frames highlight 'the cognitive and material infrastructure that underlies economic calculations of value' (p. 33). Analysts, it turns out, 'are active builders of frames, rather than passive classifiers' of data (p. 34).

Might these cognitive and material infrastructures also underlie the institutions that guide academic research? It seems likely that the notion of legitimacy-seeking lemmings and profile-seeking frame makers might also apply to data analysis. As we learned in the last chapter, there is a deductive type of approach in which research questions tied to extant theoretical frames largely govern the process of analysis. This seems to relate to the convergent thinking, and imitative and legitimacy-seeking behavior of the analysts in Beunza and Garud's (2007) empirical study. Another type of approach, which is more inductive (or perhaps abductive) and more in line with divergent thinking, allows the observational, reflective, and research-immersive work undertaken in the netnography to influence the choice of theoretical frames guiding how to break down and eventually describe the dataset. This is similar to the frame-making of analysts (who act as critics and also have 'frame controversies' that sound similar to academic debates). Neither of these strategies is preferable to the other. The former tends to be more useful for theory extension and refinement, and the latter for theory development. The former is more risk-averse. Undertaken with deliberate forethought and intent, both provide a firm basis for analysis.

Basic Principles of Qualitative Data Analysis

According to Miles et al. (2014: 10), the group who literally wrote the book on qualitative data analysis, the following operations are 'a fairly classic set of analytic moves' which they present arranged in sequential order, and which I adapt to the specific contingencies of netnographic research:

1. Coding means assigning codes or themes to the set of saved investigative data (including text, screenshots, photos, podcast files, videos), interview transcripts, and immersion journal(s).

2. Sorting and sifting through these coded materials to identify similar phrases, images, relationships, patterns, themes, categories, distinct differences (i.e., variance) between subgroups of subcategories, and common sequences.

3. Isolating these patterns and processes, as well as the commonalities and differences, and taking them out into existing or new data sites for the next wave of data collection.

4. Noting reflections or perceptions in comments on the dataset, memos, jottings, or immersion journal writing.

5. Gradually elaborating a small set of assertions, propositions, and general principles that cover the various consistencies (and discrepancies) ascertained in the dataset.

6. Comparing the generalizations with an established, extant body of knowledge consisting of constructs, categories, and/or theoretical relationships.

These operations are different from the ones I will be proposing here, for several reasons. First, Miles et al. (2014) are not dealing with netnography specifically and so their guidelines are more general. Second, the authors are focused on a particular methodological orientation related to grounded theory conducted from ethnographic data collection. And third, their steps interrelate several aspects of the qualitative research process that I decide in this book to separate for the sake of clarity. Their step three, for example, is as much about data collection as it is about data analysis and processing. That step is a useful reminder of the iterative nature of qualitative research such as netnography (and, in fact, 'iterative' could be the hidden seventh movement in netnography).

As well, and because their conception of data analysis seeks to encompass every element of the dataset, the authors note that the biggest 'challenge for all qualitative researchers is finding coherent descriptions and explanations that still include all of the gaps, inconsistencies, and contradictions inherent in personal and social life'. This is ambitious. They find the biggest risk of qualitative research to be 'forcing the logic, the order, and the plausibility that constitute theory making on the uneven, sometimes random, nature of social life'. In netnography, however, we do not necessarily always want to explain 'all of the gaps, inconsistencies, and contradictions' within our dataset. We might focus only on the deep data of exceptions from the rule, or narrow our focus for an in-depth portrait of a few black swans. At other times, we might be content to note and accept gaps, inconsistencies, and those pesky contradictions in our work. Much of the time, however, we will be seeking the same sorts of generalizations from our analysis as those which concern Miles, Huberman, and Saldaña.

DATA ANALYSIS OPERATIONS IN NETNOGRAPHY

Introducing the Five Analytic Operations

The following five subsections of this chapter will explain, outline, and provide examples to help you gain an introductory familiarity with the principles of data analysis. Because this is only one chapter, these explanations are brief and focused. In order to gain a deeper understanding, I encourage you to consult other texts, such as the ones cited in the chapter, but also moving beyond them should you want to develop a deeper and more resilient skillset. Nonetheless, these five elements should give you a solid background with which to analyze your own netnographic project and to begin, or continue, building your skills as a qualitative data analyst.

The five data analysis operations in netnography are collating, coding, combining, counting, and charting. These are described as follows:

1. *Collating* is the preparation of data for coding. Because data in netnography comes to us in various configurations and is present in a variety of formats and types (e.g., videos, photos, text), sometimes with contextual cues attached, at other times with data tags, it is necessary as a first step to collate the data, getting it into a form that can be coded.

2. *Coding* is at the heart of data analysis. Coding breaks down data into chunks and then assigns meaningful labels to it. Coding is the enactment of understanding through disassembling a phenomenon into its constituent elements and studying them. Coding is the initiation of the process of abstraction that leads to theory validation, extension, construction, or development. Coding is also a way to reflect and discover meaning. One of the key purposes of coding is to enable the researcher to detect repeating patterns across the various elements of their dataset.

3. *Combining* unites conceptually-related codes to form a new, higher-order element in analysis called a 'pattern code'. Combining merges related codes into pattern codes for the purpose of revealing more abstract structures and patterns. The act of combining is a quest for more abstract conceptual relationships. The act of combining and the pattern codes themselves become conceptual material that help the researcher discover and present research findings that answer the research question.

4. *Counting* is a quantifying procedure that allows researchers to compare various elements identified in the qualitative data. Counting is often used in content analysis, which usually quantifies data in order to describe it or relate its structural elements. Counting need not involve numbers and percentages, although

it often does. Providing quantitatively informative words, such as 'more', 'always', 'frequently', 'often', 'decreases', or 'increases', is usually sufficient.

5. *Charting* is a general term for the visualization, mapping, organization, and display of data. Whether tables, maps, charts, graphs, matrices, networks, and word clouds, data displays of various forms allow researchers to draw conclusions and gain insights from examining data transformed into a compressed and organized visual format. Researchers today have many tools for grasping a holistic sense of the data as well as a sense of its component parts and how they fit together. This chapter will consider maps, network graphs, and word clouds.

Collating, coding, combining, counting, and charting: these are the five constituent elements of the analytic process that we will develop in the remainder of this chapter, beginning with the preparatory procedures of collating.

COLLATING

Collating Operations in Data Analysis

Data comes to us in a variety of different packages. Some of them we are able to collect in exactly the format we would like. But in other cases, such as when we use automated scrapers to download entire datasets, the formats might not be exactly in a form we can use for qualitative data analysis. They need to be organized, gathered into a more sensible and useful sequence. In other words, they need to be collated.

In statistically-based analyses, such as those accompanying epidemiological studies, surveys, psychometrics, or econometrics, it is customary at the initial stage of analysis to delete and remove errors and inconsistencies from datasets to improve their quality. These operations are often called 'data cleaning', as well as 'data cleansing' or 'scrubbing' (Rahm and Do, 2000). An example of a data quality problem could be missing information, invalid dates, or misspellings that occurred during data entry. Often, there are issues with redundancies and duplicate entries that need to be either consolidated or eliminated.

Collation is preparation for coding. With netnography, we are not attempting to remove bias or errors so much as to simply make the data more amenable to coding operations. Data collation is more like a form of data organization, a systematizing that encompasses removing downloaded data that is not going to be used in the analysis. As an initial stage of data analysis, collation begins with an attempt to understand exactly which types of data and what aspects of that data you are going to be coding, and to compare that with the dataset you have on hand. Then, the data needs to be arranged and organized into a system so that it can be coded.

Three Smaller Steps: Filtering, Formatting, and Filing

There are many ways to achieve this collation. One way to think about it is to break the collating process down into three steps: filtering, formatting, and filing. These are explained as follows:

1. *Filtering*. First, you need to decide what data will be included in your coding operations. For example, because the immersion journal often contains theory and other guides to coding, and thus might guide the analysis of your data, you might decide not to include it in your dataset, or to only include parts of it, such as the entries where you stored deep data.

2. *Formatting*. Once you have decided what to include, you may need to reformat it in order to get it ready to be coded. For instance, immersion journal entries might be scribbled, contain abbreviations or acronyms that need to be expanded, or may also need to be typed into a document file. Interviews might be recorded as sound or video files, and may need to be transcribed in order to be coded. A convenient feature of many QDAS programs is functionality allowing you to import different types of files. The QDAS converts them to a single file type within the research project. If you are not using a QDAS, you will need to perform some sort of harmonizing process yourself, either by converting files into the same file format (or using a few convenient formats), or else by loading them into another type of program (e.g., inserting text, picture files, or screenshots into a spreadsheet).

3. *Filing*. Finally, you should organize the data for ease of reading, searching, and coding. It is useful to file certain kinds of data together, but only you will know exactly how to categorize the branches of your dataset so that it makes sense to you. Often, data drawn from similar sites is filed together in larger folders. Similar topics usually are filed together. But some people like to save the different types of data together so that, for example, all interviews – even ones about different topics and from different sites – are kept in one place.

Although these descriptions of the operation of data collation may seem a bit abstract at this point, they need not remain that way. This chapter and the next one offer a range of practice exercises to give you hands-on experience with these data-processing operations. They will also guide you through project exercises that will lead you to your own draft of a finished netnographic research project. In Box 12.1, you will learn about the dataset for the practice exercise, which involves a utopian YouTube video about Walt Disney's plan for a capitalist utopia. Box 12.2 provides instruction on the data-collation operations you will enact on this dataset. Box 12.3 then guides you through a data-collation operation for your own netnography project.

INTRODUCING THE ONLINE DATASET (A PRACTICE EXERCISE)

12.1

This is the introduction for the online dataset which you can download and use to follow along with the operational instructions in this book. It is distinguished as a 'practice exercise' to contrast it from the other set of exercises pertaining to your own netnographic research project, which are termed 'project exercises'.

Online, at https://study.sagepub.com/researchmethods/research-methods/kozi nets-netnography-3e, you will find a dataset based upon one that I used for a project that examined the comment and reply streams of people who posted as a response to utopian videos on YouTube. My interest in this dataset derived from engagement with the connection between contemporary utopianism, social media conversations, and activism.

The research began with an adaptation of speech that included Walt Disney's capitalist and technological utopian plan to build a permanent, corporately-sponsored futuristic community, which later developed into the Experimental Prototype Community (or City) of Tomorrow and was abbreviated as 'EPCOT'. Disney conceived of the original EPCOT not as a theme park (as it is today), but instead as a 20,000-person inhabited laboratory city that would be filled with the latest consumer innovations as a way to showcase to the world the ingenuity and imagination of the American free-enterprise system, and provide a petri dish-like city setting to be used for constant market testing by industry.

I began searching for data sites in which people discussed this plan for the original EPCOT. Although I found several discussion threads on Reddit and Facebook, the most tractable and useful was a YouTube video entitled 'Would EPCOT Have Worked?' (abbreviated here as WEHW). The WEHW video was created and narrated by Rob Plays, a Disney aficionado. First published on YouTube in May 2017, the video speculates about whether the original utopian EPCOT idea would have been workable and invites comments on the topic. It had a total of 1,072 comments and replies when I scraped it off of the YouTube site in late 2018.

To provide you with contextual background, you should first view the video, which is available at https://youtu.be/RWgKEI7Tfa8, or by searching 'Would EPCOT Have Worked?' on the YouTube search engine. An English transcription of the narration is also available on the site. If you wish to download a current set of comments, you can use a scraper program such as the YouTube comment scraper at http://ytcomments.klostermann.ca/ to do so yourself.

(Continued)

Please download the dataset of WEHW comments and replies. On the Sage site, it is provided as a CSV format file, which can be read by spreadsheet programs such as Microsoft Excel, Google Sheets, and Apple Numbers. Have a look at it. We will continue in Box 12.2 with a data-collation exercise using this dataset, which I will refer to as the WEHW ('Would EPCOT Have Worked?') dataset.

12.2 COLLATING THE WEHW DATASET (PRACTICE EXERCISE)

For the exercise, you will need to have downloaded the WEHW YouTube comments and replies dataset (see Box 12.1 if you have not done this yet). The file is a CSV spreadsheet with 1,073 rows and 14 columns for a total of 15,022 cells. Many of these cells are empty. As you may notice, the first row of the spreadsheet is labeled with a description of the variable. The first, 'id' is the exact online location of the comment or reply, specified by YouTube. The second is the username. The third is the date (expressed in relation to the time the file was downloaded). The fourth is a timestamp, and the fifth is the actual comment which was posted. You can examine the other nine columns and determine what type of data they represent.

Which of these columns is of greatest interest? Which ones contain the most meaningful data to a netnographic investigation? There will be two columns which are especially interesting (as well as a few others you might keep). You may need to scroll down the spreadsheet a few times to locate both columns. When you do so, you should expand the cell size in your viewer for these two columns so that you can read some of the text that they contain.

Your task is to clean up the dataset.

First, decide which are the most important columns you will be coding.

Second, delete any columns you do not need. (Note: do NOT delete any rows. Every row has data in it, although some data are decidedly deeper than others.)

Third, make any adjustments to the data that are helpful to your reading and coding. You may want to align rows so that, for instance, comments and replies are in the same column.

Once you have completed these steps, your dataset will be ready for coding.

COLLATING YOUR NETNOGRAPHIC DATASET (PROJECT EXERCISE)

12.3

In the project exercises in Chapters 8, 9, and 10, you were led through the collection of investigative, interactive, and immersive data. Together, the saved files from your investigative research, interviews and other exchanges from your interactive research, as well as the entries in your immersion journal, constitute your dataset for this netnography project.

Now it is time to get this data organized. If you have been rather haphazard in where you stored these files, now is the occasion to hunt them down and find all of them. What formats are they in? Do you have photographs and video files as well as text files? Data saved in word-processing documents and others contained in the cells of spreadsheets? An immersion journal written in a paper notebook?

For the analysis exercises, I will proceed on the assumption that you have placed your entire dataset into a spreadsheet or a QDAS where you can easily code it. The spreadsheet will be an easy format to use for calculating totals when you perform some basic counting functions with your coded data.

Here are the general steps you will follow, as contained in more detail in the text above:

1. *Filtering*. Decide what data will be included in, and what data excluded from, your coding operations.
2. *Formatting*. Format the data so that the file types can be read by one another, preferably in the same format (e.g., inserting pictures into spreadsheet cells). For the remaining project exercises in this chapter, I will assume you are using a spreadsheet (which is the format used for the practice exercises).
3. *Filing*. Organize the dataset in hierarchies of worksheets, files, and folders so that it makes sense to you, it is in one place, and it is relatively easy for you to locate the parts you are looking for.

Once you have completed these steps, your dataset is ready for the next stage of data-analysis operations: coding.

CODING

Coding Operations in Data Analysis

Coding is analysis. By breaking data into portions and assigning meaningful labels to it, the act of understanding through disassembling a phenomenon into its constituent elements and studying them has begun. In fact, coding is arguably the most crucial part of analysis. Codes will be used to find and combine similar pieces of data so that the researcher can cluster, display, and compare these conceptually related data with one another. Codes are flashpoints. The act of coding spurs the researcher to deeper reflection on the meaning of the data, the study, and the guiding theoretical concepts.

Coding is also a form of what Miles et al. (2014: 11) term 'data condensation', which is 'the process of selecting, focusing, simplifying, abstracting, and/or transforming the data that appear in the full corpus' or entire dataset. This is because coding enables the researcher 'to retrieve the most meaningful material, to assemble chunks of data that go together, and to further condense the bulk [of your dataset] into readily analyzable units' (p. 73).

Coding is a heuristic, a means of reflecting, and a way to discover meaning. Coding creates familiarity with your data. One of the key purposes of coding in an analytic method such as grounded theory, or in the Miles et al. (2014) style of analysis, is to enable you to detect repeating patterns across the various elements of your dataset, attuning you to the fact that something important may be happening. From those patterns, codes can be combined together into clusters, categories, or pattern codes. The interconnections of these categories with one another are the basis of higher-order constructs such as concepts, propositions, hypotheses, and theoretical relationships.

The Act of Coding

Codes are the tags you will use to assign meaning to the data collected and created during a netnography. In the process of analytic coding (which has nothing to do with the coding of computer programmers), you will attach categories to particular pieces of data. These pieces or chunks of data can be of various sizes and composed of different formats (e.g., photo, Instagram post, emoji, video, webpage, avatar). As noted in the section above on assembling and disassembling whole and parts, deciding exactly how you break data into its constituent parts is your choice.

Codes can be very literal and descriptive (e.g., talking about money), emotional and evocative (e.g., heartbreaking stories), or complex and symbolic (e.g., revelation of reflexive awareness). Codes are like book titles – they should capture the essence of the data as well as its primary content. Generating a code is, as Saldaña (2013: 4) notes, an act of 'interpreted meaning' and also the beginning of a process of 'pattern detection, categorization, [and] theory building'. Codes are usually words or short phrases that attach 'a summative, salient, essence-capturing, and/or evocative attribute' onto 'a portion of language-based or visual data' (p. 3).

Codes can be created before data collection begins, as it is in progress, or after it ends. Codes created before data collection begins are usually based on extant conceptual frameworks or key constructs that the researcher brings into the investigation. This is called 'deductive coding', for obvious reasons. As an example, one of the codes I might bring to a study investigating the power of online activists would be a master code about INFLUENCE. I would code the data looking for mentions of places and actors who manifest influence or power, such as INFLUENCE-public, INFLUENCE-boycott, and INFLUENCE-NGO.

Inductive codes emerge throughout the process of data collection, or during data analysis itself. Inductive codes may feel closer to the empirical phenomenon because they arise from contact with it. Deductive codes can be altered and revised when they do not seem to optimally fit the data, and thus take on a more inductive quality.

One of the most important operational principles of coding is its definition. Code definitions need to be coherent and straightforward so that they can be applied consistently over time and by different researchers (or others, who might be hired to help code the dataset). The definition should be precise and, if multiple coders are involved, these should be consulted in order to negotiate that its meaning is clear. Oftentimes, definitions can be improved by having two or more researchers code the same data and then discuss the results.

In Boxes 12.4 and 12.5, you will have a chance to try your hand at coding two datasets. The first one, for practice, is the downloaded utopian set. The second is the one you have collected for your research project.

Coding Examples

Seeking to study 'the resources that participants in online discussions about headlice draw upon, and in particular the part that science plays', as well as 'the forms of authority that participants hold to be convincing', 'how the dynamic of the online discussion context relates to conventional notions of medical and scientific expertise', and other related questions, Hine (2014: 578) used the Mumsnet site as her data site. She narrowed her search criteria, and ended up focusing on 62 relevant discussion threads that mentioned lice or nits in the title, giving a total of 1,127 messages (p. 579). She uploaded these messages into the NVivo QDAS program and then coded for individual remedies: 'Alongside this treatment-based coding a more grounded coding process involving several passes through the data identified a stable set of emergent themes that included risks, treatment failure, emotions, parenting expectations, sources of expertise and school policy'. After descriptively coding the data, and then presenting the results in a series of three descriptive data tables, which take up approximately four pages of the published article, she presents a subset of the themes, those relating to three elements of the phenomenon – treatment mechanisms, expertise, and notions of risk. The author gives no evidence of personal engagement in the phenomenon or the use of an immersion journal (or fieldnotes) and the work seems very similar to the more investigation-focused and content analytic-based forms of netnography. The article's research focus, as well as its interpretive conclusions, are wide-ranging, and include an emphasis on wider social concerns such as the development of public health communication efforts and the personal public understanding of science.

12.4 | DEDUCTIVELY CODING THE UTOPIAN DATASET (PRACTICE EXERCISE)

Deductive coding. Choose a theory that you are familiar with, or that you would like to be familiarized with. What can you draw from it? Conceptually, what are the key principles within it? What constructs matter most to that theory? How will you break down that theory so that its codes can be located in the WEHW dataset, which is about Walt Disney, EPCOT, utopia, consumerism, technology, money, and other things? Note: if you know a few theories (and I bet you do), you might want to choose one that has something to do with politics, hope, capitalism, activism, or some topic related to the dataset.

....

....

....

....

....

....

....

Given the constructs and principles you identified above, what would be some good deductive items to code for? What will you look for? Which words or phrases? Which concepts or ideas? (Try doing this before you have had a chance to look carefully through the data, you have only collated it, as per Box 12.2.) Write FIVE codes, or guidelines for codes. Write clear, basic, provisional definitions for all five codes. Try to word your coding definition so that it gives a yes/no answer. For example, 'DISNEY_BRILLIANT: The comment mentions the brilliance, intelligence, foresight, or other superlative mental capacity of Walt Disney/Does the comment mention the brilliance of Walt Disney?'

....

....

....

....

....

....

....

In your spreadsheet program, ADD FIVE COLUMNS. Write the names of the FIVE CODES in those columns:

- Now choose a block of 100 consecutive rows.

- Code that data using your five codes. Because you have worded your coding definition so that it gives a yes/no answer, you can then score it in the column as either a 1 (YES) or a 0 (NO). There is also no need to score the 'no' values, as these are 0. Although it is considerably more trouble to do so, you could also use a question that is open-ended and invites a thoughtful response, and code it afterwards (inductively).
- Refine these codes with someone else in the class, or find a virtual partner on one of the online qualitative research or netnography workgroups.
- Repeat as necessary to develop refined codes.

INDUCTIVELY CODING THE UTOPIAN DATASET (PRACTICE EXERCISE)

12.5

Inductive coding. We already know that you're not starting out in this project as some fictional newborn theorist. Your brain is already thoroughly polluted with other people's theories. If you are a PhD student, your brain is quite literally pickling in the juices of other people's theories.

Get as much of that theory out of your system! Purge it. Lay it out on the paper and then crumple that paper up. Blow it away like dust. Meditate on it – then release. Let it go. Dissolve it. Erase it. Delete it.

Be Zen in an Immanent Critical way.

*   *   *

Enjoy this peaceful space of no theory. Isn't it nice? You can claim tabula rasa status now (actually not, but wasn't it a nice feeling while it lasted?).

*   *   *

Then, randomly choose a number in the hundreds between 100 and 1,600. Start there and read the message threads, consecutively, for 100 or so messages. Read these first. Don't write anything yet.

After you've read the set of 100 messages once or twice, ask yourself about the key elements, the components, the sociocultural meaning-rich compositional elements of what you have read. What things matter most? How do those things connect to your pre-existing theory?

(Continued)

You have a completely open book. You can inductively code anything you detect in the WEHW dataset, which is about Walt Disney, EPCOT, utopia, consumerism, technology, and money. Write SIXTEEN codes, or guidelines for codes, with clear provisional definitions. Word your coding definition so that it yields a yes/no answer. For example, 'DISNEY_BRILLIANT: The comment mentions the brilliance, intelligence, foresight, or other superlative mental capacity of Walt Disney/Does the comment mention the brilliance (etc.) of Walt Disney?'

....

....

....

....

....

In your spreadsheet program, ADD SIXTEEN COLUMNS (you could add these one at a time, as you discover them). Write the names of the SIXTEEN CODES in those columns.

- Now, choose the block of 100 consecutive rows moving backwards from the number you chose before.
- Code that data inductively.
- Score it in the column as either a 1 (YES) or a 0 (NO). There is no need to score the absences, as they amount to zero.
- Let the code fit the data, not the other way around.
- If you want to get more subtle and do a second wave after the first wave of coding, you can start building more elaborate and subtle idea-structures in a second wave.

12.6 CODING YOUR DATASET (PROJECT EXERCISE)

Using your own project dataset, follow the example in Box 12.4, which leads you through a deductive coding exercise in which you begin with a particular theory of your choice, use it to generate codes and their definitions, and then see if any of those codes can be reasonably located in the data. If not, another theory (for example, in this case, one of political participation, clicktivism, or political communication on social media) might need to be invoked.

Again, use your own dataset. Follow the example in Box 12.5, which guides you through an inductive coding exercise in which you listen to the data first, and then find categories within it that fit.

This is your project. Use your own choice of theory. Then deductively develop some codes for it (between 10 and 20, say) and code for these. For the inductive work, you could try devising, defining, and discerning between 20 and 30 codes on the 100 or so rows of data.

COMBINING

Combining Operations in Data Analysis

Breaking apart and putting together. Smashing and merging. Fusing and blending, chopping and dividing. Combining operations, like many of the other data analysis and data interpretation operations, are concerned with uniting one or more elements in order to form a new element, which is called a 'pattern code' (Miles et al., 2014), a higher-order code, or a second cycle coding. The term 'higher-order' usefully indicates that the code represents a more abstract, more connective mode of thinking. In this data operation, we are combining codes into pattern codes for the purpose of revealing more abstract structures and patterns in the dataset. The pattern codes become conceptual material that helps you discover and present your research findings, which will answer your research question.

Combining is a process of discovery, one that resembles abduction in some way. In combining operations, you will group the initial codes into smaller numbers of categories, themes, or constructs, based on their commonalities. Using statistics, quantitative researchers might run a factor analysis or cluster analysis. In qualitative data analysis, we cluster using our intelligence, by looking across instances and contexts for meaningful similarities and other conceptual threads that connect individual codes.

Practically, combining operations usually involve going through the codes, definitions, and coded data and looking for possible connections between them. Not every code can be combined and you may find that combining more than a few is a challenging process. To assist you during your pattern-coding process, you may want to bring in additional context, by examining some of the original posts and pages. Use contextual insights from your more detailed examination to delve into what posts and participants meant when they wrote or said what they did, or what the circumstances were surrounding particular messages or other relevant questions. The same words can have very different meanings, depending on their context. And certain phrases, concepts, and situations you have already coded may be related in interesting ways in your dataset.

Remember that you are trying to generate a more inclusive and integrated conception that transcends the interactions and posts themselves. Try to find overarching categories, themes, explanations, or relationships that crosscut individual instances. It may also be helpful to return to your research question or to extant and related research in order to draw your attention to higher-order abstractions that relate to your research and your data sites.

Box 12.7 will guide you through exercises to practice combining codes into higher-order concepts. The next step is to combine these higher-order constructs into relationships or descriptions that you will present as your findings. Another technique that can assist in the process of developing your findings is to use tools and techniques to visualize your data for analysis, a data operation termed 'charting'. After the code-combining exercises in Box 12.7, the chapter presents charting, which is the last subsection in this chapter on data analysis.

12.7 **COMBINING CODES INTO HIGHER-ORDER CONSTRUCTS (PRACTICE AND PROJECT EXERCISES)**

This exercise can be performed exactly the same way for both the downloaded utopian dataset, as well as your own coded netnography project.

Follow the directions in the subsection about combining codes into higher-order constructs.

- First, read through your codes, the coding definitions, and the coded data.
- Look for commonalities between them in terms of factors such as categories, themes, explanations, or relationships that transcend and link individual instances into some sort of a pattern.
- Return to your data sites and to your captured data when you need additional context to help decipher and go deeper into your data and its codes.
- Combine the codes with similarities. Give each of these new higher-order or pattern codes a name. Define each of them precisely and with useful descriptive labels.
- These pattern codes are key outputs of the data analysis and will inform, be major characters in, or even become the research findings that you will present.

COUNTING

Counting Analysis

There may be times when describing or comparing the conceptual elements identified and coded within a netnography requires that they be quantified or counted. Conveniently, content that has been coded can also be counted. Content analysis is a technique that has a long history as a method for analyzing written, verbal, or visual communications across fields such as communication, journalism, sociology, psychology, and business (Elo and Kyngäs, 2008). Content analysis is a systematic way to describe and quantify phenomena, as well as to analyze documents and distill phrases or words into a smaller number of construct-related categories. Usually, the goals of content analysis are descriptive: to provide the concepts or categories which can describe the system, as well as to build a conceptual map of the phenomenon. Although it has been criticized as both 'simplistic' and insufficiently qualitative in nature, the approach has been found to be a helpful bridge over the divide between qualitative and quantitative data-analysis methods, and for this has developed an established position in many social scientific fields (2008: 108).

Content analysis is a field with considerable subtlety and a number of useful procedures. Sampling procedures are important, and relevant to the coding of large datasets. For instance, you have already done some (non-random, and likely non-representative) sampling in the analysis exercises in Boxes 12.4, 12.5, and 12.6. Using randomly generated number sets and confidence interval calculation to guide sampling in content analysis can be very helpful when coding large datasets in netnography. Quantitative measures of interjudge reliability can also be calculated. This chapter does not have the scope to provide greater detail, but the interested researcher should consult other texts as necessary to refine their content analysis skillset.

Regarding the quantification of data in content analysis, one of its early pioneers, Berelson (1952), argued that quantitatively descriptive words such as 'more', 'always', 'frequently', 'often', 'decreases', or 'increases' are often sufficient to provide all the information that is required. The key element of content analysis's quantification requirements is that 'the data should be amenable to statistical methods not only for precise and parsimonious summary of findings but also for interpretation and inference' (Kassarjian, 1977: 10).

Boxes 12.8 and 12.9 present exercises that will assist you in counting-based data analysis using the netnographic dataset provided, as well as your own collected project dataset.

COMPARING UTOPIAN DISCOURSE PATTERNS (PRACTICE EXERCISE)

12.8

Add up the ones and zeros of your scored elements. Compare these with one another. How can you describe the codings, what they measure, and what they reveal? How did your codes reflect the general constitution of these utopian EPCOT discourses? What can you say about their distribution? What do the relative appearances of, commonalities, and differences in these discourses tell us?

Try to visualize some of your findings using graphing (e.g., bar chart, pie chart) or other visualization programs. What does the visualization tell us?

(Continued)

What other diagrams (e.g., a relationship-type diagram) can you draw to show the relative strength of different qualities or elements of discourse that you have coded for?

How will you interpret the numbers in these analyses? What story do they tell? Are there larger patterns in them that you can detect?

12.9 COUNTING AND COMPARING YOUR DATA (PROJECT EXERCISE)

For your own netnography project, add up the ones of your coded and scored elements. What totals do they provide? How do the counted codings reflect the general constitution of the discourses and other elements of your dataset?

Which is the most commonly coded category? The three most commonly coded categories?

How does one category compare to another?

What can you say about the distribution of these conceptual categories? Are they dominated by a particular category, or are topics roughly even in their distribution?

Do you think that the sample of 100 rows was biased in some way? Do you think the results would be different if you were to code another 100 rows? A randomly chosen 100 rows? Your entire dataset?

Try to visualize some of your findings in visualization programs (e.g., bar charts, pie charts). What do the best of these visualizations tell us? What other diagrams can you draw to show the relative strength of different qualities or elements of discourse that you have coded for?

How will you interpret the counts of these analyses? What story do they tell? Are there larger patterns in them that you can detect?

Counting Analysis in Netnography: An Example

In their study of customer complaints, comments, and other feedback online, Yang and Fang (2004) employed netnography alongside content analysis to examine the service quality dimensions of online customer reviews of online securities brokerage services. After scouting relevant sites and selecting meaningful online posts, the authors downloaded 740 posts, constituting about 92,000 words in total, from two customer review platforms. The posts were imported into a QDAS and coded by the two authors using a combination of inductive and deductive methods. An inter-judge reliability score was then calculated for the two categories of codes, satisfied and dissatisfied service performance attributes.

The study revealed almost every online service dimension and subdimension identified in prior studies, and also uncovered multiple new factors that were relevant to the online service channel and its novel aspects. For the 16 major dimensions of service quality that they coded in the dataset, the researchers presented raw numbers and percentages (of the total, which they call a 'mention quotient') in a table (2004: 314–15). For example, 31.7% of the coded items related to responsiveness, 11.5% related to service reliability, and 11.1% related to ease of use. Of the 16 dimensions identified, responsiveness is by far the most mentioned. The researchers also break down each dimension into subdimensions, whose raw numbers and percentages are also presented. So, for example, the single largest subdimension in responsiveness is 'prompt response to phone calls' (9.7% of the total), followed by 'prompt order execution' (8.6%), and 'prompt services (others)' (7.1%).

Visualizing the counting results of the coded analysis of the data, the article presents a horizontal black-and-white bar chart. The chart shows the 16 dimensions of service quality, scaled from the dimension with the highest mention quotient (responsiveness), to the least (system flexibility). In addition, a different gray-colored bar on the bar chart indicates the mentions that regarded the factor being a 'satisfier' versus being a 'dissatisfier'. With these visual methods, the quantitative comparison of the different dimensions as well as their 'satisfier' versus 'dissatisfier' categories is usefully presented.

CHARTING

Charting: Data Display for Analysis

The analysis of large amounts of data is aided by visualization. Human beings are very astute processors of the details present in small amounts of rich cultural data, but their capacities are quickly overwhelmed when required to handle large datasets. The last subsection described how bar charts were used by Yang and Fang (2004) to represent some of the counting analysis of their netnographic study of the constituent elements of online service quality perceptions. This final subsection of data-analysis operations provides an overview, some examples, and some exercises that consider how data can be visualized, mapped, organized, and displayed – a general operation with many possible forms that this book terms 'charting'.

Charting is data display, and these activities can be considered a major component of analytic activity. Miles et al. (2014: 12–13) consider a data display to be 'an organized, compressed assembly of information that allows conclusion drawing and action'. Although extended text has been the most frequent form of display for quali-tative data in the past, we now have many more options that are better tools for grasp-ing both a holistic sense of the data (especially useful in interpretation) and a sense of its component parts and how they fit together (helpful in analysis). Data display can include tables, maps, charts, graphs, matrices, networks, and word clouds. All of these display forms assemble information in an organized fashion so that it is concise and comprehensible. Miles et al. (2014: 13) usefully suggest that 'the creation and use of displays is not separate from analysis – it is a *part* of analysis'. Maps, network graphs, and word clouds are three of the qualitative data display techniques we will consider in the following subsections.

Mapping: Cartographies of Netnographic Scapes

From time immemorial, people have been mapping unknown areas in order to under-stand them. Cartography is the science or practice of studying and creating maps. Map-making combines aesthetics with science, and tries to build models of reality that can communicate spatial information effectively in a visual format. Mapping shades into symbolic representation of many kinds, and there are many kinds of different maps. We can find maps of the human body with energy meridians, chakras, and acu-puncture points. Maps of the world can show differences and similarities in Internet use, birth rates, social class, religion, or even such things as preferred food and sexual habits. Recently, people have begun drawing creative maps of the Internet that depict Google and Facebook as continents with apps and games as islands. Mind maps are hierarchical diagrams that are used to visually organize and present a wide variety of different types of information and are similar to semantic networks and concept maps.

Maps in netnography can combine aspects of all of these forms of map-making. When writing in your immersion journal, you were encouraged to engage in reconnoi-tering operations (see Chapter 10). Part of the output of those operations would have been notes or sketches of different sites, pages, platforms, applications, or threads.

Where there are numerous online sites that are relevant to a netnographic inves-tigation, it can be useful to visually present them in a map-like diagram in order to analyze their similarities and differences. Quantitative researchers might use multi-dimensional scaling statistical techniques, or other clustering approaches. In some of my past netnographic work, I have assembled information into a visual form by hand, classifying and then representing the relationships between different platforms or data sites. This drawing then provides a holistic view of the different elements constituting the overall search or dataset, which can be useful both for further analysis and the display of findings. Figure 12.1 presents a diagram of different websites that all had in common their focus on recipes and meal-planning services. Rather than present this information in a table, I chose to represent it as a two-dimensional map, with similar sites grouped together, general categories labeled, and differences between sites rep-resented by the amount of space between them.

Peanut Lovers.com

Fleischmann's Yeast Bread world

Epicurious   Recipe Zaar

Kraft Kichen

Industry   Birds Eye

Food Channel   cooking.com   Campbell's Kitchen

About Seafood   Betty Crocker

Generalist   Sea-Ex Recipes for Seafood, Fish, Shellfish   Hershey Foods

Pace Foods   Mrs. Dash Home Page

Kitchen Parade.com   Cookbooks Online

A#1 Recipes   M&M's Recipes and Ideas   **Corporate**

Allrecipes.com

Chicken of the Sea

Good Morning America Recipes   King Arthur Flour Home Page

Hidden Valley Ranch Recipes   Nissin Foods-Ramen

Sun Maid Recipes

Kichen Recipes   Smucker Products

Recipe and Meal Planning Sites

Mca Master Recipes

Top Secret Recipes

COKichen.com

Weight Watchers.com   Home Canning Online   **Copycat**

GORP - Great Outdoor Cooking   Organic Tuscany Cooking School   Top Secret Recipes.com

Diet and Specialty   Chef to Chef   Mimi's Cyber Kichen   Alta's Recipe Page

Kosher Express Recipes   Joy of Baking   **Gourmet**   Anita's Recipes

Food Down Under   Maltese Traditional Recipes   Mark's Recipe Archive

Thanksgiving Recipes   **Independent**

The African Cookbook   Chef Johney's   **and Blog**

Vegan Kitchen

Ethnic   Else.com simply recipes

Chef Andy's Jell-O Pages

Vegan Cooking Recipes   German Deli

Shere's Kitchen

Greek Dishes

Figure 12.1   Conceptual map of the recipe and meal-planning space

Network Graphs in Netnographic Data Analysis

Another mode for representing complex information is the network graph. Graphs are often based on graph theory, which uses mathematical structures to model the pairwise relationships between objects. Network graphs take the form of nodes or points that are connected by lines or edges. They can feature sites, individuals, activities, or ideas. They can also reveal influence and centrality, as well as other types of social connections. Although this short introduction cannot provide many details, there is a sophisticated science behind social network analysis and its use of visual network graphs.

Recently, several scholars in different fields have noted that netnography can be usefully combined with social network analysis techniques (e.g., Whelan et al., 2016). Some published netnographies have also begun using social network analyses and related network graphs to present research findings. We might also assume that the creation and examination of these graphs played useful roles in data analysis.

In their Twitter-based study of the free open-access medical information (or FOAM) movement, Roland and colleagues (2017: 4) employed a netnographic research frame that relied heavily on the researchers' own status 'as members of the community of study [who] had an immersive and descriptive understanding of the FOAM movement'. Further, the authors gathered Twitter data from 49,459 active users who issued 429,606 tweets and created 1,258,692,900 total impressions. Social network analysis was used as the primary analytic method to understand this dataset.

The article explains that the insider understanding of the engaged netnographic stance of the researchers affirmed the community leadership status of the centrality findings from the network analysis. Figure 12.2 reprints one of the network graph depictions, showing the centrality metrics of the top 100 users of the FOAM hashtag, where the size of a node is used to represent the relative influence of that Twitter poster, and the links depict the direction and strength of the between-member communications.

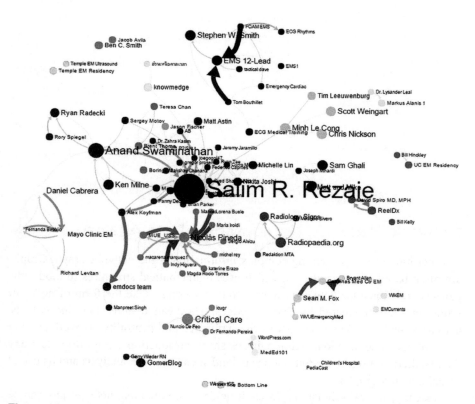

Figure 12.2 Network graph of influential FOAM movement Twitter users (reprinted from Roland et al., 2017)

Word Clouds in Netnographic Data Analysis

Word clouds are a textual visualization tool in which texts are distilled to more frequently used words, and those words are more conspicuously shown in the representation (McNaught and Lam, 2010). This form of charting qualitative data allows the recognition of more common or prominent words, and thus can lead to discerning patterns of overall or comparative word use that might otherwise go undetected. Word clouds can be a fast, widely-available, and simple way for researchers to visualize entire textual datasets, parts of them, or to compare various texts and their parts. Thus, they have the potential to be a useful tool in data-analysis operations, although it is unlikely that they would ever be the primary or only research tool used in a netnography.

Word clouds are a type of visual summary that can serve as a starting point for deeper analysis (Heimerl et al., 2014). They can help in the evaluation of whether a given text is relevant for a particular information need. For example, a data analyst might examine a word cloud of a large set of downloaded social media data to try to determine whether it is relevant or not, as part of an investigative scouting operation (this would only be part of the operation, because one would be searching for meaning in netnography, as well as the use of particular words). Word clouds have been used in literary studies to compare and contrast writing styles (Clement et al., 2008), and in education to analyze students' short written responses (Brooks et al., 2014), and also to encourage critical thinking, interaction, and engagement in students' online discussion (DeNoyelles and Reyes-Foster, 2015). In 2017, numerous journalists and bloggers used word clouds to conduct analyses of inauguration speeches and compare them (e.g., Lowkell, 2017).

One potential drawback of word clouds is that 'they provide a purely statistical summary of isolated words without taking linguistic knowledge about the words and their relations [context and meanings] into account' (Heimerl et al., 2014: 1833). Improvements and extensions to word cloud programs have been and are being made, including adding a temporal dimension to depict changes in words over time, automating the comparison of words from different sources, and combining word clouds with tree graphs to visualize the semantic relations between terms (p. 1834). In addition, numerous techniques, some involving software extension, are being developed to enhance their use as ways to provide overviews of large textual datasets (Horn et al., 2017).

Although their reported use of word clouds in published netnographic research is still uncommon, Ahuja and Shakeel (2017) highlight their use by applying them to a large dataset aggregating 1,500 tweets using the identifier handle of a transportation brand ('JetAirways'). Their interpretation of the word cloud's content is that the airline was successfully able to generate positive consumer engagement focused on its professionality and high-quality experience. In the two boxes that follow, you will be guided through practice and project exercises using word clouds in netnography.

WORD CLOUDS OF UTOPIAN YOUTUBE COMMENTS (PRACTICE EXERCISE)

Word clouds allow us to visualize the most commonly used words in large datasets, providing a chance to evaluate their contents. Using one of the free online word cloud creators (I used Wordle.net, but it no longer seems to be working in most browsers) I created the following word cloud from the downloaded dataset of all of the comments and replies to the WEHW dataset (see Figure 12.3).

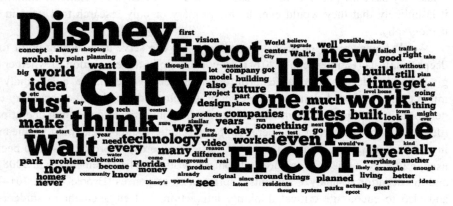

Figure 12.3 Raw data word cloud from WEHW dataset

What do you notice first about this word cloud? Which words are largest? Does this suggest anything to you? Write some of your initial reactions here before reading on.

....

....

....

....

As with other forms of analysis, sometimes we need to make data cleaning types of adjustments in order for the picture to become clearer. In this case, the word cloud is dominated by the word 'city', which is interesting and might merit further conceptual development (e.g., are commenters comparing to other cities? how are the comments related to urban planning? does this proposed utopia have special appeal because it is presented in the form of a single city?). The word cloud is also dominated by 'Disney', 'Walt', and two forms of 'EPCOT', one fully capitalized and the other spelled with a capitalized letter E. Because these latter four words are obvious, we might try to remove them from our visualization and see what else it reveals. As well, the word 'like' is so common, and so decontextualized in word clouds like this one, that it is not helpful to our analysis.

Fortunately, Wordle has a function that allows you to quickly eliminate particular words from the word cloud. Figure 12.4 is the same word cloud with 'Disney', 'Walt', 'EPCOT','Epcot', and 'like' removed.

Figure 12.4   Cleaned-up WEHW word coud

This visualization might more clearly create a picture of the overall concern, expressed as prominent words, of the entire group of comments and replies on the WEHW YouTube video. Focusing on this word cloud, you might try contemplating a few questions:

- What are the key words you detect?
- Are there conceptual links between those words? What binds them together? Do they relate to particular institutions or ideologies? Are there other patterns you can perceive?
- What does your interpretation of this word cloud make you curious about? What would you like to investigate further?

12.11 USING WORD CLOUDS IN YOUR PROJECT (PROJECT EXERCISE)

There are a number of free online programs that will produce nice word clouds. You can use a search engine and find one that interests you. Wordle (currently) offers a downloadable version, but there is a range of other sites, such as www.wordclouds.com, that (currently) work well.

Most word cloud generators do not have a size limit. This is convenient if you want to word cloud the entire Bible, all seven books of the *Harry Potter* series, or your netnographic dataset in its entirety.

Try experimenting with word clouds from different aspects of your dataset, and comparing them with each other, as well as with a word cloud of the dataset as a whole. Put all your Facebook data in, and compare it with all your Reddit data. Or compare your interview transcripts with your research webpage data. Or your investigative data with your interactional data. Does you immersion journal look very different from your other datasets?

Keep in mind that word clouds are an initial way to explore your datasets and get ideas for additional analysis and interpretation, but they are probably not refined or nuanced enough to draw more in-depth conclusions.

CHAPTER SUMMARY

Data analysis breaks phenomena down into their component parts in order to study and understand them. Chapter 12 discussed the decisions involved in analysis and linked decisions about levels of analysis to a conception of what is a whole versus what is a part. The chapter related analysis and its outcomes to sociologies of knowledge. It taught you the basic principles of qualitative data-analysis. Following that, the chapter proceeded to a more specific focus on data analysis operations for netnography. First, collating operations were explained and illustrated as the preparation of data for coding. Next, coding operations were described as initiations into the processes of abstraction and reflection that lead to theory development. Then, combining operations were detailed as procedures that merge conceptually related codes to form new, higher-order elements called 'pattern codes'. Fourth, counting operations were presented as quantifying procedures allowing netnographic researchers to more precisely compare various measurable elements in their qualitative data-sets. Finally, the chapter presented charting operations that create and use visualizations, maps, graphs, tables, and other displays of data, illustrating the concept with examples and exercises that analytically utilize maps, network graphs, and word clouds from data.

KEY READINGS

Elo, Satu and Helvi Kyngäs (2008) 'The qualitative content analysis process', *Journal of Advanced Nursing*, 62(1): 107–15.

Hine, Christine (2014) 'Headlice eradication as everyday engagement with science: An analysis of online parenting discussions', *Public Understanding of Science*, 23(5): 574–91.

McNaught, Carmel and Paul Lam (2010) 'Using Wordle as a supplementary research tool', *The Qualitative Report*, 15(3): 630–43.

Miles, Matthew B., A. Michael Huberman, and Johnny Saldaña (2014) *Qualitative Data Analysis: A Methods Sourcebook*. London: Sage.

INTERPRETING: HOW TO DISCOVER AND MAKE MEANING FROM NETNOGRAPHIC DATA

CHAPTER OVERVIEW

Interpretation is the process of making sense of, and discovering meaning in, collected and analyzed data. Hermeneutic interpretation will be introduced and clarified in this chapter. Then, the application of assemblage theory to netnographic data interpretation will be introduced and developed. The six operations of interpretation in netnography will follow thereafter. Theming is the operation which will reassemble the component pieces of an abstractly analyzed phenomenon, creating a new conceptual whole from these parts. Talenting is a way to produce theming interpretations using artistic expression. Totalizing operations will explore the reassembled conceptual whole and its meaning. Translating operations will transport the researcher as they move back and forth between worlds of data and theory. Turtling operations are based on a famous metaphor of turtles standing on each other's backs, and refer to the operation that will (re)connect data, as well as the holistic phenomenon itself to the context(s) from which they were taken. Finally, trouble-making operations are the critique of underlying and taken-for-granted notions in the service of developing a more inclusive, important, and ethical understanding. Throughout the chapter, numerous explanations and exercises will be provided to practically guide the reader through the process of data interpretation in netnography.

UNDERSTANDING INTERPRETATION

What Interpretation Is

Data interpretation is the process of making sense and discovering the significance of collected and/or analyzed data. Interpretation seeks informed conclusions and meaning from data or analysis, and encompasses its critique, as well as its extension into new and additional inquiries. Some methodologists, perhaps many, find data interpretation to be 'difficult to distinguish sharply' from data analysis and theory building (Belk et al., 2013: 147). However, most agree that interpretation is about finding more abstract constructs and that the move from analysis to interpretation involves a shift in emphasis, 'from identifying patterns in the data to attempting to find meaning in the patterns'. In the short science fiction parable that opened Chapter 11, the alien T'k'lzt-p! civilization was unable to understand and appreciate humanity because it lacked the ability to find meaning in the few human relics that remained. In a research context, interpretation is a key step to the building of theory, which can be conceptualized in social science research as 'a system of ideas or statements that help us understand some aspect(s) of the phenomenon' of interest. As it unfolds as a series of operations, procedures, or research practices, analysis and interpretation blend into one another as a nonlinear integration of understanding in which codes can expand, contract, and be revised, and during which the researcher(s) might move back and forth between codes, data, extant literature, a search for something significant to say, related readings, and the emerging theory.

In fact, all authoritative sources on qualitative data interpretation state that interpretation begins as soon as your research project does. Formulating a research question involves analysis and interpretation, taking a real-world phenomenon and focusing upon particular aspects of it that are of interest and, likely, related to extant literature and its theoretical framing. Searching and scouting for information traces, then evaluating and turning them into data by collecting them also requires interpretation. Researchers working in teams will discuss, evaluate, and interpret their project and its data in an ongoing fashion during meetings, memos, and other debriefs. As the collection progresses and researchers on the project write in their immersion journals, their interpretation of the data, their striving for the meaning of a big picture understanding, is ongoing. And as noted in Chapter 12, data operations also have many elements of interpretation about them – such as when we must devise new abstract codes, define them, and judge whether new data fits its classification scheme.

Is hermeneutic interpretation about phenomenological understanding – verstehen – or explanation? In the past, some worried about the allegedly exclusive textual nature of netnographic data (a fallacy) and its focus on social media (true). There were concerns about disembodiment, the lack of verifiable markers of social identity. There was a worrying sense that the anonymity and pseudonymity of particular platforms like Reddit, 4chan, and Twitter would inevitably attract a certain type of non-representative person and their way-out messages, giving the extreme and the crazy a platform for their forms of extreme wackiness.

However, as Geertz (1973: 20) reminds us, it is 'not necessary to know everything in order to understand something': we don't need to understand everything about social media in order to understand some things about it. Thick description, Geertz's conception, is an understanding of a cultural phenomenon that is complex, specific, and circumstantial (p. 23). This description is often affiliated with understanding as a form of description. A description that can be evocative. That can move us. That can create empathy, verstehen: deeper understanding.

Data interpretation also takes us beyond this type of evocative description into explanation. Interpretation tells us how or why a particular phenomenon has occurred in a certain manner (Wolcott, 1994). Wolcott (1994) avers that while analysis engages in acts of data *transformation*, interpretation is about *transcending* data. Interpretation goes beyond what is in the dataset itself. The process of abstraction uses the dataset as the launch point, but it is the researchers who are the rocket ships and the academic fields which are the landing places. Interpretation takes a broader vantage point shaped by the knowledge, experiences, perspectives, and imaginations of the researchers conducting it. It focuses upon a holistic perspective. Interpretation provides context. It unites elements into wholes and wholes into systems, and compares and locates those systems across other systems. Interpretations critique, revealing and questioning the assumptions behind our understandings. They may even deconstruct the various operations of data collection, interpretation, and analysis we use to reach our knowledge.

Hermeneutic Interpretation

In philosophy and biblical interpretation, hermeneutics has as its focus the understanding of texts (widely construed as including images, as well as live performances such as presentations, dance, theatre, and everyday life). Hermeneutics is a methodological discipline that provides tools to interpret human actions and texts, compare texts, and apply texts to both abstract theorizing and practical knowledge and questions (Mantzavinos, 2016). Very much like a text-based method such as the investigative data operations of netnography and the need to understand them, hermeneutic interpretation tries to use text to provide answers to questions. This sort of interpretive skill is also needed in jurisprudence, literary studies, and science.

Hermeneutic interpretation is named for Hermes, the Greek god of communication and exchange of all kinds, trade, travel, speech, astronomy, livestock, and interpretation. Son of Zeus, Hermes never failed to amuse and enchant. His words were eloquent and persuasive. But sometimes he bent the truth, with beautiful and cunning distortions. Deceptions that were often, like dreams and imagination, even more wonderful than the truth. Above all, Hermes was a traveler. While other Greek gods stayed in Olympus, Hermes constantly moved between realms, ever traveling between the worlds of gods and men. We can and will keep in mind the importance of Hermes' many talents and forms to the act of interpretation in netnography. For, like Hermes himself, the field of hermeneutics has many forms. Exegetical hermeneutics, for example, tries to penetrate the underlying meaning of authoritative texts, such as what might be meant by the stories of Adam and Eve in the Garden of Eden, other than its literal truth.

Hermeneutic interpretation is based upon the spirit of finding the whole through the individual instance and through the whole to grasp the meaning of isolated events, as philologist Friedrich Ast (1808: 178) explained. This notion, which we build directly into the interpretation operation called 'totalizing' is the foundation of the hermeneutic circle. Hermeneutic circles are also expressed in terms of parts and whole which give meaning to each other. As well, meaning is understood in a context, where the whole of something is related to a system of which it is a part, and compared with other systems and the wholes which compose them. It asks how a text means something. The way texts create meanings becomes as important in hermeneutics as what those texts mean (Mantzavinos, 2016). Interpretation is an act that tries to understand not just what words mean but also how they mean them and the significance of the concepts to which they lead. Hermeneutics is a careful unpacking of what certain conceptual networks suggest about other things such as beliefs and hidden ideologies, and the institutions, identities, and other social systems they connect to. Hermeneutic interpretation, in sum, helps qualitative researchers undertake many of the parts of their science.

Applying Assemblage Theory to Interpretation

Assemblage theory is a form of dynamic systems theory in which various different kinds of material, social, and linguistic systems self-organize into complex structures at various levels of scale. Assemblages are hybrids made of material and expressive components; they are articulations among myriad heterogeneous elements (Canniford and Badje, 2016; Slack and Wise, 2014). Assemblage theory conceptualizes a material and social world full of fluidity, hybridity, and hierarchy. It sees the world as composed of wholes composed of parts where the parts have the potential for lots of exchangeability, and in which many elements have multiple functions. Each part is like an individual, with wide degrees of freedom to do something unexpected, like disconnecting or joining another whole. Wholes are identified as wholes because of their capacity to change certain things. Relationships are not stable or fixed, but usually the overall patterns composing them are – the system is territorialized and tends towards or tries to maintain fixity. However, nothing is actually determined or fixed – even things that seem very stable or solid can change suddenly, which is called deterritorializing.

DeLanda (2016: 31) considers assemblage theory to be a 'causal' theory that is 'concerned with the discovery of the actual mechanisms operating at different spatial scales', and that also aims at finding 'the topological structure defining the diagram of an assemblage': thus assemblage theory offers many implications for explanation, description, and even visualization. One of its key concerns is 'the linkages between the micro and the macro' – a 'recalcitrant problem' to which assemblage theory's broader conceptualizing of levels of scale provides much-needed insight (p. 32). Another is its focus on different kinds of relations, which can include the various interconnections and co-constitutions of material tangible things with symbolic, semiotic, expressive elements, and so-called natural and social components (Canniford and Badje, 2016: 2). The process of 'abstraction' in assemblage theory is concerned with 'how an assemblage mobilises new compositions of material and expressive things' (p. 4). It is a non-deterministic theory, but it is concerned with the capacities of joined and unjoined elements, as well as their relations of stability and instability. Components assume a particular form by taking a territory, or territorializing other elements. When they change forms, they deterritorialize those particular elements and reterritorialize with others into another configuration. Territorialization creates the assemblage, which has various capacities. For instance, an online climate change group might have various participants who come and go. In the theory these members would be considered elements who have been territorialized. To continue the example, certain climate change groups might articulate themselves with particularly frightening or horrific expressions and symbols, like Extinction Rebellion. This articulated assemblage could be contrasted with other climate change groups, their actions and members.

Implications of Assemblage Theory for Netnography

Contained within the fragments and traces of data we investigatively locate in social media, the references in interactional interviews, and the recognitions we find in our immersion journals are assemblages piled within assemblages, cell bodies within organs within identified individuals within groups articulated to particular expressive meanings, symbols already territorialized by cultures, linked to and within societies. All social context is similarly endless: scapes within scapes, all the way through the world. Unthinkable complexity, yet structured with recurrent codes, capacities, and territories. The co-determining co-presence of permanence and impermanence at play, working within each of these elements-in-context as they interact, connect, disengage, and re-engage.

We can think of the process of netnographic interpretation as a kind of orderly structuring of concepts. Just as drawing a constellation in the sky leaves out certain celestial bodies as it includes others, so too does interpretation leave out certain patterns or constructs in order to reveal or create a particular pattern. Assemblage theory draws our attention to the act of research as the moment in which we encounter 'data' in some holistic sense. In netnography, choosing to emphasize one piece of deep data over another, to focus on this thread rather than that one, this site rather than another – all of these can have radical implications for the theory and understanding that is eventually built. Assemblage theory helps us understand both the complexity of the social phenomena we are considering in netnography and also the acts of interpretation guiding that consideration.

Further implications for interpretation of assemblage theory are drawn from conceiving theoretical structures as assemblages, and considering how those assemblages are based in contexts. DeLanda (2016) reminds us that a knife can be a kitchen tool or a weapon, depending on the context. A theory developed for a particular context or level of analysis may not work when ported to another context or level of analysis, or it may work differently there. Studying the meaning of utterances in netnography, online speech acts as they occur naturally, requires an understanding of the multiple social, cultural, institutional, ideological and even individual contexts which shape and form them and in which they occur.

A knowledge of assemblage theory in interpretation should be liberating, freeing you up to deterritorialize and reterritorialize concepts, traces, data, connections, and fields. Deleuze and Guattari intended these ideas as a combined act of political resistance and of psychological reactance shattering; they recognized the existential consequences of research and understanding. In interpretation, assemblage theory draws our attention to changes in the level of analysis, to the relationships between wholes and their parts and wholes and other wholes, to changes in forms, material-expressive articulations, and circumstances. Our interpretation is like the shifting of hierarchical chunks of different sizes of puzzle pieces. We are constantly comparing our pieces with the image that the puzzle depicts, except that in qualitative research there is not necessarily a clear guiding image for our puzzle solving. These focal elements are built into the group of interpretive procedures introduced and developed in this chapter.

INTERPRETIVE PROCEDURES

Introducing the Six Interpretive Operations

The holistic focus of triangulation, the hermeneutic circle and hermeneutic interpretation, and assemblage theory lead to a number of related but distinct procedures for data interpretation. Methodology is an interpretation of research philosophies. Scientific method abstractions of concepts such as deduction and induction, part and whole, dictate what is done in research methods by explaining why it is done.

As with data-analysis operations, these procedures can be performed sequentially, individually, or in any combination and in any order that you like. They provide an almost limitless number of different combinations to work with. Here, in their nutshells, are the basic procedures: theming, talenting, totalizing, translating, turtling, and troublemaking. These are the six overlapping operations, each related to the others, but also subtly different. Each provides a different sense and approach to interpreting. Each operation emphasizes different meanings related to the holistic tendencies of interpretation. Each results in a different peregrination of data, theory, and analysis. Theming, talenting, totalizing, translating, turtling, troublemaking: each is subtly different, and leads to a different type of transversal of the data and analysis. Reassembling the pieces. Embodying it in an artistic way. Exploring its practical implications. Linking data and theory, theory and data. Placing things in perspective by reintroducing context. Critiquing and trying to encourage positive change. Following are initial explanations of these six internally focused and externally penetrating interpretive procedures:

- *Theming*: the reassembly operation. Putting the component pieces of the abstract analysis back together again, creating a new conceptual whole from these parts.

- *Talenting*: a way to theme using art.

- *Totalizing*: exploring the whole and its meaning to the wider world.

- *Translating*: moving between the worlds of data and theory.

- *Turtling*: connecting the holism to its context and to the other conceptual systems in which it is embedded.

- *Troublemaking*: critiquing underlying and taken-for-granted notions in the service of developing a more inclusive, important, and ethical interpretation.

Theming, talenting, totalizing, translating, turtling, and troublemaking: the following sections develop them, with examples, literary bases, and practical hands-on workshop-style exercises.

THEMING

Interpretation as Thematic Pattern Recognition

Theming is an interpretive operation that seeks to conceptualize a focal phenomenon as an integrated whole. Theming is the opposite of analysis, happens subsequent to it, and in some ways, completes it. Analysis breaks a phenomenon down into components, attaches abstract classifier codes, and looks for similar patterns among them in a quest for understanding. Theming is a reassembly operation. Wherever there is fractured knowledge, the researcher uses theming to try to put the pieces of the phenomenon disassembled by the act of analysis back together again into the whole that they once presented to the world.

Theming illustrates the interrelation of analysis and (this kind of) interpretation. It is about gathering the pattern codes, and making them into larger things we can think of as 'themes', in a hierarchical pyramid of research interpretation where data is on the bottom, then codes, then pattern codes, then themes. This higher-order pattern code is the theme and it is integrative: it encapsulates a larger story in which the phenomenon is a whole made of a few thematic parts.

The naming of the interpretive operation of theming clearly relates netnography to the established practices of thematic analysis. In past overviews of published netnographies, thematic analysis has often been identified as one of the most popular, if not *the* single most popular, analytic technique. In fact, thematic analysis is such a broad and general school of qualitative research that it encompasses many of the operations of both data analysis and interpretation in netnography. Based on the idea that recurring patterns, or themes, can be located within data, the initial stages of thematic analysis follow the general coding and categorizing principles described in Chapter 12, and then are finalized with the interpretive procedures described in this chapter.

Netnography is also concerned with using naturally generated texts as units of analysis and seeking insights about the ways people structure and share their lives as narratives. Thus, it also overlaps with narrative inquiry or narrative analysis. Narrative inquiry has a range of different paradigms and theories that have been used to interpret data, including postpositivist, constructivist, Marxist, cultural studies, and feminist perspectives. However, like thematic analysis, narrative inquiry follows the basic steps of collecting data, organizing it, and then finding significance in that organization. Both thematic analysis and narrative inquiry embrace the role of metaphors in generating holistic understanding about focal phenomena. Narrative inquiry tends to be more about marginalized voices and their stories. But there is considerable overlap between the two approaches. The most important stage in both techniques, as in interpretation itself, is to gain and communicate a holistic impression of the phenomenon.

Theming interpretation is an attempt to regain the experience of the whole from its various parts, whether these are considered to be themes, pattern codes, material-expressive articulations, or narrative stories. Theming interpretation brings together the component parts of theories and data in order to study and understand the phenomenon as a holistic entity. Box 13.1 provides a theming exercise to guide you through this operation with your collected dataset.

THEMING YOUR DATASET (PROJECT EXERCISE)

13.1

Examine your entire dataset, looking for focal constructs. If you have already analyzed the dataset, these focal constructs are likely your pattern codes or

(Continued)

codes. Think of your themes as the macro-pattern codes that combine pattern codes together. Then, answer the following directed questions:

- How do these constructs or elements encompass the entire phenomenon you have studied?
- How do these constructs or elements provide a holistic answer to your research question(s)? How do they fit together into a relationship? Do they move together? What material and expressive elements do they connect together? How stable are those elements? Do they link those elements to some other elements?
- What is a process through which the phenomenon unfolds or changes?
- What does the phenomenon or its parts change? What other things does it transform, and what does it transform these other things into?
- What explains the context under which the phenomenon occurs, or the circumstances under which it changes?
- Try to write a sentence or two to capture the core idea behind what you have discovered. Be holistic and concise.

TALENTING

Using Artistic Interpretation for Intuitive Data Processing

One of the ways we understand the world around us holistically is by internalizing it as impression and experience, and then exteriorizing that experience through some kind of expression: words, symbols, body language. Talenting interpretations are systematic ways to incrementally, and, in a completely risk-free way, encourage our engagement with art as a way to analyze the data collected as part of a netnography. Doing a netnography as a team has particular advantages when using talenting operations, as they encourage us to explore both our data and our artistic self, and then report back through a performance to the other people in our research team. I know – sounds fun, right?

There is no limit to what you can do as part of your talenting. Write a little research ditty. Read your favorite theorists out loud. Play or show an artwork or performance and explain what it means to you. Screw your courage to the sticking-place and attempt something that might take you a little distance out of your usual zone of comfort. Remember that anyone can draw, even if their hand-drawn lines aren't always perfectly straight or their circles perfectly round. So what? The idea isn't to become a professional artist, but to express what you think and feel symbolically – as only you can. Art of any kind, creation of any kind, is about gaining a hidden understanding. Art is about tapping our untapped abilities to recognize larger patterns. It is an opportunity for our mind's eye to see what is difficult for our mind or eye to see.

Depict this insight in any medium you like: a poem, a sketch, a digital illustration, a video, a documentary, a short story. It's simple. And it is exactly as I stated it in the second edition of this book, *Netnography Redefined*. If you can do anything creative, then you can artify. Artifying is defined as the conversion of collected netnographic data into a form of art such as a painting, animated video, poem, or photographic image. Go ahead and be the best kind of scientist, the one who also exercises their right brain skills. Use those creative abilities to express something about your dataset in a concise, integrated fashion, designed with a style that exercises your imaginative capacities. Consider a fuller possibility space. Riff off of cool books of mythologies, horrors, heroes, archetypes, and occult symbols. Allow a chance for a moment of flight consciously realized, a more visceral, embodied, and evocative form of understanding.

In the following three boxes, you will find a selection of different exercises that you can turn to, at any time, for any interpretive project, in order to bring talenting interpretations to the fore. Feel free to attempt one, or more, or to create artistic exercises of your own.

ARTISTIC REPRESENTATION (IMAGINATION EXERCISE)

13.2

Here is a list of things to think about in relation to your netnography. If you were to make one of these artistic creations, how would you use it to express your dataset or a part of it as an artistic whole? Provide as much detail as you can, and as you like:

1. A Pixar-type movie
2. A building
3. A tattoo
4. A movie
5. A comic book
6. A dance
7. Graffiti
8. A song or symphony
9. A photograph
10. A selfie

This is of course not a complete list, as it is missing poetry and a thousand other things. Feel free to add in artistic forms like weaving, wood-working, sports, singing, and anything else you please.

13.3

TATTOO INTERPRETATION

Exercise 1: Think of a tattoo form that would express your data in a single image. What would that tattoo be? Try drawing it by hand or with a drawing program.

Exercise 2: Search online for images of tattoos linked to your concept. See how they open up your understanding of your data.

13.4

COMIC BOOK INTERPRETATION

If your research was a three- to five-page comic book, what would it say?

Create a comic book that relates to your netnography.

What would it be like? Would it be about a particular superhero? Or is it a war comic? A romance? A humorous one? What other comic book ideas might you get?

Is there a particular storyline, issue, appearance, other characters or symbols, titles of comic book lines, or anything else you wish to include?

There are numerous comic book-creating pieces of software available, including several that are online. Consider using your data and one of these tools to create a comic book interpretation.

TOTALIZING

Interpretation as Micrological Defragmentation

This is another exercise in a book full of exercises. Because what else is method if not exercises: embedded practices? Imagine your data, in a small capsule, all your data, everything you have collected, hurtling through space. And there are the T'k'lzt-p!, the insectoid civilization from Chapter 11. They are circling round again. If the T'k'lzt-p! explorers found your data one million years from now, floating in a space capsule, what might they think of it? Which pieces will you emphasize and feature so that they will be noticed? What would the T'k'lzt-p! scientists really need to know about those pieces to fully decode them? How would this deciphering of your data help the T'k'lzt-p! make sense of something else, something that is important and urgent to them, something that is wider and more universal?

What if you were to focus on a fragment of your data, one small piece, as if it were an entire universe unto itself?

What if you were to go through your immersion journal and find that something within it triggers a reverie, similar to the one that the petite madeleine triggered for Marcel Proust's narrator in *Remembrance of Things Past*? If that happened, you would definitely be totalizing. Totalizing takes a single instance of data – deep data – and attempts to expand it into a universe of its own, or into another intellectually ambitious and all-encompassing metaphor.

Totalizing is a focusing in, micrologically, on one fragment of deep data (at a time). 'Totalizing' is a term that is often used in research in a negative manner, but that is not its meaning here. Totalizing in the netnographic data interpretation context means to express elements of data as whole entities, and apply them to things like ideology and ideological interpretation. Totalizing is a psychological stance; call it an attitude about individual elements of data that temporarily elevates them into some of the most amazing pieces of data anyone has ever collected on social media. Ever.

The data one uses for a totalizing operation should not be run-of-the-mill superficial data. Totalizing should be reserved for deep data that you believe to be exceptional. Images and screenshots of data in context can be powerful forms of data to use in totalizing operations. That data could be reminiscent of the deep desires of previously identified lead users. Or a black swan. Or some other one-of-a-kind find. It should hit you emotionally in the gut. Affect you with an involuntary memory or the zap of an emotional charge, as the petite madeleine did in Proust's novel.

Totalizing is best used with fragments, smaller bites of data, because it requires a level of depth that can be difficult to sustain when data becomes lengthy and its orientations diffuse. Data can be rich or poor, but ultimately it is your reaction to the data that matters most to your interpreting of them. A tweet that pithily summarized or stated something you found meaningful might be a powerful post to totalize. Single posts can have the depth to benefit from totalizing operations, which treat them as singular wholes. Message threads or entire conversations are often rich enough to benefit from this sort of up-close and microscopic dissection. However, the risk with treating too much data in a totalizing way is that we begin to analyze it by seeing its parts, thus tearing it apart and ripping it apart from its context.

Totalizing means focusing deeply on the whole of the data, contemplating every element of that whole, and charting where it leads. In an article called 'Click to connect', I spend considerable page space analyzing a single post from a *Star Trek* group and showing its many intersections (Kozinets, 2006b: 283–5). In the first edition of this book, I do the same thing with a coffee newsgroup post of 121 words, and provide it as an exercise in hermeneutic interpretation (Kozinets, 2010: 121–5). Following this tradition, I provide the exercise in Box 13.5, which I draw from the online dataset on the YouTube EPCOT utopian comments. I leave it to you to conduct your own totalizing interpretation of these two fragments: one, a 166-word comment, provided as text; and the other, a short reply, provided as a pseudonymized screenshot. As well, you should feel free to continue to practice totalizing interpretations of particular interesting pieces of data from the dataset you collected for your own project, following the suggestions in Box 13.5.

13.5

TOTALIZING SOME DEEP UTOPIAN DATA (PRACTICE EXERCISE)

Here are two fragments of data from the downloadable dataset (available at https://study.sagepub.com/researchmethods/research-methods/kozinets-netnography-3e). The first is a quote, with the text provided, but no other context (including no poster name). The second is an image of a screenshot of a reply to a comment (also taken out of context, and pseudonymized, but with the form and images of the post intact). The spreadsheet contains many such intriguing examples.

Fragment 1:

The 'flaws' in Epcot are only an issue if the city is capitalist, this would work incredibly well as a large-scale communist city. The multilayered structure and large-scale climate control could easily be utilized to grow produce which isn't native and couldn't normally be grown in the region, creating an abundance of exotic foods for trade with other areas, combine that with the focus on advanced industry and this could be incredibly successful with oversight by anyone reasonably competent with the right goals in mind. Those within the city would have an incredible abundance so the usual stresses created by executing communism on a large scale wouldn't be issues, and the unique perks of this construction would allow the commonwealth to trade for anything they couldn't produce themselves. Communism works quite well when there is abundance, capitalism only lives in scarcity. It likely wasn't a lack of vision that prevented Epcot, but rather wealthy capitalists who were wise enough to know where it would lead.

Fragment 2:

Dionysos Jones 17 months ago
It sounds like a communist approach to capitalism. Central planning but to the benefit of industry.

👍 1 👎 REPLY

Instructions: Following the guidance provided in Box 13.6, as well as the additional detail conveyed in this subsection, create a totalizing interpretation of each of these two posts, one at a time. Then, compare your totalizing interpretations for the two fragments. If you are in a classroom, or working in a workshop situation, it may be interesting to compare and discuss your totalizing interpretation with someone else. What do you learn from the comparison about how interpretation works?

TRANSLATING

Decoding Translation/Interpretation

This section discusses translation as a form of movement between the world of data and the world of theory. It opens with a discussion of transportation, suggesting that translation requires a familiarity not merely with one world, but with many. Becoming familiar with the many different social worlds that fragments of data touch upon is to assume a comparative stance and draw on the collective works of science. Science crosses between different realms, and employing the notion of narrative transportation allows us to see the links between our own reading of scientific literatures and the necessary movement between worlds that our interpretation requires. In translation, data and theory find themselves together because they are interpreted by the research's narrator(s): you. You bring the data and theory together into an integrative arrangement through your act of translation. You broker that interpretive harmony and arrange that partnership. Translation is an operation of interpretation, then, that attempts to locate particular elements of empirical data and match them with corresponding strands of scientific abstraction, it constructs theoretical relationships in the process forming a coherent text that unites the two. It is the conscious, deliberate movement between the worlds of data and theory, weaving the parts into a coherent and, eventually, a holistic interpretation.

Translation as Transport

The translation of actual languages is very difficult to do well. Some ancient languages, such as Olmec writing, have never been fully translated, and probably never will be. Those gaps occur because the skillful translation of one language into another is not simply a transformation of words and phrases into different sounds, but a type of movement between two divergent social and cultural frameworks or ways of seeing the world. Translation is transformation from one worldview, with its rich histories, traditions, and customs, to another. Translation is temporal, geographic, bodily, gestural, and metamorphic, because language is.

Translation, then, is transportation. In the act of translation, Hermes is everywhere language is – listening to our thoughts, negotiating with the gods for us, helping us close that deal or get a better price at the market. He is the god not just of language, but also of travel. Not just of travel, but also of all kinds of exchange, wealth, and luck in life. Hermes is also the messenger god who transmits your prayer requests between the human world and the Olympian realms of the gods, as well as the emissary who escorts you, individually, to the underworld after you leave your body. Hermes is the god of astrology and astronomy as well. He teaches us about the many different worlds in our universe, even as he moves effortlessly between them.

Hermes does not simply translate, he transports. His priestesses and priests were the original mediums of narrative transportation. The psychologist Richard Gerrig (1993) coined and developed the term 'narrative transportation' as a metaphor for the experience of travel that people gain during reading a novel, as they detach from their own world and become imaginatively engrossed in the story's imaginary world. We can think of a similar operation happening during interpretation in netnography, except that we are being transported from data worlds of communication, words, images, socialities, and online experience and phenomena into the narrative worlds of abstract social science. Box 13.6 builds upon prior exercises to lead you through the translation operation.

13.6

TRANSLATING YOUTUBE COMMENTS INTO THEORY (PRACTICE EXERCISE)

Go back to Box 13.5, which you completed in the last subsection.

Look at the two fragments of data, and your interpretation of them. What are the key scientific constructs and contexts that your totalizing interpretation led you towards?

Investigate those key scientific constructs and contexts. Deepen your understanding of them. Nuance them with some reading and scholarship.

Now, return to the dataset and interpretation.

- Do the additional theoretical nuances add depth to your interpretation of the data?
- Do they contradict it?
- Do they reveal interesting elements you may have missed in your initial round of totalizing interpretation?

Repeat as needed. Continue to investigate theory, develop new perspectives from it, bring those to the data, reconceptualize your understanding of the data using your nuanced theoretical perspective, and so on, iteratively.

Translating Emic into Etic

With a research question asked, data collected, and results to find, the differences between deduction and induction can become blurry. The interpretive researcher's mind is filled with abstract theories and empirical data. During interpretive procedures, we are like Hermes, shooting back and forth between those two worlds: the Olympian realms of theory, with their abstract, distanced objectivity and the messy subjective human world of data, interests, lies, social media scruffiness, and our own pre-understandings, interests, and predilections.

Using the suffixes of the terms 'phonemic' (the significant sounds in a language) and 'phonetic' (the cross-cultural notation used to capture that sound), the linguist and anthropologist Kenneth Pike described the difference between the way native speakers use their own language and the way outside researchers conceptualized that language (Franklin, 1996). The notion of phonetic sound has the idea of cross-cultural comparison, and thus translation from one lived human context to another, built into it. Phonetics is also useful not just for studying one language at a time, and for comparing languages with each other, but for understanding the entire human phenomenon of language itself.

Pike (1967: 37) established that the 'etic viewpoint studies behavior as from outside of a particular system', the 'emic viewpoint results from studying behavior as from inside the system'. The movement from emic to etic is a type of transportation from being inside of a particular system to being outside of it (McCutcheon, 1999). What this means in the linguistic or anthropological sense is that learning a culture or language well or, for instance, gaining expert status at a particular social media activity or in a particular online context (e.g., gaming, building followers, discussion board soapboxing) is insufficient until that understanding has also become etic.

In ethnography, our data is cultural and linguistic, and in netnography this cultural data has become textual and digital. But the task is the same: form a coherent text that weaves together strands of theory with matching threads of data. According to the anthropologist Marvin Harris (1979), who criticized what he saw as Pike's emic bias, it is not enough to possess cultural experience and even expertise. What is required is to be able to translate that experience into thorough discussions of it that can systematically compare it to other related experiences. To do this, we need to have familiarity not only with the empirical world and phenomenon, with a particular language and customs, but we also need a deep familiarity with the abstract world that studies similar phenomena: the world of science and its precise, methodical, generalizations. Translation translates data into the finding of science, as Box 13.7 illustrates.

TRANSLATING YOUR DATASET FROM EMIC IN ETIC LANGUAGE (PROJECT EXERCISE)

13.7

Follow the directions from Box 13.6 above, except for this exercise use data and totalizing interpretation from your own netnographic project.

TURTLING

Systems-within-Systems within Interpretation-within-Interpretation

An Enlightened Master states to an audience of worshippers that the Earth is actually supported on the back of a tiger. After this remarkable claim, someone sassy and disrespectful calls out from the audience,

What's supporting the tiger?

The tiger is standing on an elephant.

And what's the elephant standing on?

A turtle.

A turtle. And what, may we ask, is the turtle standing on?

 At this point, the Enlightened Master smiles as if he has reached the punchline of a joke.

Yes, you may ask. The first turtle stands on another turtle.

And what does that turtle stand on? Another turtle?

asks the audacious follower, now beginning to see the pattern.

'Yes. Exactly. And what does that turtle stand on?

 The Master asks the heretical student, who is now, through the questioning, becoming enlightened himself.

Turtles. More turtles and more ...

The student, whose eyes begin to sparkle now with their own inner light, says

I can see them. It is turtles upon turtles upon turtles, to infinity. Turtles all the way down.

Defining Turtling

On June 19, 2006, Supreme Court Justice Antonin Scalia told an Easternized variant of the story with a 'guru' in *Rapanos* v. *United States*. Often the tale is attributed to a little old lady with strange views who, after a cosmology lecture confronts the great psychologist William James with her story of turtles on even bigger turtles' backs. Stephen Hawking and Clifford Geertz both wrote versions of the story. It also seems to have inspired Dr. Seuss to have written the story of Yertle the Turtle, about a king turtle who piles onto the stacked backs of his turtle subjects, trying to reach the moon. Folk songs and tales are filled with recognitions of the same contextual complexity related in this alluring metaphor. Often, they are told in cumulative forms of songs that begin with small animals and have larger and larger-sized animals, or forces, eating or affecting them. For instance, in the American nursery rhyme 'I Know an Old Lady who Swallowed a Fly' an old woman swallows a fly, then a spider, then a bird, and so on.

The popular 'turtles all the way down' metaphor is the source of the name of an interpretive procedure: turtling. What does it mean to take this story and turn it into a set of operations for qualitative data interpretation? It means connecting the holistic focal concept with its own context in a way that broadens our understanding. Thus, turtling is an interpretive act in which the researcher considers the organic system of concepts in which the focal concept is embedded in order to provide a more comprehensive conceptual explanation.

Turtling Interpretation in Netnography

Social media posts are fragments. They are messages that are also parts of holistic systems spread across every human domain. But we look at those fragments as wholes. Where did they come from? We will never completely understand even a fraction of a fragment in all of its complexity because, like the tiger on the elephant on the turtles upon turtles, the contexts that led to that fragment's existence are bound up in contexts within contexts. In the public social media data we seek and find, in the interactive conversations and interviews we conduct, in the deep data we collect in our journals, we find all of the different aspects of contemporary cultural life: social life, individual life, celebrity life, daily life, family life, national life, city life. They are stacked upon one another like turtles standing on each other's shells, using communication technologies that connect them to one another and interlink them into social and cultural systems. But though these many connecting interlinkages are not entirely distinct, they are still visible in the shards of the broken holograph we hold up to the light.

When we look at the patterns of our social media data in turtling operations, we must start by holding the telescope backwards to see the shifting kaleidoscopic grains of paths not taken. What does the entire interpretation look like, when viewed from afar? When we find utterances, or patterns of utterance, or conversational schemas, we can ask: where did they come from? what came before them? what made them possible? who else does this? where does this lead? what is the bigger view?

Turtling may be considered hermeneutic because of its connection to Hermes through the telling of tales of interconnection, and through Hermes' connection to tortoises. It is also closely related to Deleuzoguattarian assemblage theories and Koestler's related notions of holons and holarchic systems. Turtling is, in part, an attempt to consider all of these unchosen patterns. Possible assemblages, all the way down. Thus, turtling creates a conceptual space, a type of translocation beyond a particular context, that transmits interpretive frames to different theory-data worlds modulated by the researcher, such as histories, cultures, societies, fictions, alternative paradigms, and so on. Turtling breaks the boundaries of existing ways of understanding phenomena and data in the quest for new metaphors and abductive moments of unexpected connection that can bring about new insights.

Turtling requires time and patience. Like a tortoise moving, it is time-consuming but sturdy and thorough. Turtling operations will wait while you explore one more context. While you tunnel down one more conceptual labyrinth. While you expand the context and see if it fits the data better than the old one. If it helps you develop a more compelling explanation. If it brings a deeper understanding to your data interpretation. Like all of these interpretive and analytical procedures, turtling operations are better experienced in a hands-on manner than merely read about. Box 13.8 leads you through one.

13.8 MACROSCOPICALLY TURTLING YOUR INTERPRETATION

You may perform these exercises with either the practice dataset, or with your own netnographic project's data.

Exercise 1: Anchoring on Identity

The meaning in any network is a set of complex nested systems – things that have meaning are special and important, and they matter. They are things like identities – like being a German, a transperson, a teen, a Catholic. Those identities matter. They are all over the data. Find them.

- Now that you have a focus on particular identities in your dataset, telescope out, backwards from them.
- Pan backwards so we can see the whole context of the shot. What scene is playing out here in social media? What wider elements of the context, not included yet in your analysis and interpretation, might have made it happen in this way?
- What other aspects of life is your interpretation of identity connected into? For example, if the data shows people talking about their pride in being

American and capitalist, what other social elements does that discussion connect into and what higher-order systems does it connect the conversants into?

- What are the expressive and material connections facilitating and linking into the particular identity-related social media exchanges you are examining?

Exercise 2: Broadening the View

Starting point: your prior analysis or interpretation. State it as succinctly, but as thoroughly as you can. The totalizing interpretation is helpful because it encourages you to conceptualize your interpretation as a whole:

- Now, with this focus on the organic and holistic concepts established by the researcher or research team, zoom out. Try to discern the wider social, cultural, historical and other contexts in which this phenomenon and its concepts are embedded.
- What other concepts might connect to certain specific core concepts in the data and/or theory?
- Which concept do those concepts stand upon? What fields and assumptions do they depend upon to stay sturdy?

TROUBLEMAKING

Questioning Assumptions and Tipping Sacred Cows

Sacred cows are ideas, customs, or institutions that are held by those who believe them to be above criticism. Troublemaking focuses the act of interpretation as much on the questioning of sacred cows as it does on the querying of data and theory. Specifically, troublemaking refers to the questioning and critique of underlying and taken-for-granted notions in the theoretical and empirical realm, as well as in your own interpretation of it, conducted in the service of developing a more inclusive, important, robust, accurate, and morally justifiable interpretation as well as, perhaps, trying to help inspire positive change in the world.

Troublemaking is a hermeneutic act because Hermes himself was a troublemaker. When he was one day old, he stole out of his crib and took sacred cows from his brother, Apollo (he later slaughtered two of them). When a very angry Apollo figured out what he had done and confronted him, Hermes lied, pretending to be a mere baby. After Apollo called him out, Hermes bargained with his brother and gave him a lyre (made out of a tortoise shell, of course), a new musical instrument, which appeased him. This single story about Hermes teaches how language, trickery, performance, exchange, trade, the kidnapping and murder of sacred cows, and much else, are connected. It also reveals how interpretation involves constant questioning, because tricksters and liars are everywhere, even among the gods. Interpretation is an imprecise art and an inexact science, when done well. But it is more than this. It is troublemaking. A risky adventure to steal and slaughter your brother's sacred cows.

Critical Science and Interpretation

There has long been a critical function or aspect to qualitative research that comes from questioning the underpinnings of theoretical concepts and social acts. Norman Denzin, who coined and developed the integrative research term 'triangulation' in 1970, now argues that research which seeks to 'change the world' by finding 'new third ways through and around obstacles to social justice in a neoliberal world' is more important than 'mixed methods talk about designs and typologies' (Denzin, 2012: 86). In fact, he argues that 'Qualitative research scholars have an obligation to change the world, to engage in ethical work that makes a positive difference'. This work will 'confront the facts of injustice' and 'make the injustices of history visible and hence open to change and transformation'. If we are to interpret Denzin's injunctions, bringing this critical or guerrilla scholarship into netnography means that we must interpret social media data so as to make 'the murky, tragic facts of history' in that data present. We also are tasked with interpreting the likely future of the social phenomena we investigate, in order to unmake the present. An objective of this work is to build what Denzin calls 'pedagogies of hope'.

Troublemaking Applications and Examples

Troublemaking is a way to disassemble theory in the service of building new theory and thus it is intimately related to the destabilizing assemblage theory acts of deterritorialization and reterritorialization. When you question or explore the meaning, significance, valence, or taken-for-grantedness of a particular sacred cow, you are opening conceptual territory by delinking enunciations and forms of scientific expression. Usually, these epistemic disconnections occur as researchers move between research paradigms. For example, feminist or gender studies scholars focus on excluded voices, deconstruction, praxis, emotion, lived experience, and much more. Mendes (2015) used netnography along with a number of other methods to explore the relation between postfeminism, activism, and media in the third-wave Canadian anti-rape culture movement called 'SlutWalk'.

Critical theory or Neo-Marxian scholars use emancipatory theories, class, race, commodity fetishism, and many other constructs. Sandlin (2007) uses an emancipatory frame of consumer education to critically examine how the posters to a magazine's online social media site engage in a critical education in the wild that helps them understand and negotiate their role in the world as consumers. Bertilsson (2014) finds that netnography can be an excellent tool for conducting critical management research online.

Participants in netnography often reflect their own taken-for-granted assumptions about the world and how it is or should be (for example, by posting that 'socialism is the opposite of freedom'). These assumptions can be exposed and questioned as an operation of the troublemaking interpretation. Troublemaking need not limit itself to questioning theory and theorists – it can also query the participants and their data.

Queer theory tends to use reflexivity, praxis, accountability, and deconstructive methods to reveal exclusions based on gender and sexual preference. Svensson (2015) conducted a netnography of political forum discussions occurring on the Swedish queer social media platform Qruiser, analyzing it as a form of rude and antagonistic entertainment. Several of these paradigmatic frames are also related to the notions of intersectionality and intersectional netnography already explored in Chapters 4 and 5. And, if you are familiar with any of my empirical research, you are probably aware that I like to question assumptions and ask big questions. What do fans mean when they say that media texts are their 'religion'? Can consumers actually escape the market? Why is food porn considered pornographic – what's the link? Asking these short, somewhat naïve, but undeniably macro questions of empirical phenomena can be simultaneously frustrating and productive, and it is one way that we can engage in troublemaking. Boxes 13.9 and 13.10 offer two different exercises that can be performed using the practice dataset as well as by applying the dataset you have collected.

The dynamic and expanding world of social media offers us many fundamental questions to explore using troublemaking operations. What does it mean to be a mother, a soldier, a consumer, a friend, in the digital age of the social? What does play, or sex, or freedom, or youth, mean now? Making the familiar strange, holding onto the very profound strangeness that is technology, technological being, technological sociality and consociality in the current time is a key netnographic injunctive in an age where we rapidly acclimate to massive technocultural transformation. Through troublemaking, and with turtling, translating, totalizing, talenting, and theming, you will interpret these elements on your way to finally communicating your research findings to an audience.

TROUBLEMAKING WITH THEORY

13.9

You may perform this exercise with either the practice dataset, or with your own netnographic project's data.

Choose a particular frame from which to critically interpret theory. The theory that you criticize could be the theory you are using to analyze your data. Or it might be another theory or even a guiding assumption that is prevalent and has gone largely under-examined in your field.

(Continued)

The frame you adopt could be from: deconstruction, narrative inquiry, feminist theory, gender studies, ethnic studies, religious studies, Neo-Marxism, critical theory, cultural studies, queer theory, or any of a number of other critical theories:

- What concepts, ideas, and connections in the theory are sacred cows?
- What sacred cows in the theory deserve to be tipped? What does not fit well with reality? What doesn't fit well with your dataset?
- Do any of these unquestioned theories disempower people? Are there particular groups or categories of people who are disempowered?
- How might you formulate a more robust and ethical theory to encompass both the reality of the data, and the need to encourage social justice and its awareness?

13.10 TROUBLEMAKING IN THE WORLD

You may perform this exercise with either the practice dataset, or with your own netnographic project's data:

- Who is represented in your netnography? What do you know about them? Are any groups or types of people excluded? Can you tell from the discourse which groups or types of people are excluded? Are any beliefs or opinions excluded? How are these beliefs and opinions excluded?
- What do the people who are speaking on social media in your phenomenon take for granted? What are some of the invisible or taken-for-granted concepts, ideas, or power relationships? Are any of them morally problematic to you?
- What are some of the consequences of the invisibility of these excluded people, taken-for-granted concepts, ideas, and power relationships? Do they affect people's equity? Do they affect their access to resources? Do they alter their quality of life in other ways? Are there particular groups or categories of people who are especially disempowered?
- How might your theoretical formulation and writing lead to a more robust and ethical depiction of the phenomenon?
- How might other activities, such as discussion, teaching, public speaking, publication, or public intellectual activity, help you engage with the social justice issues raised by your research and its transgressive troublemaking interpretation?

CHAPTER SUMMARY

Interpretation discovers deeper meaning in collected and analyzed data. This chapter opened with a detailed explanation of the nature and meaning of interpretation. Then, it followed with an introduction and description of the uses of hermeneutic interpretation in netnography. The introduction and application of assemblage theory followed. After these introductions, you became acquainted with the six operations of interpretation in netnography: theming, talenting, totalizing, translating, turtling, and troublemaking. The subsequent subsections described and illustrated these six operations. You learned that theming is the operation that reassembles the component pieces of an abstractly analyzed phenomenon, (re)creating a new conceptual whole. Talenting produces theming interpretations using a variety of forms of artistic expression. Totalizing develops the meanings of the reassembled conceptual whole. Translating operations move the researcher back and forth between worlds of data and theory. Turtling operations reconnect data to the context, and vice versa. Finally, troublemaking operations critique underlying and taken-for-granted notions in the data, the phenomenon, and the theoretical field. Throughout the chapter, numerous explanations and exercises were provided to help guide you through the process of data interpretation on the way to developing insightful research findings to communicate to other scholars.

KEY READINGS

Belk, Russell, Eileen Fischer, and Robert V. Kozinets (2013) *Qualitative Marketing and Consumer Research*. London: Sage.

DeLanda, Manuel (2016) *Assemblage Theory*. Edinburgh: Edinburgh University Press.

Denzin, Norman K. (2012) 'Triangulation 2.0', *Journal of Mixed Methods Research*, 6(2): 80–8.

Mantzavinos, C. (2016) 'Hermeneutics', in Edward N. Zalta (ed.), *The Stanford Encyclopedia of Philosophy* (Winter 2016 Edition). Available at https://plato.stanford.edu/archives/win2016/entries/hermeneutics/ (last accessed 28 June 2019).

Wolcott, Harry (1994) *Transforming Qualitative Data*. Thousand Oaks, CA: Sage.

14

COMMUNICATING: PRESENTING AND PUBLISHING YOUR NETNOGRAPHY

CHAPTER OVERVIEW

First, this chapter will discuss some general guidelines for writing research and targeting particular research outlets. Then, the chapter will present the method-embedded research communication triangle, which will identify four key elements that must be communicated to others through the research: (1) the method of netnography; (2) the netnographic data operations; (3) the netnographic dataset; and (4) the data. The chapter will describe each of the four elements in turn, providing examples and exercises to illustrate important points. Methods must be seen as legitimate and justified. The communication of method is a rhetorical act in which strategies differ depending upon the audience, for example, whether netnography is relatively new or relatively established in this research field and outlet. Next, operations must describe, explain, and justify the particular procedures employed in this research project. Netnography currently has 25 different research operations grouped into three distinct categories of data collection and two categories of data integration operations. These operations facilitate netnographic researchers' unprecedented ability to systematically conduct qualitative social media research adapted to particular contexts, and also an unrivaled ability to communicate it to readers and fellow academics. Readers will be curious about your dataset, and you should inform them about its characteristics, including how much and what types of traces, when, and why this data was collected. Datasets, like all forms of research communication, appear more legitimate the more they are adapted to the particular representational conventions of the field and outlet to which they are targeted. Data will also need to be presented in the communication of your netnography. There are ethical concerns with data presentation in netnography that can be addressed by an appropriate application of anonymizing, cloaking, and fabrication procedures. Data is also represented for evidential, rhetorical, and discursive purposes, and sometimes for aesthetic ones. The chapter will provide numerous examples of different types of netnographic data from a variety of published netnographies, including visual and other non-textual data. The final section of this chapter will discuss some of the hallmarks of excellence in published netnographic research.

RESEARCH COMMUNICATION

Communicating your research is a culminative act in which the labors of your questioning, data collection, analysis, and interpretation operations are blended with the concepts, authors, works, and theories of particular fields, and then shared in a manner that is adapted to the conventions of your field and informational medium. By using the word 'communicating' rather than 'writing' or 'presenting', I am not limiting your research representation to text or words. Indeed, communicating your research representation encompasses the entire process of bringing your research to different audiences, whether in the form of a short social media post, an interview with a journalist, a spoken word conference presentation, a classroom discussion consisting of PowerPoint slides and verbal remarks, or a graphical or animated illustration that might be shared online. However, we must recognize that the core medium for informational scientific exchange is currently, and is likely to remain for some time, the written form. The key format for global scientific representation is text written into books, book chapters, and journal articles – usually written in English and usually published by presses headquartered in the United States and the United Kingdom. Although not focused exclusively upon this format, it is for the creation of written peer-reviewed netnographic works for these media that this chapter is most directly intended.

There are a number of helpful books on the general topic of how to write academic work in the social sciences (e.g., Devlin, 2017; Golden-Biddle and Locke, 2007; Holliday, 2016; Silvia, 2015; Thody, 2006; Wolcott, 2013). For those interested in a more universal introduction to, and development of, the topic of academic writing, I suggest consulting one of these useful guides. They offer advice about the careful planning required to write good academic research papers, the often-disembodied voice of research writing, the need to anticipate and correct potential problems with papers before submitting them, the focusing power of simplifying practices such as working titles, and the need for credibility and candidness in research accounts, as well as many other elements of this complex process. These are general guidelines applicable to the writing of research in any field, about any topic, and using any method.

CHOOSING AND UNDERSTANDING YOUR RESEARCH COMMUNICATION OUTLET

14.1

The first step in writing is understanding, and the first step in understanding is research. Before you can communicate appropriately to a particular research outlet, you need to understand that outlet. Thus, your first step in writing is to choose an outlet. What research outlet are you targeting? To which audience do you intend to communicate this research?

To acquaint yourself with the communicative characteristics of this outlet, go and investigate it. If it is a conference, read the proceedings. If it is a

(Continued)

publisher, look up their book lists, and read some sample chapters. If it is a journal, browse the last year or thereabouts of publications. Examine the titles of articles, books, proceedings, or chapters. Become familiar with the types of research being communicated. Look at the types of methods featured. Knowing your target outlet marks the beginning of your planning for academic writing.

RESEARCH WRITING FOR RIGOROUS NETNOGRAPHY

The purpose of this chapter is not to provide general advice but specific advice. It aims to help you in the specific task of effectively and efficiently writing up netnographic research for publication in a way that is rigorous. To assist in this task, we can adapt Kinneavy's (1980) communication triangle, a helpful semiotic reader response-type diagram that considers the role of the text as created by the relationship between the reader (or research audience), the writer (or researcher), and the context. For the purposes of this chapter, I will define rigorous research writing as a representational effort that appropriately situates the output of a scientific inquiry in accord with the conventions of a particular research outlet. I have followed this general principle of research writing rigour to develop Kinneavy's (1980) ideas into a new type of method-embedded communication triangle. Figure 14.1 presents a method-embedded research communication triangle that considers the act of effectively writing (or speaking, presenting, or illustrating) about research as the appropriate matching of the research communication context (i.e., the particular research field, the paradigm within the field, the theories being utilized, and the publication outlet), the representation of the method through particular data operations, the presentation of the particular dataset collected and used, and the presentation of data within the research findings. As the arrows within and between the sides of the research triangle diagram indicate, clear connections between each element – the research contexts of publication and readership, the representation of data operations, and the depiction of the dataset and also of individual instances of data – are required for the communication of the research to be seen as a methodologically rigorous and effective scientific communication by evaluators and readers.

Extending this triangle to the current context of netnography suggests that, in order to achieve methodological rigour, there are four key elements that must be communicated to audience members through the writing of the research. Those four key elements are: (1) the method of netnography, including conveying an understanding about netnography, its basis, and its applicability to the current project; (2) the netnographic

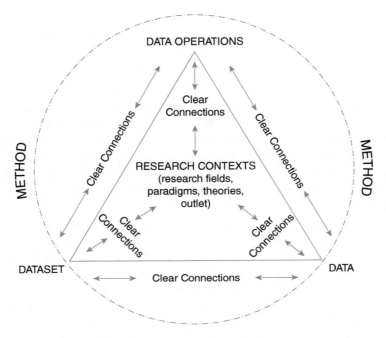

Figure 14.1 Method-embedded research communication triangle

data operations, which encompass and justify the procedures used, and what, where, when, and for how long the study took place; (3) the netnographic dataset, which overviews, describes, and justifies the data collected in the project; and (4) the data, which provides actual samples or excerpts from data in the context of the overall research presentation. A more detailed development of the guidelines and best practices for approaching a contextually and methodologically appropriate communication about these four key elements – method, operations, dataset, and data – forms the context for the subsections of this chapter that follow.

STUDYING HOW PUBLISHED NETNOGRAPHIES COMMUNICATE

14.2

For this exercise, you are required to look up and closely examine the communication strategies of one or more published netnographies in any field. The idea is to look up netnographic research in general and choose a few published works in fields that you consider close to your own. The best search engine to use for this task is usually Google Scholar. After finding and examining the work, please answer the following questions:

(Continued)

- How is netnography introduced? What terms are used? What works are cited? To which topical areas is the method linked? What communicative techniques are used to legitimize the use of the method and make it seem credible?
- Are specific data operations or research procedures described? Which ones? How are they described? Are they connected to topics, paradigms, or research fields? What level of detail is offered beyond the generic terms of 'participation', 'observation', 'interview', and 'fieldnotes'? Is information provided about particular sites and lengths of time? How much detail is given about data collection, analysis, and interpretation? What terms and citations are used? Are ethical procedures invoked, and if so, how?
- What information is provided about the dataset collected in the netnography? How is it presented? Is some description of its contents offered in a table, or in the text? How much qualitative and quantitative detail is provided? What quantities of data seem normal in this field?
- How is netnographic data presented? How much is provided? What kinds (visual, textual, links to audiovisual and auditory)? How long are the verbata? How rich is the data? How penetrating and detailed is the cultural analysis performed on the data? How are data sources cited, pseudonymized, or anonymized?
- What is your overall conclusion about how netnographic research is effectively communicated in this published work?

METHOD

Effectively Communicating about Netnography

Methods need to be seen as legitimate and justified. Although it was introduced into consumer research in 1996, and was based on cultural studies research methods that had been in publication since the early 1990s, for researchers in many fields, netnography still *seems* new. Science is a slow-moving institution. Thus, when communicating about your research, you must make arguments about why netnography is the right method for conducting *this particular piece of research*. Because netnography is used in multiple academic fields, in different types of journals, for a variety of purposes, and is also often combined with other research approaches, you will have considerable latitude in how to communicate this methodological orientation in your research. However, there are certain patterns of communicating about netnography as a rigorous methodological approach that may be helpful for you to know and understand as you begin the process of fashioning your analyzed and interpreted data, and submitting it for consideration as a piece of scientific knowledge. Readers must gain a rudimentary understanding about netnography, what it is, what legitimate fields it connects to, and why it is applicable to the problem or question at hand. This subsection considers how to communicate each of these particulars.

We can usefully think about communicating in scientific outlets as engaging in a particular form of rhetoric. Rhetoric is a language-based disciplinary field that is concerned with the role of logic, composition, style, and argument in persuading an audience to accept claims as trustworthy (O'Connor, 1996). As Locke and Golden-Biddle (1997: 1026) assert, 'as soon as scientists frame ideas for presentation to an identified audience, they are engaging in rhetoric'. Scientific rhetoric encompasses not only the content of scientific claims, but also the ways that they are supported and rendered credible in academic texts. There are a variety of different rhetorical practices identified in prior research about scientific communication (e.g., McCloskey, 1985 writes about the use of rhetoric in the field of economics). These rhetorical practices seek to enhance the credibility of the arguments developed in scientific texts (Locke and Golden-Biddle, 1997: 1026).

Communicating about any research method, including netnography, is similarly a rhetorical act of scientific writing. It follows certain rules that adapt the description and justification of a particular research method to the conventions followed by the members of a particular research field. Those rhetorical conventions tend to be different depending upon whether netnography is new or established in those particular fields. In some fields, such as psychology, organizational behavior, sociology, anthropology, and education, netnography is still quite new. In other fields, such as travel and tourism, consumer research and marketing, or communication and cultural studies, netnography is an established method. The approach to communicating the method is different in each case because the context of the research communication differs. Box 14.3 encourages you to closely examine your specific intended research context in order to understand how it communicates about method.

UNDERSTANDING EXTANT METHOD COMMUNICATION IN YOUR INTENDED RESEARCH OUTLET

14.3

Examine an information source related to your intended research outlet – whether it is the proceedings for a conference, the publication list of a book publisher, or the articles of an academic journal:

- What sorts of qualitative, interpretive, or constructivist research are featured?
- Are there ethnographies published in the outlet? Are there interviews? Are there any online ethnographies or specific forms of online ethnographies such as virtual ethnographies, digital ethnographies, or netnographies?

(Continued)

- How do they describe their methods?
- How do they justify the use of particular methods?
- What sort of rhetorical arguments do they put forward in order to make the use of this method credible?
- What types of other work do they cite in the process?

Strategies for New and Experienced Audiences

When netnography is still quite new, authors generally find it helpful to emphasize its origins in ethnography. Because ethnography is an established and legitimate process in most fields, many authors will begin their introductions of netnography by linking ethnography to netnography. For example, in a study that applies netnography to technological forecasting, Zeng et al. (2019: 208) write that 'Netnography is a qualitative research method [used] in order to observe and monitor OCs [online communities] during a specific time frame. It has its origin in ethnography.'

Similarly, netnography can be connected to a research field by reference to the prevailing use of constructivist or interpretive paradigms. In this rhetorical strategy, netnography benefits from the established tradition of qualitative research inquiry that cuts across the social sciences. Publishing their work on Chinese backpackers' group dynamics in the *Annals of Tourism Research*, Cai et al. (2019: 123) begin by positioning their research as 'underpinned by the interpretivist paradigm' and a combination of multi-sited ethnography, mobile ethnography, and netnography. They describe the combination of physical ethnography and netnography as productive, a research strategy that allows them to engage more fully in their participants' experience of backpacking journeys by following them 'across both physical and virtual spaces', covering Chinese backpackers' European travel, 'but also multiple virtual locations, such as travel discussion forums, blogs and social networking sites'. Citing Hine (2000: 123–4) as well as the second edition of this book, they describe netnography as a method 'designed to gain a reflexive understanding of online phenomena of culture and communication beyond physical spaces', and something which was conducted throughout the research process, responding to the various needs of participants to plan, conduct, and reflect upon their travel experiences using different types of social media platforms and their varying affordances.

Another way to connect netnography to research fields is to link the approach to the rise in importance of online or digital communication and its many effects on society, including the topics and areas served by the particular academic field being addressed. For example, in their general article overviewing the use of netnography in tourism research, Tavakoli and Wijesinghe (2019: 48) discuss the importance of analyzing 'cybercultures'. There are, as they note, many approaches that have helped scholars to understand online cultures – and netnography is one of those methods. Topically, netnography is particularly suited to studies involving various types of public discourses using social media, which have gained increasing relevance throughout almost every area of society. For example, Conoscenti (2019) was interested in fear discourses and studied them in the context of online conversations about Brexit and the European Union. Peeroo (2019) studied the conversations that customers initiated on retailers' Facebook pages in order to classify them and explore their implications for the design of information systems. The key implication of this type of positioning should argue that topics relating to online experience and sociality, its use, impacts, and effects, can be illuminated through a rigorous examination of public discourse or other interactions on social media. These are all legitimate reasons for using netnography.

Another common strategy for asserting netnographic rigour will point out the commonality of netnographic methods and provide a dense web of citations showing that there exist a number of important precedents to legitimize the current use of netnography. For example, Tavakoli and Wijesinghe (2019) write that 'many scholars from various disciplines have acknowledged the importance of this methodology (Bartl, Kannan, & Stockinger, 2016; Bengry-Howell, Wiles, Nind, & Crow, 2011; Nind, Wiles, Bengry-Howell, & Crow, 2013)'. There are also a growing number of articles that overview the use and utility of netnography in particular fields, such as tourism and travel or service research. If you are in a field that already possesses such an overview article, positioning your work in relation to it provides an efficient way to justify your choice of netnography.

OPERATIONS

Effectively Communicating Netnographic Procedures

Ethnography is a beguiling word. Its etymology indicates that it is concerned with writing about a people or culture. By using the similar form 'grapho', Greek for 'to write', netnography also indicates a fixation with written representation. But in this case the etymology of the word is deceiving. Both netnography and ethnography are not wholly concerned with writing about culture. They are also concentrated on *the active investigation of matters cultural*. Netnography, like ethnography, is a cultural research method, and its methods are composed of particular operations, procedures, or research practices. Thus, effective communication about your netnography must recognize that your audience wants to understand what was done (your research procedures or operations), where it was done (the data sites), why these particular procedures were followed, and how long it took. Those who are receiving the report of your research also want to know that the research was conducted in a manner that is legitimate, conducted in accord with appropriate ethical guidelines and requisite institutional approvals, based in an established literature, is internally consistent, and is sensitive to the research contexts in which it is situated. In short, they want assurances that its operations are rigorous.

What's in a name, like 'netnography', we might ask? As Chapter 1 explained, online ethnography is a generic term – and there have been plenty of other terms coined by researchers for this type of research. Thus, it makes sense that when researchers use a generic term for their research approach – such as 'online ethnography' or 'digital ethnography' – or an under-specified one – such as 'virtual ethnography' – they will often provide a detailed general accounting of the particular operations they have actually used. At the starter level are online ethnographers that offer generic, imprecise, and self-evident descriptions of an online ethnographic method as relating to combinations of participation, observation, and interview. For example, medical anthropologists Berning and Hardon (2019) explain how they use online, digital, or virtual ethnography (they use all three terms synonymously) to study how pharmacological risk and certainty are negotiated in online drug forums when users experiment with new psychoactive substances. They describe their methods as including in-depth interviews, as well as different varieties of passive and active observation. Explaining how adapted ethnographic methods allow them to penetrate the community of drug users, as well as to reflect their emic understandings, these authors offer broad and general descriptions of online ethnographic practice, such as using interviews and observation that lack the sort of methodological and operational detail that you can provide after having read this book.

One clear level of specificity that anyone can offer is to provide a clear accounting of specific data sites, as well as the length of time of engagement. For example, Saadatdoost et al. (2019) studied participant experiences in a Massive Open Online Course (MOOC), describing the research approach mainly as the naturalistic observation of a group. The article does offer some detail about the data collection, describing research operations that involved 60 online interviews, combined with fieldnote data extracted from 160 days of interaction. Are there a certain number of interviews, or a certain amount of time spent on immersive operation, which make a netnography legitimate? I do not believe there are any absolute numbers that indicate quality. There is no reason an excellent netnography could not be written without any interviews, or with only one or two excellent interviews. Similarly, a netnographer could spend a few days, a few weeks, a few months, or a few years immersed in data sites. The results of that immersion should be judged on the insights they produce, rather than on some time-centered accounting. Nonetheless, this chapter is about understanding conventions. In certain fields, certain standards and types of method description become standard. Even if one decides not to strictly adhere to them, it is always better to know what they are than to remain ignorant of them.

Clarity and Categorization of Research Practices

Communicating about particular research operations is a rhetorical strategy that legitimizes the use of a method by connecting it with the legitimacy of *separate types of research operations*, such as performing different types of observation, conducting interviews, and keeping journal notes. However, as these separate operations start to become collected into an aggregative form, whether as 'digital ethnography', 'social media ethnography', or 'netnography', they move towards an increasingly rigorous, applied, and contextualized research communication standard. For example, in their article on Chinese backpackers, Cai et al. (2019) clearly label their work as a netnography, and then offer a detailed and specific accounting of the research operations performed and why they were performed. The authors are careful to match up their use of Qyer.com and WeChat as netnographic data sites with a temporal sense of shadowing the planning, realization, and reflection of their participants' backpacking experiences. This level of precision in detailing netnographic research operations is significant, because it signals the maturing of the approach in fields that regularly publish netnographic research. Largely freed from the need to explain and justify the technique, researchers in these fields can spend time and page space providing a more precise explication of particular procedures, operations, sites, and data.

With this book, researchers now have a much wider spectrum of data collection, analysis, and interpretation operations to utilize and match to their particular fields, topics, skills, and other circumstances. As Chapters 8 to 13 detail, netnography is a set of 25 research practices grouped into three distinct categories of data collection and two categories of data integration operations. There is an immense amount of detail and flexibility in the way that netnographic researchers can apply, adapt, and combine the data-collection operations of investigation (simplification, search, scouting, selecting, and saving), interaction (interview, involvement, innovation, and informed consent), immersion (reconnoitering, recording, researching, and reflecting), and the data integration methods of analysis (collating, coding, combining, counting, and charting) and interpretation (theming, talenting, totalizing, translating, turtling, and troublemaking). As well, there is a language surrounding the detailed procedures to ensure compliance with the most rigorous current standards of research ethics practice. These operational and procedural terminologies, along with their definition and demonstration, provide a sophisticated vocabulary that is linked to existing practices and paradigms, and can be developed in much greater detail in future as various researchers focus upon and specialize in various operational elements of the process. They facilitate an unprecedented ability not just to conduct the operations of qualitative social media research that are highly adapted to the contingencies of field sites, topics, and academic fields of knowledge, but also to meaningfully communicate them to readers and fellow academics.

DATASET

Effectively Communicating Your Netnographic Dataset

The next key element for effectively communicating about your netnographic research is to provide appropriate information about your dataset. Readers will be curious about your dataset. They will want to know about the characteristics of the data you have collected in your netnography, such as how much data was collected, what types of data were collected, when the data was collected, and why this particular data was chosen. Additionally, and in order to follow rigorous and appropriate research ethics guidelines, certain legitimate procedures may need to be followed regarding communicating or cloaking the specific sources of the datasets.

You may have noticed that the word 'legitimate' appears a lot in this chapter. That is not an accident. The notion that research needs to be seen as legitimate and that there are particular strategies for achieving that legitimacy draws our attention to institutional theory. One of the founding precepts of institutional theory is that organizational actors adopt strategies of isomorphism, or assuming a similar form, in order to gain legitimacy in a process known as legitimation (DiMaggio and Powell, 1983). Applied to the communication of research in scientific outlets, institutional theory suggests that researchers can and do make their research look legitimate to particular outlets by having it resemble the research that is already considered to be legitimate by those particular outlets. In the case of netnography, we can perceive the working of legitimation in the communication contained in what is still the most exemplary single article about netnography, the netnographic Ur-text, if you will: Kozinets (2002a), an article published in a quantitative top-tier marketing journal called the *Journal of Marketing Research*. Marketing is already a field dominated by quantitative approaches, and is mostly focused on applied economics and psychological research. In that journal, this early netnography received decidedly mixed reviews. However, I adapted, or made the work more isomorphic with its surroundings. One of the ways I adapted this qualitative research technique to its quantitative surroundings was by introducing a quantitative accounting of the netnographic dataset of my admittedly 'brief netnography', provided as a short example of how a netnography was communicated and what it could reveal.

First, the data site and data procedures were described. These elements would fit into the communication of a data operations element which is described in a former section of this paper (but which, for convenience, I recount here). In Kozinets (2002a: 66–7), I began by quantitatively describing my data site, the newgroup <alt.coffee>. I quantified its traffic (approximately 75 posts per day), its rating (1,042 of all newsgroups), and its reach, which was that it was read by at least 55,939 people worldwide, a point I amplified in a footnote arguing that the 1995 statistics behind this number were probably closer to 100,000 when I conducted the data collection. By making these arguments, I was quantitatively arguing for the importance of the data site and also, by extension, its influence and representativeness of global coffee connoisseur culture. To handle sampling questions, I quoted statistics from surveys of the group indicating that posters were mainly male, well-educated, and had an average age of 48 years old. Then, after describing the data site, I turned to a quantitative description of the data procedures. I provided a discrete starting data: February 1998. I quantified the amount of time spent conducting the netnography: 33 months. I quantified the activities: reading several hundred messages.

After describing the data site and my data procedures in Kozinets (2002a: 66–7), I used quantitative information to describe the netnographic dataset. Although I had admitted previously to reading through 'several hundred' messages as part of the immersive netnographic data-collection operations, I then limited the amount of data in the dataset to 179 postings, and then further reduced this to 117 of the most important postings. These postings were described qualitatively, providing their titles and some narrative information about them, and also quantitatively, as comprising '198 double-spaced 12-point font pages, representing 117 postings containing 65 distinct e-mail addresses and user names (likely related to the number of people posting messages)' (p. 67). In later work, word counts replaced the more amorphous counting of pages.

As mentioned, the netnography provided in Kozinets (2002a) was described as 'a brief netnography' and intended as a short illustrative example. Thus, 117 postings comprising 198 double-spaced pages of data were never intended to stand as a benchmark of the typical quantity of netnographic data. In fact, the full-scale netnography I performed during my dissertation research was dramatically larger, over 550,000 words, which would equal approximately 2,200 of the double-spaced, 12-point font pages of the earlier reckoning. This amount of data is more typical of contemporary netnographies. For example, one of my most recent netnographies (Kozinets, 2019a) contained the table reproduced in Table 14.1 below, which accounts qualitatively for a research dataset including data scraped from three different YouTube data sites (and which may look familiar to those who have done the practice exercises in this book). The figures in Table 14.1 reveal that the total number of words collected from YouTube comments and replies was 487,988, a precise number described in the text as the amount of words that could be read in its totality, but which 'took some time and devotion. For comparison, Tolkien's entire *Lord of the Rings* trilogy has about 454,000 words, and Tolstoy's *War and Peace* has over 587,000 words.'

I want to emphasize that these examples are provided not because they are the only or right way to present a netnographic dataset. I present them because they are good examples of successful, published ways to communicate about a netnographic dataset in a way that fitted with the research context. Because I was publishing in a journal and in a field that favors quantification as a signal of scientific rigour, I quantified as many elements of my netnography as I could, including my descriptions of the collected data in the dataset. However, there is no magical number regarding how much data is appropriate, rigorous, or legitimate. The datasets in my published netnographies have ranged from about 50,000 words (for the brief netnography example included in Kozinets, 2002a) to over 500,000 words (in Kozinets, 2001). But there may be excellent reasons why netnographic datasets might be significantly larger than this, or smaller. The key to determining what is an appropriate size and type of dataset is how well you can communicate it as legitimate, rigorous, and credible in the scientific context you wish to present it. For some disciplines, you might not need to communicate or quantify it at all.

Table 14.1 Sample netnographic datasites and dataset descriptions (reproduced from Kozinets, 2019a)

YouTube Field Site name and brief description	Would EPCOT Have worked? (Rob Plays, fan video), abbreviated as WEHW?	The Choice is Ours (The Venus Project promotional video), abbreviated as TCi0	The Future We're Building—And Boring (Elon Musk TED Talk), abbreviated as TFWB&B	TOTALS
YouTube URL: https://www.youtube.com/	RWgKEI7Tfa8	Yb5ivvcTvRQ	zIwLWfaAg-8	
Running time of video (hours: minutes: seconds)	00:09:25	01:37:19	00:40:50	2:27:34
Total number of distinct comments and replies, at time of data collection	877	4,975	8,073	13,935
Total number of distinct user names	692	1,854	6,609	9,155
Total number of pages of single-space 12 point text	48	863	807	1,718
Total number of words in comments and replies	40,455	241,228	206,305	487,988

14.4 DATASETS IN RELEVANT PUBLISHED NETNOGRAPHIES

In Box 14.2, you were tasked with examining the general depiction of netnographic research in any particular published medium. For this exercise, you are required to look up and closely examine the communication strategies of one or more published netnographies *in the outlet you are considering targeting*. The best search engine to use for this task is usually Google Scholar. After examining this work, please answer the following questions about the presentation of the dataset:

- What information is provided about the dataset collected in the netnography? How is it presented? Is it offered in tabular form, or described in some way in the text?

- What exactly is mentioned?
- How much quantitative description of the dataset is provided?
- How is data accounted for – is it in pages, in words, in megabytes?
- What sort of qualitative detail is provided to describe the dataset?
- What other aspects of dataset communication might be relevant?

DATA

Effectively Presenting Data

The final consideration for communicating your netnography is to think about what data you will present, how much of it you will present, and in what forms and contexts you will present it. Because qualitative research inquiry seeks to convey context and rich, thick, embedded detail about its topic matter, readers want to see examples of data included as part of the analysis or interpretation. First, ethical concerns may be raised by the presentation of actual names, online pseudonyms, or the ability to back-trace data to reveal names and pseudonyms. Next, the data must be represented in the communication, and the research becomes, in this sense, a type of carefully cultivated curation. In this subsection of the chapter, these two main matters pertaining to the communication of data will be considered in turn. We will begin with the ethical aspects of representing people's posted social media data and personally identifying information. Then, the subsection will turn to discuss and provide examples of the way social media data is presented in netnography.

Ethically Presenting Data

Data communicates information intentionally, and it can also unintentionally communicate information that would have been better left unrevealed. For over two decades, Internet researchers have been cooking up strategies to deal with the fact that people can use online search engines to trace exact quotes back to their original posts and posters. For example, within days of its public release, a large and anonymized research dataset of a particular Facebook cohort was 'cracked' and identified, without ever looking at the data itself (Zimmer, 2010: 316). As Markham (2012: 334) writes, the traditional 'methods of data protection no longer suffice in situations where social researchers need to design studies, manage data, and build research reports in increasingly public, archivable, searchable, and traceable spaces'. You can experience for yourself exactly what this sort of practice feels like by doing the short exercise in Box 14.5. When traditional methods fail us, we need to invent new ones for the altered circumstances. And that is exactly what has happened.

14.5

COMMUNICATING PERSONAL REPRESENTATIONS: EXERCISE IDENTIFYING AND ANONYMIZING SOCIAL MEDIA DATA, WHILE SEEKING THE UNTRACEABLE QUOTE

Take a look at the following actual online quote, which I present in a decontextualized fashion:

> If you are a PhD student, and you can handle it, be bold. Take intellectual risks! So few of you will say something truly new that you will stand out immediately from the crowd just for being yourself. Be bold, be true to yourself!

Type the quote, or part of it, into a search engine. Can you trace the origins of the quote from the search results? Given the length of the quote, where would you guess it was posted? Try going to that platform's search engine, and then type in the quote, or part of it, such as the first sentence. Can you solve the simple mystery of this quote? If you can, then you have just 'backtraced'. Here is your next assignment: see if you can change a few words in the quote, and make it untraceable. How much changing did you need to do? How did you change it – what were the words you used? Did this substantially alter the meaning of the quote?

If you have made the quote untraceable by changing just a few words, consider this to be your hands-on introduction to data anonymization. Data anonymization can also be called 'creative data re-writing'. Now, write a concise one-page report, describing what happened as you played with and changed the data before settling on a final 'untraceable' representation to communicate.

Cloaking and Context

How you save data matters a lot. It determines what you have captured. What you have is data that is qualitative, which means that it contains a range of different qualities that can be categorized, arranged, rearranged, and are thus wide open for many forms of representation. How you represent the verbata or the direct quotes you draw from your data collection presents you with an important ethical choice.

The vividness and closeness to experience of social media data is one of its great assets, and that vibrancy comes from its rich provision of contextual detail. Thus, the more we remove of the context, the less the data have the authentic conversational and interactional elements that we are looking for in cultural research.

We must balance the following considerations:

1. The benefits deriving from contextualized data.

2. The need to protect people who are either unintentionally or voluntarily included in the study.

3. The ethical and legal responsibilities of the researcher.

If we interview someone famous and they reveal some sensitive information about their personal life than could implicate other people, because they are a type of celebrity, should we reveal their actual name? Even if the person wants to be identified – is it an ethical breach to identify them? See Box 14.6 for directions regarding further thinking about this question.

IS IT A BREACH TO ANONYMIZE SENSITIVE CELEBRITY DATA, EVEN IF THE CELEBRITY GRANTS PERMISSION TO MAKE IT PUBLIC?

14.6

Discuss the question, then report to your peers, instructor, or professor.

Protecting Confidentiality

Giving a prominent social media celebrity credit may mean exposure of sensitive comments provided in an interview. It could lead to clues that would expose the identity of an anonymized commenter on the celebrity's site. Providing actual names may mean that you are obligated to omit potentially damaging, yet theoretically valuable and insightful information from your written accounts. Thus, unless there is a good reason to use someone's actual name or pseudonym, the starting point for netnographic anonymizing is to give the participant a new pseudonym in the research presentation (including written or published work).

The answer to the question lies in the authority of the research author. It is important that the researcher and their regulatory body make the determination about anonymity and pseudonymity, and not the research participant. For justification of this guideline, it is instructive to look at Elizabeth Reid's (1996) study of an online site for survivors of abuse. In Reid's study, some participants agreed to speak to her only on the condition that they would be named. She later wrote that this was a mistake and ended up putting her participants at risk; she was the one who should have made that decision. Ultimately, it is the author's name and reputation being staked in the article, and it is the researcher who is required to be the expert on ethical rules. Participants grant consent under some conditions. They can correct accuracy using practices like the stalwart technique of member checks. And of course they can negotiate the terms of representation under other sets of practices. But it is the researcher communicating the results who decides on the most ethical and effective communication of the data gathered from participants during investigative and interactive data operations.

Three Levels of Cloaking

Several Internet researchers have recommended various methods for cloaking, disguising, concealing, or changing the identity of online sites and individual posters, for example Bruckman (2006). Whichever method you choose to use, it is important to understand why you are applying it and to always apply it consistently. I recommend the following three levels of cloaking sufficient for most netnographic projects: (a) no cloaking, where the online pseudonym or the real name of the research participant is revealed in the research representation; (b) cloaking, where the social media site is mentioned, but actual names, pseudonyms, and other potential identifiers are altered, and verbatim quotes are subtly changed so that backtracing them using a search engine fails to reveal the origin source; and (c) high cloaking, where the social media site, actual names, and pseudonyms are all altered, verbatim quotes are either changed or not used, with fabrication strategies standing in for verbatim quotes to make backtracing very difficult. I explain these three levels of cloaking further in the points that follow:

- *No cloaking*. When the risk of harm is very low, data is not sensitive, the population is not vulnerable, and where the person is already a recognized public figure such as a social media (or other) celebrity, you can use either the online pseudonym or real name of the research participant as communicated in the research representation. Generally speaking, real names should only be used for public figures (leaving you to define in context what this means), and only after considering whether any potentially harmful material is present, or needs to be omitted (again leaving you to define what this means according to your research's particular context).

- *Cloaking*. When benefits are high and the potential for harm is low, the actual name of the social media site can be provided, such as the name of a Facebook or LinkedIn group. However, all online pseudonyms, actual names, and other means of identifying people would be altered beyond recognition. The researcher should also engage in a reasonable effort to subtly alter or rephrase verbatim quotes without changing their meanings so that they cannot be linked to the original post ('backtraced') by entering the quote into a search engine. If there is a compelling reason why the quotes need to appear in the research in a form that can be traced, it should be explained.

- *High cloaking*. When the potential for harm is high, when topics are sensitive and/or the population is vulnerable, the name of the site as well as the online pseudonyms, names, and other identifying details of message posters should all be altered. In this condition, all verbatim quotes will be carefully altered to ensure that entering them in a search engine of any kind cannot backtrace them to their original postings. So-called 'fabrication' (Markham, 2012) strategies may be used to create personas or data, rather than to use actual observed persons and data. As in the cloaked condition, the researcher must take great care to maintain the meaning, and if possible the style and voice of the social media communication and its communicator.

The no cloaking condition is not used very often, but when researchers are studying celebrity content creators online, such as Marwick's (2015) study of 'Instagram famous' influencer celebrities, names can be important. Most netnography will fall into the cloaked condition. I would estimate that the ethical research standards of 80% or more of netnographic research projects would be handled by the cloaking strategy described here.

Although there are far fewer studies that use it, the highly cloaked condition is an important one to recognize and utilize where applicable. For example, Tiidenberg (2014: n.p.) studied online exhibitionism and took various precautions to protect her participants from the possibility of exposure. These procedures included acquiring informed consent from all participants, altering wordings 'to minimize their reverse-searchability', and altering published images by 'running them through a sketching application, hiding watermarks, and placing a modesty block' over exposed genitalia.

In the study my colleagues and I did on tobacco companies' social media-based promotions, we interviewed several people who had worked in various capacities to help promote tobacco use among young people. We asked them what they had been asked to do and for details about the contracts that they signed. Data security was important, and so was anonymizing the data. One participant shared a copy of a tobacco-related social media influencer contract with us. To protect the identities of the interview participants, their names were never shared with me or with the other members of the group. Actual identities were kept totally confidential. Furthermore, we removed the names from all of the documents, so that only pseudonyms and general descriptions of the individuals remained. The interviews are intact, but there is now no way to link them to actual persons.

Fabrication and Decontextualization

As mentioned above, Markham (2012) suggests something that she calls 'fabrication' as a possible solution to some of these ethical quandaries. Fabrication is a creative alteration of data into various kinds of composite renderings fictionalized narratives, layered accounts, and representational interactions, using some techniques that have been associated with remix culture (Markham, 2012: 349). The modes of these innovative activities include experimentations, collaborations, creative ingenuities and remixes. Although this is a technique applied for purposes relating to data ethics, it also involves data operations (because it is a procedure that needs to be explained) as well as data representation (because it guides how data is communicated).

Centering on individual biography and autobiography, Buitelaar (2014: 277) suggests that, in a world populated by digital doubles of people's physical identities, Internet researchers should combine narrative techniques with historiographical methods in order to uphold a principle of 'informational self-determination, with its constituent elements of human dignity and autonomy' and thus 'place the innate right of privacy in a fair position vis-à-vis the right to the freedom of expression'. Similarly, Driscoll and Gregg (2010: 20) advocate moving representation towards the autobiographical.

DuFault and Schouten (2018) studied self-quantification practices among 'one specific forum' [which they identified with the pseudonym 'mycredit.com'] relating to consumer credit reports, immersing themselves in a decade's worth of archived forum data that was publicly available. They read with purpose, subjecting their data site to careful, ongoing analysis. They also needed to grapple with ethical concerns, and it is here that the writing of their text is helpfully instructive. They began signaling their attention to data ethics by discussing how their netnographic methods were adapted to the current era of social media and its surveillance/privacy challenges:

> We devised our methods in the ongoing wake of the well-publicized news and outcry about the academic/public partnership with Cambridge Analytica and Facebook, which revealed controversial use of personal online data for a combination of academic and industry interests. We were highly conscious of new debates surrounding the use of personal online data for analysis (Markham, Buchanan and AoIR Ethics Working Committee, 2012), including the adoption of stricter GDPR (General Data Protection Regulation) privacy laws in the EU (Cornock, 2018), and proposed legislation in the US. (2018: 6)

Although they had begun their analysis by manually downloading posts from the forum, keeping pseudonyms, names, and name keys in separate files, they eventually decided not to make use of verbatim data and to delete the previously collected data from their computers, because data storage and security have proven to be such important online research ethics concerns. They consider their work on credit scores to be transpiring in 'a potentially stigmatized social space' (p. 7). The following edited paragraphs present how they communicated their use of the Markham-inspired fabrication techniques outlined in this subsection. Their description, development, and usage of the technique are exemplary for the level of detail they provide and the helpfulness of its demonstration in the context of communicating sensitive topics-based netnography:

> For this work, we decided to follow the example of social scientists who use the creative nonfiction technique of aggregating data and re-constructing composite individual narratives (Barone, 2008; Narayan, 2007; Richardson and St Pierre, 2008; Smith, McGannon, and Williams, 2015). We created two kinds of composites from our analysis of the data: composite characters, or archetypes, and composite narratives. We patterned our composite narratives from actual posts or threads in the forum. We took story lines from exemplary posts and then used creative nonfiction techniques to change the wording and details so that the meaning remained true, but the source was untraceable. We traded the composite narratives between authors to see if they resonated with the literal posts of representative members. We edited each other's prose, used bricolage, and layered accounts. We continued editing and rewriting until we could not distinguish between our composite posts and a verbatim post. We then used each composite post as a search term in various search engines to make sure they did not lead back to any specific forum post that we had used as part of our aggregated data. The composite characters reflect distinct types of forum members, which we refer to as archetypes, that emerged in our analysis.

Data Representation Examples

Netnographic data usually consists of the contextually embedded texts and/or images posted by people on various social media platforms. That data must be saved in some form, and that form requires sets of decisions that can be as much about ethics, rhetoric, and aesthetics as they are about theoretical contribution. Data must be represented in the communication, and the research becomes, in this sense, a type of carefully cultivated curation. Data is collected, analyzed, and then presented as examples or parts of a rhetorical argument substantiating particular descriptions and claims of theoretical contribution, but also one that seeks to represent a human cultural activity, and provide a rich description and a sense of what the temporally and (usually visually) embodied social experience feels like. This subsection of the chapter examines, with examples, some of the different ways social media data is effectively presented in netnography.

DATA COMMUNICATION IN RELEVANT PUBLISHED NETNOGRAPHIES

In Box 14.2, you were tasked with examining the general depiction of netnographic research in any particular published medium. For this exercise, you are required to look up and closely examine the communication strategies of one or more published netnographies *in the outlet you are considering targeting*. The best search engine to use for this task is usually Google Scholar. After examining this work, please answer the following questions about the presentation of data in the published work:

- How is netnographic data presented? How much is provided? What percentage of the findings of the paper, approximately, are made up of presentations of data?
- What kinds (visual, textual, links to audiovisual and auditory) of data are presented?
- If verbata are presented, about how long are the verbata? How are verbata attributed? What is the form of the citation of data? What is the range of length of verbata presented?
- How rich is the presented data in terms of detail, context, and emotional content?
- How large on the page are particular pieces of non-textual data such as screenshots and images?
- Is the netnographic data cited, pseudonymized, anonymized, or fabricated? What visual and rhetorical signals accompany the presentation of data?

Micrologically Unpacking Social Media Fragments

In the section above, you learned about how DuFault and Schouten (2018) used the heavy cloaking strategy of creating a composite narrative to communicate forum post data. In one, they provide the signature line that appears under the posts of one of their participants, 'Pat' (p. 11):

October 2017: VantageScore 3.0: 820. January 2017: EX 840; EQ 820; TU 835. 2009: EX 600 EQ 610 TU 630. AAoA10: 7.2 years. Credit line total: $50K. Utilization: 0%. Cards: Chase 0/$10K; BofA 0/$25K; Citibank 0/$15K. Moral: Just pay your bills and the rest takes care of itself

Their analysis of this untraceable data fragment follows. They begin by summarizing the quantification involved in the signature line: 'Pat's signature line, like many on this forum, is essentially a short credit bio – a financial self-portrait communicated in numbers'. Then, they proceed to translate the various elements that constitute it, performing an analytical act of interpretation:

> We see his FICO 8 credit score history from the three major credit bureaus, now in the 800s (excellent), from the low 600s (fair) in 2009, and his new use of the VantageScore model, also excellent. We see his total credit available across all cards, the number of credit cards, and which cards he holds, the credit limits and balances per card, and the average age of accounts.

In a micrological analysis that 'unpacks' the meanings in the verbatim quotes the way carefully folded laundry can be unpacked from a suitcase, the authors tell us about the cultural role of this particular embedded communication. The scores and what they stand for are 'all well-known to members as components of credit-score calculations'. In fact, this accounting is a common activity, ranging from boasting to confession, one which has several meanings pertaining to the group members' shared goals and their reinforcement through self-display: 'Many other members have similar signatures. They most often show upwardly trending scores – sometimes dramatically so – and are inspirational. New users post their modest gains proudly and are congratulated by the community.' The data and its detailed unpacking are good examples of netnographic data analysis. Not only is data provided, it is also carefully interpreted and related to the larger questions about what is happening on the mycredit.com site and what might be its wider implications. From the careful interpretation of DuFault and Schouten (2018), we not only learn what was said about this sensitive topic of personal credit scores and histories (and in an untraceable, ethically sound manner), we also get some explanation about why it was said, and why it was posted in that manner.

Cultural Depiction Using Deep Data

Throughout your immersion journal, you will have been noting your noticing of particularly rich and contextually informative data: deep data. Now that you are curating the research representation that will communicate them, you will want to feature instances of data that illustrate major points of contribution. Resonant data conveys to its audience a personalized and sensitizing connection with the human experience. Part of what we are searching for in our reconnoitering is resonant data. We seek traces that will be emotionally and intraceptively appealing, subjectively important and imaginatively productive. When we are considering the communicative potential of our netnographies we must evaluate data based upon whether we believe it will speak meaningfully and deeply to our intended audience. Is it visceral? Does is induce particular moods or emotional states? Does it relate, as anthropologist Ruth Behar (1996) asks us contemplate, to our vulnerability as engaged observers of humanity?

In Estonia, a supposedly non-religious country, Uibu (2013: 70, 74) found a supportive, open and 'remarkably benevolent' Internet forum called 'The Nest of Angels' acting as a 'religious-spiritual incubator' where people discuss spiritual and religious ideas in relation to their own 'seemingly abnormal experiences'. Using the representation of this data skillfully, we get a sense from Uibu of the power of these communications. For example, consider the following data fragment, which also holistically represents the way that contact with the spiritual world of angels is fused with an account of mundane actions (such as cleaning one's kitchen cupboards), and extended into a description of emotions, caring, and feelings of self-affirmation and self-love.

> The signs from angels are miraculous and they leave the soul full of love. E.g., I cleaned the cupboard where my relatives keep their dishes and utensils. And suddenly, there are wonderful golden wings, certainly broken off from a Christmas decoration ... But when I looked at them I felt such a miraculous feeling of love, with praise and gratitude. Such feeling that angels are caressing and saying that you are good. (Uibu, 2012: 76)

West and Thakore (2013: 251) open their article about race in the online world with a piece of data from their online toy collection forum, which they renamed 'The Playhouse'. The data was a simple greeting:

> Hi, TansyTen! Welcome to the Playhouse ... You should look around for Sandrine10 and MskratMlly. I think that they will be good friends for you!

The authors use this choice piece of data to lead us into the online world of toy collectors and introduce their central topic of racial exclusion. They explain that the role of moderators is to both welcome people and to police, to some extent, the social media space. Rhetorically foreshadowing a contrast, the authors state: 'On the surface, this is a very welcoming gesture, in that it helps the new member make connections with other users. However, a little context reveals a more complex situation: In her introduction to the forum, TansyTen identified herself as a Black woman. The two members suggested by the moderator are also Black' (pp. 251–2).

Because the authors had also conducted interviews with online participants, they are able to then deepen the analysis with the additional data. TansyTen then says that the moderator 'thought I'd be friends with these other people, but we don't have anything in common except we're Black ... I mean, really, I mean, it's hard to find Black people on the internet but I can find them on my own. Like, am I not supposed to talk to the White people?' (p. 252). The verbatim quote, with outrage apparently expressed in the 'I mean, really' section, is a powerful introduction to the idea that adult women coming together to discuss the collecting of American Girl dolls is also a rich site to examine the power of race and the patterns of racial exclusion as they occur through social media interaction. The presence of the data in the introduction to the paper and the site draws the reader into this new social world in a compellingly dramatic fashion.

Communicating Visual and Non-textual Data

As well as providing resonant, summative, and compelling textual data, social media offers a range of other ways to connect readers to phenomena. The different visual forms of data can make for powerful communication devices. Tenderich et al. (2018) used netnography to show how social media is used by people with diabetes for empowerment and peer support. The article provides many illustrations from visual posts captured from Instagram, Reddit, Twitter, Facebook, and diabetes forums. These screengrabs are highly effective at conveying the emotional reality of diabetes. For instance, Figure 14.2 features two annotated screenshots illustrating 'diabetic pride' where people, including those living with Type 1 diabetes, show off various parts of their lives. In one, a message poster shows off their 'diabetic ink', a tattoo expressing the reality of being diabetic, a bold and positive approach that is common, with many boards on Pinterest allowing people with diabetes to peruse diabetes tattoo designs. The other shows an athletic rock climb, and was posted with the hashtag #T1DLooksLikeMe (T1D is a short form for Type 1 Diabetes). The rich data carries a strong emotional message that amplifies as well as exemplifies the assertions made in the text of the article.

Social media is allowing patients to turn the traditional experience of shame and isolation on its head. (Numbers indicate the instances of each hashtag on Instagram alone through October 2017.)

Figure 14.2   Diabetes visual examples from Tenderich et al. (2018: 5).

In some recent netnographies, the visual form of data is extended to mobile phone screenshots. Rambe and Mkono (2018) used a 'netnography of WhatsApp-based supervisor–supervisee consultations and in-depth interviews to unravel how WhatsApp-mediated postgraduate supervision fosters the social construction of relational and existential authenticity in resource-constrained contexts'. Their use of 31 figures, each of them a mobile screenshot of a WhatsApp message window, provides a powerful and dramatic way to tell the story of the ups and downs, high and lows, challenges, frustration, mystifications, and triumphs of postgraduate supervision in a South African educational context. For example, Figure 14.3 provides a screenshot of the exchange between a postgraduate student and a supervisor, demonstrating not only the emotional commitment present in the relationship (conveyed with lots of exclamation points, emojis, and inspiring messages), but also the

Figure 14.3 WhatsApp screenshot that captures the communicating of excitement about postgraduate academic accomplishments, from Rambe and Mkono (2018: 18)

role of technological devices and platforms in its contemporary manifestation. In a single snapshot, a singular piece of data frames a number of arguments developed further in the article, such as the negotiation of hierarchies, self-expression, and the management of anxiety. These themes are explored in a wider context in which social media devices shrink the social distances between hierarchical relationships in education and other contexts.

The permutations and combinations of data communication in netnography are virtually limitless. Isbell (2018) provides multilingual data from a Reddit forum dedicated to learning the Korean language. After providing a figure illustrating the different elements of the online 'activity system' (p. 84), the author supplies a series of 'excerpts' that illustrate the discussions, negotiation, and disclosure transpiring around the translation of the Korean language into English. In all, the presentation of the data is invaluable to the author's goal of 'painting a vivid picture of activity in the r/Korean' online informal language learning community (p. 97). After these encounters, the English language reader comes away more knowledgeable not only about the Korean language and about translation, but also about the role of subreddits such as this one and the general role of social media in informal language learning and other forms of learning in the wild.

O'Leary and Carroll (2013) provide rich and revealing excerpts of data that relate dialog that reveal a range of cooperative, competitive, ego-driven, and hierarchical relationships manifesting through online discussions of online poker games. Although we might assume that online poker is a highly individualist pursuit, conducted with the self-representational equivalent of a poker face, O'Leary and Carroll's (2013) data is conversational and interactive. Conveyed in a scripted dialog form, it is filled with informal, joking, helpful, angry, problem-solving, and many other kinds of communication. Their data vividly illustrate the social richness of the world of online poker players and intimately bring it to life for readers.

There are many different ways to effectively communicate your netnography using social media data. This subsection has provided some examples. For example, one data communication strategy involves introducing rich fragments of data and then translating their various elements in order to provide evidence of general principles at work. Another strategy presents particularly powerful examples. Some will open with verbata from the data and then slowly expand upon and explain their greater significance. Other types of data are visually rich and thus richly informative. Others introduce us to a different cultural world through scripts or mobile phone screen grabs. With all of these strategies, the netnographer is utilizing the data to illustrate the origins and support for core theoretical assertions. Also, the data familiarize us, as readers of an ethnography, with the look, sound, and feel of a distinctly different and unique social and cultural world.

14.8 GETTING IN THE GAME

If you have been following and completing the exercises in this book, you will already have a research question (which may need to be refined), a dataset, analysis and interpretation (which may need to be refined), as well as plenty of guidelines about how to communicate netnographic research in your targeted field and outlet. Now, it is time to start working on a draft to submit.

Your Exercise: Do it.

As you begin writing, consider that you are not alone. When I began writing the first edition of this book in 2008, I had to search to find examples of netnographic research that weren't written by me or by authors already familiar to me. Today, early in 2019, I am notified every time someone publishes work that uses netnography, and I receive these notifications almost every day. At present, midway through 2019, Google Scholar returns about 2,070 mentions of netnography that have occurred since 2018. Google Trends shows me a gradual rise in the number of worldwide inquiries about netnography over the past decade, which currently stand somewhere around 60–70 queries per day. At regular intervals now, different fields are beginning to publish overview articles spotlighting the role and use of netnography in their field. In 2014, while I was writing the second edition of this book, there were already many more authors using netnography in a much wider variety of research fields than there had been six years before when I was writing the first edition. I drew heavily upon their use of the method to develop that book.

For this, the third edition of the book, there was another dramatic increase in the number of netnographies and other online ethnographies available to include as research examples. Those many articles and chapters helped me develop and refine the 25 netnographic research operations presented in this book. As you combine all the separate elements of your netnography together into your research communication, you should feel excited. At this moment, with this new information in your hands, you have an unheard-of opportunity to develop and communicate new thinking about the worlds of social media communication and the realms it touches and that touch it. You have a chance to contribute to important ongoing discussions about the matters closest to your heart, the things that concern you, and the ones that you delight in. Research is a chance to make a difference. To other scholars, certainly, and to your research field, but also to students, to journalists, to policy makers, and to the public. Like social media itself, research is an opportunity to take part in a great conversation, a discourse of knowing and discovering.

Doing research is important. Communicating your research changes things. As you write your netnography, remember the hundreds and even thousands of people who have gone before you, and have accomplished their goals using these procedures – and, to be honest, with much weaker descriptions of them than you have here. Do not be intimidated – simply take the process step by step. Follow the guidelines. Go back and look over the exercises and descriptions. Think about the systematic way you can follow these directions to create a netnography that is completely your own. Visualize yourself following these directions and seeing your hard work communicated, presented, published, perhaps rewarded and awarded. Put the pieces together.

One day, I am confident, when all your efforts are complete, my Google Alert will send me a message, and it will be your netnography cited in the alert, sitting in my email inbox. A brand new article or chapter or book – something unique and exciting. Thank you for reading this book. It will be my great honor to return the favor and read your work. I honestly cannot wait to one day click on that link and read what you've been working on!

THE HALLMARKS OF GREAT NETNOGRAPHY RESEARCH

The choices of examples in this chapter were not accidental. They were chosen from published research that achieved the most important goals of netnography. A good netnography will educate us about what is happening in the world of social media. It will follow some topic or some group, filling us in about what is being said and how it works as a social system. It will often achieve these goals by focusing on a particular characteristic such as the categories of the contents of the interactions in public social media of different types, or the communication strategies, or the types of communications or connections.

A high-quality netnography must also present data well. It must explain its particular data operations in a way that makes clear their connection to a research field, its constructs, theoretical orientation, and the data sites used. Data sites are the launchpads for the inquiry, and a knowledge of their context is vital. In all, these elements are contained in netnography, with its six stages of initiation, investigation, interaction, immersion, integration, and instantiation.

Strong netnographies will also alternate between the use of the telescope and the microscope. They will combine penetrating systems-level insights with microscopic-level examinations of what seem like minutiae. They will use micrological methods to examine small fragments and expand them into major illustrations of holistic conclusions. They will provide black swans, exceptions to the rule, and lead users. They will offer strong explanations about why things happen, not just descriptions of them happening. These causal explanations will make intuitive leaps and offer bigger understandings than mere piecemeal approaches. All of these are elements that can help make a good netnography into a great one.

Often, guides to academic writing and publishing such as those of Holliday (2016), Silvia (2015), and Wolcott (2013) will emphasize that your goal should be long-term research impact rather than simply the short-term goal of achieving publication. Your work should be aimed not only at answering important questions – and thus tying up loose ends – but also at stimulating further inquiry, which in a way is pulling at loose strings to unravel additional intriguing questions. Does your work contribute new ideas, concept, frameworks, structures, or knowledge of their relationships or progressions over time or through other sources of difference and variance? Does your research relate to central questions, debates, or issues in your academic field? Does it reveal something new that could be applicable to other researchers, policy makers, or thinkers?

A great netnography needs to do more than this. Besides offering excellent theoretical contributions, illustrating them well, and extending them through judicious analysis and interpretation, a great netnography needs to provide us with a window on a different communicative world. To be great, it needs to do more than just make this strange new world familiar, it needs to make us care about it and the real people populating and affected by it. A great netnography needs to activate first the head and imagination, and then the heart of the reader. It needs to arouse that most important of emotions: empathy for others. A sense of our own shared humanity. We can think about the various steps of netnography as a way to try to re-experience and curate the humanity of the people whose communicative traces are caught in, then scraped and captured from, public social media. The process is a bit like reading ancient bear tracks in the muddy clay of an old cave.

Once you have arrived at a powerful narrative, which can stir the heart and awaken a human connection between those you are writing about and those you are communicating it to, what then? Might you suggest some awareness, some new awakening? What is your troublemaking specialty? What institution would you erode, undermine, and actively work to topple? What new and better process, understanding, or action would your work recommend? That is your research axiology. Ultimately, it is either a form of activism or non-activism. You either reflexively take a side, or you unreflectively take the side of those who claim not to be taking a side. Your work either seeks to reinforce a system or it incites changes to a system. Combined with the need for novelty, for saying something new and unique, for being theoretically sound and useful, for arousing empathy, moving the heart, and perhaps stimulating action, these criteria are key elements not only to communication, representation, and publication but also to achieving the important goal of having a lasting academic impact. And perhaps even an impact that stretches beyond academia, into the other social spheres where together we all reside.

CHAPTER SUMMARY

This chapter began by discussing some general guidelines for writing research and targeting particular research outlets. After that, it offered the method-embedded research communication triangle as a way to understand four key elements of research communication. These four elements are: (1) the method of netnography; (2) the netnographic data operations; (3) the netnographic dataset; and (4) the data. Each of the four elements was described and developed in turn, with examples and exercises illustrating important points. The communication of method is a rhetorical act in which strategies differ depending upon the audience. Operations draw upon the 25 different netnographic research operations to describe, explain, and justify the particular procedures employed in the specific research project. Netnographers need to provide details about the netnographic dataset, including how much and what types of traces were searched and scouted, when, and why this data was collected. Data representation in netnography presents ethical concerns that can be addressed by appropriate procedures such as anonymizing, cloaking, and fabricating. The chapter then offered several examples of different types of netnographic data from a variety of published netnographies, including visual and other non-textual data. Its final section discussed the hallmarks of excellence in published netnographic research before wishing the reader well on their journey of discovery.

KEY READINGS

Bruckman, Amy (2006) 'Teaching students to study online communities ethically', *Journal of Information Ethics*, 15(2): 82–95.

Locke, Karen and Karen Golden-Biddle (1997) 'Constructing opportunities for contribution: Structuring intertextual coherence and "problematizing" in organizational studies', *Academy of Management Journal*, 40(5): 1023–62.

Markham, Annette (2012) 'Fabrication as ethical practice: Qualitative inquiry in ambiguous internet contexts', *Information, Communication & Society*, 15(3): 334–53.

Tavakoli, Rokhshad and Sarah N.R. Wijesinghe (2019) 'The evolution of the web and netnography in tourism: A systematic review', *Tourism Management Perspectives*, 29: 48–55.

Wolcott, Harry (2013) *Writing Up Qualitative Research*. London: Sage.

15

THE FUTURE OF
NETNOGRAPHY

15.0 THE NEXT CHAPTER

Continuity

Congratulations for making it through all 14 prior chapters of this book. At times, it was not easy reading. But reading is just a bit easier than writing. And it is your time to write.

Of all the forces in the world right now, social media may represent the most interesting and powerful one. Poised between surveillance capitalism and the utopian ideals of free public spheres, perhaps more than anything else social media currently reveal the collective promise and constraints of the citizen-consumer. Social media communications open a window on others and ourselves, and what we might see is a bundle of potentials that can and are socially, politically, and economically activated. The modern-day citizen-consumer/social activist: possibly a new form of screen-hypnotized couch potato, or else the most powerful change agent in the contemporary world.

In a quarter of a century researching social media, I have learned a few things, and I have tried to convey as many of them as I could to you in this book, jam-packing it with histories, cultural explorations, academic theories, and workbench-level procedures and tools. We need more tools for cultural exploration of these increasingly familiar, yet deeply strange, realms. Online, we may be deeply intimate with our own online neighborhoods, our everyday cellphone search and shopping decision practices and habits. But we are also profoundly perplexed and overwhelmed in the face of social media's overall vastness. We are swept away in connections to agencies and forces we dare not dream about. We are inhabitants not of some sort of Gibsonian matrix cyberspace simulation, not yet. We are more like willing travellers within a largely textual and audiovisual cyberplace, cultural locations, McLuhanesque villages of gathered people, places, and activities. These are warm social cyberplaces, rather than cold digital cyberspaces. When we visit them, as we ought to, as embedded and immersed cultural explorers, travelers through the towns and cities of cyberplaces, we become qualitative social media researchers: netnographers.

Virginia Heffernan (2016) writes about how basic human experiences are raised up aesthetically and made magic through social media, just as many of the physical and emotional experiences of the world we knew a decade or two ago are simultaneously vanishing. This sense of what she calls magic and loss is too deep and too monumental for any single cultural commentator to handle on their own: it takes a global village. The next chapters of this crowdsourced work, this gigantic and collaborative piece of realist artwork, will be written by you. This book is already my curation, now it becomes yours.

The book about social media research that you hold right now in your hands is, after all, still in a literary form that reminds us of our past, our embodiment, our physicality. It is an incitement to take a break from screens and cyberspaces. The few blank pages that follow are a space dedicated to you. Indeed, the margins throughout this book are a happy encouragement for you to capture your own words on these pages, mingling and merging them with my own. This is a callout to use the last few pages of this book, to take them and make them your own as you create and co-produce, narrate and deliver your research pre-sentation and representation for audiences of your own. Thank you for being an audience for this work. Now, it is time to plan you own performance. What impassions you? What matters in your world? What is the story you will tell? Find a way to free it.

the current

of netnography

is free

to connect into the future

of netnography

is yours to

create

SUPERCONNECTIVITY

1. The phenomenon of almost perfect transmission of communication and information throughout the human habitations of the universe, via computers.
2. The interconnections of all social and economic institutions as a result of communication via computer networks. (*The Online Dictionary of the English Language*, unabridged: 2067; Hiltz and Turoff, 1993: 455)

' There is always a point at which the terrorist ceases to manipulate the media gestalt. A point at which the violence may well escalate, but beyond which the terrorist has become symptomatic of the media gestalt itself. Terrorism as we ordinarily understand it is innately media-related. '

(William Gibson, 1984)

REFERENCES

Agee, Jane (2009) 'Developing qualitative research questions: A reflective process', *International Journal of Qualitative Studies in Education*, 22(4): 431–47.

Ahuja, Vandana and Moonis Shakeel (2017) 'Twitter presence of jet airways-deriving customer insights using netnography and wordclouds', *Procedia Computer Science*, 122: 17–24.

Aitamurto, Tanja (2013) 'Balancing between open and closed: Co-creation in magazine journalism', *Digital Journalism*, 1(2): 229–1.

Alang, Sirry M. and Marcel Fomotar (2015) 'Postpartum depression in an online community of lesbian mothers: Implications for clinical practice', *Journal of Gay & Lesbian Mental Health*, 19(1): 21–39.

Alvesson, Mats (2003) 'Beyond neopositivists, romantics, and localists: A reflexive approach to interviews in organizational research', *Academy of Management Review*, 28(1): 13–33.

Amit, Vered and Nigel Rapport (2002) *The Trouble with Community: Anthropological Reflections on Movement, Identity and Collectivity*. London: Pluto.

Anderson, Benedict (2006) *Imagined Communities: Reflections on the Origin and Spread of Nationalism*. London: Verso.

Appadurai, Arjun (1990) 'Disjuncture and difference in the global cultural economy', *Theory, Culture & Society*, 7(2–3): 295–310.

Arnould, Eric J. and Melanie Wallendorf (1994) 'Market-oriented ethnography: Interpretation building and marketing strategy formulation', *Journal of Marketing Research*, 31(4): 484–504.

Arvidsson, Adam (2005) 'Brands: A critical perspective', *Journal of Consumer Culture*, 5(2): 235–58.

Ashman, Rachel, Anthony Patterson, and Stephen Brown (2018) '"Don't forget to like, share and subscribe": Digital autopreneurs in a neoliberal world', *Journal of Business Research*, 92: 474–83.

Askew, Kelly (2002) 'Introduction', in Kelly Askew and Richard Wilk (eds), *The Anthropology of Media: A Reader*. Malden, MA: Blackwell.

Association of Internet Researchers Ethics Working Group (2012) *Ethical Decision-making and Internet Research: Recommendations from the AoIR Ethics Working Committee (Version 2.0)*. Available at: http://aoir.org/reports/ethics2.pdf.

Ast, Friedrich (1808) *Grundlinien der Grammatik, Hermeneutik und Kritik*. Landshut: Jos. Thomann, Buchdrucker und Buchhändler.

Atmananda, Brother (2016) 'Moral strength: The foundation of spiritual freedom'. *Public Facebook page* available at www.facebook.com/YoganandaDisciples/posts/moral-strength-the-foundation-of-spiritual-freedom-excerpts-brother-at-manandai-w/1075625162470726/

Babbie, Earl (2004) 'Laud Humphreys and research ethics', *International Journal of Sociology and Social Policy*, 24(3/4/5): 12–19.

Bakardjieva, Maria (2005) *Internet Society: The Internet in Everyday Life*. London: Sage.

Baker, Sally (2013) 'Conceptualising the use of Facebook in ethnographic research: As tool, as data and as context', *Ethnography and Education*, 8(2): 131–45.

Bakhtin, Mikhail (1981) 'Forms of time and the chronotrop in the novel', in Michael Holquist (ed.), *The Dialogic Imagination* (pp. 259–442). Austin, TX: University of Texas Press.

Bardzell, Shaowen and William Odom (2008) 'The experience of embodied space in virtual worlds: An ethnography of a Second Life community', *Space and Culture*, 11(3): 239–59.

Bartl, Michael, Vijai Kumar Kannan, and Hanna Stockinger (2016) 'A review and analysis of literature on netnography research', *International Journal of Technology Marketing*, 11(2): 165–96.

Bartlett, Richard A. (2013) *The World of Ham Radio, 1901–1950: A Social History*. Jefferson, NC: McFarland.

Bauman, Zygmunt (2013) *Liquid Modernity*. New York: Wiley.

Baym, Nancy K. (1993) 'Interpreting soap operas and creating community: Inside a computer-mediated fan culture', *Journal of Folklore Research*, 30: 143–76.

Baym, Nancy K. (1995) 'The Emergence of community in computer-mediated communication', in Stephen G. Jones (ed.), *Cybersociety* (pp. 138–63). Thousand Oaks, CA: Sage.

Beaulieu, Anne (2004) 'Mediating ethnography: Objectivity and the making of ethnographies of the internet', *Social Epistemology*, 18(2–3; April–September): 139–63.

Behar, Ruth (1996) *The Vulnerable Observer: Ethnography that Breaks Your Heart*. Boston, MA: Beacon.

Belk, Russell W. (ed.) (2006), *Handbook of Qualitative Research Methods in Marketing*. Cheltenham, UN and Northampton, MA: Edward Elgar Publishing.

Belk, Russell (2014) 'The labors of the Odysseans and the legacy of the Odyssey', *Journal of Historical Research in Marketing*, 6(3): 379–404.

Belk, Russell, Eileen Fischer, and Robert V. Kozinets (2013) *Qualitative Marketing and Consumer Research*. London: Sage.

Belk, Russell, John F. Sherry Jr, and Melanie Wallendorf (1988) 'A naturalistic inquiry into buyer and seller behavior at a swap meet', *Journal of Consumer Research*, 14(4): 449–70.

Belk, Russell, Melanie Wallendorf, and John F. Sherry Jr. (1989) 'The sacred and the profane in consumer behavior: Theodicy on the odyssey', *Journal of Consumer Research*, 16(1): 1–38.

Bell, Colin and Howard Newby (1974) 'Capitalist farmers in the British class structure', *Sociologia Ruralis*, 14(1–2): 86–107.

Bengry-Howell, Andrew, Rose Wiles, Melanie Nind, and Graham Crow (2011) 'A review of the academic impact of three methodological innovations: Netnography, child-led research and creative research methods', ESRC Research Innovation Series, University of Southampton.

Beniger, James R. (1987) 'Personalization of mass media and the growth of pseudo-community', *Communication Research*, 14(3): 352–71.

Berdychevsky, Liza and Galit Nimrod (2015) '"Let's talk about sex": Discussions in seniors' online communities', *Journal of Leisure Research*, 47(4): 467–84.

Berdychevsky, Liza and Galit Nimrod (2017) 'Sex as leisure in later life: A netnographic approach', *Leisure Sciences*, 39(3): 224–43.

Berelson, Bernard (1952) *Content Analysis in Communications Research*. Glencoe, IL: The Free Press.

Berning, Moritz and Anita Hardon (2019) 'Virtual ethnography: Managing pharmacological risk and uncertainty in online drug forums', in Anna Olofsson and Jens O. Zinn (eds), *Researching Risk and Uncertainty* (pp. 77–101). Cham: Palgrave Macmillan.

Bertilsson, Jon (2014) 'Critical netnography: Conducting critical research online', in Emma Jeanes and Tony Huzzard (eds), *Critical Management Research: Reflections from the Field* (pp. 135–52). London: Sage.

Bertram, Stewart and Keith Ellison (2014) 'Sub Saharan African terrorist groups' use of the Internet', *Journal of Terrorism Research*, 5(1): 5–26.

Beunza, Daniel and Raghu Garud (2007) 'Calculators, lemmings or frame-makers? The intermediary role of securities analysts', *The Sociological Review*, 55 (2): 13–39.

Bingham, Christopher (2017) 'An Ethnography of Twitch Streamers: Negotiating Professionalism in New Media Content Creation', unpublished doctoral dissertation.

Biraghi, Silvia and Rossella Chiara Gambetti (2018) 'How to use digital diaries in data collection to engage networked consumers', *Mercati e Competitività*, 4: 105–23.

Bjork-James, Sophie (2015) 'Feminist ethnography in cyberspace: Imagining families in the cloud', *Sex Roles*, 73(3–4): 113–24.

Boellstorff, Tom (2007) 'Queer studies in the house of anthropology', *Annual Review of Anthropology*, 36 (April): 17–35.

Boellstorff, Tom (2008) *Coming of Age in Second Life: An Anthropologist Explores the Virtually Human*. Princeton, NJ: Princeton University Press.

Boellstorff, Tom, Bonnie Nardi, Celia Pearce, and Tina L. Taylor (2012) *Ethnography and Virtual Worlds: A Handbook of Method*. Princeton, NJ: Princeton University Press.

Bosk, Charles L. and Raymond G. De Vries (2004) 'Bureaucracies of mass deception: Institutional review boards and the ethics of ethnographic research', *The Annals of the American Academy of Political and Social Science*, 595(1): 249–63.

Boyd, Danah (2004) 'Friendster and publicly articulated social networks', *Proceedings of ACM Conference on Human Factors in Computing Systems* (pp. 1279–82). New York: ACM Press.

Boyd, Danah and Jeffrey Heer (2006) 'Profiles as conversation: Networked identity performance on Friendster', *Proceedings of the 39th Annual Hawaii International Conference on System Sciences (HICSS'06)*, 3: 1–10.

Boyd, Danah M. and Nicole B. Ellison (2007) 'Social network sites: Definition, history, and scholarship', *Journal of Computer-mediated Communication*, 13(1): 210–30.

Brooks, Bill, Debra Gilbuena, Stephen Krause, and Milo Koretsky (2014) 'Using word clouds for fast, formative assessment of students' short written responses', *Chemical Engineering Education*, 48(4): 190–8.

Brown, Stephen, Robert V. Kozinets, and John F. Sherry, Jr. (2003) 'Teaching old brands new tricks: Retro branding and the revival of brand meaning', *Journal of Marketing*, 67(July): 19–33.

Brubaker, Jed R., Gillian R. Hayes, and Paul Dourish (2013) 'Beyond the grave: Facebook as a site for the expansion of death and mourning', *The Information Society* 29(3): 152–63.

Bruckman, Amy (2002) 'Studying the amateur artist: A perspective on disguising data collected in human subjects research on the Internet', *Ethics and Information Technology*, 4(3): 217–31.

Bruckman, Amy (2006) 'Teaching students to study online communities ethically', *Journal of Information Ethics*, 15(2): 82–95.

Buchanan, Ian (2015) 'Assemblage theory and its discontents', *Deleuze Studies*, 9(3): 382–92.

Buchanan, Elizabeth, Annette Markham and Charles Ess (2010) 'Ethics and internet research commons: Building a sustainable future', *Association of Internet Researchers 11th Annual Conference Workshop*, Gottenburg, Sweden.

Buitelaar, J.C. (2014) 'Privacy and narrativity in the internet era', *The Information Society: An International Journal*, 30(4): 266–81.

Büscher, Bram (2016) '"Rhino poaching is out of control!": Violence, race and the politics of hysteria in online conservation', *Environment and Planning A*, 48(5): 979–98.

Cai, Wenjie, Scott A. Cohen, and John Tribe (2019) 'Harmony rules in Chinese backpacker groups', *Annals of Tourism Research*, 75: 120–30.

Canniford, Robin and Domen Badje (2016) 'Assembling Consumption', in Robin Canniford and Domen Badje (eds), *Assembling Consumption: Researching Actors, Networks and Markets* (pp. 1–18). London and New York: Routledge.

Carey, James W. (1989) *Communication as Culture: Essays on Media and Society*, revised edn. London: Routledge.

Carey, James W. (1993) 'Everything That Rises Must Diverge', in Philip Gaunt (ed.), *Agendas: New Directions in Communications Research* (pp. 171–84). Westport, CT: Greenwood.

Carey, James W. and John J. Quirk (1970) 'The mythos of the electronic revolution', *The American Scholar*, 39(2–3): 395–424.

Castells, Manuel (1996) *The Information Age: Economy, Society, and Culture, Volume I: The Rise of the Network Society*. Oxford: Blackwell.

Castells, Manuel (2007) 'Communication, power and counter-power in the network society', *International Journal of Communication*, 1(1): 238–66.

Chaffey, Dave (2018) 'Global Social Media Research Summary 2018', available at www.smartinsights.com/social-media-marketing/social-media-strategy/new-global-social-media-research/ (last accessed 30 April 2019).

Chatfield, Tom (2018) *Critical Thinking: Your Guide to Effective Argument, Successful Analysis and Independent Study*. London: Sage.

Chuter, Robin (2018) 'Finding companionship on the road less travelled: A netnography of the Whole Food Plant-Based Aussies Facebook group', unpublished Bachelor's thesis, Edith Cowan University, available at http://ro.ecu.edu.au/theses_hons/1517/ (last accessed 30 April 2019).

Clark, Lynn Schofield (2016) 'Participants on the margins: #BlackLivesMatter and the role that shared artifacts of engagement played among minoritized political newcomers on Snapchat, Facebook, and Twitter', *International Journal of Communication*, 10: 235–53.

Clement, Tanya, Plaisant, Catherine, and Vuillemot, Romain (2008) 'The story of one: Humanity scholarship with visualization and text analysis (Tech Report HCIL-2008-33)', College Park, MD: University of Maryland, Human-Computer Interaction Lab. Available at http://hcil.cs.umd.edu/trs/2008-33/2008-33.pdf (last accessed 30 April 2019).

Clerc, Susan J. and David Lavery (1996) 'DDEB, GATB, MPPB, and Ratboy: The X-Files' media fandom, online and off', in David Lavery, Angela Hague and Maria Cartwright (eds), *Deny All Knowledge: Reading the X-files* (pp. 36–51). London: Faber & Faber.

Clifford, James (1997) *Routes: Travel and Translation in the Late Twentieth Century*. Cambridge, MA: Harvard University Press.

Clifford, James and George E. Marcus (eds) (1986) *Writing Culture: The Poetics and Politics of Ethnography*. Berkeley, CA: University of California Press.

Cohen, Anthony P. (1985) *The Symbolic Construction of Community*. London: Tavistock.

Coleman, E. Gabriella (2010) 'Ethnographic approaches to digital media', *Annual Review of Anthropology*, 39: 487–505.

Collins, Patricia H. (1990/2000) *Black Feminist Thought: Knowledge, Consciousness, and the Politics of Empowerment*. New York: Routledge.

Connelly, Louise (2010) 'Virtual Buddhism: An analysis of aesthetics in relation to religious practice within Second Life', *Online-Heidelberg Journal of Religions on the Internet*, 4(1): 12–34.

Conoscenti, Michelangelo (2019) 'Big data, small data, broken windows and fear discourse: Brexit, the EU and the majority illusion', *De Europa: European and Global Studies Journal*, 1(2). Doi: http://dx.doi.org/10.13135/2611-853X/2914.

Correll, Shelley (1995) 'The ethnography of an electronic bar: The lesbian cafe', *Journal of Contemporary Ethnography*, 24(3): 270–98.

Costello, Leesa, Marie-Louise McDermott, and Ruth Wallace (2017) 'Netnography: Range of practices, misperceptions, and missed opportunities', *International Journal of Qualitative Methods*, 16(1): 1609406917700647.

Couldry, Nick (2012) *Media, Society, World: Social Theory and Digital Media Practice*. Cambridge: Polity Press.

Crenshaw, Kimberlé (1989) 'Demarginalizing the intersection of race and sex: A Black feminist critique of antidiscrimination doctrine, feminist theory and antiracist politics', *University of Chicago Legal Forum*, 1(8): 139–67.

Creswell, John (2009) *Research Design: Qualitative, Quantitative, and Mixed Methods Approaches*, 3rd edn. London: Sage.

Cresswell, Tim (2002) 'Introduction: Theorizing place', in Ginette Verstraete and Tim Cresswell (eds), *Mobilizing Place, Placing Mobility: The Politics of Representation in a Globalized World* (pp. 11–32). Amsterdam: Rodopi.

Cronin, James M., Mary McCarthy, and Alan Collins (2014) 'Creeping edgework: Carnivalesque consumption and the social experience of health risk', *Sociology of Health & Illness*, 36(8): 1125–40.

D'Ambra, John, Concepcion S. Wilson, and Shahriar Akter (2017) 'Affordance theory and e-books: Evaluating the e-reading experience using netnography', *Personal and Ubiquitous Computing*: 1–20. http://dx.doi.org/10.1007/s00779-017-1086-1.

Dame, Avery (2016) 'Making a name for yourself: Tagging as transgender ontological practice on Tumblr', *Critical Studies in Media Communication*, 33(1): 23–37.

Daniels, Jessie (2009) *Cyber Racism: White Supremacy Online and the New Attack on Civil Rights*. Lanham, MD: Rowman & Littlefield.

Davis, Erik (1998) *Techgnosis: Myth, Magic + Mysticism in the Age of Information*. New York: Harmony Books.

Davis, Teresa (2010) 'Third spaces or heterotopias? Recreating and negotiating migrant identity using online spaces', *Sociology*, 44(4): 661–77.

DeLanda, Manuel (2006) *A New Philosophy of Society: Assemblage Theory and Social Complexity*. London: A&C Black.

DeLanda, Manuel (2016) *Assemblage Theory*. Edinburgh: Edinburgh University Press.

Denning, Peter J. (1989) 'The science of computing: The ARPANET after twenty years', *American Scientist*, 77(6), 530–4.

DeNoyelles, Aimee and Beatriz Reyes-Foster (2015) 'Using word clouds in online discussions to support critical thinking and engagement', *Online Learning*, 19(4).

Denzin, Norman K. (2012) 'Triangulation 2.0', *Journal of Mixed Methods Research*, 6(2): 80–8.

Denzin, Norman K. and Yvonna S. Lincoln (1994) *Handbook of Qualitative Research*. Thousand Oaks, CA: Sage.

Devlin, Ann Sloan (2017) *The Research Experience: Planning, Conducting, and Reporting Research*. London: Sage.

DiMaggio, Paul and Walter Powell (1983) 'The iron cage revisited: Institutional isomorphism and collective rationality in organizational fields', *American Sociological Review*, 48: 147–60.

Diniz, Marisa Victoria, Sue Y. Sun, Claudia Barsottini, Mauricio Viggiano, Roney C. Signorini Filho, Bruna Sanches Ozane Pimenta, Kevin M. Elias, Neil S. Horowitz, Antonio Braga, and Ross S. Berkowitz (2018) 'Experience with the use of an online community on Facebook for Brazilian patients with gestational trophoblastic disease: Netnography study', *Journal of Medical Internet Research*, 20(9): e10897.

Doheny-Farina, Stephen (1998) *The Wired Neighborhood*. New Haven, CT: Yale University Press.

Driscoll, Cathrine and Melissa Gregg (2010) 'My profile: The ethics of virtual ethnography', *Emotion, Space and Society*, 3: 15–20.

DuFault, Beth Leavenworth and John W. Schouten (2018) 'Self-quantification and the datapreneurial consumer identity', *Consumption Markets & Culture*: 1–27. https://doi.org/10.1080/10253866.2018.1519489.

Dyck, Noel (2002) '"Have you been to Hayward Field?": Children's sport and the construction of community in suburban Canada', in Vered Amit (ed.), *Realising Community: Concepts, Social Relationships, and Sentiments*. London and New York: Routledge.

Edgar, Eugene and Felix Billingsley (1974) 'Believability when N = 1', *The Psychological Record*, 24(2): 147–60.

Effrat, Marcia Pelly (ed.) (1974) *The Community: Approaches and Applications*. New York: The Free Press.

Eiland, Howard (2014) *Walter Benjamin*. Cambridge, MA: Harvard University Press.

Eiler, Alicia (2012) 'How Photographs on Instagram Differ From Flickr', *readwriteweb*. Available at https://readwrite.com/2012/04/27/how_photographs_on_instagram_differ_from_flickr/ (last accessed 30 April 2019).

Ellul, Jacques (1964) *The Technological Society*. New York: Random House.

Elo, Satu and Helvi Kyngäs (2008) 'The qualitative content analysis process', *Journal of Advanced Nursing*, 62(1): 107–15.

Elvey, Rebecca, Jennifer Voorhees, Simon Bailey, Taylor Burns, and Damian Hodgson (2018) 'GPs' views of health policy changes: A qualitative "netnography" study of UK general practice online magazine commentary', *British Journal of General Practice*, 68(671): e441–e448.

Emerson, Robert M., Rachel I. Fretz and Linda L. Shaw (1995) *Writing Ethnographic Fieldnotes*. Chicago, IL: University of Chicago Press.

Emerson, Robert M., Rachel I. Fretz and Linda L. Shaw (2011) *Writing Ethnographic Fieldnotes*, 2nd edn. Chicago, IL: University of Chicago Press.

Eriksson, Henrik, Mats Christiansen, Jessica Holmgren, Annica Engström, and Martin Salzmann-Erikson (2014) 'Nursing under the skin: A netnographic study of metaphors and meanings in nursing tattoos', *Nursing Inquiry*, 21(4): 318–26.

Escobar, Arturo (1994) 'Welcome to Cyberia: Notes on the anthropology of cyberculture', *Current Anthropology*, 35(3): 211–23.

Ethnography Matters (2012) 'Writing live fieldnotes: Towards a more open ethnography'. Available at http://ethnographymatters.net/blog/2012/08/02/writing-live-fieldnotes-towards-a-more-open-ethnography/ (last accessed 30 April 2019).

Evans, Harry, Steve Ginnis, and Jamie Barlett (2015) '#SocialEthics: A guide to embedding ethics in social media research'. Available at www.ipsos.com/sites/default/files/migrations/en-uk/files/Assets/Docs/Publications/im-demos-social-ethics-in-social-media-research-summary.pdf (last accessed 31 April 2019).

Farquhar, Lee (2013) 'Performing and interpreting identity through Facebook imagery', *Convergence*, 19(4): 446–71.

Fernback, Jan (1997) 'The individual within the collective: Virtual ideology and the realization of collective principles', in Steve G. Jones (ed.), *Virtual Culture* (pp. 36–54). Thousand Oaks, CA: Sage.

Fiedler, Casey and Nicholas Proferes (2018) '"Participant" perceptions of Twitter research ethics', *Social Media + Society*, 4(1): 2056305118763366.

Flickr Stats and Facts (2018) Available at https://expandedramblings.com/index.php/flickr-stats/ (last accessed 2 September 2018).

Forte, Maximilian (2002) 'Another revolution missed: Anthropology of cyberspace', *Anthropology News*, 43(9): 20–1.

Fox, Susannah and Lee Rainie (2014) 'The Web at 25 in the U.S.', Pew Research Center: *Internet & Technology*. Available online at www.pewinternet.org/2014/02/27/the-web-at-25-in-the-u-s/ (last acccessed 8 June 2019).

Franklin, Karl J. (1996) 'K.L. Pike on etic vs. emic: A review and interview', *Summer Institute of Linguistics*, 27.

Friedman, P. Kerim (2005) 'Folksonomy', *Anthropology News*, 46(6).

Frömming, Urte Undine, Steffen Köhn, Samantha Fox, and Mike Terry (2017) *Digital Environments: Ethnographic Perspectives Across Global Online and Offline Spaces*. Bielefeld, Germany: Transcript Verlag.

Gadamer, Hans-Georg (2006) 'Classical and philosophical hermeneutics', *Theory, Culture & Society*, 23(1): 29–56.

Gambetti, Rossella C. and Guendalina Graffigna (2010) 'The concept of engagement: A systematic analysis of the ongoing marketing debate', *International Journal of Market Research*, 52(6): 801–26.

Garcia, Angela Cora, Alecea I. Standlee, Jennifer Bechkoff and Yan Cui (2009) 'Ethnographic approaches to the internet and computer-mediated communication', *Journal of Contemporary Ethnography*, 38(1)(February): 52–84.

García-Álvarez, Ercilia, Jordi López-Sintas, and Alexandra Samper-Martínez (2017) 'The social network gamer's experience of play: A netnography of Restaurant City on Facebook', *Games and Culture*, 12(7-8): 650–70.

Garey, Michael R. and David S. Johnson (2002) *Computers and Intractability*, 29. New York: W.H. Freeman.

Gaspar, Rui, Cláudia Pedro, Panos Panagiotopoulos, and Beate Seibt (2016) 'Beyond positive or negative: Qualitative sentiment analysis of social media reactions to unexpected stressful events', *Computers in Human Behavior*, 56(March): 179–91.

Geertz, Clifford (1973) *The Interpretation of Cultures*. New York: Basic Books.

Geertz, Clifford (1998) 'Deep hanging out', *New York Review of Books*, 45(16): 69–72.

Gehl, Robert W. (2016) 'Power/freedom on the dark web: A digital ethnography of the Dark Web Social Network', *New Media & Society*, 18(7): 1219–35.

Gerrig, Richard J. (1993) *Experiencing Narrative Worlds: On the Psychological Activities of Reading*. New Haven, CT: Yale University Press.

Gibson, James J. (1986) *The Ecological Approach to Visual Perception*. Hillsdale, NJ: Lawrence Erlbaum.

Gibson, William (1984) *Necromancer*. New York: Ace.

Ginsburg, Faye, Lila Abu-Lughod, and Brian Larkin (2003) 'Introduction', in Faye Ginsburg, Lila Abu-Lughod, and Brian Larkin (eds), *Media Worlds: Anthropology on New Terrain* (pp. 1–57). Berkeley, CA: University of California Press.

Goffman, Erving (1969) *Strategic Interaction*. Philadelphia, PA: University of Pennsylvania Press.

Golder, Su, Shahd Ahmed, Gill Norman, and Andrew Booth (2017) 'Attitudes toward the ethics of research using social media: A systematic review', *Journal of Medical Internet Research* 19(6). Available at www.ncbi.nlm.nih.gov/pmc/articles/PMC5478799/ (last accessed 30 April 2019).

Golden-Biddle, Karen and Karen Locke (2007) *Composing Qualitative Research*. London: Sage.

Gómez Cruz, Edgar and Elisenda Ardèvol (2013) 'Some ethnographic notes on a Flickr group', *Photographies*, 6(1): 35–44.

Gopaldas, Ahir and Eileen Fischer (2012) 'Beyond gender: Intersectionality, culture, and consumer behavior', in Linda Tuncay Zayer and Cele Otnes (eds), *Gender, Culture, and Consumer Behavior* (pp. 394–408). London: Routledge.

Grabher, Gernot and Oliver Ibert (2014) 'Distance as asset? Knowledge collaboration in hybrid virtual communities', *Journal of Economic Geography*, 14: 97–123.

Gretzel, Ulrike (2017a) 'The visual turn in social media marketing', *Tourismos*, 12(3): 1–18.

Gretzel, Ulrike (2017b) 'Social media activism in tourism', *Journal of Hospitality and Tourism*, 15(2): 1–14.

Gretzel, Ulrike (2017c) '#travelselfie: A netnographic study of travel identity communicated via Instagram', in Susan Carson and Mark Pennings (eds), *Performing Cultural Tourism: Communities, Tourists and Creative Practices* (pp. 115–28). New York: Routledge.

Gubrium, Jaber F. and James A. Holstein (eds) (2001) *Handbook of Interview Research: Context and Method*. Thousand Oaks, CA: Sage.

Guidry, Jeanine, Kellie Carlyle, Marcus Messner, and Yan Jin (2015) 'On pins and needles: How vaccines are portrayed on Pinterest', *Vaccine*, 33(39): 5051–6.

Guidry, Jeanine, Yuan Zhang, Yan Jin, and Candace Parrish (2016) 'Portrayals of depression on Pinterest and why public relations practitioners should care', *Public Relations Review*, 42(1): 232–6.

Guo, Ken H. (2018) 'The odyssey of becoming: Professional identity and insecurity in the Canadian accounting field', *Critical Perspectives on Accounting*, 56: 20–45.

Gurrieri, Lauren and Hélène Cherrier (2013) 'Queering beauty: Fatshionistas in the fatosphere', *Qualitative Market Research: An International Journal*, 16 (3): 276–95.

Gustavsson, Anders (2013) 'Death and bereavement on the internet in Sweden and Norway', *Folklore: Electronic Journal of Folklore*, 53: 99–116.

Hannerz, Ulf (2016) *Writing Future Worlds: An Anthropologist's View of Global Scenarios*. Stockholm, Sweden: Springer.

Harris, Marvin (1979) *Cultural Materialism: The Struggle for a Science of Culture*. New York: Random House.

Hart, Matt (2015) 'Youth intimacy on Tumblr: A pilot study', *Young*, 23(3): 193–208.

Haslanger, S. (2000) 'Gender and race: (What) are they? (What) do we want them to be?', *Nous*, 34(1): 31–55.

Hayles, Katherine (2012) *How We Think: Digital Media and Contemporary Technogenesis*. Chicago, IL and London: University of Chicago Press.

Hearne, Evelyn and Marie Claire Van Hout (2016) '"Trip-sitting" in the black hole: A netnographic study of dissociation and indigenous harm reduction', *Journal of Psychoactive Drugs*, 48(4): 233–42.

Heffernan, Virginia (2016) *Magic and Loss: The Internet as Art*. New York: Simon & Schuster.

Heimerl, Florian, Steffen Lohmann, Simon Lange, and Thomas Ertl (2014) 'Word cloud explorer: iText analytics based on word clouds', in *47th Hawaii International Conference on Systems Science* (pp. 1833–42). Published by The Institute of Electrical and Electronics Engineers.

Heinonen, Kristina and Gustav Medberg (2018) 'Netnography as a tool for understanding customers: Implications for service research and practice', *Journal of Services Marketing*, 32(6): 657–79.

Henderson, Katie, Girish Prayag, and Sussie Morrish (2017) 'Dimensionality of consumer engagement in fashion blogs', in Patricia Rossi (ed.), *Marketing at the Confluence between Entertainment and Analytics* (pp. 917–20). New York: Springer.

Henriques, Flávio Medeiros and Severino Joaquim Nunes Pereira (2018) 'Authenticity and classic rock consumption: A netnography on Facebook', *REAd. Revista Eletrônica de Administração (Porto Alegre)*, 24(1): 1–29.

Herrman, John (2018) 'Twitter's misguided quest to become a forum for everything', *New York Times*, 15 August.

Hiltz, Starr Roxanne and Murray Turoff (1978) *The Network Nation: Human Communication Via Computer*. Cambridge, MA: MIT Press.

Hiltz, Starr Roxanne and Murray Turoff (1993) *The Network Nation: Human Communication Via Computer* (revised edition). Cambridge, MA: MIT Press.

Hine, Christine (2000) *Virtual Ethnography*. London: Sage.

Hine, Christine (2014) 'Headlice eradication as everyday engagement with science: An analysis of online parenting discussions', *Public Understanding of Science*, 23(5): 574–91.

Hine, Christine (2015) *Ethnography for the Internet: Embedded, Embodied and Everyday*. London: Bloomsbury.

Holden, Alexander and Heiko Spallek (2018) 'How compliant are dental practice Facebook pages with Australian health care advertising regulations? A netnographic review', *Australian Dental Journal*, 63(1): 109–17.

Holliday, Adrian (2016) *Doing and Writing Qualitative Research*, 3rd edn. London: Sage.

Horn, Franziska, Leila Arras, Grégoire Montavon, Klaus-Robert Müller, and Wojciech Samek (2017) 'Discovering topics in text datasets by visualizing relevant words', arXiv preprint arXiv: 1707.06100.

Howard, Lyz (2018) 'Casting the "Net" in autonetnography: Exploring the potential for analytic autonetnography as an emerging e-research methodology', in Jeroen Huisman and Malcolm Tight (eds), *Theory and Method in Higher Education Research* (Volume 4) (pp.163–87). Bingley: Emerald.

Howard, Philip N. (2002) 'Network ethnography and the hypermedia organization: New media, new organizations, new methods', *New Media & Society*, 4(4): 550–74.

Hubbs, Delaura L. and Charles F. Brand (2005) 'The Paper Mirror: Understanding reflective journaling', *Journal of Experiential Education*, 28(1): 60–71.

Hudson, James M. and Amy Bruckman (2004) '"Go away": Participant objections to being studied', *The Information Society*, 20(2): 127–39.

Hutchby, Ian (2001) 'Technologies, texts and affordances', *Sociology*, 35(2): 441–56.

Isbell, Daniel R. (2018) 'Online informal language learning: Insights from a Korean learning community', *Language Learning & Technology*, 22(3): 82–102.

Isupova, Olga (2011) 'Support through patient internet-communities: Lived experience of Russian in vitro fertilization patient', *International Journal of Qualitative Studies on Health and Well-being*, 6(3). Doi: 10.3402/qhw.v6i3.5907. Available at www. tandfonline.com/doi/full/10.3402/qhw.v6i3.5907 (last accessed 27 June 2019).

Jackson, Jean E. (2016) 'Changes in fieldnote practice over the past thirty years in U.S. anthropology', in Roger Sanjek and Susan W. Tratner (eds), *eFieldnotes: The Makings of Anthropology in the Digital World* (pp. 42–64). Philadelphia, PA: University of Pennsylvania Press.

Jackson, Kristi, Trena Paulus, and Nicholas H. Woolf (2018) 'The Walking Dead genealogy: Unsubstantiated criticisms of qualitative data analysis software (QDAS) and the failure to put them to rest', *The Qualitative Report*, 23(13): 74–91.

Jackson, Michael (1998) *Minima Ethnographica: Intersubjectivity and the Anthropological Project*. Chicago, IL: University of Chicago.

Jary, David, John Horne, and Tom Bucke (1991) 'Football "fanzines" and football culture: A case of successful "cultural contestation"', *The Sociological Review*, 39(3): 581–97.

Jeacle, Ingrid and Chris Carter (2011) 'In TripAdvisor we trust: Rankings, calculative regimes and abstract systems', *Accounting, Organizations and Society*, 36(4): 293–309.

Jenkins, Henry (1992) *Textual Poachers: Television Fans and Participatory Culture*. New York: Routledge.

Jenkins, Henry (1995) '"Do You Enjoy Making the Rest of Us Feel Stupid?": alt. tv. twinpeaks, the Trickster Author, and Viewer Mastery', in David Lavery (ed.), *Full of Secrets: Critical Approaches to Twin Peaks* (pp. 51–69). Detroit, MI: Wayne State University Press.

Jick, Todd D. (1979) 'Mixing qualitative and quantitative methods: Triangulation in action,' *Administrative Science Quarterly*, 24(4): 602–11.

Johns, Mark D., Shing-Ling Sarina Chen and G. Jon Hall (eds) (2003) *Online Social Research: Methods, Issues, and Ethics*. New York: Peter Lang.

Jones, Stephen G. (ed.) (1995) *Cybersociety*. Thousand Oaks, CA: Sage.

Jones, Steve (ed.) (1998) *Cybersociety 2.0: Revisiting Computer-mediated Community and Technology* (Volume 2). Thousand Oaks, CA: Sage.

Kantanen, Helena and Jyri Manninen (2016) 'Hazy boundaries: virtual communities and research ethics', *Media and Communication*, 4(4): 86–96.

Kaplan, Sheila (2018) 'Big tobacco's global reach on social media', *New York Times*, 24 August. Available at www.nytimes.com/2018/08/24/health/tobacco-social-media-smoking.html (last accessed 30 April 2019).

Kassarjian, Harold H. (1977) 'Content analysis in consumer research', *Journal of Consumer Research*, 4(1): 8–18.

Kavakci, Elif and Camille R. Kraeplin (2017) 'Religious beings in fashionable bodies: the online identity construction of hijabi social media personalities', *Media, Culture & Society*, 39(6): 850–68.

Kavanaugh, Andrea L. and Scott J. Patterson (2001) 'The impact of community computer networks on social capital and community involvement', *American Behavioral Scientist*, 45(3): 496–509.

Khan, Shamus (2018) 'The subpoena of ethnographic data', *Sociological Forum*. Doi: 10.1111/socf.12493.

Kiesler, Sara, Jane Siegel, and Timothy McGuire (1984) 'Social psychological aspects of computer-mediated communication', *American Psychologist*, 39(10): 1123–34.

Kiesler, Sara, D. Zubrow, A.M. Moses, and V. Geller (1985) 'Affect in computer-mediated communication: An experiment in synchronous terminal-to-terminal discussion', *Human-Computer Interaction*, 1: 77–104.

King, Storm (1996) 'Researching internet communities: Proposed ethical guidelines for the reporting of results', *The Information Society*, 12: 119–28.

Kinneavy, James L. (1980) *A Theory of Discourse*. New York: Norton.

Koestler, Arthur (1967) *The Ghost in the Machine*. London: Hutchinson.

Kozinets, Robert V. (1997a) 'To Boldly Go: a Hypermodern Ethnography of *Star Trek* Fans' Culture and Communities of Consumption', unpublished PhD dissertation, Queen's University, Kingston, Canada.

Kozinets, Robert V. (1997b) '"I Want To Believe": A netnography of *The X-Files*' subculture of consumption', in Merrie Brucks and Deborah J. MacInnis (eds), *Advances in Consumer Research*, Volume 24 (pp. 470–5). Provo, UT: Association for Consumer Research.

Kozinets, Robert V. (1998) 'On netnography: Initial reflections on consumer research investigations of cyberculture', in Joseph Alba and Wesley Hutchinson (eds), *Advances in Consumer Research*, Volume 25 (pp. 366–71). Provo, UT: Association for Consumer Research.

Kozinets, Robert V. (2001) 'Utopian Enterprise: Articulating the meanings of Star Trek's culture of consumption', *Journal of Consumer Research*, 28(June): 67–88.

Kozinets, Robert V. (2002a) 'The field behind the screen: Using netnography for marketing research in online communities', *Journal of Marketing Research*, 39(February): 61–72.

Kozinets, Robert V. (2002b) 'Can consumers escape the market? Emancipatory illuminations from Burning Man', *Journal of Consumer Research*, 29(June): 20–38.

Kozinets, Robert V. (2006a) 'Netnography 2.0', in Russell W. Belk (ed.), *Handbook of Qualitative Research Methods in Marketing* (pp. 129–42) Cheltenham, UN and Northampton, MA: Edward Elgar Publishing.

Kozinets, Robert V. (2006b) 'Click to connect: Netnography and tribal advertising', *Journal of Advertising Research*, 46(September): 279–88.

Kozinets, Robert V. (2010) *Netnography: Doing Ethnographic Research Online*. London: Sage.

Kozinets, Robert V. (2015) *Netnography: Redefined*. London: Sage.

Kozinets, Robert V. (2016) 'Amazonian forests and trees: Multiplicity and objectivity in studies of online consumer-generated ratings and reviews, a commentary on de Langhe, Fernbach, and Lichtenstein', *Journal of Consumer Research*, 42(6): 834–9.

Kozinets, Robert V. (2019a) 'YouTube utopianism: Social media profanation and the clicktivism of capitalist critique', *Journal of Business Research*, 98: 65–81.

Kozinets, Robert V. (2019b) 'Consuming technocultures: An extended JCR curation', *Journal of Consumer Research*, 46 (3): 620–27.

Kozinets, Robert V., Kristine de Valck, Andrea Wojnicki, and Sarah Wilner (2010) 'Networked narratives: Understanding word-of-mouth marketing in online communities', *Journal of Marketing*, 74(March): 71–89.

Kozinets, Robert V. and Jay M. Handelman (1998) 'Ensouling consumption: A netnographic exploration of the meaning of boycotting behavior', in Joseph Alba and Wesley Hutchinson (eds), *Advances in Consumer Research*, Volume 25 (pp. 475–80). Provo, UT: Association for Consumer Research.

Kozinets, Robert V. and Richard Kedzior (2009) 'I, Avatar: Auto-netnographic research in virtual worlds', in Michael Solomon and Natalie Wood (eds), *Virtual Social Identity and Social Behavior* (pp. 3–19). Armonk, NY: M.E. Sharpe.

Kozinets, Robert, Anthony Patterson, and Rachel Ashman (2017) 'Networks of desire: How technology increases our passion to consume', *Journal of Consumer Research*, 43(February), 659–82.

Kretz, Gachoucha and Kristine de Valck (2010) '"Pixelize Me!": Digital storytelling and the creation of archetypal myths through explicit and implicit self-brand association in fashion and luxury blogs', in Russell W. Belk (ed.), *Research in Consumer Behavior*, Volume 12 (pp. 313–29). Bingley: Emerald.

Kulavuz-Onal, Derya and Camilla Vásquez (2013) 'Reconceptualising fieldwork in a netnography of an online community of English language teachers', *Ethnography and Education*, 8(2): 224–38.

Lange, Patricia G. (2007) 'Publicly private and privately public: social networking on YouTube', *Journal of Computer-mediated Communication*, 13(1): 361–80.

Laurel, Brenda and S. Joy Mountford (1990) *The Art of Human-computer Interface Design*. Boston, MA: Addison-Wesley Longman Publishing Co.

LeBesco, Kathleen (2004) 'Managing visibility, intimacy, and focus in online critical ethnography', in Mark D. Johns, Shing-Ling Sarina Chen and G. Jon Hall (eds), *Online Social Research: Methods, Issues, and Ethics* (pp. 63–79). New York: Peter Lang.

Leipämaa-Leskinen, Hanna (2011) 'Cultural analysis of dieting consumers' construction of bodies and identities', *Qualitative Market Research: An International Journal*, 14(4): 360–73.

Leonardi, Paul M. (2011) 'When flexible routines meet flexible technologies: Affordance, constraint, and the imbrication of human and material agencies', *MIS Quarterly*, 35(1): 147–67.

Lincoln, Yvonna S. and Egon G. Guba (1985) *Naturalistic Inquiry*. Thousand Oaks, CA: Sage.

Litchman, Michelle L., Dana Lewis, Lesly A. Kelly, and Perry M. Gee (2018) 'Twitter analysis of #OpenAPS DIY artificial pancreas technology use suggests improved A1C and quality of life', *Journal of Diabetes Science and Technology*: 1932296818795705.

Liu, Liping, Chan Li, and Dan Zhu (2012) 'A new approach to testing nomological validity and its application to a second-order measurement model of trust', *Journal of the Association for Information Systems*, 13(12), Article 4.

Locke, Karen and Karen Golden-Biddle (1997) 'Constructing opportunities for contribution: structuring intertextual coherence and "problematizing" in organizational studies', *Academy of Management Journal*, 40(5): 1023–62.

Logan, Ashleigh (2015) 'Netnography: observing and interacting with celebrity in the digital world', *Celebrity Studies* 6(3): 378–81.

Lorenz, Ursula (2017) 'The working lives of freelance female musicians in the United States music industry: A netnography', Unpublished Ph.D. dissertation. Schottsdale, AZ: Northcentral University.

Lowkell (2017) 'Word clouds: Trump's inaugural speech compared to Obama's, Bush 43 & 41's, Clinton's, Reagan's, Carter's', bluevirginia.us. Available at https://bit.ly/2BCbT8a (last accessed 1 May 2019).

Lubet, Steven (2018) *Interrogating Ethnography: Why Evidence Matters*. Cambridge: Oxford University Press.

Madianou, Mirca and Daniel Miller (2013) 'Polymedia: Towards a new theory of digital media in interpersonal communication', *International Journal of Cultural Studies*, 16(2): 169–87.

Maldoff, Gabe (2018) 'How GDPR changes the rules for research', iapp. Available at https://iapp.org/news/a/how-gdpr-changes-the-rules-for-research/ (last accessed 1 May 2019).

Mantzavinos, C. (2016) 'Hermeneutics', in Edward N. Zalta (ed.), *The Stanford Encyclopedia of Philosophy* (Winter 2016 Edition). Available at: https://plato.stanford.edu/archives/win2016/entries/hermeneutics/ (last accessed 28 June 2019)

Marcus, George (1995) 'Ethnography in/of the world system: the emergence of multi-sited ethnography', *Annual Review of Anthropology*, 24: 95–117.

Markham, Annette (1998) *Life Online: Researching Real Experience in Virtual Space*. Lanham, MD: AltaMira.

Markham, Annette (2012) 'Fabrication as ethical practice: Qualitative inquiry in ambiguous internet contexts', *Information, Communication & Society*, 15(3): 334–53.

Martin, Kirsten and Katie Shilton (2016) 'Putting mobile application privacy in context: An empirical study of user privacy expectations for mobile devices', *The Information Society*, 32(3): 200–16.

Marwick, Alice E. (2015) 'Instafame: Luxury selfies in the attention economy', *Public Culture*, 27(1): 137–60.

McCloskey, Deirdre N. (1985) *The Rhetoric of Economics*. Madison, WI: University of Wisconsin Press.

McCutcheon, Russell T. (ed.) (1999) *The Insider/Outsider Problem in the Study of Religion*. London: Cassell Academic.

McLaughlin, Margaret L. (1995) 'Standards of conduct on Usenet', in Steve Jones (ed.) *Cybersociety: Computer-mediated Communication and Community* (pp. 90–111). Thousand Oaks, CA: Sage.

McLuhan, Marshall (1994) *Understanding Media: The Extensions of Man*. Cambridge, MA: MIT Press.

McNaught, Carmel and Paul Lam (2010) 'Using Wordle as a supplementary research tool', *The Qualitative Report*, 15(3): 630–43.

McQuarrie, Edward F., Jessica Miller, and Barbara J. Phillips (2013) 'The megaphone effect: Taste and audience in fashion blogging', *Journal of Consumer Research*, 40(1): 136–58.

McVeigh, Jim, Jennifer Germain, and Marie Claire Van Hout (2016) '2, 4-Dinitrophenol, the inferno drug: A netnographic study of user experiences in the quest for leanness', *Journal of Substance Use*, 22(2): 131–8.

Mead, George Herbert (1934) *Mind, Self and Society*. Chicago: University of Chicago Press.

Medrado, Andrea Meyer and Ana Paula Muller (2018) 'Maternal rights digital activism and intersectional feminism: an analysis of the independent media platform "Cientista Que Virou Mãe"', *Brazilian Journalism Research*, 14(1): 174.

Mendes, Kaitlynn (2015) *Slutwalk: Feminism, Activism and Media*. Dordrecht: Springer.

Mezirow, Jack (ed.) (2000) *Learning as Transformation: Critical Perspectives on a Theory in Progress*. New York: Jossey-Bass.

Miles, Matthew B., A. Michael Huberman, and Johnny Saldaña (2014) *Qualitative Data Analysis: A Methods Sourcebook*. London: Sage.

Minowa, Yuko, Luca M. Visconti, and Pauline Maclaran (2012) 'Researchers' introspection for multi-sited ethnographers: A xenoheteroglossic autoethnography', *Journal of Business Research*, 65(4): 483–9.

Mkono, Muchazondida (2011) 'The othering of food in touristic eatertainment: A netnography', *Tourist Studies*, 11(3): 253–70.

Moeller, Kim, Rasmus Munksgaard, and Jakob Demant (2017) 'Flow my FE the vendor said: exploring violent and fraudulent resource exchanges on cryptomarkets for illicit drugs', *American Behavioral Scientist*, 61(11): 1427–50.

Moraes, Caroline, Nina Michaelidou, and Rita W. Meneses (2014) 'The use of Facebook to promote drinking among young consumers', *Journal of Marketing Management*, 30(13–14): 1377–401.

Moreillon, Judi (2015) '#schoollibrarians tweet for professional development: A netnographic case study of #txlchat', *School Libraries Worldwide*, 21(2): 127–37.

Moreno, Megan A., Natalie Goniu, Peter S. Moreno, and Douglas Diekema (2013) 'Ethics of social media research: Common concerns and practical considerations', *Cyberpsychology, Behavior, and Social Networking*, 16(9): 708–13.

Moreno, Megan A., Alison Grant, Lauren Kacvinsky, Peter Moreno, and Michael Fleming (2012) '"Older adolescents" views regarding participation in Facebook research', *Journal of Adolescent Health*, 51(5): 439–44.

Morris, Isla-Kate (2016) 'E-ethics and Higher Education: Do Higher Education challenges make a case for a framework for digital research ethics?', *Networking Knowledge: Journal of the MeCCSA Postgraduate Network*, 9(5).

Mortara, Ariela and Simona Ironico (2013) 'Deconstructing Emo lifestyle and aesthetics: A netnographic research', *Young Consumers*, 14(4): 351–59.

Mumford, Lewis (1967) *The Myth of the Machine: Technics and Human Development*, Volume 1. London: Secker & Warburg.

Muniz Jr, Albert M. and Hope Jensen Schau (2005) 'Religiosity in the abandoned Apple Newton brand community', *Journal of Consumer Research*, 31(4): 737–47.

Munt, Sally R. (ed.) (2001) *Technospaces: Inside the New Media*. London: Continuum.

Murthy, Dhiraj (2008) 'Digital ethnography: An examination of the use of new technologies for social research', *Sociology*, 42(5): 837–55.

Nardi, Bonnie A. (2016) 'When fieldnotes seem to write themselves: Ethnographyo, in Roger Sanjek and Susan W. Tratner (eds), *eFieldnotes: The Makings of Anthropology in the Digital World* (pp. 192–209). Philadelphia, PA: University of Pennsylvania Press.

Nelson, Michelle R. and Cele C. Otnes (2005) 'Exploring cross-cultural ambivalence: A netnography of intercultural wedding message boards', *Journal of Business Research*, 58(1): 89–95.

Nind, Melanie, Rose Wiles, Andrew Bengry-Howell, and Graham Crow (2013) 'Methodological innovation and research ethics: Forces in tension or forces in harmony?', *Qualitative Research*, 13(6): 650–67.

Nissenbaum, Asaf and Limor Shifman (2017) 'Internet memes as contested cultural capital: The case of 4chan's/b/board', *New Media & Society*, 19(4): 483–501.

Norman, Donald A. (1990) *The Design of Everyday Things*. New York: Doubleday.

O'Connor, Ellen S. (1996) 'Lines of authority: Readings of foundational texts in the profession of Management', *Journal of Management History*, 2(3): 26–49.

O'Leary, Killian and Conor Carroll (2013) 'The online poker sub-culture: dialogues, interactions and networks', *Journal of Gambling Studies*, 29(4): 613–30.

Orsolini, Laura, Gabriele Duccio Papanti, Giulia Francesconi, and Fabrizio Schifano (2015) 'Mind navigators of chemicals' experimenters? A web-based description of e-psychonauts', *Cyberpsychology, Behavior, and Social Networking*, 18(5): 296–300.

Ortner, Sherry B. (1984) 'Theory in anthropology since the sixties', *Comparative Studies in Society and History*, 26(1): 126–66.

Palo, Annbritt and Lena Manderstedt (2017) 'Beyond the characters and the reader? Digital discussions on intersectionality in *The Murderer's Ape*', *Children's Literature in Education*: 1–17. Available at: https://link.springer.com/article/10.1007/s10583-017-9338-2 (last accessed 28 June 2019).

Parker, Michael (2007) 'Ethnography/ethics', *Social Science & Medicine*, 65(11): 2248–59.

Patton, Michael Quinn (2002) 'Qualitative interviewing', *Qualitative Research and Evaluation Methods*, 3: 344–7.

Pearce, Nick and Sarah Learmonth (2013) 'Learning beyond the classroom: Evaluating the use of Pinterest in learning and teaching in an introductory anthropology class', *Journal of Interactive Media in Education*. Doi: http://doi.org/10.5334/2013-12.

Peeroo, Swaleha (2019) 'Customer-initiated conversations on Facebook pages of Tesco and Walmart', in Suresh Chandra, Satapathy Vikrant, Bhateja Radhakrishna, Somanah Xin-She Yang, and Roman Senkerik (eds), *Information Systems Design and Intelligent Applications* (pp. 43–51). Singapore: Springer.

Peeroo, Swaleha, Martin Samy, and Brian Jones (2015) '*Customer engagement manifestations on Facebook pages of Tesco and Walmart*', Computing, Communication and Security (ICCCS), 2015 International Conference on IEEE. Doi: 10.1109/CCCS.2015.7374166.

Penley, Constance and Andrew Ross (eds) (1991) *Technoculture: Cultural Politics*. Minneapolis, MN: University of Minnesota Press.

Pentina, Iryna and Clinton Amos (2011) 'The Freegan phenomenon: Anti-consumption or consumer resistance?', *European Journal of Marketing*, 45(11/12): 1768–78.

Perren, Rebeca and Robert V. Kozinets (2018) 'Lateral exchange markets: How social platforms operate in a networked economy', *Journal of Marketing*, 82(January): 20–36.

Pettigrew, Simone, Melanie Pescud, Wade Jarvis, and Dave Webb (2013) 'Teens' blog accounts of the role of adults in youth alcohol consumption', *Journal of Social Marketing*, 3(1): 28–40.

Pew Research Center (2017) Social Media Fact Sheet. Available at www.pewinternet.org/fact-sheet/social-media/ (last accessed 2 July 2019).

Phillips, Barbara J., Jessica Miller, and Edward F. McQuarrie (2014) 'Dreaming out loud on Pinterest: New forms of indirect persuasion', *International Journal of Advertising*, 33(4): 633–55.

Piacenti, David Joseph, Luis Balmore Rivas, and Josef Garrett (2014) 'Facebook ethnography: The poststructural ontology of transnational (im)migration research', *International Journal of Qualitative Methods*, 13(1): 224–36.

Pike, Kenneth (1967) *Language in Relation to a Unified Theory of the Structure of Human Behavior*, 2nd edn. The Hague: Mouton.

Pink, Sarah (2017) 'Foreword', in Urte Undine Frömming, Steffen Köhn, Samantha Fox, and Mike Terry (eds), *Digital Environments: Ethnographic Perspectives Across Global Online and Offline Spaces* (pp. 9–11). Bielefeld, Germany: Transcript Verlag.

Pink, Sarah, Heather Horst, John Postill, Larissa Hjorth, Tania Lewis, and Jo Tacchi (eds) (2015) *Digital Ethnography: Principles and Practice*. London: Sage.

Pittman, Joseph W., M. Elizabeth Bennett, Lorne D. Koroluk, Stacey G. Robinson, and Ceib L. Phillips (2017) 'Characterizing the orthodontic patient's purchase decision: A novel approach using netnography', *American Journal of Orthodontics and Dentofacial Orthopedics*, 151(6): 1065–72.

Postill, John and Sarah Pink (2012) 'Social media ethnography: The digital researcher in a messy web', *Media International Australia*, 145(1): 123–34.

Potts, Liza and Angela Harrison (2013) 'Interfaces as rhetorical constructions: Reddit and 4chan during the Boston marathon bombings', *Proceedings of the 31st ACM International Conference on Design of Communication*, pp. 143–50.

Priyadharshini, Esther and Amy Pressland (2018) 'Analysis as assemblage: Making sense of polysemous texts', *Critical Studies in Media Communication*, 35(5): 420–39.

Protection of Human Subjects, US Federal Code Title 46, Section 46 (2018). Available at www.ecfr.gov/cgibin/retrieveECFR?gp=&SID=83cd09e1c0f5c6937cd9d7513160f-c3f&pitd=20180719&n=pt45.1.46&r=PART&ty=HTML (last accessed 1 May 2019).

Puri, Anjali (2007) 'The web of insights: The art and practice of webnography', *International Journal of Market Research*, 49(3): 387–408.

Putnam, Robert D. (2000) 'Bowling alone: America's declining social capital', in Lane Crothers and Charles Lockhart (eds), *Culture and Politics: A Reader* (pp. 223–34). New York: Springer.

Quinton, Sarah and Nina Reynolds (2018) *Understanding Research in the Digital Age*. London: Sage.

Quinton, Sarah and Damien Wilson (2016) 'Tensions and ties in social media networks: Towards a model of understanding business relationship development and business performance enhancement through the use of LinkedIn', *Industrial Marketing Management*, 54: 15–24.

Rahm, Erhard and Hong Hai Do (2000) 'Data cleaning: problems and current approaches', *IEEE Data Engineering Bulletin,* 23(4): 3–13.

Rainie, Lee and Barry Wellman (2012) *Networked: The New Social Operating System*. Cambridge, MA: MIT Press.

Raitanen, Jenni, Sveinung Sandberg, and Atte Oksanen (2017) 'The bullying-school shooting nexus: Bridging master narratives of mass violence with personal narratives of social exclusion', *Deviant Behavior*, 40(1): 96–109. Doi: https://doi.org/10.1080/0 1639625.2017.1411044.

Rambe, Patient and Muchazondida Mkono (2018) 'Appropriating WhatsApp-mediated postgraduate supervision to negotiate "relational authenticity" in resource-constrained environments', *British Journal of Educational Technology*, 50(2): 702–34.

Reed, Adam (2005) '"My blog is me": Texts and persons in UK online journal culture (and anthropology)', *Ethnos*, 70, 220–42.

Reichertz, Jo (2007) 'Abduction: The logic of discovery of grounded theory', in Anthony Bryant and Kathy C. Charmaz (eds), *The SAGE Handbook of Grounded Theory* (pp. 214–28). London: Sage.

Reid, Elizabeth (1996) 'Informed consent in the study of on-line communities: A reflection on the effects of computer-mediated social research', *The Information Society*, 12: 169–74.

Rhazzali, Khalid (2015) 'Islam online: A netnography of conversion', in Daniel Enstedt, Goran Larsson and Enzo Pace (eds), *Annual Review of the Sociology of Religion: Religion and Internet* (pp. 164–82). Leiden: Brill.

Rheingold, Howard (1993) *The Virtual Community: Homesteading on the Electronic Frontier*. New York: Addison-Wesley.

Rice, Ronald E. (ed.) (1984), *The New Media, Communication, Research, and Technology*. Beverly Hills, CA: Sage Publications.

Rice, Ronald E. and Everett M. Rogers (1984) 'New methods and data for the study of new media', in R.E. Rice (ed.), *The New Media, Communication, Research, and Technology* (pp. 81–99). Beverly Hills, CA: Sage Publications.

Rieber, Robert W. and David K. Robinson (eds) (2013) *The Essential Vygotsky*. New York: Springer Science & Business Media.

Ritzer, George and Douglas J. Goodman (2008) *Modern Sociological Theory*. New York: McGraw-Hill Higher Education.

Rogers, Everett M. (1962) *Diffusion of Innovations*. New York: Free Press of Glencoe.

Roland, Damian, Jesse Spurr, and Daniel Cabrera (2017) 'Preliminary evidence for the emergence of a health care online community of practice: Using a netnographic framework for Twitter hashtag analytics', *Journal of Medical Internet Research*, 19(7).

Roth-Cohen, Osnat and Tamar Lahav (2018) 'Going undercover: Online domestic tourism marketing communication in closed and open Facebook groups', *Journal of Vacation Marketing*, 25(3): 349–62. Doi:https://doi.org/10.1177/1356766718796054.

Ruvio, Ayalla and Russell Belk (2018) 'Strategies of the extended self: The role of possessions in transpeople's conflicted selves', *Journal of Business Research*, 88(July): 102–10.

Saadatdoost, Robab, Hosein Jafarkarimi, Alex Tze Hiang Sim, and Jee Mei Hee (2019) 'Understanding MOOC learners: Insights from participation in Coursera MOOC', *International Journal of Web-Based Learning and Teaching Technologies (IJWLTT)*, 14(1): 93–112.

Saboia, Inga, Ana Margarida Pisco Almeida, Pedro Sousa, and Cláudia Pernencar (2018) '"I am with you": A netnographic analysis of the Instagram opinion leaders on eating behavior change', *Procedia Computer Science*, 138: 97–104.

Saldaña, Johnny (2013) *The Coding Manual for Qualitative Researchers*, 2nd edn. London: Sage.

Salmons, Janet (2009) *Online Interviews in Real Time*. London: Sage.

Salmons, Janet (2011) *Cases in Online Interview Research*. London: Sage.

Salmons, Janet (2017) 'Getting to yes: Informed consent in qualitative social media research', in Kandy Woodfield (ed.), *The Ethics of Online Research* (Advances in Research Ethics and Integrity, Volume 2) (pp.109–34). Bingley: Emerald.

Sandlin, Jennifer A. (2007) 'Netnography as a consumer education research tool', *International Journal of Consumer Studies*, 31(3): 288–94.

Sanjek, Roger and Susan W. Tratner (eds) (2016) *eFieldnotes: The Makings of Anthropology in the Digital World*. Philadelphia, PA: University of Pennsylvania Press.

Schiele, Kristen and Mine Ucok Hughes (2013) 'Possession rituals of the digital consumer: A study of Pinterest', in Gert Cornelissen, Elena Reutskaja, and Ana Valenzuela (eds), *European Advances in Consumer Research*, Volume 10 (pp. 47–50). Duluth, MN: Association for Consumer Research.

Schouten, John W. and James H. McAlexander (1995) 'Subcultures of consumption: An ethnography of the new bikers', *Journal of Consumer Research*, 22(1), 43–61.

Schuler, Douglas (1996) *New Community Networks: Wired for Change*. Boston, MA: ACM Press/Addison-Wesley.

Schuman, Donna L., Karen A. Lawrence, and Natalie Pope (2018) 'Broadcasting war trauma: An exploratory netnography of veterans' YouTube Vlogs', *Qualitative Health Research*, 29(3): 357–70. Doi: https://doi.org/10.1177%2F1049732318797623.

Schütz, Alfred (1962) *Collected Papers*, 3 Volumes, trans. Martinus Nijhoff. The Hague: Springer.

Senft, Theresa M. (2008), *Camgirls: Celebrity & Community in the Age of Social Networks*. New York: Peter Lang.

Setiadarma, Dani and Mariko Rizkiansyah (2018) 'Netnography studies in Indonesia and international YouTube community at 411 rallies in Jakarta', *Malaysian Journal of Social Sciences and Humanities*, 3(1): 79–90.

Shakeela, Aishath and David Weaver (2016) 'The exploratory social-mediatized gaze: Reactions of virtual tourists to an inflammatory YouTube incident', *Journal of Travel Research*, 55(1): 113–24.

Shaw, Frances (2013) '"These wars are personal": Methods and theory in feminist online research', *Qualitative Research Journal*, 13(1): 90–101.

Shelton, Martin, Katherine Lo, and Bonnie Nardi (2015) 'Online media forums as separate social lives: A qualitative study of disclosure within and beyond Reddit', iConference 2015 Proceedings.

Shen, Anyuan (2014) 'Recommendations as personalized marketing: Insights from customer experiences', *Journal of Services Marketing*, 28(5): 414–27.

Sherry, John F., Jr. and Robert V. Kozinets (2001) 'Qualitative inquiry in marketing and consumer research', in Dawn Iacobucci (ed.), *Kellogg on Marketing* (pp. 165–94). New York: Wiley Books.

Silver, Christina and Ann Lewins (2014) *Using Software in Qualitative Research: A Step-by-Step Guide*, 2nd edn. London: Sage.

Silvia, Paul J. (2015) *Write It Up: Practical Strategies for Writing and Publishing Journal Articles*. Washington, DC: American Psychological Association.

Slack, Jennifer Daryl and J. McGregor Wise (2014) *Culture and Technology*. New York: Peter Lang.

Smith, Aaron and Monica Anderson (2018) 'Social media use in 2018'. Washington, DC: Pew Internet & American Life Project. Available at: www.pewinternet.org/2018/03/01/social-media-use-in-2018/ (last accessed 3 May 2019).

Snelson, Chareen (2015) 'Vlogging about school on YouTube: An exploratory study', *New Media & Society*, 17(3): 321–39.

Sproull, Lee and Sara Kiesler (1986) 'Reducing social context cues: Electronic mail in organizational communication', *Management Science*, 32(11): 1492–512.

Stacy, Christopher C. (1982) *Getting Started Computing at the AI Lab*, AI Lab working paper no. 235, 7 September, (p. 9). Massachusetts Institute of Technology.

Statista (2018) 'Most famous social network sites worldwide as of July 2018, ranked by number of active users (in millions)'. Available at www.statista.com/statistics/272014/global-social-networks-ranked-by-number-of-users/ (last accessed 2 May 2019).

Steiner, Georg (1989) *Real Presences*. Chicago, IL: University of Chicago Press.

Stephens-Davidowitz, Seth (2017) *Everybody Lies: Big Data, New Data, and What the Internet Can Tell Us About Who We Really Are*. New York: HarperCollins.

Stone, Allucquere Rosanne (1991) 'Will the real body please stand up?', in Michael Benedict (ed.), *Cyberspace: First Steps* (pp. 81–118). Cambridge, MA: MIT Press.

Sugiura, Lisa, Rosemary Wiles, and Catherine Pope (2017) 'Ethical challenges in online research: Public/private perceptions', *Research Ethics*, 13(3–4): 184–99.

Sultana, Shaila, Sender Dovchin, and Alastair Pennycook (2014) 'Transglossic language practices of young adults in Bangladesh and Mongolia', *International Journal of Multilingualism*, 11: 449.

Sumiala, Johanna Maaria and Minttu Tikka (2013) 'Broadcast yourself – global news! A netnography of the "Flotilla" news on YouTube', *Communication, Culture & Critique*, 6(2): 318–35.

Svensson, Jakob (2015) 'Participation as a pastime: Political discussion in a queer community online', *Javnost – The Public*, 22(3): 283–97.

Svensson, Lennart and Kyriaki Doumas (2013) 'Contextual and analytic qualities of research methods exemplified in research on teaching', *Qualitative Inquiry*, 19(6): 441–50.

Tavakoli, Rokhshad (2016) 'My journeys in Second Life: An autonetnography', in Catheryn Khoo-Lattimore and Paolo Mura (eds), *Asian Genders in Tourism* (pp. 104–20). Bristol: Channel View.

Tavakoli, Rokhshad and Paolo Mura (2015) '"Journeys in Second Life": Iranian Muslim women's behaviour in virtual tourist destinations', *Tourism Management*, 46: 398–407.

Tavakoli, Rokhshad and Sarah N.R. Wijesinghe (2019) 'The evolution of the web and netnography in tourism: A systematic review', *Tourism Management Perspectives*, 29: 48–55.

Taylor, Erin B. (2018) 'GDPR for qualitative researchers'. Available online at https://erinbtaylor.com/entry/gdpr-for-qualitative-researchers (last accessed 2 May 2019).

Taylor, James R. (2001) 'Toward a theory of imbrication and organizational communication', *American Journal of Semiotics*, 17(2): 269–98.

Tenderich, Amy, Burghardt Tenderich, Tanner Barton, and Sarah Elizabeth Richards (2018) 'What are PWDs (People With Diabetes) doing online? A netnographic analysis', *Journal of Diabetes Science and Technology*: 1932296818813192.

Thody, Angela (2006) *Writing and Presenting Research*. Thousand Oaks, CA: Sage.

Tierney, Patrick (2001) *Darkness in El Dorado: How scientists and journalists devastated the Amazon*. New York: WW Norton & Company.

Tiidenberg, Katrin (2014) 'Bringing sexy back: Reclaiming the body aesthetic via self-shooting', *Cyberpsychology: Journal of Psychosocial Research on Cyberspace*, 8(1): article 3.

Tobacco-Free Kids (2018) 'New investigation exposes how tobacco companies market cigarettes on social media in the U.S. and around the world', Tobacco Free Kids press release. Available at www.tobaccofreekids.org/press-releases/2018_08_27_ ftc (last accessed 3 May 2019).

Tönnies, Ferdinand ([1887] 1957), *Gemeinshaft und Gesellschaft* (trans. Charles P. Loomis). East Lansing, MI: Michigan State University Press.

Tratner, Susan W. (2016) 'New York parenting discussion boards: eFieldnotes for new research frontiers', in Roger Sanjek and Susan W. Tratner (eds), *eFieldnotes: The Makings of Anthropology in the Digital World* (pp. 171–91). Philadelphia, PA: University of Pennsylvania Press.

Triggs, Teal (2010) *Fanzines*. London: Thames & Hudson.

Tuikka, Anne-Marie, Chau Nguyen, and Kai K. Kimppa (2017) 'Ethical questions related to using netnography as research method', *ORBIT Journal*, 1(2).

Turkle, Sherry (1995) *Life on the Screen: Identity in the Age of the Internet*. New York: Simon & Schuster.

Turkle, Sherry (2011) *Alone Together: Why We Expect More From Technology and Less From Ourselves*. New York: Basic Books.

Turner, Victor (1969) 'Liminality and communitas', in Victor Turner (ed.), *The Ritual Process: Structure and Anti-Structure* (pp. 94–113). Chicago, IL: Transaction Publishers.

Uibu, Marko (2013) 'Creating meanings and supportive networks on the spiritual internet forum "The Nest of Angels"', *Journal of Ethnology and Folkloristics*, 6(2): 69–86.

Van der Nagel, Emily (2013) 'Faceless bodies: Negotiating technological and cultural codes on Reddit Gonewild', *Scan: Journal of Media Arts Culture*, 10(2): 1–10.

Van Dijck, José (2013) *The Culture of Connectivity: A Critical History of Social Media*. Oxford: Oxford University Press.

Van Gelder, Lindsy (1991) 'The strange case of the electronic lover', in Rob Kling (ed.), in *Computerization and Controversy: Value Conflicts and Social Choices* (pp. 364–75). San Diego, CA: Academic.

Van Hout, Marie Claire and Evelyn Hearne (2015) '"Plant or poison": A netnographic study of recreational use of 1, 3-dimethylamylamine (DMAA)', *International Journal of Drug Policy*, 26(12): 1279–81.

Van Hout, Marie Claire and Evelyn Hearne (2016) 'Confessions of contemporary English opium-eaters: A netnographic study of consumer negotiation of over-the-counter morphine for misuse', *Journal of Substance Use*, 21(2): 141–52.

Van Maanen, John (1988) *Tales of the Field: On Writing Ethnography*. Chicago, IL: University of Chicago Press.

Veer, Ekant and Mai Barakat (2009) 'Validation, community, and control through exhibitionism: Sufferers of anorexia nervosa and their YouTube Vlogs', Consumer Culture Theory Conference (pp. 11–14). University of Michigan, Ann Arbor, MI.

Virilio, Paul (ed.) (1994) *The Vision Machine*. Bloomington, IN: Indiana University Press.

Von Hippel, Eric (1986) 'Lead users: A source of novel product concepts', *Management Science*, 32 (July): 791.

Wallace, Ruth, Leesa Costello, and Amanda Devine (2018) 'Netnographic slog: Creative elicitation strategies to encourage participation in an online community of practice for Early Education and Care', *International Journal of Qualitative Methods*, 17(1): 1609406918797796.

Walther, Joseph B. (1992) 'Interpersonal effects in mediated interaction: A relational perspective', *Communication Research*, 19: 52–90.

Walther, Joseph B. (1995) 'Relational aspects of computer-mediated communication: Experimental observations over time', *Organization Science*, 6(2): 186–203.

Walther, Joseph B. (2002) 'Research ethics in internet-enabled research: Human subjects issues and methodological myopia', *Ethics and Information Technology*, 4: 205–16.

Wang, Yi-Sheng (2018) 'Addiction by design: using netnography for user experiences in female online gambling game', *International Journal of Human–Computer Interaction*, 34(2): 774–85.

Ward, Katie J. (1999) 'Cyber-ethnography and the emergence of the virtually new community', *Journal of Information Technology*, 14(1): 95–105.

Wargo, Jon M. (2015) 'Spatial stories with nomadic narrators: affect, Snapchat, and feeling embodiment in youth mobile composing', *Journal of Language and Literacy Education*, 11(1): 47–64.

Warner, Leah (2008) 'A best practices guide to intersectional approaches in psychological research', *Sex Roles*, 59(September): 454–63.

Walther, Joseph B. (1992) 'Interpersonal effects in mediated interaction: A relational perspective', *Communication Research*, 19: 52–90.

Webb, Eugene J., Donald T. Campbell, Richard D. Schwartz, and Lee Sechrest (eds) (1966) *Unobtrusive Measures: Non-Reactive Research in the Social Sciences*. Chicago, IL: Rand McNally.

Wei, Yujie, Detmar W. Straub, and Amit Poddar (2011) 'The power of many: An assessment of managing internet group purchasing', *Journal of Electronic Commerce Research*, 12(1): 19–43.

Wellman, Barry, Janet Salaff, Dimitrina Dimitrova, Laura Garton, Milena Gulia, and Caroline Haythornthwaite (1996) 'Computer networks as social networks: Collaborative work, telework, and virtual community', *Annual Review of Sociology*, 22(1): 213–38.

Wertham, Fredric (1973) *The World of Fanzines: A Special Form of Communication*. Carbondale, IL: Southern Illinois University Press.

Wesely, Pamela M. (2013) 'Investigating the community of practice of world language educators on Twitter', *Journal of Teacher Education*, 64(4): 305–18.

West, Rebecca J. and Bhoomi K. Thakore (2013) 'Racial exclusion in the online world', *Future Internet*, 5(2): 251–67.

Whalen, Elizabeth A. (2018) 'Understanding a shifting methodology: A content analysis of the use of netnography in hospitality and tourism research', *International Journal of Contemporary Hospitality Management*, 30(11): 3423–41.

Whelan, Eoin, Robin Teigland, Emmanuelle Vaast, and Brian Butler (2016) 'Expanding the horizons of digital social networks: Mixing big trace datasets with qualitative approaches', *Information and Organization*, 26(1–2): 1–12.

White, Patrick (2017) *Developing Research Questions*, 2nd edn. London: Palgrave.

Williams, Matthew (2015) 'Towards an ethical framework for using social media data in social research'. Social Research Association Ethics Workshop Institute of Education, UCL, London, 15 June. Available at http://socialdatalab.net/wp-content/uploads/2016/08/EthicsSM-SRA-Workshop.pdf (last accessed 3 May 2019).

Williams, Raymond (1976) *Keywords: A Vocabulary of Culture and Society*. Oxford: Oxford University Press.

Wirth, Louis (1964) *On Cities and Social Life*. Chicago: University of Chicago Press.

Wogan, Peter (2004) 'Deep hanging out: Reflections on fieldwork and multisited Andean ethnography', *Identities: Global Studies in Culture and Power*, 11(1): 129–39.

Wolcott, Harry (1994) *Transforming Qualitative Data*. Thousand Oaks, CA: Sage.

Wolcott, Harry (2013) *Writing Up Qualitative Research*. London: Sage.

World Internet Stats (2018) World Internet Users Statistics and 2018 World Population Stats. Available at www.internetworldstats.com/stats.htm (last accessed 2 July 2019).

Worth, Sol and John Adair (1972) *Through Navajo Eyes: An Exploration in Film Communication and Anthropology*. Bloomington, IN: Indiana University Press.

Wu, Mao-Ying and Philip L. Pearce (2014) 'Chinese recreational vehicle users in Australia: A netnographic study of tourist motivation', *Tourism Management*, 43: 22–35.

Yang, Zhilin and Xiang Fang (2004) 'Online service quality dimensions and their relationships with satisfaction: A content analysis of customer reviews of securities brokerage services', *International Journal of Service Industry Management*, 15(3): 302–26.

Yeager, Jennifer (2012) 'Survivors online: A netnographic analysis of the emerging role played by the internet as a source of support for survivors of sexual violence'. PhD dissertation, University of East London.

Zeng, Michael A., Hans Koller, and Reimo Jahn (2019) 'Open radar groups: The integration of online communities into open foresight processes', *Technological Forecasting and Social Change*, 138: 204–17.

Zhang, Yang and Michael John Hitchcock (2017) 'The Chinese female tourist gaze: A netnography of young women's blogs on Macao', *Current Issues in Tourism*, 20(3): 315–30.

Zimmer, Michael (2010) '"But the data is already public": On the ethics of research in Facebook', *Ethics and Information Technology*, 12: 313–25.

Zuboff, Shoshana (2019) *The Age of Surveillance Capitalism: The Fight for the Future at the New Frontier of Power*. New York: PublicAffairs.

Zwick, Detlev, Samuel K. Bonsu, and Aron Darmody (2008) 'Putting consumers to work: co-creation and new marketing govern-mentality', *Journal of Consumer Culture*, 8(2): 163–96.

INDEX

NOTE: page numbers in *italic* type refer to tables, figures and boxes.